KARL LAGERFELD
A LIFE IN FASHION

An eye for Paris: Karl Lagerfeld presents his 1972 collection
for Chloé on the Esplanade du Trocadéro.

ALFONS KAISER

KARL
LAGERFELD
A LIFE IN
FASHION

With 53 illustrations

On the jacket:
Christian Weber/Contour by Getty Images

First published in the United Kingdom in 2022 by
Thames & Hudson Ltd, 181A High Holborn, London WC1V 7QX

This paperback edition first published in 2023

Translated from the German by Isabel Adey

British Library Cataloguing-in-Publication Data
A catalogue record for this book is available from
the British Library

ISBN   978-0-500-29753-7

Printed and bound in the UK by CPI (UK) Ltd

Be the first to know about our new releases,
exclusive content and author events by visiting
thamesandhudson.com
thamesandhudsonusa.com
thamesandhudson.com.au

Contents

Appendix

'Karl For Ever': tribute at the Grand Palais on 20 June 2019

In Loving Memory

It was a familiar scene, as at any major Chanel show. Young men in black suits being briefed in their role as stewards on the stairs to the Grand Palais. Traffic jams on Avenue Winston Churchill caused by double-parked black limousines. Women in tweed suits hovering outside the immense Beaux-Arts building, waiting to be snapped one last time before making their way inside. The sun angling down on the glass palace, casting a melancholy light through the dome on this last evening of spring.

But nothing was the same in Paris on 20 June 2019. At the centre of all the feverish preparations, the eager anticipation and the displays of vanity was an empty space. Karl Lagerfeld, the guiding light of the strange parallel universe of fashion, had died four months earlier, and now everyone who once moved in his orbit had gathered again. 'Karl's family', as his most intimate colleagues were always known, and his extended family, all came to bid him farewell. Some two and a half thousand guests came from all over the world, many of them dressed in black, others in pink or white because they knew he didn't like people to mourn.

The title of the official Parisian tribute was 'Karl For Ever'. For a designer who preferred not to dwell on the past, and even refused to attend family funerals, this was never going to be a memorial in the traditional sense. Instead, it was a joyful evening of celebration that began with a parade of famous faces, video homages, musical performances and dance interludes, and ended with a champagne reception. Two and a half thousand people gathered in his honour: this was the perfect tribute to a man who excelled at bringing people together.

Le Tout Paris pulled up outside the Grand Palais. Among them were France's First Lady Brigitte Macron – whom Lagerfeld had always liked because her husband, Emmanuel Macron, had taken over from François Hollande, not exactly his favourite French president – and former First Lady Carla Bruni-Sarkozy, whose long career in modelling had included a stint with Chanel. Caroline of Monaco, one of the fashion designer's closest friends, donned a white shirt with a black silk bow. She was joined by her daughter, Charlotte, who wore a black ankle-length dress. Lagerfeld's former muses, Inès de la Fressange, Claudia Schiffer and Caroline de Maigret, made their way down the steps of the glass palace, taking their time to keep their composure so there would be no bad photographs. Model Gigi Hadid, clearly moved, told the cameras: 'When I come to the Grand Palais, I always feel like I'm going to see Karl... I got ready today as if I was getting ready to see him.'

The man who was closest to the fashion designer in his final years smiled enigmatically for the cameras. Sébastien Jondeau, Lagerfeld's former bodyguard, driver and confidant, stepped out in a three-piece suit, surrounded by an air of mystery that would linger long after the memorial was over. Lagerfeld wanted his ashes to be combined with the ashes of his mother and those of his life partner, Jacques de Bascher, who had died thirty years before him. The responsibility fell to Jondeau, who had taken Lagerfeld's ashes to an undisclosed location following the cremation at the Crématorium du Mont-Valérien in Nanterre. The fashion designer disappeared exactly as he wanted – without leaving a trace.

Karl Lagerfeld showcased his world four times a year at the Grand Palais up until the couture show in January 2019, which he was unable to attend due to ill health. The palace, originally built for the 1900 Exposition Universelle, was the setting for his two annual ready-to-wear collections and his two haute couture collections for spring/summer and autumn/winter. But this time the show was not about the next season's fashions. These two hours were all about one man's life, about all the different roles he had played over eighty-five years, how he thought, talked, behaved and lived. As became clear by the end of the star-studded event, Karl Lagerfeld was more than just a fashion designer: he was an originator of ideas, books, sketches, maxims, logos, expressions, careers and ideals.

Former clients, fans, managers, models, dressmakers and actors were not the only people on the list on this evening of remembrance. Other faces appearing at the memorial included Lagerfeld's personal florist, Caroline Cnocquaert, who arrived on the avenue in one of her Lachaume delivery vans. Marina Krauth of the Felix Jud bookstore travelled in from Hamburg, while Hervé Le Masson and Catherine Kujawski from Librairie 7L, Lagerfeld's own bookstore on the other side of the Seine, attached a handwritten note to the glass door to let customers know that the shop would be closed from 4.30 that afternoon. Jewelry designer Aaron Cyril Bismuth sported a necklace with large, colourful gemstones, the same as the one that Lagerfeld had kept for special occasions. Birte Carolin Sebastian talked about starting out as a model in the 1990s, when Lagerfeld gave her a wink and the encouragement she needed in a world that was still completely new to her.

The spotlight was not on fashion on this last evening of spring in the Grand Palais; it was on the man behind the designs.[1] Hanging from the steel framework of the vast hall were fifty-six gigantic photographs of Lagerfeld from different eras of his life, sometimes sporting a beard or a monocle, elsewhere holding his beloved cat. These images charted his extensive career in fashion, spanning six and a half decades, starting from his time as Pierre Balmain's assistant in 1954. They also documented his love of showmanship, remembering the romantic young man with a side parting and a white handkerchief in his breast pocket, the hyper-photoshopped global celebrity who fancied himself as a rock star, and the quirky-looking dandy with his Birman cat.

Those portraits watched over the Parisian high-society event hosted by Chanel, Fendi and the designer's signature Karl Lagerfeld brand. The indefatigable creator had worked for all three companies to the last, and now his image was gazing out over the kind of elite spectacle he loved to witness when he was alive. Bernard Arnault, who had incorporated Fendi into his LVMH empire, the biggest luxury conglomerate in the world, might now have his sights on the other two brands as well. But, as if to put paid to any such rumours on an evening like this, France's richest man set business aside and engaged in polite conversation with Alain Wertheimer, who privately co-owns Chanel together with his brother Gérard. The insatiable brand collector is unlikely to have been content with mere pleasantries, however. With the Wertheimer brothers both in their seventies, and having spent decades in the luxury sector, their interest in the superlative brand could well be starting to wane. After all, Lagerfeld had orchestrated Chanel's revival for the last three and a half decades. What was going to happen now he was gone?

There were enough renowned designers under one roof at 'Karl For Ever' to stage an entire fashion week. Valentino Garavani, for one, spoke of his great admiration for the friend he had known since the 1950s, while Stella McCartney, Lagerfeld's successor at Chloé, paid her respects in a black lace veil. Tommy Hilfiger, a true champion of the Karl Lagerfeld name, travelled up from Nice, while Ralph Lauren joined from London, where he had just been awarded an honorary knighthood by Prince Charles. Gucci designer Alessandro Michele hugged Fendi chief Silvia Fendi. Two designers previously rumoured to be possible successors to the Chanel throne, Alber Elbaz and Haider Ackermann, were also among the famous faces at the memorial event.

Karl Lagerfeld was not much of a family man. What mattered to him most was the family he made for himself. 'That was his strength: his ability to use the people around him and draw upon them for his creativity, for his own life and knowledge, to find out what was happening on the street,' Sébastien Jondeau said in one of the video homages that opera director Robert Carsen had compiled, along with live performances, for this evening-long tribute on the second longest day of the year. 'He was the original multi-tasker, a man who did everything at once,' said *Vogue* chief Anna Wintour. 'Karl loved parties, he loved people, but he was protective of his private life...

[He] often said that when he died, he wanted to disappear. Well, that cannot happen.'

And, in fact, it did not happen. An unusually vocal Alain Wertheimer reminisced about their working relationship, which began in 1982, when he appointed Lagerfeld to revamp Chanel, and soon turned into a friendship. Bernard Arnault compared the designer to Picasso, another legend who kept reinventing himself throughout the different stages of his career. Tilda Swinton took to the stage to perform an excerpt from one of Lagerfeld's favourite novels, Virginia Woolf's *Orlando*: 'Clothes that wear us and not we them... They change our view of the world and the world's view of us.' The charming Cara Delevingne recited a poem about cats by French writer Colette; Lang Lang performed Chopin's *Grande valse brillante* in E-flat major on a limited-edition Steinway piano designed by Lagerfeld himself; Pharrell Williams sang his hit song 'Gust of Wind'; and Helen Mirren quoted some of her favourite 'Karlisms', including 'personality begins where comparison ends'.

'Karl For Ever' was an uninhibited tribute to the myth that Karl Lagerfeld had created for himself during his lifetime. This man had poured so much of his creativity into his own personal brand during his career, and now the legend was here to stay. He was the author of his own image, his own master of ceremonies, the ruler of his own public perception. His fame was also due to his perfectly orchestrated public appearances. He entertained audiences far and wide with his words of wisdom and his quips. He won over millions of people in the visual era with the logo he created in his own self-image.

'No second option' was one of Lagerfeld's favourite sayings: he made a commitment, and he saw it through. In an era of infinite possibilities, where endless options lead to arbitrary decisions, particularly in fashion, this decisive attitude was as antiquated as his stand-up collar. But his steadfast commitment was a real breath of fresh air, the antithesis to a society in which obligations vanish into thin air and allegiances crumble. Karl Lagerfeld was living proof that it was possible to keep a commitment while staying true to oneself.

Lagerfeld's characteristic rigour, the strict work ethic that never failed to amaze the French, leads us all the way back to his roots. It would be impossible to fully understand the life of this man without his grandparents and parents, his sisters and friends, teachers and classmates. The dazzling career of this German in Paris would never have been a reality were it not for the Prussian officials, the Hanseatic merchants, and all the other people who came before him. Until now, so many of the details of Karl Lagerfeld's early life have been lost in the fog of history, making it easy to lose sight of the people behind the legend. In the stories he told and the webs he wove, the designer blurred the traces of his biography, laying false trails for those who tried to find out more. With journalists all too happy to believe the picture he painted of who he was, and with so many of us consumed by our fascination for this figure – at once timeless and inextricably bound to his place in history – we have lost sight of the people who made him.

Although that evening in the Grand Palais was bright and beautiful, much remained hidden in the dark. What those portraits didn't show was how the designer's early years shaped him, and how he later sought to control more than just his own life. They didn't show the trauma he suffered in his early childhood, or what drove him to his endless pursuit of productivity, nor why he strove to become a master of so many disciplines, including product design, photography, set design, interiors, illustration, caricatures, collecting, books and publishing.

This book aims to get a little closer to a man who always kept himself at a safe distance. It is based on conversations with over a hundred of Lagerfeld's relatives, friends, acquaintances, classmates, neighbours, colleagues, business associates and employees in Germany, France, Italy and the US. It also features new insights from previously unseen letters and faxes from Lagerfeld's personal archive, as well as recently uncovered letters, notes and photographs that belonged to his parents. It includes previously unpublished material from two interviews between the author and Lagerfeld in

2015 and 2017. Private archives, church records, local and national archives proved invaluable when researching this book, specifically in Baden-Baden, Bad Bramstedt, Beckum, Hamburg, Yakutsk, Kiel, Münster, Neumünster, Neustadt in Holstein, Palm Beach Gardens, Paris, Reggio Emilia, Schleswig and Vladivostok.[2]

There was one thing the eager crowd missed all too easily on that evening before the solstice in the Grand Palais: the myth was a real person. He was a man with ideas, skills and weaknesses. He was a man who made mistakes. Yet again, the fashion scene held an inward gaze, revolving around itself. But, legend though he was, this man did not simply appear out of nowhere. When people spoke of the energy in the room that evening, they were talking about someone who once lived, someone with roots. But where did he come from? Even if we choose to look back on a life from when it ended, the beginning is always the best place to start.

11 April 1930, 3 Dürerstrasse, Münster: Otto Lagerfeld and Elisabeth Bahlmann (centre row, left) celebrate their wedding. The marriage is witnessed by the bride's sister Felicitas Ramstedt (right) and her husband Conrad (back row, left), whose daughters Eva (front, left) and Tita (front, second left) would become Karl Lagerfeld's favourite cousins. The mother of the bride, Milly Bahlmann, is shown in the centre of the photograph.

Prologue

Father

One of Otto Lagerfeld's best customers lived right under his roof: the evaporated milk entrepreneur's son, Karl, was fed straight from the tin. His mother, Elisabeth, had no desire to breastfeed: 'I didn't marry a dairy merchant only to be forced to surrender my breasts. There's always canned milk,' she said.[1] In his mother's eagerness not to 'spoil her bosoms',[2] little Karl was nursed on the same evaporated milk that his father produced in his factory. Fortunately, it seemed not to do him any harm.[3]

Otto Lagerfeld, born in Hamburg on 20 September 1881, also owed a great deal to evaporated milk. He was set up for life when he founded the Glücksklee brand, but only after serving his time as a young, aspiring Hamburg merchant, travelling the world and exposing himself to real danger. While learning the ropes in the coffee trade, Otto Lagerfeld discovered the true meaning of international trade, experiencing first-hand how global history can strike.

His father, Otto Lagerfeld Sr (b. 1845), was also a merchant. His name is given in the 1910 Hamburg telephone directory with the description 'Wine shop and authorized wine importer, general warehouse of the Grande-Chartreuse (Pères Chartreux in Tarragona)'. The liquor dealer sold his imported products, including herbal liqueur, at 74 Rödingsmarkt in Hamburg's old town, close to the inland harbour.[4] His son Otto built him a house for his old age in the Ottensen neighbourhood, at number 70 on the famous thoroughfare known as the Elbchaussee, which joins the Elbe suburbs with the district of Altona and the inner city. This was the address for letters of condolence when Tönnies Johann Otto Lagerfeld passed away on 22 June 1931 at the age of eighty-five. The house overlooking the River Elbe was also on the obituary notice for his wife Maria Lagerfeld (née Wiegels) when she died on 13 March 1936.[5] In those days, the whole Elbchaussee area – including the Ottensen end, where the Lagerfelds lived – was an even more sought-after residential district than it is today. Back then there were hardly any cars, so there was no disadvantage to living in one of the even-numbered houses, on the right-hand side on the way out of town. These days, one has to cross a busy street in order to reach the banks of the Elbe on the other side.

One of eleven children, Otto Lagerfeld Jr followed in his father's footsteps when he decided to become a merchant. He completed an apprenticeship with a Hamburg-based coffee exporter, was called up for military service, then travelled to Maracaibo in Venezuela on assignment for the Hamburg company Van Dissel, Rode & Co. in late 1902. Venezuelan coffee was in high demand in Hamburg around this time, but travelling to the country to secure supplies was extremely dangerous.[6] By undertaking the assignment in Maracaibo, Otto Lagerfeld was putting himself at risk of catching the rampant yellow fever that was spread by mosquitoes around the marshy terrain. He was also exposing himself to political unrest in the region on the back of falling coffee prices. Uprisings in Colombia, with the start of the Thousand Days' War in 1899, brought trading with the neighbouring country to a complete standstill. Guerrilla warfare made work increasingly difficult on the plantations. Then came the Venezuelan crisis of 1902 to 1903, a naval blockade against the country by Great Britain, Germany and Italy, which resulted in many German citizens being arrested.

Despite all the social and political unrest in the region, the twenty-one-year-old still decided to take passage to Venezuela in 1902 aboard a merchant vessel.[7] He was taken prisoner in Maracaibo, where he claims he only survived yellow fever because an Indigenous woman rubbed oil into his skin both day and night.[8] Otto Lagerfeld Jr continued his quest for superior coffee beans on his travels through Colombia on muleback. The political conflicts, which only ceased when a treaty was signed in March 1903, showed the young merchant that there was no way of trading successfully if the political situation was too unstable.

Realizing that the job offered little in the way of prospects, Otto Lagerfeld terminated his contract after a few years in the role.[9] He travelled to the United States, where his brothers Joseph and Johannes were already living, and arrived in San Francisco on 16 April 1906.[10] This was just two days before a massive earthquake struck the city, killing more than three thousand people and igniting several devastating fires in its wake. According to his granddaughter Thoma Schulenburg, he witnessed the fires from Sausalito, on the other side of the Golden Gate strait.[11]

Otto Lagerfeld remained in San Francisco until at least December 1906.[12] He then continued northwards to Kent, near Seattle, in Washington State, where the Carnation Evaporated Milk Company, still in its infancy, was looking for an ambitious young travelling salesman for its export business. He travelled onwards to Japan, Manila and Hong Kong, before reaching Vladivostok in 1907, where he set up an office on the company's behalf.[13] Evaporated milk was still a fairly new product at the time. It was the result of a relatively recent development by scientists in the nineteenth century: they had discovered a way to kill the germs in milk by heating the liquid and removing water through inspissation. Homogenization helped to reduce the fat particles, making the milk easy to digest and preventing the milk from creaming so quickly. The demand for long-lasting condensed milk was highest in regions where fresh milk was in scarce supply, which in those days was the norm since the domestic fridge had yet to be invented.

But why Russia, of all places? And why Vladivostok, 5,000 miles from Hamburg? Karl Lagerfeld, who spoke a great deal about his mother but said very little about his father, repeatedly stunned people when he told them about his father's professional exploits. 'My father even sold condensed milk in Vladivostok.' He clearly prided himself on his father's entrepreneurial spirit and his thirst for adventure. Andrei Sidorov, a local historian, discovered one of Otto Lagerfeld's advertisements in a Vladivostok reference book from 1912.[14] According to the advert, the products he sold besides

Advertisement from 1912: Otto Lagerfeld sold canned milk and other
American products, including flycatchers, ropes and tools, in Vladivostok.

condensed milk included other American exports such as flycatchers,
dried fruits, manila rope and files, as well as other metal tools like
mining drills and agricultural equipment.

The city at the eastern limit of the Russian Empire was the perfect
base for a merchant, with convenient links to various manufacturing companies. The Trans-Siberian Railway, completed in various
stages up to 1916, brought the Far East closer to Europe. From 1903,
this development contributed to an economic upturn in the region,
as the most important Russian seaport by the Pacific Ocean became
an international trading hub. Otto Lagerfeld sold the canned milk
under the Russian trademark 'Gvozdika' (Carnation).

As a Russophile who also spoke the language, it must have been
particularly painful for Otto Lagerfeld to witness all the changes
that took hold when World War I broke out. On 1 August 1914, when
Germany declared war on Russia, he requested permission from the

Russian authorities to leave for the United States via Japan because he could no longer run his business due to the 'suspension of trading operations with London and Hamburg'.[15] A few days later, however, he was one of several Germans arrested on suspicion of espionage.[16] He applied for Russian citizenship while in Vladivostok prison but his request was denied, even though he had lived in the country for seven years and was conversant in both Russian and English.[17] American citizen Eleanor L. Pray watched from the platform at the train station when Otto Lagerfeld was deported with his fellow countrymen.[18]

After journeying over 1,250 miles north, presumably mostly by boat, Otto Lagerfeld and the other prisoners were transferred to Verkhoyansk, a remote village located just above the Arctic Circle in Siberia. The republic of Yakutia was traditionally the destination of choice for exiles, even during the Tsarist period. The original outcasts were the peasants and the workers, the Old Believers and the sectarians; then came the political outcasts in increasing numbers. In Stalinist times, the region became known as a 'prison without bars'. In a landscape so isolated, with conditions so harsh, it was hard to even imagine trying to flee, especially given the absence of railways and proper roads. Verkhoyansk was home to 470 residents, three shops and one church.[19] The area was under the control of the local police rather than the military authorities. There were no POW camps: the whole of Verkhoyansk was a place of exile by definition.

The only insights into the living conditions come from indirect accounts – for instance, from the reader's letter that Otto Lagerfeld sent to the *Frankfurter Allgemeine Zeitung* in 1956 in response to a newspaper report on 'Blocks of Milk': 'Milk is sold in blocks throughout northern Siberia, not only in Yakutsk... The milk is collected in a deep dish in the winter and frozen while the cows are being milked, then again straight afterwards. The farmers' wives remove the milk by skimming the dish over the top of a fire and tossing the blocks of milk into a sack. People buy milk by the bag in northern Siberia, and they store it in an ice hole at home. If they need milk, they simply go in, chip a bit off the block and thaw it over the open hearth. I was held near Yakutsk on the northern section of the Lena for four years during World War I. Temperatures averaged between fifty and fifty-five degrees below zero in the winter there.'[20]

What a chilly picture he paints! Life in exile must have been brutal. The barometer hit minus 67.8 degrees on 5 February 1892, the lowest temperature on record at the time. From then on Verkhoyansk was deemed the northern 'Pole of Cold', colder than all the other inhabited regions in the northern hemisphere; in other words, it was the 'coldest town in the world'. Still, Otto Lagerfeld makes no mention of suffering or deprivation, choosing instead to write objectively about milk as if very little else happened in this remote settlement. His account is a reflection of the traditional masculine attitude that prevailed at the time, playing it cool and not letting things show. It might also be characteristic of the Hanseatic tendency towards understatement in the telling of real-life stories, and perhaps the use of repression as a survival tactic that was so common in the twentieth century.

Otto Lagerfeld made it back to Hamburg via Saint Petersburg in 1918 amid the chaos of revolution. Then in 1919, he started importing cans of Carnation milk through his company, Lagerfeld & Co.[21] His name was entered onto the commercial register on 1 March 1919 along with Johannes Jacob Lagerfeld, his brother, who was also registered as a merchant of the Groß Flottbek quarter of Hamburg. Carl Wübbens, a friend who had likewise been exiled from Vladivostok with him, was later listed as a co-shareholder on 26 August 1922.[22] As cans of evaporated milk slowly became popular, Otto Lagerfeld established his own company in 1923 under the brand name Glücksklee (German for 'four-leaf clover'). The red and white label, designed by the man himself, featured a green four-leaf clover with a cow's head at the centre. Karl Lagerfeld's father set him a great example of how to build a brand. Evidently he was proud of his father's achievements: even when the designer was in his seventies, he still wore a gold clover pin on his lapel.[23]

The offices of Lagerfeld & Co. were located by the Alster river in Hamburg (at 52 An der Alster). The Carnation milk importer was probably the first German company to specialize in evaporated milk. Imports of the product originally cost the managing director US$5 per crate,[24] but this increased when import duty hikes were imposed in 1922. From then on, according to Otto Lagerfeld's records, every crate of milk was subject to a customs charge of 20 marks. To work around this predicament, he convinced his American licensors that it would be cheaper to produce the tins using German manpower and to use German milk. He went on to establish Glücksklee Milchgesellschaft mbH in 1925, profiting from the modest prosperity of the 'Golden Twenties' in the early years of the business.

Production began on 1 May 1926 in the new factory at Neustadt harbour. The location was perfect from a logistical point of view: it was within easy reach of numerous dairy farms in East Holstein and benefitted from direct access to the Baltic Sea for distribution. The four-leaf clover was a hit. Long-life milk was a long-awaited treat for the people of Germany. They could use it to make hot chocolate and desserts, or to make coffee more palatable, or they could simply add water and drink it cold. A 1930 advert sold Glücksklee milk under the heading 'Please, mother, can I have some more?' with the tagline: 'Even children who don't like vegetables ask for seconds when you add a little Glücksklee milk.'

Though Otto Lagerfeld tried to stay on the right side of the Nazis when they came to power in 1933, his business still fell upon hard times in the years that followed. The company added two more factories in 1937, one in Waren (Mecklenburg), the other in Allenburg (East Prussia), but World War II soon put the brakes on production. In a letter from 9 April 1941 the factory director wrote, 'If it isn't coal, then we're out of cans, vats or sheet metal. Every day there's something else. You cannot imagine what it is like to accept 130,000 litres of milk a day, not knowing whether you will be able to package it.'[25] The company soon had to change tack and started making cheese, butter and powdered milk instead. The factories in Waren and Allenburg fell victim to the war, but the director did not go without during this time. According to the information provided on his denazification survey,

Otto Lagerfeld had a steady gross annual income in excess of 50,000 marks from 1935, rising to 70,000 marks per year from 1940 to 1944.[26]

Tragedy struck in the Bay of Lübeck on 3 May 1945, when the war was almost over. The British Royal Air Force targeted the *Cap Arcona*, *Thielbek*, *Deutschland* and *Athen*, mistakenly assuming that enemy troops were on board. When the bombs hit, they killed more than eight thousand prisoners from Nazi concentration camps, who were travelling aboard the German ships. Chaos erupted in Neustadt. Survivors stole food from the Glücksklee warehouses, and a freight train carrying cheese wheels, sacks of sugar and packs of butter was ransacked. Residents, migrant workers and prisoners of war raided the food warehouses, too.[27] Appalling deaths followed: exhausted former prisoners gorged themselves on butter and were unable to digest the rich food, perishing 'in great numbers'.[28] It is not clear whether the Glücksklee director was arrested in connection with the incident, having stockpiled food supplies without inform-ing the authorities. In any case, Otto Lagerfeld was allegedly taken into custody in Neumünster, which was 'extremely embarrassing' for his wife.[29]

Soon enough, the lucky clover returned to form when the German Currency Reform was introduced in 1948. Historian Ulrich Herbert writes: 'Homeowners and landowners benefitted greatly from the unilateral depreciation of financial assets and the stability of material assets, as did commercial enterprises and businessmen.'[30] By 1952 the company was processing 535,000 litres of milk a day. The Glücksklee brand became a major employer in Neustadt, as well as being the town's biggest taxpayer and an excellent customer to the dairy farmers based in East Holstein.

When Karl Lagerfeld was young, his father was constantly travel-ling to his factories or working at the company's headquarters at 36 Mittelweg in Hamburg.[31] 'The only thing he cared about was canned milk,' the designer once said.[32] 'My father wasn't much of a talker, but when he did talk, it was mostly about business. He was Hanseatic through and through. I never had any deep conversations with him.'[33]

Evidently he was a *Pfeffersack* (literally, a 'sack of pepper', a term used to describe many a wealthy yet boorish Hamburg merchant).[34] Karl Lagerfeld never got a real feel for his father's business dealings. As out of place as he was in the Holstein countryside, this Grand Burgher's son only visited the Glücksklee factory in Neustadt once. His cousin Kurt Lagerfeld remembered the event: it was in May 1952, at the factory's twenty-fifth anniversary celebration in nearby Grömitz. A farmer asked Karl if he wanted to drink a beer with him, but the eighteen-year-old said no: he only drank champagne.[35] It wasn't long before he headed for Paris.[36]

Otto Lagerfeld stayed on as the director of Glücksklee until 1957. Despite the company's success under his leadership, it started to fall behind its Swabian competitor, Bärenmarke, which was doing particularly well in the southern German market. By 1963, Glücksklee's share of the market was between 16 and 17 per cent, considerably lower than the 26–28 per cent share boasted by its competitor.[37] In the mid-1960s, the thousand or so employees at the company generated somewhere in excess of 100 million marks.[38] Very little remains of Otto Lagerfeld's legacy today. In 1985 Glücksklee's American licensor was acquired by the Swiss Nestlé corporation, then on 17 September 1987 Glücksklee GmbH was dissolved and incorporated into Nestlé Deutschland AG, the German subsidiary of the multinational company.[39] The factory in Neustadt by the Baltic Sea closed its doors on 31 December 2002, after seventy-six years in operation, even though it was still productive and the order books were full. All of a sudden the long brick building on the harbour was empty. The residents of Neustadt were disappointed in Nestlé. The evaporated milk division was sold to Hochwald Foods in Rhineland-Palatinate in 2003; since 2008 Hochwald has been the only manufacturer of evaporated milk in Germany. Sales of canned milk have been on the decline for years, as consumers increasingly opt for a low-fat diet. Nowadays, old-age pensioners are the only people who are likely to poke a couple of holes into a tin of this high-fat milk and pour it into their coffee drip by drip.

Otto Lagerfeld, a pleasant but reserved gentleman, tried to give his granddaughter Thoma a taste of some of his life experiences in his later years. She once accompanied him to a Chinese restaurant he liked in Wilhelms-Platz (now known as Hans-Albers-Platz) in the St Pauli neighbourhood, and he surprised her by chatting to the owners in Chinese. Thoma was very impressed, both by his language skills and by the food. There is no conclusive proof of Karl Lagerfeld's claims that his father had learned nine languages in his years of apprenticeship and travel.[40] But in any case, he certainly spoke English, French, Spanish, Russian, and a little Chinese. And now he was happy to have someone he could show.[41]

Otto Lagerfeld moved to Baden-Baden with his wife Elisabeth in March 1960. Though he had retired by this time, he gave 'consultant director' as his profession when registering at his new address[42] – clearly he was not ready to put his life's work behind him yet. In his son's words, the life of a pensioner was no thrill: 'He had no work, he felt useless. For ten whole years he did nothing but read the newspaper all day.'[43] Evidently his father 'died of boredom': 'He dozed off reading the newspaper at the age of ninety.'[44] In fact, Otto Lagerfeld was eighty-five years old when he died in the Black Forest retirement haven on 4 July 1967 – the same age as his father and his son when they died.

Karl Lagerfeld often claimed that his mother only told him the sad news three weeks after his father had died. But he didn't mind, he would say, he didn't like funerals anyway.[45] Two days after Otto Lagerfeld's death, his obituary was published in the *Frankfurter Allgemeine Zeitung* on behalf of Glücksklee. 'From humble beginnings,' it read, the former director had built 'one of the most important businesses in the German dairy industry'.[46] Was Karl's mother oblivious to the notice in the newspaper? Had she really risked her son in Paris learning of his father's death from the press and not from her? Of course not. It can't have taken that long for Karl to find out about his father's death: the burial was at Nienstedt Cemetery in Hamburg on 10 July 1967, and he was there.

Well, not exactly. The funeral was one last reminder of Karl Lagerfeld's rather curious relationship with his father. Instead of joining his family at the burial, he waited in a nearby hotel called the Louis C. Jacob on the Elbchaussee until the funeral party appeared.[47] His family was outraged. 'Aunt Ebbe' also fell out of favour that day. Karl's cousin Kurt remembers Elisabeth Lagerfeld telling her in-laws that the relationship was over, and that they should use the formal 'Sie' (for 'you', instead of the informal 'Du') to address each other from now on. The family must also have been angered when Karl later claimed that the Lagerfeld dynasty would end with him. After all, Otto Lagerfeld's siblings had children, grandchildren and great-grandchildren of their own. There are lots of people named Lagerfeld in Germany and the US, but most of them are not listed in the phone book.

One thing Karl Lagerfeld cannot be accused of is neglecting the family grave in plot 16D of Nienstedt Cemetery, where his grandfather, his grandmother and two of his aunts were also buried. According to the cemetery office, Karl later extended the term of the six-person burial plot until 2042, much longer than the norm.[48] When his resting place is finally levelled out, Otto Lagerfeld – the last person to occupy the family grave – will have been dead for seventy-five years.

Mother

Karl Lagerfeld found his father distant and aloof. He was closer to his mother, who was home more and always had something to say. As well as revealing her dark sense of humour, this woman's frank comments expressed an unrelenting strictness and impossibly high standards. With all the anecdotes and biting remarks her son aired to an astonished public over the years, Elisabeth Lagerfeld hardly seemed like the most maternal person. She had no filter when it came to projecting her high expectations onto her son, exasperating and motivating him at the same time.

Lagerfeld once talked about the time she threw away his old diaries. 'You don't want everyone to know how stupid you are, do you?'[49]

'Never wear a hat, you look like an old lesbian.'[50]

'You look like me but not as good.'[51]

'Your nose is like a potato. And I think I should order curtains for the nostrils!'[52]

'You could have made more of yourself, but what you've managed to achieve is okay given your lack of ambition.'[53]

'Please speak faster, so you can hurry up and finish talking all that nonsense.'[54]

'With fat fingers like those, you should never smoke or play the piano.'[55]

'It's a pity you can't see yourself walking across the yard. If you could, you'd see how fat your bottom is these days.'[56]

The impact of tough motherly love on a child is hard to measure. Such cutting, oddly spiteful words have been uttered to many a youngster by many a critical parent. Still, these harsh remarks from his mother made it hard for the young Karl to identify with who he was supposed to be as a child. Feeling like an outsider in his age group, he was spurred on by his mother's criticisms and wanted to grow up as quickly as possible so that he could be free from the shackles of childhood. There is another explanation, however: perhaps Karl's mother didn't mean everything she said and was simply trying to put her motherly pride into perspective through jibes and put-downs.

If we are to interpret Elisabeth's behaviour, we must step back and take a closer look at her story. The daughter of the district administrator for Beckum, she was raised in the rather provincial setting of this town between Münster and Paderborn in North-Rhine Westphalia, whose population was less than ten thousand around the turn of the twentieth century. Coming from a family that moved around a lot, Elisabeth and her older sister Felicitas Bahlmann grew up knowing that their roots were elsewhere. They also occupied a prominent position in this provincial environment because their father was the district administrator, which made it easier for them to escape certain patterns of childhood – unlike the children of people who had lived in the town much longer.

Poise was everything: sisters Felicitas (left) and
Elisabeth Bahlmann enjoyed a privileged upbringing
in the former administrative centre of Beckum.

Karl Bahlmann (1859–1922) was more than just a local politician.
He was born in Neustadt in Upper Silesia and completed his secondary-school education in Recklinghausen in 1881. He then studied law in
Freiburg, Greifswald and Berlin, and became a doctor of law in Jena
in 1884. He served as a government assessor, and was appointed as
a senior administrator in Gammertingen on the Swabian Jura from
1891 to 1899, before finally taking on the post of district administrator
of Beckum from 1899 to 1922. He also represented the Centre Party in
the Provincial Diet of the Province of Westphalia for the constituency
of Beckum from 1911 to 1920. He did not live to witness the gradual
descent of the Centre Party, the rise of the Nazis, or the dissolution
of the Provincial Diet when the Nazis came to power in 1933.

Karl Bahlmann, who later lent his first name to his grandson, was
an erudite, proactive man who was well-versed in politics, justice and

the bureaucracy of the German Empire and the fledgling Weimar Republic. His father, Wilhelm Bahlmann (1828–1888), had been a judge and a senior civil servant in Prussia. Karl Bahlmann was personally appointed as district administrator by the German Emperor Wilhelm II. The Emperor's letter, dated 23 August 1899, has been preserved with Bahlmann's personal file in the Westphalia section of the regional archive of North Rhine-Westphalia. It begins 'We, William, King of Prussia by the grace of God…' and states that Bahlmann was appointed by the Emperor himself.[57]

The Bahlmanns moved to Beckum and did not look back. The twentieth century was in its infancy, and things were going well for the young family. As a reserve officer, the new district administrator requested leave from the regional council for 'military service', which he completed at least in 1900, 1905 and 1907, usually for four weeks at a time. Karl Sr's requests for leave can also be found in the regional archives of Münster, along with his holiday requests. In 1901 he asked for four weeks' leave to travel to Norderney, then in August 1904 it was three weeks in Switzerland, four weeks in Tyrol in summer 1905, and four weeks in Switzerland in July 1907.

The family wanted for nothing around this time. From 1 October 1904, the district president of Münster boosted the district administrator's salary of 5,400 marks with an additional allowance of 600 marks. An extra 600 marks per year were added to these 6,000 marks on 1 October 1907. And by 1 October 1910, this annual sum of 6,600 marks rose to 7,200 marks. This was a lot of money at the turn of the century, when the average worker earned around 1,500 marks per year and just over one mark could buy a hundredweight of coal or a kilogram of pork. In 1911, the district administrator was also given a car for official business.

Elisabeth was born in Gammertingen in the district of Sigmaringen (Baden-Württemberg) on 25 April 1897, and she was two when she moved to Beckum with her family. She and her elder sister Felicitas must have felt like princesses. They lived in a large official residence on the ground floor of the Kreisständehaus building in Beckum. Now known as the 'Altes Kreishaus', the magnificent neo-Gothic building dating from 1886 or 1887 was a wonderland for children, with its impressive proportions and its sprawling back gardens. Elisabeth's first school was in Beckum. She then attended the Lyceum, 3 miles away in Ahlen, from 1911 to 1913, and left after completing her exams.[58]

Soon enough, cracks started to appear in this pretty picture. In the spring of 1908, Karl Bahlmann suffered what was assumed to be a heart attack when he was not even fifty years old. He received medical treatment in Wiesbaden in April and May 1908, then in Cologne in October of the same year. Even before his health took a turn for the worse, he was frequently away from home, travelling around the district and being called up for reserve training. From 1911, he frequently had to take leave to attend hearings at the Provincial Diet and he was away from home even more than before. And now he was also travelling to Bad Nauheim, a spa town in Hessen renowned for its specialist treatments for cardiovascular disease, several times a year.

Karl Bahlmann continued to attend to his official duties regardless, as shown by the various distinctions he received in the following years. Records show that he and fellow district administrator Max Gerbaulet, representing Beckum and Warendorf respectively, were awarded the 'rank of Most Gracious Privy Government Council' on 19 January 1915 'by the highest decree' of His Majesty and the Minister of the Interior. A note from 1917 states that Bahlmann received the military decoration of the 'Eiserne Kreuz am weiss-schwarzen Bande' (iron cross on a black and white ribbon). On 19 April 1921, his status was raised to that of 'Großes Landratsamt', a senior district administrator post that also brought with it a higher salary. Then on 6 March 1922, the district secretary delivered the following news to the chairman of the regional council: 'The district administrator and Privy Councillor Dr Bahlmann passed away this morning.' He was laid to rest at the Elisabethfriedhof cemetery in Beckum.

Kahl Bahlmann's untimely death on his sixty-third birthday was a blow to the family. His widow, Emilie ('Milly') Bahlmann, had to vacate the official residence in Beckum to make way for the new district administrator. She wanted to move to Münster, where her elder daughter Felicitas lived, but as she stated in a letter to the chairman of the regional council, she was unable to find an apartment there due to 'difficulties in the housing market'. The late district administrator's widow, 'Frau Wwe. Landrat Bahlmann', therefore apologized that she would be unable to move out of the official residence until the following year, and since inflation had sky-rocketed, she requested financial assistance on 31 March 1923 to help with the costs of the move.[59] On 11 September 1923, the chairman of the regional council granted her a removal allowance of 3,037,376 marks.

Emilie Bahlmann initially lived on Achtermannstrasse before moving into the new house at 3 Dürerstrasse in the spring of 1929. The house was located in the up-and-coming Kreuzviertel district, one of Münster's most popular residential areas, which borders the ring of fortifications that once protected Münster's Old Town and now serves as the 'Promenade'. The district administrator's widow was the first tenant on the first floor, the *piano nobile*. The owner's granddaughter, Ruth Brandt (b. 1922), still remembers having to curtsey whenever she bumped into the widow on the stairs or outside the building. Emilie Bahlmann, who had a maid in keeping with her social status and always wore black, had to be addressed as 'Madame Privy Councillor' or 'Mrs District Administrator'.[60]

Her daughter Felicitas, Karl Lagerfeld's aunt, lived around the corner. She was born on 16 November 1892 and married Conrad Ramstedt in 1920, a surgeon and the medical director of the Raphaelsklinik in Münster. Felicitas Ramstedt's grandson, Gordian Tork, recalls that she was 'very elegant, ahead of her time, and very independent'. From the 1950s, she drove through North-Rhine Westphalia in a car for her work as a pharmaceuticals representative. Sometimes Gordian, the son of her younger daughter Felicitas ('Tita', married name Tork), was allowed to accompany her. And while 'Frau Professor', as she was known, introduced herself to the doctors, her grandson would be outside cleaning the car, a Ford Taunus.[61]

The 1920s were not an easy time. Elisabeth Bahlmann was twenty-four years old when her father died, and her mother's precarious situation meant that she had to become independent fast. Presumably this didn't bother her; she wanted to get out of the dull countryside anyway. She was guided by feminist principles. Even at a young age she was politically minded, as evidenced by certain aspects of her appearance. Karl Lagerfeld once talked about how his mother cropped her hair 'around 1919', so very early on: 'She was very much the feminist. Her hair was very long in the photographs from her childhood, but for the rest of her life she always had short hair.'[62] In the 1920s, before the bob came into fashion, short hair-cuts on women were seen as a feminist statement, an expression of female emancipation.

Elisabeth was politicized by the women's movement, which had campaigned for political participation for decades. 'One of her heroes was Hedwig Dohm, who started to be a feminist in Germany in the 1800s when women had not a great position,' Karl Lagerfeld said in 2015.[63] In the 1870s, when Dohm's first books were published, women's rights were limited to the three C's: children, cooking, and the church. Lagerfeld was a child when he first heard about the Berlin feminist, whose granddaughter Katia later married Thomas Mann. 'People remember the English suffragettes but the first to care about women's rights was Hedwig Dohm.'[64]

In her day, Hedwig Dohm (1831–1919) was already campaigning for rights that would only become a reality in the twentieth century. The feminist trailblazer wanted girls to have the same opportunities for education and training as boys. She also said that women needed to be financially independent in order to enter into a partnership of equals with men, and she called for women to finally be given the right to vote. Dohm took aim at the chauvinistically based male claim to power and argued that motherly love was acquired rather than being a natural instinct. Her argument was therefore that women could continue to work after giving birth, and that institutions could take care of the housework and raising children.

Motherly love: not an instinct but something that women acquire? This is very reminiscent of how Elisabeth Lagerfeld treated her son. Perhaps this man's path through life was inspired not only by his mother's ambition and rigour, but also by her feminist drive?

When Elisabeth Bahlmann was a young woman aged between eighteen and twenty-one, she must have been delighted with the growing number of rights being afforded to women. From 1908, women were allowed to join a political party in Germany for the first time, and soon women would finally be allowed to vote. On 30 November 1918, the *Reichswahlgesetz* (Electoral Act), the regulation concerning the elections for the constituent German national parliament, ruled that all German men and women aged twenty-one and over could vote. The twenty-one-year-old Bahlmann would have been among the women who cast their votes for the elections on 19 January 1919. There were 37 women among the 423 members of the German National Assembly, which convened in Weimar in September and later in Berlin: 19 of these seats were for the Social Democratic Party (SPD), 6 were for the Centre Party, and the numbers were even lower for the other parties. It can be assumed that this hard-won success by the women's movement also sparked arguments in the Bahlmann household: as a member of the moderately conservative Centre Party, Elisabeth's father was hardly likely to have been in favour of women's suffrage.

Affection played only a minor role in child-rearing in the German Empire, hence Elisabeth Bahlmann's upbringing was generally quite strict. In those days, affection was reserved for one's spouse and the Fatherland. Militarism, authoritarianism and – in the state of Münster – Catholicism resulted in an unforgivingly stern approach to parenting. Tenderness was not part of the regime. 'My mother abhorred physical proximity,' Karl Lagerfeld once said. 'I must have inherited that trait from her.'[65] Gordian Tork (b. 1951) says that his grandmother Felicitas and her sister Elisabeth were subjected to a strict upbringing in that Prussian civil servant's household in Beckum: 'Etiquette and manners were very important. They had to treat their parents with the utmost respect and were not allowed to show their feelings.' All the same, he also says that the family were loving towards one another. 'Aunt Ebbe wasn't as overbearing as he often makes her out to be,' Tork said, referring to how his uncle twice-removed used to speak about Elisabeth. 'She had a sharp tongue, but she was also funny.'[66]

Elisabeth Bahlmann left provincial life and the patriarchy behind her as a young woman when she moved to Berlin. Karl Lagerfeld's cousin Kurt recalls that she worked as a lingerie sales assistant in a department store there.[67] But according to Thoma Schulenburg, whose mother was Elisabeth's stepdaughter Thea, she completed an apprenticeship as a dressmaker in Berlin and worked as a manageress in a fashion boutique: 'She had this incredible knowledge of fabrics and did all kinds of needlework with real passion and flair.' It was a treat to accompany her to the Seiden Brandt store at the Hamburg Rathaus after the war: 'She inspected the fabric through a monocle and exercised moderation when disciplining the sales staff – because she wanted to come back, of course.'[68]

Elisabeth Bahlmann's work as a sales assistant was not at odds with her need for independence. Quite the opposite: unlike most women her age in Beckum, she had managed to free herself from the role of housewife and mother that was earmarked for girls who lived in rural areas. Ulrich Herbert writes that the female worker represented a 'new, modern kind of woman', who embodied a new 'womanly independence and served as a clear contrast to the Wilhelmine image of women, whose prototypes were the female farmer, the haggard working-class woman with lots of children, and the conservative, middle-class "lady" of refined society, who kept a distance from working life'.[69] Female workers were associated with growing options for consumers and leisure activities that revolved around life in the city.[70]

It is unclear when exactly Elisabeth Bahlmann left home. 'She lived in Munich and then in Berlin as a young woman,' Karl Lagerfeld said.[71] Her name is not listed in the annual editions of the directories for Berlin and Greater Munich. And she was always vague when she mused to her son over the temptations of what was then the imperial capital. 'You can ask me anything about my childhood and the time after I met your father,' she told him. 'What happened in between is none of your business.' So he knew 'basically nothing' about his parents, but he didn't need to know, either. 'It's their life, it's none of my business,' he said in his characteristically offhand way.[72]

Perhaps Karl's mother didn't want her son to know that she had been married before. He only ever mentioned this fact in passing – and there was never any indication of where or when she got married, nor any mention of who this husband was. The story of how Elisabeth Bahlmann met Otto Lagerfeld also remains shrouded in mystery. We have never found out for certain how this young woman, eager for new experiences, crossed paths with this older man, who had already had more than his fair share of experiences. Some believe they met in the department store in Berlin, where she was selling the wares that he would have been buying.[73] However, she still had plans following her time in Berlin, and it is unlikely that she would have pursued those plans if she had already been with Otto Lagerfeld at that time. On 1 April 1929, she moved to Cologne.

The entry for Elisabeth Bahlmann in the 1930 Cologne directory contains the following information: 'Kindergymnastik, Salierring 43hp, Tel. 217 472.' The address is for a children's gymnastics club on a mezzanine floor.[74] And in two letters to her mother from Cologne, she writes about her new life, saying that 'everything is in good order' – she just had to wait for the children to sign up now. She sounds eager to get her business 'up and running', and tells her mother that she is proud of the sign when she sees it 'lit up from afar'. She talks about the playroom, which is evidently a room in her apartment, and about her visits to various doctors. It can be assumed that she would have been visiting them to introduce herself as a children's gymnastics teacher, so that they could recommend her services. 'I'm sure it will be alright, the children will come eventually,' she writes to Milly Bahlmann – and she seems to be encouraging herself with these words.[75]

Elisabeth was long gone from Berlin by this point, so Otto Lagerfeld may well have met his bride-to-be on holiday during the summer of

1929. Karl Lagerfeld's version of events seems quite plausible, if this is so: 'She had invited her nieces to the Baltic Sea on holiday,' he once said. 'My father, who was a widower, was there with his daughter too. He thought she was also a widow when they met, but she wasn't.'[76] Like Elisabeth, Otto Lagerfeld had been married before – to Theresia Feigl, a merchant's daughter, born in Hamburg on 20 March 1896. The entrepreneur was forty years old when they got married on 31 January 1922.[77] Theresia sadly died during childbirth that same year, at the age of just twenty-six. Her daughter, who was born the same day – 30 November 1922 – was called Theresia (Thea for short) after her mother. This was another heavy blow for Otto Lagerfeld, who had only recently survived the trials of World War I. His sisters took care of little Thea, who would spend the rest of her life burdened by the knowledge that her mother had died giving birth to her.

'Otto Lagerfeld Jr' (address: '70 Elbchaussee') and Elisabeth Bahlmann ('Münster i. Westf., Dürerstr. 3') announced their engagement in the local *Hamburger Nachrichten* newspaper on 8 March 1930. They got married in Münster on 11 April 1930. Otto was forty-eight at the time, and Elisabeth was thirty-two. The marriage record on file in the Münster register office states that Elisabeth Josef Emilie Bahlmann had 'no profession', while the word 'housewife' has been inserted next to the entry for her sister Felicitas, who was one of the witnesses, along with her husband Conrad Ramstedt.[78] A photograph (see p. 16) shows the small wedding party standing outside the building on Dürerstrasse. The women are wearing cloche hats, the men are in top hats, and the bride and groom are beaming. The mother of the bride is standing in the centre, clearly proud that her younger daughter has 'married well', as people used to say in those days: her first son-in-law was a professor, and her second son-in-law was a company director.

The marriage started well. Glücksklee barely felt the impact of the economic crisis that allowed the Nazis to gain an increasingly strong hold in the country. Otto Lagerfeld's healthy income then allowed him and Elisabeth to move further out of town, where life was even

more picturesque and tranquil. On 25 March 1930, he purchased the
manse at 4 Baurs Park from Auguste Baur, the daughter of Georg
Friedrich Baur, who had created this leafy landscaped park lined with
impressive houses.[79] Before long, on 7 April 1933, the family moved
to 3 Baurs Park, where they enjoyed even more stunning vistas of the
Elbe; the steep slope down to the river meant the view was completely
unimpeded. But they couldn't quite settle there either, and so they
moved from Hamburg to Bad Bramstedt when the children Martha
Christiane ('Christel'; b. 1931) and Karl (b. 1933) were still small. Otto
Lagerfeld sold the house at 3 Baurs Park in 1935. It was bought by the
National Socialist Joachim de la Camp, the then-Vice President, and
later President, of the Hamburg Chamber of Commerce.[80]

But what could have made the family leave one of the most prestigious addresses in the whole of the municipality of Blankenese?
The threat posed by the Nazis may have been a factor. Otto Lagerfeld
had survived the Venezuela Crisis and World War I, and now violent
conflicts were on the horizon once more. 'Altona Bloody Sunday'
happened virtually on their doorstep in Blankenese: on 17 July 1932,
a march by the National Socialist Party's 'Storm Trooper' paramili-
tary faction turned violent, and eighteen people were shot dead.
By moving to the small Holstein town of Bad Bramstedt, which benefitted from good rail connections from Hamburg and was on route
to the Neustadt factory, the Lagerfelds would manage to maintain a
safe distance from the political upheavals. Importantly, they would
also have a good supply of food.[81]

According to a contemporary witness, however, the fear of impending war was not the motivation for the move. Helmut Junge (b. 1930)
was the son of lawyer and notary Kurt Junge, who worked for Otto
Lagerfeld. Young Helmut lived at 5 Baurs Park with his family and
often played with Christel Lagerfeld. The nanny, Sister Meta, also
took care of him – Junge says this was 'a gift' for his mother Gertrud.
But Mrs Junge did not get along with her neighbour Mrs Lagerfeld.
And neither did little Helmut. One morning when he was three or
four years old, he stopped by next door and rang the doorbell to

call for Christel. It was so early that he woke Elisabeth Lagerfeld up. 'She huffed and puffed at me, asking what I wanted so early in the morning.' It seems she was unhappy living in Blankenese and didn't mind letting everyone know. According to Helmut Junge, she was the 'problem' in the family.[82]

Elisabeth Lagerfeld later told her step-granddaughter that she was unhappy in Blankenese. Rather than making her calm, the view of the river crushed her spirits: 'The ebb and flow gave me depression,' she told Thoma Schulenburg. In the tidal waters of the Lower Elbe, the water level varies by more than 10 feet between low and high tide. When the tide is out, the large mudflats that appear on either side of the channel are not necessarily the prettiest sight. 'But perhaps that was just a pretext,' notes Schulenburg.[83] In any event, it is fair to say that Elisabeth Lagerfeld felt out of place in Blankenese. Perhaps part of the reason was that only people who had lived in Hamburg for generations had the privilege of belonging to the upper echelons of society.[84]

Whatever her reasons, Elisabeth wanted to get out of Hamburg. After escaping provincial life for Germany's four biggest cities in her twenties, living in Munich, Berlin, Cologne and Hamburg, she was now returning to the countryside for a quieter life. In 2004, her son said she was 'bored to death' in Bad Bramstedt,[85] a small rural town that can only have reminded her of Beckum. With a well-off husband, plenty of domestic staff, and three children – two of her own and one stepdaughter – she no longer had to work. So she stayed at home in the manor behind the trees, cut off from the rest of the world in a rather eerie setting.

The children in the neighbourhood were intimidated by this well-to-do couple from Hamburg, whose bearing, gestures and style were like something from another world. 'Mrs Lagerfeld always seemed like an English lady to me,' says former neighbour Karl Wagner.[86] 'She didn't want to have anything to do with anyone else,' notes Sylvia Jahrke, whose family were given temporary accommodation in the Lagerfelds' manor house towards the end of the war. 'She never cracked a smile, even though she had a nice life and didn't have to work. I would just creep past her and curtsey, then scarper. I was afraid of the woman.'[87]

The three C's were never going to be enough for this feminist. As well as negotiating childcare, cooking and church, she became a rather colourful character during her time in the countryside. She could play the strict teacher, the overbearing head of a large household, the escapist who retreated from reality in marathon reading sessions, the consumerist who loved luxury products and fashions, or the violinist who practised three times a day only to abandon the hobby and never play again.[88] She spent a lot of time working on her image. 'She had manicured hands, which was rare in those days,' Sylvia Jahrke recalls. 'She had white collars and wore a brooch.' Elisabeth Lagerfeld read fashion magazines, enjoyed going on shopping sprees in Hamburg, and made sure her children were always well turned-out. Even her husband fit in perfectly with this self-modelled urbane image: he wore a signet ring – Sylvia had never seen anything like it in her life.

Out in the sticks in Holstein, bored like Madame Bovary in Yonville, how did Elisabeth Lagerfeld find inspiration? Like the wife of Gustave Flaubert's country doctor, she devoted herself to the fine arts. Apparently she always had her head in a book: 'I remember her being on the couch reading and telling other people what to do,' her son recalled.[89] She often read French books because she wanted to improve her language skills, and this habit also rubbed off on her son. 'I spent my childhood in the country and started reading even before going to school. There was nothing else in my life but sketching and reading.'[90]

Emma Bovary, the protagonist of Flaubert's novel, sought refuge in an ill-fated love affair in the countryside. It seems that Elisabeth Lagerfeld, too, had her head in the clouds at times. Her son claimed he was told that she was the 'first woman in Europe to get an aviator's licence'.[91] 'She flew her own plane in 1919,' he said,[92] though admittedly he 'never saw her fly'.[93] No doubt he wasn't the only one who never saw his mother in the cockpit. In any case, there are photographs from 1924 showing her sister Felicitas standing beside a single-engine LVG C.VI, a former reconnaissance and artillery-spotting aircraft that was used for sightseeing trips and long-distance flights after World War I.[94] The photos may have been taken by Elisabeth; perhaps the two sisters booked a sightseeing flight together. If Elisabeth had been the pilot, surely there would have been photos of the occasion in her sister's estate.

Karl Lagerfeld also spoke of his mother wearing a wedding gown designed by Madeleine Vionnet, a couturier who was very successful in Paris at the time.[95] This certainly was not the norm in Germany. Author Raphaëlle Bacqué claims that this elegant past and the visits to the Parisian fashion boutique were something that Elisabeth's son 'invented' in order to 'sustain the comparison' with Yves Saint Laurent and his mother.[96] Lucienne Andrée Mathieu-Saint-Laurent was truly an elegant vision, and Yves even introduced her to Christian Dior once.[97] But Elisabeth Lagerfeld also knew a thing or two about fashion. She had worked in the industry and adored Paris. A copy of the first edition of German *Vogue* was discovered in her estate, along with issues of other German fashion magazines such as *Beyers Mode für alle*, *Ullstein Moden Album*, the *Hamburger Illustrierten*, and even the *VTZ* (*Vereinigte Textil- und Bekleidungszeitschrift*), a journal published from 1937 to 1943 to support exports of German textiles and clothing.[98] She was therefore knowledgeable on the subject and had good taste. All the same, the dress shown in the photograph from her wedding is unlikely to be an original Vionnet. Fashion houses in Hamburg and Berlin used to buy dressmaking patterns (*patrons couture*) from Paris around this time, then they would produce the designs in the original fabrics with a simpler cut. The dress she wore was therefore probably a simplified version of a Vionnet dress.

For a woman raised in Westphalia, being aware of what else was out there didn't mean that Elisabeth Lagerfeld lost touch with reality. Her feet were firmly on the ground, and the Lagerfelds stayed together for thirty-seven years until Otto died in 1967 – unlike the couple in Flaubert's *Madame Bovary*, where Emma dies an agonizing death and Charles loses his wife. As happens in any marriage, sacrifices were made along the way. Elisabeth was often left alone with the children. 'She was probably unhappy because her husband was away so much,' says Sylvia Jahrke. 'Maybe that's also why she was so dominant and so harsh.'

Whenever Otto Lagerfeld returned home to Bad Bramstedt from Hamburg or Neustadt in his chauffeur-driven car, he had to toe the line and acquiesce to his wife's demands. 'She would always tell the men around her how things should be done,' Karl Lagerfeld said in 2015. 'She was very tough, and very nasty. My father was very sweet and her victim. My father found exactly the wife that was not for him. He could never relax.'[99] In the documentary film *Lagerfeld Confidential*, he even went so far as to say, 'She made slaves of everyone.' And: 'She was relatively distant, her favour had to be earned.'[100]

Karl Lagerfeld sought to earn his mother's favour for as long as she lived. And no doubt he was still trying to meet her approval even after she died. 'It seems that his mother chose her only son as a kind of male life partner, a kind of stand-in husband to make up for the frequent absences of his mild-mannered father,' says Parisian psychotherapist Daniela Tran. 'He was this fantastic projection screen for her, becoming her own creation – and, of course, her work had to be perfect. No child can ever measure up to that kind of projection; no matter what he did, it was never good enough for her.'[101] This combination of psychological factors gave rise to Karl Lagerfeld's unconscious lifelong mission to please his eternally dissatisfied mother.

'When I was young, my mother always said to me that I was stupid,' he once said. 'I've probably just been overcompensating ever since.'[102] This was an interesting choice of words coming from someone like Karl Lagerfeld, a man who was extremely sceptical of any kind of introspection.[103] The psychologist Alfred Adler defined overcompensation as an exaggerated attempt to make up for certain physical, mental or social shortcomings. Following this logic, it is hardly surprising that the young Karl believed he would eventually become famous. His formidable self-assurance and his indefatigable work ethic – a sort of addiction that gripped him well into old age – could well be interpreted as a reaction to the humiliations the designer suffered early in his life. Paradoxically, his career could have been the outcome of all the disparagements and put-downs he endured as a youngster.

As merciless as his mother could be, Karl still identified with her. He understood where she was coming from, and he often said that he thought she was right to say the things she did.[104] 'I was so megalomanic as a child that I needed to be put in my place every once in a while.'[105] In 2011, he said that modern parenting often involves 'too much coddling and not enough discipline'. It seems he saw the character-forming benefits of tough love. 'I hate how children are praised to the skies, only to drop back down to earth with a thud when it all comes to nothing.' In France they use the term 'angélisme' to describe the naïve humanist idealism of an anti-authoritarian upbringing: 'I'm not sure if that's a good thing.'[106]

So why did Karl Lagerfeld repeatedly mention his mother's vicious remarks in his interviews? 'By doing so, he made her words less potent,' says psychologist Daniela Tran. 'When we say something that is weighing on our mind, we no longer have to carry it around with us. The thought takes shape outside of the soul and we rid ourselves of it by turning it into an external object, something that exists outside of us.'[107] There were also certain very practical advantages to portraying his mother as an imposing figure after she died. People identified with Karl Lagerfeld when they spoke to him, and that couldn't do him any harm. Journalists were both horrified and entranced when the designer repeated his mother's sensational remarks. And not only did he become a legend over the decades, but so did the woman behind the scenes.

Elisabeth Lagerfeld never lost sight of her long-term goal of moving to the big city. After a decade or so in Hamburg (from 1949) and almost a decade in Baden-Baden (from 1960), she was finally edging closer to this goal. In the spring of 1968, following the death of her husband, she moved from the River Oos of Baden-Baden to the Seine. She left behind her existence as a widow in her retirement idyll to spend the last phase of her life in the capital of the student movement. Finally she would be close to the son she criticized so fiercely but loved so dearly.

The young Karl Otto, *c.* 1938

1933 to 1951

Birth

Karl Lagerfeld came into the world in Hamburg on 10 September 1933. This sentence is much more complex than it looks, as Lagerfeld was never quite satisfied with this as his date of birth. 'Empress Elisabeth of Austria was murdered in Geneva on 10 September 1898,' he said. 'The Formula One driver Wolfgang Graf Berghe von Trips was killed in an accident on 10 September. I hate retrospectives. I hate birthdays.' And 10 September was also too close for comfort to the anniversary of the 9/11 disaster: 'Am I really supposed to celebrate now, on the eve of this terrible date?'[1]

The day and year of Lagerfeld's birth were also historically significant for another reason: 10 September 1933 was the day the German Reich ratified the *Reichskonkordat*, the treaty negotiated between the Vatican and emergent Nazi Germany. It was a momentous occasion for the new Chancellor of the Reich and soon-to-be dictator Adolf Hitler. The State–Church agreement between the German Reich and the Holy See produced a huge surge in the 'international credibility and legitimacy' of the Nazi regime, which had only recently come to power, not to mention allowing the regime to gain the 'approval of the German Catholics'.[2] On the day Karl Lagerfeld was born, the 'Führer' had therefore consolidated his absolute dominion, and within just a few months the regime had 'almost completely stripped away the principles of liberalism, democracy and the rule of law'.[3] It all happened extremely fast. Seizure of power on 30 January 1933; Reichstag Fire Decree, eliminating political opposition, on 28 February; federal elections on 5 March; Enabling Act, giving Hitler power to make laws without parliamentary consent, on 24 March: the dictatorship was rapidly established according to the *Führerprinzip* ('leader principle'). Arrests, waves of terror and intimidation meant that by autumn 1933 'almost all the political and social institutions and organizations had either been brought in line with the new regime or outlawed'.[4]

Lagerfeld never spoke about any of this, because he claimed he wasn't even born when it all happened. Ever since the 1960s, he had been claiming that his birth year was 1938, effectively making himself five years younger than he really was. Only in private did he drop the charade: 'I was born in a terrible year,' he told his publisher Gerhard Steidl.[5] 'He had to make himself out to be younger,' says fashion historian Peter Kempe. 'That way, he wouldn't be taken for a Nazi.'[6] He had to protect himself when he went to Paris in 1952, because every German who could have been a soldier in the war was treated with suspicion at that time.

Lagerfeld also had another issue with that fateful year in German history. Apart from the shame of it all, being born in 1933 made him seem old. He and his favourite cousin, Tita Tork from Münster, decided early on that they were going to make themselves out to be younger. The pair had learned the importance of appearances from their mothers: Elisabeth and Felicitas Bahlmann had social roles to perform as young women, they wore corsets and stood up straight, they made an impression and placed great importance on beautiful clothing – and, of course, they kept quiet about their age. In the end, their children Tita and Karl got one up on the past. Tita made herself four years younger: her gravestone in the Lauheide Forest Cemetery in Münster says that her date of birth was 17 October 1925, rather than 17 October 1921.[7] For Karl, the gap between fact and fiction was five years long.

The fashion scene provided an additional incentive to cover up his age: Lagerfeld's friend-cum-rival Yves Saint Laurent was three years younger than him. Ironically, the debate about Lagerfeld's real age only served to boost his profile over the years, adding to the myth and fuelling the guessing game around the facts regarding his life. Ultimately his reputation even outgrew that of Saint Laurent. He remained the topic of much discussion and continued to work on his legend, seeing no need to justify his claims with hard evidence. This only benefitted him and served as proof of his supremacy.

But even the mighty must fall, and a few days before Lagerfeld's seventieth birthday the *Bild am Sonntag* outed him as a liar.[8] The game was up, and the designer was forced to justify himself. He tried to brush the rumours off in later interviews, saying that he was born sometime 'between '33 and '38'.[9] He even went one step further: 'I wasn't even born on 10 September. As for whether it was 1933 or 1938... I decide my age. I'm intergenerational, so my age doesn't matter – I'm free from all that.'[10]

When the debate surrounding his age appeared in the press, Karl's employee Sophie de Langlade told him about her grandmother, who came from the Caribbean island of Martinique and was forced to flee in 1930 when Mount Pelée erupted. The young woman claimed that her papers had been lost to the fire, and when she applied for new documents in France she lied about her age – probably out of vanity. On paper at least, she became five years younger as a result.[11] This story may have been what prompted Lagerfeld to create his own version of events: 'Altona was bombed and my birth certificate was burned,' he suddenly claimed. 'I don't know if I was born on 10 September, and the year is probably in fact somewhere between 1933 and 1938. What good would it do for me to tie myself down?'[12] It is true that the old town hall was completely destroyed when Altona was bombed in the summer of 1943. But this was not where his birth was registered. Instead, his birth certificate is still exactly where it always was: at the register office in Hamburg North.[13]

In an appearance on the German talk show 'Menschen bei Maischberger' on 5 December 2006, it was obvious that the designer did not take these discussions of his age lightly after all. He was confronted with statements made by two of his former neighbours from Bad Bramstedt, Siegfried Werner and Karl Wagner, both of whom were roughly the same age as him. A pre-recorded clip showed the 72-year-old Wagner saying, 'He was happy when he had his sketchpad and a pencil with him, or when he was left to play with dolls.' Watching from the studio, Karl Lagerfeld grew visibly agitated. 'I don't know them,' he said. 'I never played with children, I hated children. Please get those horrible old men away from me!'

Two days later, the German tabloid newspaper *Bild* published an article with the headline 'Lagerfeld swears on TV' and Karl Wagner responded to the incident: 'Karl has probably lost his grip on reality. We played together a lot as children. We sat on the terrace, daydreaming together. We wanted to build a tramline to school so we wouldn't have to walk those four kilometres anymore.'[14] These days, Wagner believes that his childhood friend reacted the way he did because he was trapped by the lie he had concocted for himself: 'He got himself into a mess when he made himself out to be five years younger, and then he couldn't get the monkey off his back.'[15] His real age was confirmed a few years later when the birth announcement published in the *Hamburger Nachrichten* entered the public domain.[16] 'Otto Lagerfeld and Elisabeth Lagerfeld (née Bahlmann), of Baurs Park, Blankenese ... announce the joyful birth of a healthy boy on Sunday 10 September.' Slightly offset at the top left and typed in semi-bold script is the name of the newborn baby: 'Karl Otto'.[17]

It was a boy! Otto Lagerfeld must have been delighted. Just ten days from celebrating his fifty-second birthday, he was already on the old side for a new father. But since he had only been blessed with two daughters thus far, he had – in keeping with patrilineal ideas – been keeping his fingers crossed for a male successor to continue his lineage. As proof of the family's pride, the baby was named Karl after his maternal grandfather Karl Bahlmann. This was what his godfather (and uncle) Conrad Ramstedt wanted, too – for the boy to be named according to the traditional pattern. Karl Lagerfeld later said that he would have preferred to have been named Conrad, after his godfather. However, Ramstedt assured him that 'Karl' meant 'man' or 'master' in Old High German, and his father explained that *kral* was the word for 'king' in Slavic languages.[18] And so the young Karl was happy with his first name after all. His middle name was also something of a family tradition: his father was called Otto, his

Karl Otto

ntag. 10. September 1933

Otto Lagerfeld und Frau Elisabeth
geb. Bahlmann

Hamburg-Blankenese
Baurs Park

There is no mistaking the date of birth on the announcement
to relatives, friends and neighbours.

grandfather was Tönnies Johann Otto Lagerfeld, and one of his aunts on his father's side was named Ottilie. The youngster would be Karl Otto, and that was that.

The decision to name this Sunday child Karl was a stroke of luck. According to a reasonably representative study of names given to boys in Germany in 1933, the most common, in order of popularity, were: Hans, Günter (Günther), Horst, Carl (Karl), Werner, Gerhard, Heinz, Klaus (Claus), Helmut (Helmuth) and Walter (Walther).[19] It is fair to say that it wouldn't have been quite so easy for a Günter, Horst or Walter Lagerfeld to build a global career for himself. The fact that Karl Lagerfeld had a clear, monosyllabic, internationally recognizable first name that he could use for his public image must have been a contributing factor to his success. Karl didn't have the same Nazi ring to it as Horst, and it didn't take an umlaut, like Günter. It was also short and snappy, lending itself to buzzwords that boosted self-promotion in later years: 'Karlisms' are his best sayings, 'Karlikaturen' are his political caricatures, 'Karleidoscope' is a perfume from 2011, and the 'Karlito' – the small talisman accessory by Fendi – also

Baby in Baurs Park: little Karl only spent
the first year of his life in Blankenese.

became a commercial hit from 2014. In addition, Fendi launched the
'Karligraphy' bag in the autumn of 2019. His conveniently snappy first
name certainly paid off over time.

Even as a child, this boy was the pride of the family, a joy to behold.
Paul Sahner describes the scene as if he had been there to witness it:
'When godfather Conrad places his thumb in the baby's palm to test
his reflex, the parents are delighted. Karl Otto grasps hold energeti-
cally.' Lagerfeld also described himself as a baby: 'I slept well, I had a
huge appetite, and I smiled at everyone.'[20] He once claimed that his
earliest memory involved hearing the signals from the ships on the
Elbe. But in truth, the pride of the family was still in nappies when
the Lagerfelds set off for the greener pastures of the countryside.

Bissenmoor

Very little remains of the Bissenmoor Estate today. Christel Friedrichs,
the daughter of Karl's childhood friend Siegfried Werner, lives right
behind the spot where the manor once stood. Everything is peace-
ful here, just outside Bad Bramstedt. Stray stones from the former
foundations stick out of the foliage, along with the remnants of an
old stone bench. A slight clearing in the woods hints at the stately
driveway that once led to the building. Up ahead, on the tarmacked

road, is one of the pillars from the old entranceway; the other is in ruins. A portrait of the late Karl Lagerfeld has been spray-painted onto a utility box. It is the only reminder of the fashion designer who spent his early years here.

It is difficult to believe that this same spot was once home to a manor built in 1907.[21] It takes a great deal of imagination to look at these ruins and picture a white mansion with a cobbled forecourt, where the master of the house would pull up in his chauffeur-driven car when returning from his trading post in Hamburg or factory in Neustadt. Illustrations in old books about Bad Bramstedt fill out the gaps in the picture. This was a grand building that looked almost enchanted with its staircase, its veranda, the turret on the roof ridge, and its mullioned windows. Even in 2013, Lagerfeld could still draw the house from memory without a second thought: in Loïc Prigent's film *Karl Lagerfeld Sketches his Life*, he conjured the image of his old family home with its frontage, the iron gate on the left, and his bedroom window on the right-hand side of the first floor.

The house stood out against the backdrop of farm buildings with stables, barns and sheds. It was impressive – and slightly unsettling. The large, gloomy hallway had black-and-white terrazzo flooring, and a huge old-fashioned painting adorned the wall. But outside was a different story: the house was surrounded by gardens, meadows and woodland, so the children were in their element there. According to Thoma Schulenburg, the daughter of Karl's half-sister Thea, Elisabeth Lagerfeld was practically minded: the farm was 'a solid self-sufficient operation', though the lady of the house 'rarely lent a hand' in the garden.[22]

Otto Lagerfeld geared up for the long haul. On 20 September 1934, not long after the family moved in, he requested permission for a series of renovations.[23] He had a garage built in the basement and two new windows installed in the dining room on the ground floor. The manor house also boasted a relatively modern interior for its time, and, unlike most other families, the Lagerfelds had their own telephone. The number ('telephone no. 50') is written in the header of a letter from Otto Lagerfeld in 1935.[24] Even by the time the 1947 directory was issued, there were only just over fifty connections listed for Bad Bramstedt, and the majority of these numbers were for public institutions such as the municipal office or large companies like the Lentföhrden peat factory.

Otto Lagerfeld quickly expanded the farm with the addition of a 'dung heap with cesspool' and a wooden road bridge across the Lentföhrden floodplains. The only project that faltered involved his plan to build a huge granary. Though his request was provisionally approved on 22 June 1935 – on the condition that the granary should be 3.5 metres away from the boundary line – the district administrator suddenly announced on 17 September that it would actually have to be 'at least 6.0 metres' from the boundary. Perhaps the councilman thought that too much was happening too fast over at Bissenmoor.

Otto Lagerfeld was also earning a bit of a reputation for himself down at the town hall. Friedrich Utermarck, who became the full-time mayor of Bad Bramstedt on 4 December 1934, stumbled upon the following piece of information in the local newspaper on 17 July 1935: 'The new owner of Bissenmoor farm has carried out substantial works on the property recently. The manor house has been thoroughly renovated inside and out, the splendid grounds have been tidied up, and trees have been planted. Now a new granary and a double silo are being built on the farm.' So on 3 August, Utermarck wrote a letter to the police sergeant Ehmke, enclosing the newspaper cutting and asking him to find out whether structures were being built without the necessary building warrants. This was followed by the mayor's demand for a 6-metre distance from the boundary line on 14 October. Otto Lagerfeld responded to the order on 22 October, explaining that the distance of 3.5 metres had been verified by the master builder. He signs off with a 'Heil Hitler!' – evidently he was adapting to the new tone in the Bad Bramstedt town hall.

The Lagerfelds owned the property at Bissenmoor for around fifteen years. When they sold it after the war, the building gradually fell into disrepair. The subsequent owner, Walter Rust, turned the

mansion house into a guesthouse, and then an old people's home
a few years later. But evidently neither of these endeavours was
successful. The building, rotten from woodworm, was taken over by
Bad Bramstedt council in the 1970s. But it seems that no efforts were
made to preserve Bissenmoor over the years. On 7 January 1979, the
ballet maestro Nikita Gsovsky from Hamburg proposed relocating his
renowned 'international boarding school for ballet' from the nearby
municipality of Quarnstedt. He offered to renovate the building 'in
the style of a manor house' and said he would pay a sum of 100,000
marks for the privilege.[25] But without further ado, the council gave
the order to demolish the building on 18 January. On 22 January
1979, the invoice for the demolition work was issued to the building
authorities, and for 32,743.20 marks, the once magnificent house was
swiftly razed to the ground.[26] The town of Bad Bramstedt showed
its indifference to the memory of Karl Lagerfeld, who had long been
famous by the 1970s. An opportunity was missed: a white mansion
in the forest would have been a fantastic tribute to celebrate the
town's most famous son, with a museum of a scale and style akin
to the Christian Dior Museum in Granville, high above the cliffs
of Normandy.

Childhood

It might sound as if little Karl Otto grew up in a rather sedate environment, but that isn't really the case. Whenever his father was around
– which, granted, wasn't often – he was busy with his renovation
projects and expanding the family home. His mother managed the
household and issued orders to the housekeeper and the nanny.
There were pigs and chickens in the barn next door and cows grazing
in the fields with their calves. Karl's big sister Christel liked to play
with the boys in the neighbourhood, but most of the time Karl himself
sat on the sidelines, daydreaming and drawing in his sketchpad.

The young Karl never quite fit into this provincial setting. It wasn't
that he had his head in the clouds, he was simply convinced that he
was destined for better things. He knew he wanted to take centre

stage: 'I was six years old,' he recalled. 'I was sitting on my mother's desk in the country estate, in the big house – on her desk, where I was not supposed to sit and sketch – and I said to myself: "You will become very famous."'[27] Even as a child, it seems, he felt like one of the chosen few.

This little boy was older than his years and had no interest in people his own age. Apparently he had no real friends, just 'two or three' children whom he 'used as slaves'. They did all the things he didn't want to do, like cleaning his bike. 'But of course I never let them do my homework – they were too average for that. I hated being a child. I wanted to talk to the adults and to be thought of as one of them.'[28]

Karl's nanny Martha Bünz (b. c. 1907) was a kind woman with no children of her own, and she showered the boy with affection. She lived in Bissenmoor with her husband and made a bit of money on the side through work for the Lagerfelds. 'She got on with the boy, and he was fond of her,' says Elfriede von Jouanne, her niece twice-removed, who exchanged letters with Karl Lagerfeld in the 1990s.[29] Martha Bünz often had to stand in for Karl's parents. Otto was always busy, and Elisabeth was away for her fair share of the time, too. For instance, she joined her husband on a business trip to the US from 1 to 29 April 1934, and in 1950 she accompanied him stateside once again.[30] After returning from a long trip in 1937, Elisabeth Lagerfeld wrote to her mother in Münster: 'The children were delighted when I got back,' she said in her letter. Apparently Karl kept asking, 'You're not going away again, are you?'[31]

Karl Wagner was born in July 1934 and also grew up in Bissenmoor. He has fond memories of his friend's older sister: 'Christel was a real tomboy. She used to climb trees with us. We'd take crows' eggs from their nests, then blow out the eggs and thread the shells onto string.' It seems she was quite different from Karl Otto (as he was known to his classmates and the local children), who never joined in their games. 'Whenever we played in Bissenmoor, he would just sit outside the house sketching and dressing up his dolls.'[32] Apparently

With the nanny: the home help often looked
after the boy of the house in the countryside.

his half-sister Thea was once given a puppet theatre for Christmas,
and he took the jointed puppets and repeatedly dressed them up in
different clothes.[33]

Adventures didn't really appeal to this son of a well-to-do family.
Perhaps he had learned from experience that it was better to be
safe than sorry. One such experience involved being thrown off a
horse called Saturn, a gift from one of his father's friends, Hamburg
ringmaster Willy Hagenbeck: 'Since then, I've never liked horses.
I was thrown off the saddle once, and that was that. My love of
horses was no more.'[34] Karl never joined the local lads when they set
out to catch slippery lampreys by hand in the nearby waters. And
when they were ordered to fetch eggs so that his mother could bake
a cake, he lingered outside the barn holding his nose in disgust. He
also hated the cowshed because of its stench. 'We didn't take him
seriously,' Karl Wagner says. 'And he didn't take us seriously either.'

It would appear that the young Karl Otto was extremely gifted, especially when it came to languages. 'I could speak German, French and English at the age of six,' he claimed in 2015. 'I had a private tutor for French. She was a refugee who had been a German teacher at a French school for well-heeled girls before World War I. Both my parents spoke French and I couldn't understand a word, so I was desperate to learn French. She gave me lessons because she needed the money.'[35] This penchant for French must have baffled the neighbours, who would have interpreted it as misplaced elitism and lofty educational aspiration. His childhood friend Siegfried Werner's family, for instance, didn't even speak High German at home; they only spoke Low German until long after World War II.[36]

Karl allegedly learned to read at the age of five. He started with the picture book *Molle und der grüne Schirm* (Molly and the Green Umbrella) and soon moved onto the German mythological saga *Nibelungen*. When he was older, he would sit in the attic flicking through issues of *Simplicissimus*, the satirical German weekly magazine from the pre-war era. He also liked to browse through his mother's magazines. 'There were no picture books available to buy at that time, so he would colour in the black-and-white photographs with crayons,' Paul Sahner writes.[37] These intensive reading sessions in the attic helped him to work on his artistic skills and sharpen his wit. Putting his thoughts onto paper allowed him to provoke a reaction while simultaneously creating a safe space for himself. Through his art, he cultivated the detached air of someone who can fit in anywhere but doesn't belong anywhere, someone who enjoys company but floats above it all, someone who participates in life but prefers to take his observations and feed them into his own symbolic world.

'Karl Otto was aloof, but he had this strong charisma,' says Sylvia Jahrke.[38] He was her favourite playmate back then. She recalls the time he helped her ride a bike that was propped against the wall of the house. 'In Hamburg, where we came from, people didn't ride bikes.' So even though she was ten years old, she still didn't know what to do. She sat on the bike seat and Karl Otto held on to stop her falling off while she found her balance. Someone told her off for helping herself to the bike – she can't remember who it was – and the nine-year-old Karl defended her.

Karl wasn't at all down-to-earth like the farmers' sons from the neighbourhood, who had to help out in the barn and the fields. 'He was very smart and well-groomed,' recalls Sylvia Jahrke. 'I noticed that his fingernails were clean. The other boys had black fingernails.' He didn't have many friends, she says, and the other children didn't go to his house to see him. As far as Sylvia was concerned, it seemed that the Lagerfelds lived in their own 'bubble'.

Karl's niece Thoma Schulenburg was often at Bissenmoor as a small child, and many of her earliest memories are linked to the time she spent there. Her mother, Karl's elder half-sister Thea von der Schulenburg, worked for *Die Welt* newspaper in Hamburg in the late 1940s, and she often had to stay late at the office. The mother and daughter lived on the top floor of the Glücksklee premises at 36 Mittelweg, and Otto Lagerfeld often took his granddaughter back to the countryside with him. The little girl always looked forward to seeing her uncle, who was only eleven years older than her. Karl looked after her and used his pocket money to buy her a paper cone full of gifts for her first day at school. His sister Christel spun wool from her sheep and used it to knit clothes for her niece. 'She made me a sweater and mittens, which were terribly itchy.'

Everyone in the family called him Mule, and not even Thoma could refer to him as Uncle Karl. Some people have speculated that Karl earned his nickname by being so stubborn,[39] but family members tell a different story. Apparently Karl's mother picked it up in the Münster region. In Low German, and in the Münster dialect, the word 'Mule' means 'mouth' and appears in sayings about not mincing one's words and keeping one's mouth shut: for example, 'Kien Blad vüör de Mule niëmen' ('Kein Blatt vor den Mund nehmen'; 'Don't mince words'), or 'Holle Mule!' ('Halt's Maul!'; 'Shut up!'). Even as a child, Karl had earned himself a reputation for his sharp tongue and racing mouth.

In a letter to her sister Felicitas in January 1937, his mother wrote: 'He's such a character – he has a real mouth on him!'[40]

Even though he was often an outsider and he wasn't exactly in his element growing up in the countryside, Karl Lagerfeld never tried to distance himself from this aspect of his background. 'In a way, we are bound to a certain past, a certain tradition, a certain kind of upbringing.'[41] This attachment manifested itself in curious details later in his life: even as an old man, he still carried a cushion he had kept since his childhood whenever he flew on his private jet. 'I hate travelling without it.'[42] He had a nervous stomach, so he liked to hold the cushion against it for comfort. By this point, the old thing was so faded that the embroidery of a train and the words 'Gute Reise' (Have a good trip) were barely visible.

Was there too little in the way of inspiration in his rural environment? Or did he simply need a different kind of visual stimulus? For whatever reason, this boy's imagination was always taking him far away. Sometimes it even took him all the way back to the eighteenth century – the time when Frederick II established Prussia as a European superpower, when the Age of Enlightenment was dawning but the era of bourgeois society had not yet begun, and when the absolutist monarchs were depicted in the most magnificent of paintings. One day, the young Karl noticed a copy of Adolph von Menzel's *Frederick the Great and his Round Table* hanging in a gallery in Hamburg. He loved the painting and told his mother he wanted it for Christmas. 'That's how life should look,' he told her,[43] insisting that he wouldn't be able to sleep unless he had the painting for himself. But even though it was just a copy, it was still very expensive. So, instead, his parents decided to buy him a chromolithograph of another wonderful Menzel composition, *Frederick the Great Playing the Flute at Sanssouci*, which was much more affordable. 'Apparently I sulked so much that they ended up asking the gallery for the other picture.' His parents even managed to persuade the gallery owner to open on Christmas Day so that the boy could finally get his very own *Round Table*.[44]

The painting represented 'a kind of ideal I have been striving to achieve ever since', said Lagerfeld. 'It was 1945 and it sold for 3,000 marks, which was a lot of money at the end of the war and a very valuable gift for a child of my age.'[45] But what was it he liked so much about the picture? The scene depicts King Frederick II in the beautifully illuminated Marble Hall at Sanssouci Palace in Potsdam. Frederick the Great is shown in the centre, with the French philosopher Voltaire sitting in the second chair to the left, engaged in an animated discussion with another guest across the table. The rococo hall of a castle, complete with gilded mouldings, a glittering chandelier, classical marble columns: the scene summoned by this painting stirred the young boy's imagination.

Menzel's art may also have given Lagerfeld a glimpse of what the future had in store for him. Perhaps he saw a vision of himself reflected in the grandeur of this king, whom Menzel refrained from artificially elevating and instead depicted as an enlightened monarch in good company. 'It is not only the composition that accords a central position to the king; he also had a central role to play, namely that of arbiter,' writes art historian Werner Busch. 'He gave free rein to his circle of salaried wits but reserved the right of the last word.'[46] Lagerfeld later held round tables in his apartment on the Rue de l'Université and in his château in Brittany, almost as if to pretend the eighteenth century had never ended. This debonair ideal also foreshadowed his life as a creative director: he always reviewed his collections while sitting at a large table, surrounded by assistants, journalists and dressmakers. Everyone was free to voice their opinion, but the final judgment always rested with the enlightened ruler.

Lagerfeld often talked about his childhood ambition, painting the picture of a strong-willed boy who was never going to settle for anything but the very best. He told the story of a pertinacious youngster who fuelled his imagination to turn a less than exciting life in rural northern Germany into a font of fascination and escapism. Inspired by his idol Frederick the Great, little Karl saw himself as Karl the Great.

War

At some point, commuting from the trading post in Hamburg to Bad Bramstedt became too much for Otto Lagerfeld. Until his mother's death in 1936, he would often stay the night with her in her house at 70 Elbchaussee. Then, in or around 1939, he bought a town house at 46 Innocentiastrasse in Harvestehude, one of the most beautiful parts of Hamburg. With its lovely view of the gardens in Innocentiapark, the new house was only about half a mile away from the director's office at 36 Mittelweg, making it much more accessible than the Elbchaussee, which – beautiful though it may have been – was a longer commute.[47]

The family lived there for a few years. Previously, it was thought that the Lagerfelds only retreated to Bissenmoor when the heavy air raids began in Hamburg in late July 1943.[48] In fact, by this point Elisabeth Lagerfeld and the children had already been in the countryside for a while. In a letter she sent from Bad Bramstedt in the summer of 1942, she told her sister that she had bought her daughter a rabbit hutch.[49] And shortly before Christmas 1942, the eleven-year-old Christel wrote a letter to her aunt saying, 'Mule and I are getting a little Christmas tree this year. We never had one in Hamburg.'[50] Otto Lagerfeld joined them in July 1943.[51]

Despite the rural location, even Holstein felt the effects of the war. Still, one man claimed he didn't notice. 'I was lucky; I escaped everything,' Karl Lagerfeld said in 2004. 'I saw nothing of the war.'[52] He said he was in 'the only place where nothing happened', and was 'incredibly lucky' that the war didn't reach him in the countryside.[53] But there was no way that the Lagerfelds could have missed the war, try as they might to pretend it wasn't happening. People were being bombed out of the cities, and the impact on their lives was profound. Sylvia Jahrke is a case in point. Born on 16 November 1934, she lived through numerous air raids in Hamburg as a child. But the fear hit a completely new level when 'Operation Gomorrah' struck the city between 24 July and 3 August 1943. The relentless campaign of air raids from British and American planes created a firestorm to which some 34,000 people fell victim. Sylvia, who was eight years old at the time, recalls running out of the cellar in a panic during one of the air raids – and seeing the people running across from Bethesda hospital vanish into thin air when the phosphorous bomb struck.[54] Sylvia, her mother, and her sisters Rosemarie and Ingrid were transported by truck from Hamburg to Bad Segeberg. They then continued on foot to Bad Bramstedt because their mother was from the town and one of their aunts lived in Bissenmoor. Their salvation finally came when they were temporarily put up in a room at the Lagerfelds' house in 1943. While Sylvia lay awake in her shared room on the first floor because she was haunted by the horror of the firestorm, Karl Otto was sound asleep just a few feet away.

The Lagerfelds had no say over the matter. 'Any living space that was available was subject to strict controls,' says local registrar Manfred Jacobsen. 'It was down to the city council to decide which refugees were to be accommodated where.'[55] The owners of the manor house were forced to make several rooms available to those who had been displaced by the war. Now the Lagerfelds found themselves living on the ground floor, sharing their bathroom and toilet with strangers.[56] 'No doubt Mrs Lagerfeld would have preferred us not to be there,' says Sylvia Jahrke. Homeowners and farmers were often reluctant to take in refugees in those difficult times, but they had no choice. And now refugees were arriving in droves: between 1942 and 1945, the population of Bad Bramstedt grew from around 3,300 to around 7,000.

What were the children supposed to do with their time? 'We had no toys because we had been driven out of our homes due to all the bombing,' says Sylvia Jahrke. 'We weren't allowed to stray far from the house either, because the war was still happening.' So they would just sit on the terrace steps or in front of the house, chatting. The children had to be careful, just like their parents. 'In the latter years of the war we were afraid of low-flying aircraft on their way to Kiel or Neumünster,' recalls Karl Wagner. 'They shot at everything that moved. We skirted along the fronts of the houses or walked through the woods so they couldn't see us.'[57]

No one in Bad Bramstedt could possibly have been oblivious to the threat of disaster.[58] All the lights had to go out at night during wartime. The Lagerfelds also had blackout panels for their windows. An air raid warden stood guard, keeping an eye on the Allied aircraft. In late March 1942, the Hanseatic city of Lübeck just 30 miles away was attacked and 'half the city was razed to the ground'.[59] Young people had to do air-raid duty. Rheumatic patients had been vacated from the local sanatorium following the Russian campaign in 1941 and 1942, and now the building was full of wounded German soldiers. With the floods of refugees arriving towards the end of the war – up to 1,200 people – the spa town was desperately overcrowded. A bomb struck Bad Bramstedt during the night of 27 July 1942, probably as the result of an emergency drop. It killed ten people in the centre of the town, injured nineteen, destroyed three houses and damaged several more. Then in April 1945, a low-flying attack by the Allies on an open truck transporting German soldiers by the marl pits killed fifteen members of the German armed forces and two civilians. The war had been over for three weeks on 30 May 1945, when a British storage facility full of confiscated munitions exploded at Schäferberg. Sylvia Jahrke, who lived in the area with her family from the end of the war, was on her way to Bissenmoor to fetch milk when it happened. 'The blast sent me flying through the air and I fell on the ground,' she recounts. 'An Englishman pulled me into the ditch. The missiles only narrowly missed us.'

Is it really possible that all this eluded the Lagerfelds, who lived just a few hundred feet from the marl pits and a mere couple of miles from the town centre? Did their son – a curious boy aged ten or eleven – really fail to see what was going on? 'I didn't even notice that it happened,' Lagerfeld said in 1984.[60] 'I have no memory of seeing my parents anxious, but they probably avoided talking about politics.'[61] There was no way, however, that he could have missed the attacks on Hamburg, less than 30 miles away. 'Yes, I saw the red sky and the aeroplanes,' he finally admitted in one of his last interviews. 'We went up on a platform to look at the fires in the distance.'[62]

The Lagerfelds would also feel the after-effects of the war, because the British were coming and change was afoot. Otto Lagerfeld wrote to the mayor of Bad Bramstedt on 18 July 1945, saying that a British officer from the occupying forces (Captain Bruce of the '8 Corps District German Mobilisation Centre Control Unit') had forced him to vacate the house and the administrative building on 16 July. This move affected twenty-seven people. He, the custodian and the foreman temporarily moved into the Lagerfelds' cowshed along with their families. Knowing that the cows would have to go back into the shed in late September, Otto Lagerfeld made a request for all three families to be given appropriate living quarters in good time. He also asked the mayor to erect a storage shed because the sheds where the grain and straw were kept had been requisitioned by the occupying forces. 'Presently, the only place I have to cook is on an open hearth in the farm.' He received a reply from the mayor on 4 August 1945 to the effect that such living quarters were 'no longer available'.[63]

The merchant enclosed a breakdown of the costs incurred as a result of the occupation, along with an itemized list of the things that had been confiscated. These items included: a chair, a sofa, a circular saw, a workbench, four clay pipes, a large linen tablecloth, eight porcelain cups and saucers, eight breakfast plates, a dessert plate, a sugar bowl, a coffee pot, and five wicker chairs (with 'special braiding'). The English soldiers had barely spent a few weeks in the manor house when the incensed merchant was forced to intensify his complaint. On 15 September 1945 he wrote to the mayor once again, this time complaining of torn-out doors, cut-up beams, used firewood, and much more. The English soldiers had destroyed three windows in the shed and up to six windows in the barn – damage he claimed was mostly caused by them 'playing football against my shed and on my farm'. A large central window in the house was also smashed 'as the result of careless driving'.

It seemed there was barely anything left of the supplies and the house's sophisticated interior décor by the time the soldiers were done. Around eighty hundredweight of coke had been taken from the boiler room, and an electric oven was missing from the kitchen, along with two cupboards from the store room. Various items had disappeared from the entrance hall, among them a grandfather clock, a corner unit full of books, thirty gramophone records, a Telefunken radio with a built-in record player, and an oil painting. The dining room was missing a sideboard, various oil paintings and copper etchings, and there was no sign of the chandeliers, wall mirrors, wash basins, stoves and curtains that used to be in the bedrooms. The British occupying forces had even helped themselves to the bidet, the toilet and the bathtub from the bathroom – all this in the space of just a few weeks.

As of 15 July 1945, the family was forced to live in the cowshed before moving into the granary. Then seven long months later, on 15 February 1946, they were finally notified by the mayor that the building had been 'vacated by the British occupying forces' and they could move back into their home without further ado. Otto Lagerfeld painstakingly listed the costs of all the rental losses, damages and other losses incurred in a letter to the mayor on 9 March 1946, which in total amounted to a sum of 3,084.37 marks in compensation. Evidently he was reimbursed for most of the damages he had suffered. Then, on 29 January 1947, he compiled a list of issues that had yet to be addressed by the authorities in Bad Segeberg. The list mentioned the 'gymnastics equipment' that had been 'removed and burned', and the 'repairs for the radio apparatus and built-in gramophone'. He received 1,038.50 marks for his trouble, as well as eighty hundredweight of coke as 'compensation in kind'.

But still it wasn't over: this lengthy back-and-forth with the authorities went on for years. Otto Lagerfeld's final letter on the subject is dated 10 December 1951 and is still held on file in the Bad Bramstedt municipal archives. It includes copies of the original supporting documents he sent to the mayor's office and a note to say that the total losses amounted to roughly 3,200 marks. On 11 December 1951, the mayor passed the letter and its contents on to the tax department responsible for dealing with war damages and expenses from the occupation of Germany: 'The statements made by Mr Lagerfeld are plausible.' It can be assumed that this admission marked the end of a long chapter; otherwise there would surely have been more letters from the relentless merchant, who had since moved back to Hamburg with his family.

So it seems that even the Lagerfelds experienced hardship in the war and its aftermath. Still, they were lucky compared to the millions who suffered a far worse fate. Fortunately, Otto Lagerfeld was too old to serve in the Wehrmacht and Karl Lagerfeld too young. Though they must have experienced fear and difficult times, they were never persecuted or displaced in the true meaning of the word. They were also spared most of the material consequences of World War II. Beyond the relatively sheltered realm of Bissenmoor, poverty and food shortages were rife. The war had destroyed businesses, homes and transport links. The economy was in tatters. The school meals provided by the British forces weren't enough to satisfy hungry little mouths. The 'winter of starvation' from 1946 to 1947, the coldest winter of the twentieth century in the North Sea region, tormented the numerous refugees from eastern Germany, who were often forced to live in wretched conditions. Ulrich Herbert writes that 'the floods of refugees were directed first and foremost to rural regions' following the devastation of Germany's towns and cities. 'The proportion of displaced people in the countryside of Northern Germany was around 50 per cent,' he writes, 'whereas in Hamburg and Bremen it was just 7 per cent, and in Berlin it was 2 per cent.'[64]

Karl's friend Sylvia, who left Bissenmoor in 1945 when she returned to the city with her family, suffered from nutritional oedema. Her father had survived the war, but now he could barely support his family. The children at school talked about their terrible experiences. Many men had been injured or were still being held as prisoners, and when they finally returned they were very hard on their sons, many of whom had been raised by women in their absence. Fortunately for Karl, the Lagerfeld family was also spared this fate.

'In memory of 12 March 1938': a four-year-old Karl looks over at the swastika flag, while his sister stands next to the flagpole.

Nazi Party

The Austrian Anschluss, the annexation of Austria by Germany on 12 March 1938, was an important step for the Nazis on the path to achieving their dream of building a 'Greater German Reich'. Forming a political union with the Austro-fascist 'Federal State of Austria' allowed the German Reich to expand its dominion considerably. The excitement was palpable in both Austria and Germany. And as the Führer legend grew exponentially, a systematic campaign of terror was launched against Jews, intellectuals, dissidents and minorities in Austria – or *Ostmark*, as it was known by the Nazis.

The Lagerfelds were among the many people who welcomed the Austrian Anschluss, as evidenced by a private photograph from 1938. It shows the house in Bissenmoor and a flagpole just outside, flying a swastika flag at least 20 feet high. The young Karl Lagerfeld can be seen in the foreground wearing a knitted jumper, shorts and knee-length socks. The four-year-old is standing on the lawn, looking towards the house and the flag that is flapping in the wind.[65]

There was no obligation for citizens to fly the party flag on private property on national holidays or other occasions in Nazi Germany. But people who chose not to do so did attract a degree of suspicion. 'If people didn't raise the flag in Bad Bramstedt, it was usually because they didn't have one,' explains Manfred Jacobsen, head of the municipal archive. 'The mayor and many of the residents were staunch Nazis, or at least professed German nationalists, and the annexation of Austria wasn't particularly contentious, so it is fair to say that raised flags would not have been a rarity.'[66]

In the Lagerfelds' case, the decision to fly the flag was not purely driven by a sense of duty. This much is indicated by a note on the back of the photograph, which was developed at 'Photo Hoffman' in Bad Bramstedt. It looks like Elisabeth Lagerfeld's handwriting: 'In memory of 12 March 1938.' There is also a short description, which is partly illegible: 'Chr. is standing by the flagpole ... checking the flag.' A closer look at the photo reveals little Christel standing in the background next to the flagpole, her head pointed upwards. The fact that a photo was taken to celebrate the annexation, and that the day itself was regarded as a memorable occasion, implies approval for the regime and its foremost symbol.

So was this approval a sign of enthusiasm, or mere willingness to move with the times? Either way, it would appear that Otto Lagerfeld and his wife sympathized with the Nazis. Karl's father offered his services to the regime as soon as the Nazis came to power. His denazification form indicates that he joined the National Socialist German Workers' Party (*Nationalsozialistische Deutsche Arbeiterpartei* – NSDAP) in May 1933 and remained a member until the dictatorship ended in May 1945.[67] His statement on the form issued by the 'Military Government of Germany' reveals that he had applied to join in early May 1933 and was accepted at the end of May. He never held office or had any special rank in the party, but he did join various associations. So from 1934 he was obliged to become a member of the German Labour Front (*Deutsche Arbeitsfront* – DAF) and, in the same year, he also became a member of the National Socialist People's Welfare organization (*Nationalsozialistische Volkswohlfahrt* – NSV). Then from 1936 he also voluntarily served in the National League of Germans Abroad (*Volksbund für das Deutschtum im Ausland* – VDA), followed by the German Colonial League (*Reichskolonialbund*) from 1937. According to Horst Gies, a Berlin-based historian specializing in Nazi agricultural policy, the decision to voluntarily join the latter two organizations was an 'expression of a certain political stance'. On the other hand, if he wanted to continue trading dairy products, Otto Lagerfeld had no choice but to sign up for sub-organizations of the State Food Corporation (*Reichsnährstand* – RNS), a government agency established with the aim of regulating food production and the market.[68]

The facts surrounding Otto Lagerfeld's party affiliations are remarkable in a number of respects. In 1933, most of the members of the Nazi Party were unmarried young men, and the average age was less than thirty-five,[69] whereas Otto Lagerfeld was already fifty-one when he joined early that same year. Moreover, so many people were eager to join the NSDAP following the German parliamentary election on 5 March 1933 that the party imposed a freeze on the uptake of new members on 1 May 1933 in an attempt to ward off an onslaught of opportunists.[70] Exceptions to this rule were members of the Hitler Youth, the SA and the SS, as well as members of the National Socialist Factory Cell Organization (*Nationalsozialistische Betriebszellenorganisation* – NSBO), an association of party members representing large companies. Given that none of these criteria are likely to have applied to Otto Lagerfeld, it is all the stranger to note that he was admitted to the Nazi Party at the end of May 1933.

When the war was over, he tried to fashion himself as a critic of the regime. 'As a representative of American interests, my relationships with the party were extremely tense,' he told the denazification committee on 24 July 1947, citing issues with the dairy commissioner, the main association for the German dairy industry and the Dairy

Federation. With the introduction of the new Hereditary Farm Law in 1933, the German government established an elaborate system of regional marketing associations and national associations for all agricultural products. The powers granted to these organizations were almost limitless, allowing them to control everything from production, packaging, shipping and distribution to prices, volumes and quality requirements. Milk-processing companies were forced to cooperate with the new system.[71] Otto Lagerfeld must have been afraid of losing control of Glücksklee.

He told the denazification committee that the regional economic consultant appointed to advise the Gauleiter (local party leader) had alleged that the American proprietors were Jewish, in order 'to undermine my reputation and that of the company'. Apparently 'a storm was brewing' when he tried to purchase the factories in Allenburg (East Prussia) and Waren (Mecklenburg) from the Red Cross in 1937: 'I probably would have had it coming to me had I not been representing American interests,' he claimed. The situation was getting in the way of him running the company, and after the Americans entered the war 'certain circles' tried to 'swallow up Glücksklee's business', he said. He managed to ward off the threat, albeit not without 'great difficulty'. Clearly the committee considered him an opportunist rather than an ardent supporter of the Nazi Party. He was classed as an unscrupulous 'hanger-on'. The Glücksklee works council also exonerated him, and on 15 October 1947 the advisory committee ruled that he would be allowed to stay on as director of Glücksklee.[72]

Otto Lagerfeld's wife also completed a 'questionnaire from the state commissioner for denazification and the categorization of the Hanseatic City of Hamburg', which is held on file in the Hamburg state archives. Elisabeth Lagerfeld ('occupation: wife') was hoping to travel to the US with her husband and needed a 'political clearance certificate' in order to do so. The certificate, dated 23 March 1950, stated that she was 'neither a member of the NSDAP nor of any of its organizations'. She was considered 'politically unencumbered', hence there were 'no objections' to her embarking on a trip to the

US. The stamp dated 22 March 1950 states that she was not subject to classification in any of the categories employed in the denazification efforts.[73]

In all probability, this assessment was misguided. Among the former belongings of Felicitas Bahlmann is a typewritten letter with the heading: 'Why did I become a member of the N.S.D.A.P.?!' Although the declaration is not signed, it can clearly be attributed to Elisabeth Lagerfeld, as it was kept alongside all the other letters she wrote to her sister in Münster over the decades, many of which she composed on a typewriter.[74] In the five-page letter, she refers to herself as the daughter of a 'sovereign Prussian district administrator' and the chair of a 'patriotic women's association' – none other than Karl and Milly Bahlmann, of course. She also talks about her experiences in Berlin and Hamburg, where she once lived, and there is a note in the margin, clearly in her handwriting. The characteristic style, the placement of commas and the orthography also give her away as the author of the letter.

As to why she became a member of the party – well, that question was easy enough to answer, she writes. Her explanation: 'Because I thought it was best for Germany, and not just for Germany but for all of Europe.' She believed that it was 'completely possible that Hitler was capable of taking control of the disunity among the German people, subordinating them to an idea, putting an end to all the discord in the party, and establishing order both domestically and abroad'. She also believed that Hitler could restore social justice, and that a 'healthy Germany' would protect Europe from Bolshevism. She writes that the East had been a threat 'for centuries' – more so than ever with the 'Bolshevist era' – and this threat 'could only be countered with a healthy Germany and with the conviction of all nations, particularly the people of England'.

It seems she underestimated what the Führer was capable of when he came to power: 'One could not have imagined that Hitler would not know how to handle this power once it was his, or that he would allow the other people who shared in his power to completely disregard the big idea. Or that he would become beholden to his megalomania and would only have time for advisors around him who submitted to his will; that he would not tolerate any healthy opposition; that he would not allow far-sighted men with proper skills to go anywhere near him; or that he would ban every element of free speech.' But at some point, like many people, she was unable to summon the courage to leave the Nazi Party. According to historians, the number of resignations fell when the NSDAP came to power.[75] 'I will never claim that I did not belong to the party,' she wrote. 'I acted in good conscience. It was torture enough to have been so disappointed.'

In her letter, Elisabeth Lagerfeld explains the historical reasons for her political leanings: 'One came from a century which was still more or less living and breathing the spirit of Prussia, where the decency and reliability of the civil services and the German people in general were established values.' And as the 'daughter of a sovereign Prussian district administrator', the concepts of 'patriotism' and 'correctness' came naturally to her. She writes that 'chaos' ensued after the collapse of the Austro-Hungarian Empire in 1918, exposing people to the 'hardship of unemployment' and, later, the 'burden' of the Treaty of Versailles. 'What else could one do but welcome a firm hand that had what it took to establish order and take positive action, allowing people to earn their daily bread through work once more!'

Elisabeth Lagerfeld saw for herself the kind of 'drudgery' people were subjected to and how they were 'exploited' when she visited a dressmaker's atelier in Hamburg. She also criticized the working conditions in the Berlin department store Kaufhaus Gerson, where she was said to have worked in the 1920s: 'So much needs to be done in order to improve the conditions for the working population. Women of the property-owning class, in particular, have no idea what it is like to spend every day working under time constraints in unpleasant spaces.'

She was right to point out that conditions were precarious for those working in the textile industry: 'Most of the ready-to-wear fashion in

Berlin was produced in small sewing shops or in the cottage industry,' explains historian Gerda Kessemeier. 'And this usually happened in dingy, run-down settings. The workers were paid based on their output, they had no health insurance or pension arrangements in place, and they were at the mercy of middlemen who in turn delivered the pieces to the fashion houses.'[76] Elisabeth could not help but notice the severe gap between the rich and the poor, between the seamstresses and the customers at Gerson. And as an impassioned feminist, this well-heeled daughter must have been appalled to see that women, first and foremost, were the ones being exploited by the system. After the war she told her step-granddaughter Thoma Schulenburg that she had hoped the Nazis would provide a solution for social problems of this kind.[77]

Though Elisabeth claimed she was never actively involved in the party, she did say she believed that the NSDAP had the capacity to create the ideal 'ideological and political conditions' for Germany. 'That's why I joined the party,' she wrote in her declaration. Another reason she gave for her approval of the new regime was her enthusiasm for Hitler's energetic style of leadership. In a letter to her sister in 1937, she made a loose connection between Immanuel Kant's 'Categorical Imperative' and Hitler's basic attitude: 'I thought of Hitler... There is no such thing as impossible when it comes to the effort of will. You see his achievement, which seems superhuman. There you have it: this is a maxim of the [individual] will, extreme effort. Nevertheless, despite believing that one has reached an extreme of the will, one has only just arrived at a minimum, which cannot yet be considered a principle of universal law.'[78]

Elisabeth Lagerfeld's great-nephew Gordian Tork knows from family stories that she and his grandmother Felicitas initially supported National Socialism in Germany. The two sisters truly believed that things were looking up for the country when the 1936 Olympic Games were held in Berlin. But all this changed quite abruptly for his grandmother when the events of Pogromnacht transpired in November 1938. Like many other Germans, however, Elisabeth's enthusiasm for the Nazis continued into the early years of the war.[79] Her optimism only began to fade one day when she 'saw the Jews creeping over to their assembly points in Hamburg at dawn'. The Jews of the city were rounded up and deported to the ghettos and concentration camps in the East in October 1941, at a time when the Lagerfelds had returned to Hamburg for a short spell. A large percentage of the residents in Harvestehude were Jewish, and there was no ignoring all the persecution and the deportations. 'I was shocked by the way things were going with the solution to the Jewish question and the handling of religion. I thought that addressing these questions with violence was dangerous, inhumane and foolish. Once I had come to this realization, I was never seen wearing the party insignia ever again.'

It took Elisabeth a while to distance herself from the overarching ideology. 'At first I was in denial about the alleged misconduct among people in positions of power,' she wrote. 'Having it slowly dawn on you that your most sacred feelings have been betrayed is the most terrible experience. And on top of all that, there was this terrible war happening! Gaping abysses were appearing!' And yet she says that 'for the sake of my children and my husband', she found herself powerless to leave the party. 'They tried to make it difficult for us in all sorts of ways, threatening to take the farm away from us and things like that.' It seems she was paralysed by the fear of persecution. The picture she paints is bleak: 'Now here we stand in front of the heap of ruins that once was Germany, our ideals shattered and our hearts bleeding. The individual losses and experiences of war are nothing compared to this betrayal of our best intentions. The people who so patiently endured all the hardships of war are now subjected to incomparable misery and adversity! The elements and corruption now taking hold eclipse anything that happened in 1918. The finest young people that Germany had to offer have bled to death, and the rest of us have grown old. We are old in our hearts. All the rest is just resignation!' What is striking about this written declaration is how Elisabeth Lagerfeld is trying to make excuses while simultaneously asking herself some rather probing questions. In fact, she is probably more critical and scrutinizing than most other Germans who played their part in National Socialism. She did not remain silent – apart from when she was forced to present herself to the state commissioner for the purposes of denazification.

One of the anecdotes Karl Lagerfeld shared time and time again provides different insights into his mother's thoughts about the era. When Elisabeth Lagerfeld and her son were on their way to the dentist in Bad Bramstedt one day after the war, they ran into one of Karl's teachers. He asked her, 'Couldn't you tell your son to cut his hair occasionally?' She grabbed the teacher's tie, flung it in his face, and replied, 'Why? Are you still a Nazi?'[80] When he appeared on a German talk show in 2012, Karl Lagerfeld grabbed hold of presenter Markus Lanz's tie and tossed it in the air, hitting him in his right eye – and making him wince in pain as he covered his eye with his hand.[81]

School

Karl Otto Lagerfeld was not a fan of school. He was not an exceptional student, most of the subjects bored him, he sang off-key in music lessons, he was like a fish out of water in physical education, and he was often the butt of his classmates' jokes. And to make matters worse, the walk from Bissenmoor to Jürgen-Fuhlendorf school was more than one and a half miles.

The youngster just about managed to bumble through in music. Karl Otto knew that he could not hit the notes, perhaps because his voice was about to break, but, like the rest of the children, he still had to sing in front of Miss Hinzpeter in class. Thankfully he had a plan: Peter Bendixen, who sat next to him and had a talent for music, would play the notes on the piano and accompany him, so that it wouldn't be so obvious when he hit a bum note. So that's what they did: Peter played and Karl sang, though they didn't make it all the way to the end of the song because 'before long the performance was drowned out by all the laughter; even Miss Hinzpeter was laughing'. Karl's performance was graded 'satisfactory' – not bad by his

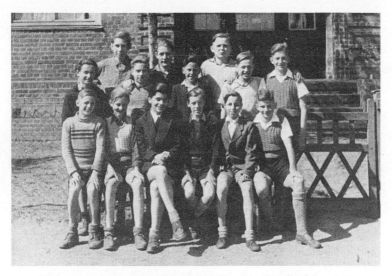

With a tie, a signet ring and a quiff: Karl Otto (front row, third from left)
stood out among the other boys at school.

standards – while Peter's 'satisfactory' was not up to his usual form.[82]
The young Karl didn't excel in physical education, either. One day the
children were told to pair up with the person next to them for a boxing
match. In a bid to curtail the undignified spectacle, Karl made another
deal with his opponent: all Peter had to do was clobber him on the
chest and he would fall over, allowing Peter to declare it a knockout.
Unfortunately the teacher cottoned on that it was all an act: the
two boys had to sit next to each other for two hours and write an
essay as a punishment for cheating. Then there was the embarrassing incident during a cross-country relay race. Some of the runners
tried to save time by throwing the baton up ahead towards the next
runner, but the clumsy Karl threw the baton into a ditch and then
took ages to find it.[83]

Just as well, then, that he was so resourceful. Sometimes Karl wrote
the answers to questions he thought might come up in exams 'inside

the double cuff of his shirt'.[84] He also got into the habit of writing his own notes to get out of class because his parents were away so much and he knew he could get away with it. 'If the weather was bad then I would say I was sick. I was a dab hand at copying my mother's handwriting.' He once even claimed that he was suffering from polio so that he could stay at home: 'I told my parents that everything hurt and I could no longer move.'[85] He did such a good job of faking his illness that he 'really couldn't move for half an hour'. But Mrs Lagerfeld was no pushover, and she quickly solved the problem: 'My mother gave me a clip around the ear, and I was cured.'[86]

Karl also considered school surplus to his requirements. 'I was hardly ever at school,' he once claimed. 'I didn't need to go. There wasn't much competition in rural Bad Bramstedt, so it wasn't all that difficult to keep up with the others.'[87] But his former classmates remember things differently. Ursula Scheube, for one, remembers her old classmate being a 'completely normal pupil, not super gifted'.[88]

Strictly speaking, he was lucky to have the chance to attend school in the first place. 'You had to have the right parents if you wanted to go to secondary school,' says Christel Friedrichs, who was named after Karl's sister. Her father, Karl's neighbour Siegfried Werner, 'was the son of a farmer, which meant that was never a possibility for him'.[89] Money was never an issue for the Lagerfelds, so things were different for them. Still, trying to get any child of ten or twelve to think of going to school as a stroke of luck was probably asking too much.

The journey to school became easier later on, when Karl befriended his classmate Dorothee Großekettler (married name Böge, 1934–2012). It was a short walk from Bissenmoor to Kurhaus station, which was on the AKN railway line that ran between Altona, Kaltenkirchen and Neumünster. From here, the two children travelled to the next stop, Bad Bramstedt station. Their 'private secondary school', founded on 1 May 1908, was within easy reach, close to the train station. And the journey was bound to seem quicker with his friend Dorothee there for company. Karl bravely walked alongside her, even when the others teased them with jibes about the 'bride and groom'. He also once drew a Punch and Judy for Dorothee, who he said was the only girl who really interested him at that time.[90] According to former classmates, Dorothee was a nice, sociable child from a good family. Her father was the director of the local health clinic – a detail which, it is safe to assume, is unlikely to have escaped Karl Otto's parents' attention.

The secondary school had changed its name to the Jürgen-Fuhlendorf-Schule in 1937. Local hero Jürgen Fuhlendorf, a *Fleckenvorsteher* (mayor) who 'saved the farmers of Bad Bramstedt from serfdom in the seventeenth century', was the inspiration for the new name, one which was finally deemed fitting for the institution.[91] More and more pupils flocked to the school when World War II broke out. Families were relocating to low-key areas, or at least sending their children to school there to escape the heavy air raids over Hamburg and Neumünster. In 1939 there were 72 pupils at the Jürgen-Fuhlendorf-Schule, and by 1944 there were 253.

Not everyone who went to private school had to pay for the privilege; sometimes the council paid. Families in need of financial assistance received full or half scholarships, while parents suffering cash-flow problems were allowed to defer their payments. Faced with the hardships of wartime, even the children became resourceful. Paper was scarce, there were no colouring pencils, and the pupils often had to share books. Hans-Joachim Bronisch, who died in the same year as his former classmate, recalled sharing a Latin book with Karl Otto and the other children: they handed the book over on Ohlau Bridge at 4 p.m. so that two pupils could use it in a single afternoon.[92]

Paper was never in short supply for Karl – sometimes he even got it from his father's business associates in America. On one occasion when he asked his father to bring back some paper from Hamburg, Otto Lagerfeld told him, 'If you run out, you can always draw on the back of the sheet.' Karl was having none of that: 'I'll never draw on the other side, never!'[93] With all this paper, he was free to work on his drawing skills to his heart's content. 'Karl Otto was very good at art,' his classmate Inge Ludwig recalls. 'He once drew the maths teacher struggling over a beef roll with a knife and fork. The picture even made it onto the wall of the classroom. The resemblance to the teacher was uncanny; Karl Otto had a real eye for faces.'[94] The girls were always saying: 'Draw us a dress!' And then at breaktime he did just that, in a few simple strokes – much to the girls' delight.

His art teacher Heinz-Helmut Schulz was also impressed by his talent. 'He completely accepted Karl Otto and encouraged him,' recalls Barbara Dieudonné.[95] Schulz himself said that he noticed Karl 'because even at a young age, he had an ability to work independently'.[96] But not even Karl's supportive teacher was spared his student's sharp tongue. Schulz liked to paint landscapes and said to Karl: 'You're good at drawing people, but you'll never be a landscape artist.' His student's response: 'I wouldn't want to be [any good] if that meant drawing the kinds of pictures you do.' And so he completely avoided landscapes.[97] Schulz would leave an impression on Karl Lagerfeld for the rest of his life: this important figure was one of the few people from Bad Bramstedt he stayed in touch with long after he had moved to France.

The student also liked to show off his language skills: 'My main hobby was interrupting the French teacher to let him know his pronunciation was off.'[98] His speaking skills were impressive. 'He already spoke very well back then,' Inge Ludwig notes. His talent for communication obscured his otherwise rather average performance. He once admitted that 'swagger' was the only reason he made it through school.[99]

Karl Otto lived in his own world. He didn't cause a scene with adolescent escapades, nor did he torment the teachers or smoke by the little shed in the schoolyard like the other boys. He seemed like some kind of messenger from a foreign land: 'As well as looking upper-class, he behaved that way, too, perhaps inadvertently drawing attention to the fact that he was different because he came from the city,' writes former classmate Peter Bendixen.[100] His privilege came across in the way he presented himself: 'He was polite, well-behaved, and always extremely well-dressed,' says Barbara Dieudonné. 'He was the only boy at the school ball to ask other mothers to dance,' recalls Inge Ludwig. 'And he loved spending time with us girls.'

He behaved differently with the boys. One anecdote from his former classmate Fritz Andresen shows just how cheeky he could be.[101] A lot of children wore old clothes after the war because money was short and their families couldn't afford to replace them. People were happy that they had something to eat, so that's just how things were. 'We refugees were given clothes that had been sewn together from hand-me-downs,' says Inge Ludwig. 'Shoes were hard to come by, and lots of people wore army jackets.'

Fritz Andresen also had to wear old clothes after the war, specifically the trousers, leather belt and brown shirt he had worn as a uniform in the 'Deutsches Jungvolk' (German Youth). 'I had joined the Jungvolk at the age of nine because I thought it sounded exciting,' says Andresen. 'We did things like hauling coal for old people,' he says, referring to his time in the sub-section of the 'Hitler Youth' for boys aged between ten and fourteen. Under the pretext of the *Volksgemeinschaft* (people's community) this youth organization provided physical and ideological training in the Nazi regime, with the intention of preparing these children to serve in the war.

Even though the war had ended, Fritz was still wearing the thick cotton uniform to school. His grandmother had removed the Nazi insignia, but everyone knew where the notorious outfit had come from. And not everyone liked it, least of all his classmate Karl Otto, who never joined the Jungvolk. It must have been 1946 when Fritz's classmate hissed at him in the schoolyard: 'They should give you potato skins instead of school meals, you Nazi pig.' Karl Otto would have been better off holding his tongue. Though Fritz Andresen was slightly younger, he was actually bigger. He grabbed hold of young Karl, dragged him over to the long-jump pit, threw him in, and shoved his face into the sand. Andresen recalls Karl Otto getting such a face full that he had to go to the eye doctor in Kiel the next day to make sure everything was okay.

The jibe from this sneering twelve-year-old comes across as downright condescending. Around this time, Otto Lagerfeld had commissioned his tailor, Staben of Hamburg, to make his son his first tailored suit.[102] The situation was quite different for Karl's classmate Fritz, who may well have been grateful that he had anything to wear at all: his father was still a prisoner of war, and now he was being raised by his grandmother and had to sell home-made honey to earn his money for school.

Teaching ground to a halt during the final chaos of the war in April 1945, when the school building was temporarily used to house refugees. Lessons resumed by order of the military government on 28 November – with 'woeful resources', according to Lagerfeld's former classmate Peter Bendixen.[103] This situation continued for a long time, and in the period from 1 January 1949 to 31 March 1950 the teachers at the school had to forego 25 per cent of their salary.[104] The private school became a state-funded selective secondary school in the 1950s, before eventually moving into a generously proportioned new building on the hillside in 1972. The old school became a primary school known as the 'Grundschule am Bahnhof'. Decades later, the science labs still serve as a reminder of the building's past as a selective secondary school.

Karl Otto left school in 1949 when he moved back to Hamburg with his family. But from 27 to 29 July 1949 he joined his classmates on a big trip to an area known as 'Holstein Switzerland' – a natural park of hilly upland noted for its resemblance to a Swiss landscape. The children cycled around the area and jumped into the lakes at Ukleisee, Kellersee and Dieksee. A photograph from 29 July shows Karl Otto in the Ukleisee lake with a group of boys. He is standing up to his chest in the water and waving his arms in the air. Is he pretending to drown and begging to be rescued? Is he calling out to the two boys on the shore? Or is he just trying to be the centre of attention because he knows that a photograph is being taken?

Another photo from this school trip still makes his classmate Ursula Scheube laugh. It shows Karl Otto emerging from the background wearing shorts, a double-breasted jacket and a tie, and seven girls sitting in a clearing having a picnic in front of him. 'He had the girls at his feet,' says Scheube, who appears to his right in the front of the picture, wearing a pale dress and with her dark hair in a long braid. 'And that's how it stayed from then on, for the rest of his life.'

Many of the girls from his class left school before their senior year, either because higher education was still off-limits to them or because they had to go out and earn a living. Ursula Scheube left school after eleventh grade and went to the vocational college for women in Neumünster. Inge Ludwig left after completing her secondary-school leaving certificate and became a kindergarten teacher in Neumünster. She has thought about her famous classmate on many occasions since then. Once, when she spotted the fashion designer in a magazine on a visit to the hairdresser, she bragged: 'I went to school with him.' To which the hairdresser's son sarcastically replied: 'And I went to school with Michael Jackson.'

Humiliation

Karl Otto wasn't like the others. His classmates could sense it, and so could he; they just didn't have a name for it yet. The difference is clear from two school photographs taken in 1948. One of these shows him sitting in the front row, smiling, with one leg crossed over the other, surrounded by the rest of the boys in his class (see p. 75). He stands out from the crowd in his dark double-breasted jacket with its peak lapel. A closer look at the picture reveals a signet ring on his right hand – a most unusual accessory for a boy of his age, and a sign of his provenance. The other photograph was taken on a school trip to the Baltic seaside resort of Laboe in Kiel in August. The rest of the children on the boat are wearing shorts, whereas Karl is sporting trousers, a tie and a double-breasted jacket. He is the only one sitting down for the photograph (see p. 82). He stares into the camera, as if fully aware of his charisma. His hair is perfectly coiffed. The other boys' hair has been whipped up by the breeze from the Baltic Sea.

Not like the others: Karl Otto (front, left) is easy to spot
on a school trip to the Baltic seaside resort of Laboe.

That hairdo. The young Karl's carefully groomed hair positively
gleams in the sunlight. 'We always had buzzed sides and long hair
on top,' says Karl Wagner, describing the typical Hitler Youth haircut
so many boys had around that time. 'Whereas his hair was swept
back and pomaded.'[105] Other boys started to grow their hair out after
the war, but there was still one big difference: most of the children
in northern Germany had blond or mousy hair, whereas this young
boy stood out from the crowd with his dark mane.

Karl Otto was different. 'He was often by himself at breaktimes,'
says Ursula Scheube, who also went to his school. 'He was a loner,'
agrees former classmate Fritz Andresen. 'We left him out because
he was such an oddball.'[106] Inge Ludwig also remembers the boys

making fun of him at school. All the elements of his personal style, his 'behaviour, his appearance, his clothing and his baroque head of hair' made people want to tease him. 'Even the teachers poked fun at him,' writes Peter Bendixen.[107] According to Karl's former headmaster Hans-Otto Jarren, his fellow pupils' behaviour towards him was sometimes so threatening that 'he was only allowed to go home if he was escorted by older pupils'.[108] Apparently the students and teachers even took up a collection once – to raise money to send him to the hairdresser.

Just imagine: this boy is teased by everyone at school, even his teachers; they make fun of his hair, taunting and pressuring him into going to the hairdresser; he has to make his way home escorted by an older student for protection. All this verbal and physical aggression was about more than just his privilege; it was about the affected appearance and mannerisms of this young boy, who was aware of his nascent homosexuality in early puberty.

'It all begins with an insult,' writes French sociologist Didier Eribon.[109] 'Sometimes no gesture is even necessary: one's appearance or clothing suffice to provoke an act of hatred.'[110] It seems almost as if Eribon is staring directly at this boy. Lagerfeld never really spoke about the impact of such childhood experiences on his life. How could he? This boy, who was already an outsider because he lived outside of town, would have been traumatized by the persecution he suffered at school. According to Eribon, acts of hatred leave a mark on the consciousness, 'inscribing shame in the deepest levels' of the mind: The 'permanent insult', he says, is 'a more or less definitive sentence, for life', because the child learns that he is 'someone who can be looked at or talked about in a certain way and who is stigmatized by that gaze and those words'.[111] Homosexual people therefore sought out 'means to flee insult and violence, whether it be by way of dissimulation or by way of emigration to more hospitable locations'. Examples of 'more hospitable locations' included big cities like Berlin and Paris.[112] So, in a sense, his flight to Paris some years later was psychologically mapped out for him all along.

As far as his worldly parents were concerned, being gay was no big deal. He asked his mother about homosexuality when he was eleven years old. Her response: 'Some people are this way, some are that way.'[113] And 'some people are blond and some people have dark hair'.[114] And in a similar vein: 'It's like having a particular hair colour, nothing more. What can it matter to civilized people?'[115] In his own words, he didn't struggle with the realization that he was gay. 'I was lucky to have very open-minded parents. And I'm not convinced that they were all that innocent themselves when they were young.'[116] In a manner of speaking, he was free to do as he pleased. 'It may have been forbidden for some people, but nothing was out of bounds where I lived.'[117]

This may well have been the case. With the liberal upper-class attitude that prevailed in the Lagerfeld household, there was no place for disapproving of those who led a different lifestyle. Still, his father was disappointed, and no doubt his son could sense it. Moreover, despite the picture of tolerance that Lagerfeld paints in his recollections, the reality of life in Germany at that time was quite different. Even though the war was over, and with it all the years of persecution and murder of homosexuals by the Nazis, the country was still gripped by homophobia. Germany's notorious 'gay paragraph' continued to apply after World War II. Paragraph 175 of the German Criminal Code, which criminalized same-sex relations between men, had been part of the legislation since 1871. The Nazis redrafted the legislation in 1935, increasing the maximum sentence from six months to five years, and expanding the definition of what constituted a crime so that physical contact was no longer the key criterion. The Nazi wording of the 'gay paragraph' was officially adopted by West Germany when the republic was founded in 1949. Up to that point there had been more than a thousand final convictions every year since the war ended, and after 1950 the numbers rose to more than two thousand per year. Particularly in the countryside, gay men were derided, baited, slurred and reported to the authorities around this time, even after the Nazi era was over.

In the words of Wolfgang Joop, 'The gay child feels like a black child in a white class.'[118]

Sneering glances, spiteful remarks and tangible persecution: these were just a few of the reasons why Karl Otto didn't like going to school. This kind of treatment also drove him to start picturing a world for himself outside of Holstein, and may have factored into his preference for subjects that required the use of his imagination. He was an enthusiastic member of Miss Jüngst's drama group at school, appearing in Molière's *Tartuffe*. He loved art, and reading was his favourite pastime, even as a child. According to Didier Eribon, culture in the broadest sense came to play an important role in how gay men defined themselves. Research into the subject of homosexuality has identified a general 'orientation toward "artistic professions"', linking 'the feeling of being "different" with a yearning for an "artistic" life'.[119] But where was he supposed to go if he wanted to turn his artistic leanings into a career? It was never going to happen in Bad Bramstedt – he knew that much already.

Sisters

Karl Lagerfeld's sisters, Theresia and Christel, kept a low profile over the years, preferring not to give into temptation and ride on their little brother's coattails. Ever since the 1950s, when Karl parted ways with the family to make a new life for himself in Paris, their relationship with him had been distant. According to Didier Eribon, dissonance within the family had a lasting effect on gay men, often fuelling a 'project of self-restructuration' in their lives.[120] 'Friends who have been met in gay locales replace ... family relations that have been abandoned to a greater or lesser extent,' Eribon writes.[121]

Martha Christiane Lagerfeld, Otto and Elisabeth's first child, was born in Hamburg on 11 May 1931. She was only two years older than Karl, and since she didn't go to boarding school for as long as their half-sister Thea, she was very close to her brother as a child – even though he lacked some of her more practical leanings.[122] Karl's childhood friend Sylvia Jahrke said she always found him 'a bit prim and

A rare photo: Thea (back left), who spent most of her youth at boarding
schools, appears with her father Otto Lagerfeld and her half-siblings
Christel and Karl Otto in this picture taken around 1936.

proper', whereas Christel was quite the opposite: 'She was a wild child,
always running around the place.'[123] It seems that as a five-year-old
she was so unruly that her parents decided to enlist a specialist to
analyse her handwriting and give them insights into her personality.
The expert concluded that she was 'prone to considerable mood swings
due to her emotional excitability'.[124] But as unpredictable as she may
have been in her early years, she calmed down as she got older. 'All
the whining and wailing has completely stopped,' Elisabeth wrote in
a letter to her sister in 1942, when Christel was eleven: 'Such a funny
child, and so well-behaved.' The only problem was with her schooling:
'I promised her a hundred marks if she studies hard enough to avoid
being held back next autumn; I believe that will work.' Evidently the
child-rearing and all the other jobs were taking their toll on the lady
of the house. 'Just imagine: the house, the garden, the chickens, the
children, and then Christel's homework, which can be a real struggle

sometimes!' In the same letter, she talks about picking and preserving fruit, patching clothes and doing the washing. 'I doubt Madame Privy Councillor would have done this. But I take it slowly and will get help.' Then she throws in for good measure: 'Other than that, the three of us have an extremely comfortable life here and love each other very much.'[125]

Otto Lagerfeld was more concerned with making sure his children received a practical education than an academic education. After leaving high school, Christel studied hotel management and completed part of her training at her grandparents' favourite hotel, the Four Seasons in Hamburg. She also worked in Berchtesgaden, Bavaria.[126] She left Germany in 1957, when she accepted a job as an au pair in Seattle, Washington. This was where she met her future husband Robert Johnson, who was more than eight years her senior. He was working as a tax inspector when they met, having previously served in the US Navy during World War II. The couple got married in 1959 and moved from the West Coast to the East Coast, settling in the small town of Portland in Connecticut. Christel was an uncommon name in America, so she reverted to her birth name and became known as Christiane Johnson. She and Robert had four children: Caroline, Roger, Paul and Karl.

Their son Karl, named after his uncle, died in a motorcycle accident at the age of eighteen in late May 1980 – on a bike given to him by his uncle. 'Perhaps that's why Karl was always so afraid of motorcycling,' says Lagerfeld's close confidant Sébastien Jondeau. He too was a passionate motorcyclist, and had a narrow escape when he broke his spine in two places in December 2016. The fashion designer took care of Jondeau after the motocross crash, perhaps partly because he was still haunted by what had happened to his nephew.[127]

Christel's children only saw their uncle once, when he flew out to the US and pulled up in Portland in a black limousine. 'He stayed just for the afternoon,' Christiane Johnson recalled. 'I went over to visit him a couple of years later, I think.' Every once in a while he sent letters or Christmas cards. In spring 2014 he wrote to her saying that he had had a cat for two and a half years: 'I didn't know that a pet could be so great.' And: 'I just cannot believe that you will be 83 and I will soon turn 81.'[128] At least he was honest about his age in his letters to his big sister.

Even though Lagerfeld was often in Manhattan, just a few hours' drive from Portland, his sister was too far away for his tightly scheduled life. He thought that being in the US was like being 'on another planet'. He said his sister was completely caught up in her life there: 'She doesn't want to leave her husband alone for a single day; she has some really lovely, charming children.'[129] He called her 'an undeniably nice person, unlike me'. He also commented on how charitable she was: apparently, whenever he sent her something from Chanel she gave it straight to poor people.[130] As well as being devoted to her family, she was very active in the Protestant community, where she did a lot of charity work.[131] Her brother sometimes sarcastically referred to her as 'The Saint' for this very reason.[132] Christiane Johnson passed away on 9 October 2015 at the age of eighty-four. She is buried at the Swedish Cemetery in Portland, along with her husband Robert, who had died a year earlier. Her brother did not attend the funeral.

The fact that Karl's half-sister Thea took a completely different path in life is probably indicative of the centrifugal forces at play in this family. Born on 30 November 1922, Thea was nine years older than Christel and eleven years older than Karl. Other people who lived in the neighbourhood rarely mention her in their childhood stories of Bissenmoor, no doubt because Thea started boarding school when her siblings were still very young. 'We had no idea that he had an older half-sister,' says Karl's former classmate Barbara Dieudonné.[133] He wasn't as close to Thea as he was to Christel. This would also be a cause of family discord later on.

Thea Lagerfeld started attending a Catholic boarding school in the 1930s. 'She wanted to get away from the house because of her stepmother,' her daughter Thoma Schulenburg says.[134] She then attended the Reinhardswaldschule, commonly known as the 'women's school', in Kassel. This boarding school was founded shortly before World War

I by high-school teacher Eleonore Lemp, whose goal was to enable girls to attain 'a solid education'. In addition to 'girls' subjects' such as nursing, the curriculum at this progressive school also included economics and civic education.[135] Former student Gertrud Scheele recalls sitting by the fire with the other girls on Sunday evenings and listening intently as the ambitious headmistress read aloud from works by Goethe and Schiller.[136]

The educator was determined to give her students a complete education at her 'elite school'. The girls had to work in the garden, on the poultry farm and in the dairy. The curriculum also included a 'practical year', which likely replaced the German National Labour Service – a period of national service which, from the beginning of the war, was made compulsory for young women as well as young men. Thea Lagerfeld spent this time working in the home of the aristocratic Schulenburg family in Tylsen, a rural community in the district of Salzwedel in Saxony-Anhalt. Here, she fell in love with the family's youngest son, Thomas Graf (i.e., Count) von der Schulenburg.

The welcoming environment in the Schulenburgs' family home was like a sanctuary away from her stepmother's hostility. It would appear that Elisabeth Lagerfeld didn't take kindly to Thea's presence in her home, as evidenced by a letter she wrote to her sister in 1942, expressing her relief that Thea had not turned up in Bad Bramstedt. Evidently the nineteen-year-old Thea lived with her father in Hamburg during the summer. 'She never comes to the telephone when Otto calls me in the evenings,' a rather incensed Elisabeth writes. 'But the next time I see her I shall tell her what I think of her snotty tone. I certainly won't let her get away with how she thinks she can behave towards me.' Apparently even Otto complained about the bratty attitude of the little madam.[137]

No wonder Thea Lagerfeld got engaged to Thomas von der Schulenburg so quickly. She would have liked to marry him immediately, but Otto Lagerfeld was adamant that his daughter should wait until she was of full legal age.[138] But that was too far away, and so she married the Wehrmacht officer (b. 1 October 1919) on 3 April 1943, when she was still just twenty years old. The couple had only been living together as man and wife for three weeks – honeymooning at Lake Constance – when Thomas von der Schulenburg was called back to the Front. He left behind his now-pregnant wife, who often set out from their apartment in Sondershausen (Thuringia) and travelled around 125 miles to visit her mother-in-law, Theodora von der Schulenburg, in Tylsen and over 190 miles to see her father in Hamburg. Thea-Friederike von der Schulenburg, known as Thoma, was born on 16 January 1944 in Neumünster and baptized in Wallstawe, Tylsen. In the full throes of the war, devastating news arrived from the Eastern Front, and suddenly everything changed for the young family. On 4 March 1944, less than a year after marrying Thea, Thomas von der Schulenburg was confirmed dead at the age of twenty-four. According to the obituary notice, First Lieutenant von der Schulenburg, commander of a Panzer motorized reconnaissance division, died 'on the front line in the East'.[139] Thea von der Schulenburg became a widow at the age of just twenty-one, and little Thea-Friederike had lost one of her parents after only seven weeks in the world. Soon she would be called Thoma, in honour of her late father.

Thea von der Schulenburg was eager to become independent. She and her daughter were living at the Glücksklee headquarters at 36 Mittelweg when she marched up to the editorial office of German newspaper *Die Welt*. Dressed in a dark blue suit with a white-collared shirt and long gloves, she introduced herself to her prospective employer. 'I haven't studied, but I want to work,' she said.[140] Her determination paid off, and she was employed as the newspaper's picture editor for a number of years in the late 1940s.[141] A nanny looked after little Thoma while she was at work.

Thea moved to Frankfurt in 1950 with her six-year-old daughter and her boyfriend, graphic designer Julius Stahlberg, whom she married in 1951. She got a job as an account manager in the German office of McCann, an American advertising agency, and was based in

Oberlindau, in the affluent Westend district of the city. Her daughter went to boarding school, just as she had done in her childhood. Soon the couple moved west of Frankfurt to Niederjosbach because Julius Stahlberg had been suffering from tuberculosis since the war and needed a change of environment. The air was better in the Taunus region, plus there was a respiratory clinic nearby in Naurod. Despite their best efforts, Stahlberg died in the late 1950s, making Thea a widow for the second time before the age of forty. She abandoned the surname Stahlberg, reverted to calling herself von der Schulenburg, and moved to Wiesbaden.[142]

Eventually she got together with Horst Joachim Wilke, an account executive at McCann. Wilke dealt with one of the company's major clients, Neckermann, and ended up making a name for himself following a flash of inspiration in 1960. The company had been forced to abandon its slogan 'Besser dran mit Neckermann' (Better off with Neckermann) when one of its rivals took action and a court ruling banned the slogan on the grounds of comparative advertising and unfair competition. Now the mail-order company was desperately trying to come up with an alternative: 'We stayed up late into the night brainstorming,' Josef Neckermann wrote in his memoirs. 'All kinds of suggestions were put forward and discarded.' That was until Wilke – who had nothing to do with the creative side of things – blurted out the perfect solution: 'Neckermann macht's möglich' (Neckermann makes it possible). Josef Neckermann was excited. The partner of Karl Lagerfeld's half-sister had just come up with what was to be one of Germany's best-known slogans.[143]

Over the years, relationships within the family became more and more strained. Lagerfeld said that his half-sister 'did not behave well' after their father's death in 1967; apparently he 'never saw her again' after that.[144] Her daughter Thoma Schulenburg remembers the issue involving disagreements over the family's inheritance. But in fact the two of them did stay in touch, albeit rather loosely. In 1989, Karl wrote the following in a letter to his cousin Kurt: 'Christel is doing well over in the US. I don't hear much from Thea.'[145] All the same, he continued to send her cards with photographs of himself on the front: 'For Thea, [from] your Mule, Easter 1985.' Or: 'Dear Thea, Here is a self-portrait. Love, M. 10.4.94.'[146] And when Thea von der Schulenburg found herself in emotional and financial straits, Lagerfeld did his bit to help by offering reassurance and money.

When asked about his now-deceased half-sister in 2005, he replied in his typically off-hand way: 'I didn't see her for thirty years, and now she's dead.'[147] He later claimed she was a lesbian and fled school 'for sleeping with the teachers'.[148] A fellow student from the Reinhardswald school has no memory of such affairs: 'And if anything had happened back then, we would have heard about it.'[149] Thea von der Schulenburg's daughter also thinks his story is absurd: 'That's nonsense,' she says.[150]

No matter what Thea did, Elisabeth Lagerfeld was never satisfied. 'In the latest news, Theresa has got remarried again,' she wrote in a letter to her sister in December 1972, outraged by her stepdaughter's marriage to Horst Joachim Wilke. 'It seems Theresa has married her old beau, although what is old – he's five years younger than her. She turned fifty on 30 November… How is that possible?'[151] All the same, Elisabeth was attentive to Thoma, who often visited her during the holidays; no doubt she thought her stepdaughter was incapable of looking after the child herself. Karl Lagerfeld never saw his half-sister again following the dispute over their inheritance in the late 1960s,[152] and Thea von der Schulenburg passed away on 1 October 1997 at the age of seventy-four. She was buried in Wiesbaden, where she died. Her half-brother did not attend the funeral.

Prussia

It was a routine trip for Matthias and Andrea Wirthwein, the proprietors of Die Wortfreunde, a second-hand bookshop in Mannheim. Christopher Pfleiderer, an antiquarian bookseller friend, had tipped them off that there were lots of old books to be had at a house clearance in Baden-Baden. So that hot summer's day on 22 July 2009, they drove out to the spa town in the Black Forest to take a look. When they pulled up outside the apartment building at 142B Lange Strasse, the house clearance vans from Strasbourg were already parked in the yard and the workers were making their way down the stairs heavily laden with the contents of the apartment. When the Wirthweins went inside, however, they were greeted by a sad sight. The house clearers were shaking the books off the shelves so that they could get to what they wanted: the slightly yellowing lacquered shelves.[153]

The whole thing made Matthias Wirthwein want to turn around and leave: 'Such a disgraceful way to treat books,' he noted. He did, however, manage to stumble upon a stack of volumes by the popular German author Karl May, so it wasn't all bad. But when Wirthwein started packing the green tomes away, the man from the house clearance company said he had already reserved them for himself. That was the final straw. Wirthwein turned to his wife and suggested that they leave. But Andrea had been on a hunt of her own, and she had laid her hands on a couple of old magazines, including a first edition of German *Vogue* from 1928. She took the magazines and boxed them up, along with a lavish old volume about Frederick the Great, even though she knew her history buff of a husband wouldn't think much of it. All in all, there were four or five crates' worth to take back to the bookshop.

Weeks later, Matthias Wirthwein finally unpacked the contents in his shop. He was already familiar with the book about Frederick the Great; the title usually fetched between 15 and 30 euros online. He was weighing up whether to pitch the price higher and put it online or to sell it in the shop for less when he stumbled upon Conrad Ramstedt's dedication to his nephew 'Carl Otto Lagerfeld'.

Carl Otto Lagerfeld? Was that who they thought it might be? The next day Matthias and Andrea Wirthwein started to do a bit of detective work. They wrote to the University of Münster, where Conrad Ramstedt had been a professor, and they compared the signature in the book with the signatures on his letters. Now they knew for certain that the dedication had been written by the surgeon from Münster who had married Karl Lagerfeld's aunt Felicitas Bahlmann.

Conrad Ramstedt dedicated a book to his godson and nephew, 'Carl [*sic*]
Otto Lagerfeld', on his confirmation, Easter 1948: 'When you read this
book, which describes our unforgettable Prussia under Frederick the
Great, you should realize that the state of Prussia probably no longer
exists at the moment, but its spirit will <u>never</u> disappear.
May you still experience the resurrection of Prussia.'

The same Conrad Ramstedt (1867–1973) had been the senior consultant on the surgical ward at Münster's Raphaelsklinik from
1909 to 1947, his faithful service only interrupted by World War I.
He had made a name for himself for successfully carrying out a
pyloromyotomy on a colleague's 22-day-old son for the first time
on 18 June 1911. From then on the surgical procedure, used to treat
the intestinal condition of pyloric stenosis, was referred to as the
'Ramstedt–Weber' operation.[154] Ramstedt was chief surgeon at
the Raphaelsklinik from 1944 to 1947, and in recognition for his
achievements after the hospital was devastated in World War II, he
was awarded the Grand Cross of the Order of Merit of the Federal
Republic of Germany in 1962. Karl Lagerfeld's uncle and godfather,

who was twenty-five years his wife's senior, was another major authority in the family.

Until now, the only mention of Conrad Ramstedt in the literature about Karl Lagerfeld was in a rather significant anecdote. The ten-year-old Karl was walking with his uncle in Münster one day when they passed by Freiligrathstrasse, a street named after the German poet Ferdinand Freiligrath. When the boy asked who this 'Freiligrath' was, his godfather was furious that he didn't already know, and gave him a clip around the ear for his ignorance. Later on, back at his house, he let his sister-in-law know exactly what he thought: 'Elisabeth, your son is a nitwit,' Ramstedt complained. 'And that's all your fault for being so superficial.'[155]

The professor was born in the nineteenth century, like Freiligrath, and still cherished the old educational ideals from that time. The tribute to Prussia he wrote in his dedication in the book at the age of eighty-one is therefore only logical. Also interesting to note is the mention of Karl's confirmation, as he had always described himself as unreligious. 'I wasn't allowed to go to church,' the designer once said. 'I had no religious education.'[156] In 2011, he said that he had no interest in religion per se and was more concerned with the influence of religion on history and culture. He said he studied this phenomenon much like the biologist Jean Rostand looked at ants.[157] The designer explained that he was a child of Catholic parents living in a Protestant area. 'So I never had to go to church. I didn't get con-firmed, I don't even know what that is.'[158] And when German television host Johannes B. Kerner mentioned 'communion or confirmation', he claimed he had done neither of these things.[159] Perhaps these overly zealous reactions were just a way of deflecting. A fortune-teller had once told his mother: 'You're pregnant, you're going to have a boy, and he will be a bishop.'[160] When Lagerfeld was a boy in Bad Bramstedt, getting confirmed was a matter of course. The Christian rite of passage is a requirement for attending communion, and the confirmation records for the local church parish do indeed include an entry for 'Karl Otto Lagerfeld': he is listed under the number 17 in 1948. According to the Evangelical-Lutheran Church Parish of Altholstein, the confirmation ceremony was held at Bad Bramstedt church on Palm Sunday, 21 March 1948.[161] Although he preferred not to acknowledge any religious ties in his life, the little Karl was also baptized at the Catholic Church of St Antonius in the Hamburg district of Winterhude.[162]

Karl Lagerfeld's parents were not as unchurched as he later made them out to be. Catholicism was, and still is, widespread in the Münster region. The designer once said: 'My father's parents and my mother's mother were hysterical, so my parents were tired of [religion]. My mother used to say: "There is one God for everybody and all the religions are shops."'[163] In fact, Elisabeth Lagerfeld's denazification questionnaire states that she became an Old Catholic in 1936 'out of conviction'.[164] In all likelihood, her husband would have convinced her to join the faith, as he was an Old Catholic. Over the years, the Lagerfelds maintained their ties to the Catholic Church. The couple donated a sanctuary lamp to the Maria Grün Catholic Church in Blankenese, and it would continue to burn for a long time: the lamp was only replaced when it was gifted to a parish in Poland during renovation works in 2005 and 2006.[165]

So just how did the great Prussian king end up in Baden-Baden, in the form of this tome entitled *Fridericus Rex*? According to information in state archives, Otto and Elisabeth Lagerfeld registered a change of address on 9 March 1960 when they moved from 85 Harvestehuder Weg in Hamburg to 16a Hahnhofstrasse in Baden-Baden. After Otto Lagerfeld died on 4 July 1967, Elisabeth Lagerfeld gave notice of another change of address on 9 April 1968 and set off to Paris to join her son. It is possible that she left the magazines and the old tome with a friend before she left – along with the old volumes of Karl May's work that the house clearer claimed for himself.

The Wirthweins wrote to Karl Lagerfeld in Paris to tell him about their discovery in 2009. They did not hear back from him – well, this fashion designer never was one for reminiscing. The couple have since been offered four-figure sums for the book, but they are unlikely to part with it. In any case, the book serves to demonstrate certain religious and familial lines of tradition. As for the 'resurrection of Prussia' that Karl Otto's godfather called for in his dedication (see p. 94), Karl Lagerfeld, the *roi prussien*[166] (Prussian king), brought Prussia back to life in the person he came to be: 'Basically it's true: I'm Prussian by nature.'[167]

Awakening

Where is Karl? Is he the young man with a side parting and a bow tie standing by the stairs (7:51 minutes in), gazing at the fashion models in awe? Or is he the young man in a tie sitting to the left of the front row, next to a woman who appears to briefly lean over to him (8:35 minutes in)? This YouTube footage of Parisian label Dior's appearance at a major Hamburg fashion show, from a documentary about life in the city in 1949 ('Filmaufnahmen über und aus Hamburg 1949'), is evocative but inconclusive. Just where is Karl? No matter how many times you watch it, it is impossible to tell.

Perhaps the young Karl Lagerfeld didn't even make it into the footage from the Hotel Esplanade. The invitations in the Dior archives[168] reveal that three shows were held over the course of two days: two at evening galas on 12 and 13 December 1949, and one at an afternoon-tea event at 4 p.m. on 13 December. Lagerfeld, who had just left school at the time, often talked about attending one of these shows with his mother. The experience was a kind of epiphany for him. Up to that point he wasn't quite sure what to do with his artistic talents. But when he went to the show and witnessed the work of one of the world's greatest fashion designers, his eyes were opened to opportunities he had never imagined could exist.

Events like this had been a rarity in Hamburg since 1945. As other excerpts of the film show, the residents of this megalopolis had more pressing things on their minds around this time. Hamburg was still reeling from the devastating aftermath of the war. People were dealing with material and moral crises. In 1949, a new school opened in the Iserbrook district for the first time since the war, but the children had to be taught in two or three shifts due to the lack of space. In March of the same year, a huge floating crane by the Versmannkai promenade was blown up by the occupying forces as part of the post-war effort, even though First Mayor Max Brauer had tried to convince the British to let it stay. On 23 April 1949 the film director Veit Harlan, who faced charges of contributing to the Holocaust with his antisemitic propaganda film *Jud Süß* (Süss the Jew), was acquitted of the charges on the grounds of insufficient proof. A second trial in 1950 also ended with an acquittal. Then on 8 May, citizens voted for the Basic Law (*Grundgesetz*) and Hamburg officially signed up to becoming a state of the Federal Republic of Germany.

Much of life in those days revolved around coping with the long-term effects of the Nazi era. But, as time went on, things started to take a turn for the better. The currency reform of 20 June 1948 laid the foundations for economic recovery, while the formation of the Federal Republic of Germany on 23 May 1949 paved the way for political stability. The strongest political parties at the first parliamentary elections on 14 August 1949 were the Christian Democratic Union of Germany (*Christlich Demokratische Union Deutschlands* – CDU), with 31 per cent of the votes cast, and the Social Democratic Party of Germany (*Sozialdemokratische Partei Deutschlands* – SPD), with 29.2 per cent. Most of West Germany's citizens had turned their backs on the right-wing parties, and the country found its way to political stability under Konrad Adenauer (CDU), who was elected Federal Chancellor on 15 September 1949. He was re-elected three times – in 1953, 1957 and 1961.

The birth of newspapers such as *Die Welt* (1946), *Hamburger Abendblatt* (1948) and *Hamburger Morgenpost* (1949) also heralded a change for the better. A raft of new magazines also appeared around this time, among them *Stern* (founded in Hanover in 1948, before moving to Hamburg in 1949), *Der Spiegel* (which was established in Hanover in 1947, and relocated to Hamburg in 1952) and *Bild* (1952), as well as women's magazines such as *Film und Frau* (1949) and *Constanze* (1948). In just a few years, these new publications transformed Hamburg into Germany's media capital. Newspaper and magazine enthusiast Karl Lagerfeld, whose half-sister worked at *Die Welt*, came up with some very inspired ways of making the most of what his hometown had to offer.

By the close of the 1940s, a new era was also dawning for the Lagerfelds. Business was looking bright for the Glücksklee director. Elisabeth Lagerfeld was done with the tedium of country life in a place that reminded her a little too much of her younger years in Beckum. 'My mother was bored to death in the countryside,' her son later said. 'And I was desperate to get out of there as soon as I could.'[169] He left school, his parents sold Bissenmoor, and they said goodbye to Bad Bramstedt. When they moved back to Hamburg, the house on Harvestehuder Weg was still under construction and the house in Innocentiapark was being rented out, so they moved into the Hotel Esplanade for a while. It just so happened that they were in the right place at the right time. The impressive building – which was a hotel from 1948 to 1951 – brought yet another sign of future prosperity. Christian Dior had declared that the modest post-war years were over in 1947 when he unveiled his extravagant 'New Look' in Paris. Since then, he had started touring his new collection around the world several times a year – to give it 'a breath of fresh air', he later wrote.[170] After his acclaimed debut, Dior's fashion house experienced rapid growth and was soon more sought after internationally than any other competitor. His models, whom he referred to as his mannequins, travelled as far afield as Japan, South Africa, Greece, Scotland and South America, with a team of stylists and press coordinators, eager to tap into new markets.

Now the team even made it to Hamburg. 'Yesterday morning, four dainty women with four colossal trunks arrived at the central station on the Nord-Express from Paris,' the *Hamburger Abendblatt* newspaper reported in an article on 12 December 1949. 'The first French fashion envoys since the war, trailblazers from the Christian Dior fashion house, which is showcasing a collection of eighty designs at the Hotel Esplanade today and tomorrow at the invitation of *Constanze*.'[171]

Publishers John Jahr and Axel Springer created *Constanze* after obtaining a licence from the British Military Government to publish a women's magazine. The indefatigable editor-in-chief Hans Huffzky quickly made *Constanze* a hit – and just a year after the magazine was launched, readers were impressed to learn that Paris's top fashion designer had accepted its invitation to Hamburg. Well, almost. Sadly, the man himself wouldn't be making a personal appearance; he was busy in France on the Côte d'Azur, working on designs for his next collections.

The first to appear were Dior's right-hand woman Suzanne Luling, press coordinator Mademoiselle Le Bidois, a French journalist, and Madame Castelnot, also known as the *Reine des Cabines* (the Queen of the Fitting Rooms). They unpacked the trunks of clothes in the Hotel Esplanade and prepared the dresses for the show with the help of two German ironers, whom they praised for their skills: 'We would take them back to Paris with us in a heartbeat.' The models would be under the watchful eye of Madame Castelnot and the police – as was the all-important 'Cygne Noir' (black swan) dress that the fashion designer had created for one of his muses, Marlene Dietrich.

The models – France, Sylvie, Jane, Julie, Simone and Tania – arrived a day later on the night train. One can only imagine the impression they made, especially France, Sylvie and Tania, whom Dior would later, in his autobiography, refer to as his 'star mannequins': 'They alone can bring my clothes to life,' he wrote.[172] Karl Lagerfeld could still remember the names Simone and France a whole sixty-eight years after the event.[173] Each of the six young women received a bouquet of roses as soon as they pulled into the station. Photographer Norbert Leonard, whose real name was Norbert Levy, and who had only narrowly survived the terror of Nazi rule, photographed the models amid a landscape of ruins. When Jacques Chastel – the managing director, and apparently the only man among the eight hundred or so employees at Dior – misplaced his bow tie before the start of the big fashion parade, the staff at *Constanze* quickly bought him a new one for six marks. The mannequins waited behind a velvet curtain

CONSTANZE

Beifall für France!

Modekönig Dior schickte seine
6 schönsten Mädchen und seine
80 schönsten Kleider zu Constanze

1. Heft · 3. Jahrgang · Erscheint alle 14 Tage mittwochs · Preis 60 Pfennig

Hosted by *Constanze* magazine: Christian Dior showcases
his fashion in Hamburg, December 1949.

that separated them from the guests in the large hall. Axel Springer
greeted the guests as the Esplanade orchestra played 'Parlez-moi
d'amour'. This evening wasn't about business, he said, it was about
fashion as an art form.

The clothes on display at this Dior show truly were works of
art. The audience went into raptures over the dresses in taffeta,
silk, brocade and velvet; the furs, necklaces and sequins, beading
and gemstone embroideries; the models' perfect poise, adroit twirls

and exaggerated poses. 'It is significant', an article in *Die Zeit* newspaper read, 'that he only uses a few basic colours – black, red, brown and their pastel tones – which he combines in a way that is so awash with unexpected beauty and sensational sophistication that they met with cries of excitement and admiration in the banquet hall.' The compères whispered the names of the dresses into the microphone – 'Poudre et Sucre', 'Matisse', 'Christian Bérard' – just as the boss wanted them to, with no other comments. The film crew's footage is fogged in places – because the smoke from the cigars was getting into the picture.

Der Spiegel reported that Dior's designs wowed the audience because of the 'simplicity of the lines' rather than their 'extravagance'. The verdict from *Constanze*: 'The women devoured the dresses with their eyes', while it was 'not only the dresses' that caught the attention of the men in the audience. *Die Zeit* raved about the 'ravishing girls from Paris, who captured the flair of that enchanting city with their spectacular gowns, racy fragrances and sparkling jewelry', calling them 'emissaries of a world that is still out there, somewhere: the big, wide world where there is no wreckage, no work – only parties, air travel and formal dances'.

The report from *Der Spiegel* was more sedate: 'On the Seine, a Dior dress costs between 100,000 and 120,000 francs, the equivalent of 1,200 to 1,400 Deutschmarks.' But *Die Zeit* was still caught up in raptures: 'The charm and sensibility of this country, the creativity and flair for colour of its couturiers, their eroticism and extremely refined taste, which earn this fashion designer ... his unrivalled international reputation.' The reporter was certain that the new style would give business a boost: 'A simple glance at Dior's creations will breathe new life into German ready-to-wear clothing.'

This statement was almost like a prophecy. Karl Lagerfeld was at the show and loved what he saw – and, of course, he would take French and German ready-to-wear clothing to a whole new level in later years. 'I can still clearly remember the Dior show,' he told German *Vogue* before a trip to Hamburg to celebrate Chanel's Métiers d'Art show at the Elbphilharmonie in December 2017.[174] Almost seven decades down the line, and also in the run-up to Christmas, this major show was a late response to the old master. The Dior show was legendary, but the Chanel show was unsurpassable. This Hamburg boy had long since outrun the great idol of his youth.

Christian Dior was grateful for everything that happened in Hamburg. When the staff from *Constanze* visited him in his atelier on Avenue Montaigne, he showed them the 'little light-blue day dress in pure silk' that he had named after the magazine. The pleated shirt dress known as the 'Constanze' was then modelled for *Constanze* by a mannequin named Jane.[175] It was clear that this man knew how to inspire dreams and how to speak to women, with his relatively uncomplicated clothes. He also knew how to get on the right side of the media – no doubt Karl Lagerfeld couldn't help but notice this, too.

Fashion was Lagerfeld's calling. Any doubts he still had after the Dior show were put to rest after one other experience. His mother, who encouraged his artistic skills, approached the director of the Hamburg Academy of Fine Arts at Lerchenfeld and showed him some of her son's sketches. Instead of inviting her son to try out for the academy, the director told her: 'Your son is not interested in art at all; he's interested in fashion. Look closer at what he draws: bold dresses. He could be a costume designer for the theatre.' The youngster later had to concede: 'My sketches were not up to the standards of painting at that time.' His mother was irritated: 'You're too lazy, you have no ambition, you don't try hard enough to make something of yourself.'[176]

Elisabeth Lagerfeld wanted more for her son. After the war, Hamburg no longer had so much to offer; all that remained of the big city was mass destruction. 'My mother always said that Hamburg is the gateway to the world, but only the gateway,' the designer said. Her advice: 'You have to get out of here!'[177] But she didn't want him to venture eastwards: 'Berlin stopped being Berlin when the Jews were driven out. From 1933, Berlin was out of the question,' her son later said.[178] The German capital had played a crucial role in Elisabeth

Connected to the world: Karl Lagerfeld was still living
with his parents in Hamburg in the early 1950s ...
but soon he would be leaving.

Lagerfeld's life in the 1920s, but to her mind it had been 'broken' ever
since the war. 'This was another reason why she didn't want to go
back to the city,' her son said. 'She wanted to keep the picture she had
in her mind from when she was still young, sprightly and happy.'[179]

The ambitious woman quietly let her son know what kinds of
possibilities were out there. But if Karl was to pursue the kind of cos-
mopolitan life his mother secretly longed for, he would also have

to turn his back on the kind of humdrum business life his father wanted for him. Karl had his heart set on something completely different. Germany bored him – unsurprising, really, given the 'peculiar inflexibility'[180] of the stuffy, cautious conservatism underpinning the country's economic upturn and growing political stability at the dawn of the Adenauer era.

The family moved into the large house at 65 Harvestehuder Weg in 1950.[181] Karl had a small room with a bunk-style bed. 'He hung out there most of the time,' says his niece Thoma Schulenburg. 'He didn't want to go to school anymore.'[182] His goal was clear, and he was now certain that he wouldn't be able to take much more of Hamburg. 'I started to prepare myself for Paris. I went to French lessons for three hours, five times a week. Not many school kids do that.'[183] He dashed to these classes in the evenings for three years – 'to make sure my French was perfect,' he once said on a German talk show.[184] But Karl's longing for Paris didn't help matters at home. His father hated the fact that Karl wasn't living up to his expectations, says Thoma Schulenburg: 'They had lots of disagreements. It was essentially quite a cruel relationship.' The 'petulant child' couldn't quite put his finger on what it was that he wanted to do. And this only served to make his father even angrier.

Things weren't looking good for Karl at the start of the 1950s. He had disappointed his mother with his lack of artistic ambition, and nothing he did was enough to satisfy his father. Perhaps he was even disappointed in himself, not knowing how to turn his dreams into reality. He did have an inkling of what he wanted to do – after all, Dior had shown him what was possible – but nothing was straightforward. He had entered a strange incubation period in his formative years. An idea had taken hold, and now he just had to let it develop. There was only one thing for it: he had to depart for a different world to bring his ideas to life.

Karl Lagerfeld wasn't the only one who harboured these kinds of hopes around this time. Many other young Germans wanted to take their homeland's tarnished image and change it for the better.

Some were drawn to the world of fashion, like former anti-aircraft auxiliary F. C. Gundlach (b. 1926), who transported his compatriots into elegant visual worlds they had never even dreamed of, with his fashion photography. Wolfgang Joop (b. 1944), whose father came back late from the war and demanded discipline and obedience, broke away from this strict environment and sought solace in the fictional worlds of art and fashion. The photographer Peter Lindbergh, who was born in 1944 in Reichsgau Wartheland (German-occupied Poland) and grew up in Duisburg as the child of exiled parents, is credited with establishing the era of the supermodels. And Jil Sander, who was born in 1943 and survived the hardships of post-war life just 40 miles away from Bad Bramstedt, would come up with her pristine style in the decades that followed.

Fashion also brought the promise of a higher-order existence for the young Karl Lagerfeld. It offered a brighter, more beautiful reality away from the mundanity of everyday life – a freer, more open lifestyle than his father's closed worldview. And fashion did not dwell on the entanglements of German guilt; instead, with every new season, it looked to the future.

1952 to 1982

Paris

Next stop: Paris. Allegedly Karl Lagerfeld arrived into the Gare du Nord on a train from Hamburg on 28 August 1952. 'I came to attend secondary school here for two years. But my stay in Paris ended up being rather longer than that.'[1] In another version of the story, he travelled by plane and was welcomed at the airport by his father's business associates.[2] Whatever mode of transport he took, he was indeed looked after by the head of the French office of Carnation, one of his father's acquaintances from work.[3] The secretary of the evaporated milk company's office in Paris, 'a horrible woman with googly eyes', found lodgings for the young man at the Hôtel Gerson, which was located opposite the Sorbonne library at 14 Rue de la Sorbonne.[4] Lagerfeld later wrote that this was a residence 'for minors and students' to give the impression that he had moved to Paris at the age of fourteen, but on 10 September 1952 he would have already turned nineteen years old.[5]

By all accounts, he was neither nervous nor afraid in this unfamiliar city. He talked about this in an interview recorded towards the end of his life: 'People said to my mother, "You know, it's dangerous. He will be lost." But my mother said, "There are few people who get lost and few people who don't get lost. My son is from the part of the people who are not getting lost."' He continued, 'I mean, in those days you were scared of nothing because nothing was dangerous. It's not like today.'[6] Besides, he was up on the fifth floor in his two rooms with a balcony, hovering above it all – his life reminded him of the French film *Under the Paris Sky*. When he left his lodgings and ventured out onto the street below, he entered a lively student quarter full of shops and cafés.

Even as a young man, he changed addresses frequently. In 1955 he moved to 32 Rue de Varenne. Then in 1957, perhaps to escape the watchful eye of his landlady, he moved to 31 Rue de Tournon, where writer Katherine Mansfield once lived: 'Finally I had my own apartment in a building from the 18th century! No one was there to "keep an eye on me". I could finally do what I wanted!'[7] In 1958 and 1959 he lived in an apartment overlooking the courtyard at 19 Rue Jacob: 'The view of the gardens and Delacroix's studio was very poetic.' Then from 1959 to 1963 he resided on the ground floor at 7 Quai Voltaire, not far from the building where Voltaire had once lived: 'You could never open the windows in summer because there was so much noise from the traffic.'[8]

Voltaire, Eugène Delacroix and Katherine Mansfield – even in his first ten years in Paris, the young Karl was immersed in a world of philosophy, art and literature. All the apartments were located within a 1,500-foot radius of the Café de Flore, one of his favourite haunts. He was so fond of the Left Bank that he remained forever faithful to the quarter. So faithful, in fact, that he never slept on the other side of the Seine, in the eighth arrondissement.[9]

Lagerfeld perfected his language skills at the Alliance Française, a cultural institute offering French courses for foreigners. It seems he caught the teacher's attention: 'The good woman suggested that I help her with the courses for German pupils, but I told her that wasn't why I had come to Paris.'[10] He preferred to be out and about in the city: 'I spent all my time walking around. I could be a Paris tour guide! I also went to the cinema, from the first showing to the last, to work on my French accent.'[11] He claimed he saw *Les Enfants Terribles* – the 1950 film named after Jean Cocteau's tragic book about an incestuous brother and sister – five times in a single day.[12]

'Le Champo', on the corner of Rue des Écoles, was less than 300 feet from his first apartment. The arthouse cinema, which added a second screening hall in the basement in 1956, was a school in the art of seeing. This little cinema, with its impressive Art Nouveau façade, was frequented by some of the future stars of French cinema, including

Claude Chabrol and François Truffaut, both of whom were slightly older than Lagerfeld. The young man also visited the 'Cinémathèque française' and the cinemas on the Champs-Élysées. The films he loved the most were the old ones that took him back to the 1930s.[13] 'I went [to the cinema] whenever I could. I saw all the Gloria Swanson films, including *The Cabinet of Dr Caligari*. I couldn't sleep for three nights afterwards because I thought that the puppet was going to come into my room from the balcony and kill me.'[14]

It seems that the young Karl got to know the city by wandering aimlessly through its streets and arcades. Walter Benjamin's description of the *flâneur* in his *Passagen-Werk* (The Arcades Project) also applied to the young German in Paris: 'Dialectic of flânerie: on one side, the man who feels himself viewed by all and sundry as a true suspect and, on the other side, the man who is utterly undiscoverable, the hidden man.'[15] As someone who was easily stimulated visually and even referred to himself as a 'voyeur',[16] Lagerfeld was free to give in to his urge to people-watch anonymously – though he, too, was secretly being observed by others. The city seemed to him like something from a pre-war-era film, such as *Under the Roofs of Paris* (1930). 'At that time Paris was a gloomy, almost sinister city because of all the coal heating. On the walk from the train station to the city centre, the most beautiful city in the world didn't seem particularly clean.' The colours and smells were what had changed the most since then, he said.[17]

These early years in Paris were a period of apprenticeship and travel, in a city where private life happens on the streets. 'Parisians make the street an interior,' wrote Walter Benjamin.[18] With no school to go to and no job to speak of, the young Karl could often be found strolling casually around the city, not like a worker dashing for the metro or a tourist trying to find the right street. He later spoke of how all sorts of social classes would mix within a neighbourhood, or even an apartment block, which made life all the more exciting. He found his way around this public space by wandering from street to street. He would linger by the windows of the bookstores and antique shops of Saint-Germain-des-Prés, then cross the bridges over the Seine to the Right Bank and amble past the Louvre, through the Tuileries Garden and the arcades of Rue de Rivoli. He time-travelled through entire centuries on his walks, following in the footsteps of the existentialists who used to meet at the Café de Flore and marvelling at the grandeur of the Louvre, which had served as the royal palace until 1682, when Louis XIV moved his court to Versailles.

All these sights and experiences would have a defining impact on the young Karl. The world he was discovering became an integral part of who he was, and from this point forward he was never away from Paris for more than a few weeks at a time. As he glanced out of the window in his apartment on the Quai Voltaire during the final decade of his life, he could see the Seine and the other side of the river in the distance, and trace the routes of the walks he used to go on in his younger days. To his left he looked onto the Tuileries, and to his right he could see all the way up to the immense courtyard of the Louvre, almost right up to the museum's landmark – the iconic glass pyramid designed by architect Ieoh Ming Pei in 1989.

These extended walks also helped to shape the young man's later career. 'The flâneur is the observer of the marketplace,' Walter Benjamin wrote just fifteen years earlier in his philosophical fragments. 'His knowledge is akin to the occult science of industrial fluctuations. He is a spy for the capitalists, on assignment in the realm of consumers.'[19] And indeed, this people-watcher would repeatedly consult his memory in his career as a designer, searching for ways to exploit the zeitgeist for material gain. As he wandered around the avenues of his mind, revisiting the sights he had seen, inspiration emerged completely transformed.

Slowly but surely, he found his bearings in Paris. Among the acquaintances he made along the way was German student Peter Bermbach, who had regularly visited the city since the mid-1950s and decided to move there in 1960. The pair hit it off immediately. 'He hadn't done his Abitur [high-school graduation certification], perhaps because he was so sure of himself, but he was very erudite,'

Bermbach noted. 'He read a lot and liked listening to music.' Karl tested his newfound friend's knowledge: 'Have you heard of Elisabeth Charlotte, Princess Palatine?' he asked. Yes, Bermbach had read the risqué letters from the princess who had married the homosexual brother of Louis XIV. 'From that day on we were friends.'[20]

The two young men were also connected by certain things that went unsaid. Peter Bermbach had been held in prison in Munich for a week, allegedly for 'attempted seduction' under paragraph 175a of the German Criminal Code. The young republic of West Germany interpreted the 'gay paragraph' strictly, banning all homosexual acts between men. Then with the 1969 reform, the definition of a punishable offence changed to intercourse with a man under the age of twenty-one. It wasn't until relatively recently, in 1994, that the paragraph was completely abolished. Across the border in comparatively liberal France, however, life was already better for gay men: the age of consent had been twenty-one since 6 August 1942. 'We never talked about homosexuality,' says Bermbach. The constant legal threat was cause enough for him to head for the land of freedom, equality and fraternity: 'Homosexuality was more tolerated here.'

Karl Lagerfeld must have had a similar experience when he embarked on this new stage in his life. He was entering a period when, according to sociologist Didier Eribon, all the wounds inflicted during childhood 'nourish the energies through which gay people create or recreate personalities for themselves'.[21] Lagerfeld had finally landed in a society where it was acceptable to be gay. 'The advantages of the fashion world', he said in 1996, 'are the absence of racism and homophobia.'[22]

But despite living in this relatively laissez-faire environment, the two men didn't have it easy in Paris. When they first arrived in the city, they belonged to another minority: they were German. 'There was a strong anti-German sentiment at that time, even among the younger generation,' says Bermbach. 'The war had only been over for a decade or so,' he explains. In 1940, the Wehrmacht had marched into Paris and swiftly seized the whole country. Many residents were forced to flee the capital, some 92,000 French soldiers were killed in the struggle against the invaders, and 10,000 Jews were deported to concentration camps in the East, where they were killed. Many French workers were pressed into service and forced to work in Germany; some were even sent to the Glücksklee factory in Neustadt and the Lagerfelds' farm in Bad Bramstedt.

France had suffered the imperious presence of the occupying forces and endured humiliating treatment at the hands of the Germans. The stronger France's opposition to the occupiers, the worse Germany's reign of terror became. More than 20,000 members of the resistance movement were killed in the liberation struggles before the Allied Forces and the resistance fighters finally freed France from the Germans' clutches. In September 1944, the period referred to by President Charles de Gaulle as the 'Thirty Years War' – from the start of World War I in 1914 to the 'Libération' in 1944 – finally came to an end.[23] Peter Bermbach often sensed a degree of reservation from the French. 'We two Germans were both outcasts, so to speak, so we got along easily.'

The two friends spent a lot of time together in Karl's apartment at 7 Quai Voltaire. 'He lived in a furnished ground-floor flat with high ceilings,' Bermbach recalls. A small staircase without a banister led to the bedroom, which was just 5 feet in height. 'The room was lined with black-and-white material. We would lie there on the bed together like two school friends, listening to music. There were stacks of 33-rpm records lying around the place.' They nicknamed this part of the flat 'the Oblomov room', inspired by Ivan Goncharov's nineteenth-century novel about a daydreamer who was as well-bred as he was passive.

Karl was always working on his musical education. 'Once when I was in Madrid I bought a record called *Concertos for Two Organs* by the baroque musician Antonio Soler, also known as Padre Soler,' Bermbach recalls. 'Karl had never heard of it before, and he was desperate to have it. We didn't have the equipment to make a copy, and the record wasn't available to buy in Paris. So he suggested we do a swap: he'd give me his new album of Lotte Lenya chansons, and I'd give him my Padre Soler. I still have the Lenya [record] today.'[24]

Although the two young men got along well, Bermbach's companion still kept himself to himself: 'He didn't talk about his personal life much.' He also had a habit that Bermbach didn't like at all: 'Whenever I rang the doorbell he would leave me standing there waiting... It always annoyed me, but I didn't want to sound petty so I never said anything.' Perhaps his rather private friend needed his peace and wanted a few more minutes to himself. But then again, perhaps this was his aristocratic side showing through: maybe this son of a Grand Burgher was trying to keep up appearances, like a nobleman trying to show that his house was rather large and the maid should have answered the door by now. 'He was very good at selling himself,' says Bermbach. He was in his mid-twenties, he looked good, his manners were impeccable, and he was very well groomed. 'The first time I saw a cotton bud was in his bathroom,' Bermbach recalls. Karl was surprised when he asked him what it was for: 'What, you've never seen one before?' He also made sure things smelled right. The housekeeper had the habit of pouring rather pungent Eau de Javel into the laundry as a bleaching agent. 'I always have to keep an eye on her and make sure she doesn't do it,' Karl said. 'I don't want to end up smelling like poor people.'

The young Peter Bermbach was disposed to the fine arts, but he had never come across an illusionist like Karl before. This much is clear from an episode in one of Karl's Paris apartments, where a signed picture of one of Paul Klee's angels adorned the wall. Karl claimed it was an original, but the art historian instantly saw through the masquerade. 'It was a reproduction, of course.' Clearly his imaginative friend didn't always have a strict relationship with the truth.

Beginnings

Karl Lagerfeld even made his first step into the world of major fashion seem effortless. Lovers and students of fashion in Paris all knew about the International Wool Secretariat (IWS), the international extension of a marketing organization primarily representing Australian sheep farmers. The IWS was promoting virgin wool at a time when synthetic fibres were on the rise, and it organized a competition for young designers as part of its work in Paris. Budding couturiers were invited to submit their sketches in the hope of securing a job as a designer's assistant. In 1954 the 'Concours du Dessin de Mode' was writ large on huge placards featuring a fashion illustration by René Gruau.[25]

Apparently luck was kinder to Karl than to the other applicants. The designer would later claim that he did no preparation whatsoever for the competition. 'By the time I received a telegram six months later telling me I had won a prize, I had completely forgotten that I had submitted a design for a coat. I hate coats.'[26] He said that he gave away many of the coats from his own wardrobe, even though they were tailored. One time when his father was in Paris and Karl went to meet him at the fittingly upmarket Hotel George V, where he was staying, Otto Lagerfeld insisted on buying his son a coat because of the cold weather. Evidently Karl didn't hesitate to state his demands. He pointed out a navy blue cashmere coat in the shop opposite and insisted it had to be that one or nothing at all. Of course he got what he wanted. 'My father indulged my every wish.'[27]

The deadline for the award later known as the Woolmark Prize was 31 October, and so prospective designers eagerly submitted their fashion illustrations in the hope of winning. The best designs from three categories were then produced in the ateliers of three fashion designers: the coat was made by Pierre Balmain, the suit by Jacques Fath, and the gown by Hubert de Givenchy.[28] The evening of 11 December 1954 would be a memorable event – not just because the young man who so hated coats was crowned the winner of the coats category.

The three winners stood on the stage at the cocktail reception. A twenty-one-year-old Karl presented his canary-yellow coat, complete with three-quarter-length sleeves, deep V-shaped neckline at the back and quirky belt-buckle collar, paired with a grey felt hat and grey gloves. 'Very ladylike,' he later sneered. 'It looked new at the time.'[29] Up there

Bashful winners: Karl Lagerfeld, Yves Saint Laurent and Colette Bracchi showcase their designs for the 'Concours du Dessin de Mode' fashion competition in 1954.

on the stage with him was another newcomer: the eighteen-year-old Yves Saint Laurent had made it to third place the year before and was now being awarded the prize for best dress. As Lagerfeld and Saint Laurent stood there in the company of Colette Bracchi – winner in the suits category – and the three models, they looked like two schoolboys in suits: slim, well-behaved, and serious. Karl the Great still looked like Little Karl. He almost could have passed for sixteen, the age he later claimed to be when he won the prize. But already he was sporting his grown-up signature look: white handkerchief in his breast pocket and a signet ring on his right ring finger.

Thelma Sweetinburgh, who was in charge of the IWS Paris office at the time, presented the prize. 'She was very stylish,' Lagerfeld said after she passed away in 2007. Even half a century later, he could still draw Sweetinburgh in the Jacques Fath suit she was wearing that day. 'She was the first person I met from the world of fashion,' he said. He later went to the florist Lachaume, whose most loyal customer he would become, and bought her a bouquet to show his appreciation.[30]

The winter ceremony marked the beginning of a long friendship that would ultimately turn into an even longer-lasting feud. Fashion history was written when these two men graced the stage: Yves Saint Laurent and Karl Lagerfeld were set to become the two most important designers of the next half century. The members of the jury – designers Balmain, Fath and Givenchy, illustrator René Gruau, and journalists including Simone Baron, editor-in-chief of French *Elle* – were impressed by the designers' talents. As well as receiving job offers, the aspiring couturiers each won 300,000 francs: 'Quite a lot of money for such a silly schoolboy,' Lagerfeld later said.[31] The prize fund was actually the equivalent of less than US$1,000, but it was a lot of money all the same.

Yves Saint Laurent had a stroke of luck: Christian Dior, whom both designers idolized, ultimately hired him as his assistant on the recommendation of Michel de Brunhoff. The then editor-in-chief of *Vogue* was also on the jury, and had already been taken by the young designer's sketches when he received letters from Saint Laurent's father.

Pierre Balmain offered Karl a job as his assistant when he visited the Balmain studio where the coat was being made for the prize-giving ceremony. Later on, Lagerfeld revealed that he had also received an offer from Cristóbal Balenciaga (1895–1972),[32] but he didn't want to start his career there – possibly because he was put off by the designer's strict forms, his relentless elegance and his monastic, secretive ways. Instead, Karl decided to go with the younger designer,

Balmain (1914–1982), who rose to international acclaim in 1954 after designing the dress Audrey Hepburn wore to marry Mel Ferrer: a striking gown with a flared skirt and a wasp waist.

Until the young Karl got his first job working for Balmain, he had been drifting somewhat aimlessly through life. Now the time had come to be more focused. He was still wet behind the ears and hadn't formally studied fashion, so he was in for a surprise: 'I had my own idea about it all, but it was completely removed from reality,' he later said.[33] The young designer learned the basics at Balmain, studying 'techniques from the 1920s and 1930s that no longer exist, for fifteen to twenty hours a day'. During his time at the fashion house, he learned to produce the kinds of sketches that contain all the information required in order to produce the garment. 'I can draw every last detail so that no one needs to ask about the measurements, the spacing, what kind of buttons to use or where to insert the sleeves. Everything is right there in the sketch; it's all correct.'[34]

By all accounts, he wasn't overly fond of this strict period of intensive apprenticeship. 'For me, the worst thing at Balmain was having to stand behind the stage during the fashion galas,' he said. In those days, fashion shows were much more drawn-out than they are today, and Lagerfeld found that he hated the environment there.[35] But he figured out how to work things to his advantage. 'I remember one time, my little sister Ria was desperate to get her hands on a fur coat,' Peter Bermbach recalls. 'Karl suggested dark brown beaver fur, an affordable and – in his opinion – flattering fur for a young woman in her early twenties. He sketched a design for her, with a scarf instead of a collar and just three large buttons at the top. The Balmain furrier accepted the design and Ria became the proud owner of a very valuable and unique Lagerfeld–Balmain coat. With a label, of course.'[36]

Friends

Even though Karl Lagerfeld worked long days in Paris, he still found time to make new friends. He was on duty in the Balmain atelier when he made the acquaintance of Bronwen Pugh, who was one of his boss's muses. Pierre Balmain thought she was one of the most beautiful women in the world, putting her in the same league as Greta Garbo, Vivien Leigh and Marlene Dietrich. Born in London in 1930, Pugh joined a wave of British models that had arrived on the scene, among them Barbara Goalen and Fiona Campbell-Walter. These new models heralded the dawn of the British era in the fashion world, when models like Jean Shrimpton and Twiggy represented the quintessential modern woman, and designers like Mary Quant and Ossie Clark captured the spirit of the times. Even Parisian fashionistas could be found scouring Carnaby Street and later King's Road for the latest trends.

Bronwen Pugh got along well with Balmain's young assistant, Karl Lagerfeld, who was a foreigner like her. She lived with the English model Christine Tidmarsh and the Russian/English model Svetlana Lloyd, both of whom worked at Dior as in-house mannequins and were fond of his assistant Yves. In 1956, the three young women invited both budding designers to join them for dinner in their tiny apartment with a view of the Eiffel Tower. 'They thought they were coming to a proper sit-down dinner,' Pugh later said, remembering the designers appearing at the flat-share on Avenue de la Bourdonnais. 'But (a) we had no money, and (b) we only had this small flat without any chairs. So we put a couple of cushions on the floor instead. They were polite but taken aback when they arrived. The French love a proper evening meal.'[37]

These were frugal times for the models, who were only paid poorly, if at all. Karl hadn't hit the big time yet: his contributions to the Balmain collections were based more on vague ideas than actual designs. But he had lofty aspirations. Pugh remembers the day he piped up and announced he was going to be rich and famous. 'We just laughed at him,' she said. This quirky twenty-two-year-old was an endless source of amusement for the girls. 'Karl had this unusual way of dancing,' Pugh reminisces, referring to the times she and her flatmates ventured out to the clubs on the Left Bank, accompanied by their two couturier friends. 'We had never seen anything like

For a friend: Karl Lagerfeld gave
this drawing to Victoire Doutreleau
in 1961. Perhaps the young boy
in the picture is him. Today, the
former model sees the sketch as
an expression of Lagerfeld's
secret wish to have a child.

it before.' They asked: 'What kind of dance is that?' His response:
'It's modern dance, see!'[38]

Karl also met Victoire Doutreleau, one of Christian Dior's favourite mannequins, through Bronwen Pugh. 'She introduced us at the
Bar des Théâtres on Avenue Montaigne,' Doutreleau recalls.[39] Karl
instantly liked her, and she knew she liked him: 'We were both still
kids, you know. He had this romantic side, but even then he had a
strong personality.' His French accent tickled her, and it never ceased

to amaze her how quickly he skipped from one subject to the next. Before long he gave her the pet name 'Vichnou'. Lagerfeld's sketch from 1956, which he called 'Victoire à toutes ses époques', shows her modelling dresses from all different eras, as if she had travelled through time from the 'Lady of the Camellias' to Coco Chanel, from the Belle Époque to the present day. The large drawing still takes pride of place on the wall of her apartment in Paris.

So Dior was the common denominator. It was Dior who connected his assistant Yves Saint Laurent with the model Victoire Doutreleau and with Anne-Marie Poupard (later Muñoz), his colleague at the atelier, whose uncle – composer Henri Sauguet – was friends with Christian Dior. 'When Yves came to Dior in 1955, I was already one of the star mannequins,' says Doutreleau, who was possessed of a powerful sensual allure. They were a tight-knit group: Yves remained close to Victoire for years and Anne-Marie for decades. Anne-Marie followed him when he opened his own fashion house on Rue Spontini, and she remained his most important employee until he retired from fashion in 2002. 'It was a wonderful time,' says Doutreleau. 'There was no grudge between Karl and Yves in those days.' But in the long run, a design god like Yves Saint Laurent would refuse to tolerate another god by his side. And it went both ways.

'For years we all went out as a group,' Doutreleau notes. Sometimes they would set off in Karl's VW Beetle Cabriolet and take it for an extra spin around the Arc de Triomphe. 'Yves and Karl lived their present in the past,' she writes in her memoirs, her tone both poetic and ironic.[40] While Doutreleau loved the 'triangle' of Brasserie Lipp, the Café Deux Magots and the Café de Flore on Boulevard Saint-Germain, her two designer friends had slightly more refined tastes and preferred the 'Old Trinity' of the Café de la Rotonde, the Café du Dôme and the restaurant La Coupole on Boulevard du Montparnasse. But they also liked to frequent the Macumba or the Éléphant Blanc together for dancing.

Nightlife didn't exactly do it for Karl: he only ever drank Coca-Cola, he didn't smoke or take drugs – not even when they were all the rage – and in fact he rarely danced. He was definitely more of a people-watcher. When Victoire told her friend Yves that he had drunk too much yet again, Karl had an interesting solution. 'My children, you should do the same as me and drink Coca-Cola instead,' he proposed. 'Then you wouldn't be under the impression that you're enjoying yourselves.'[41]

He liked his new friends. They were young, beautiful and success-ful, like him. Finally he was moving in important circles, socializing with sophisticates and models who had worked for Dior, the kind of women who held their cigarette at a right angle between their dainty fingers. It was a wonderful time. These bright young things were in demand and the fashion scene was booming. The whole world was mad about Dior, and some people were crazy for Balmain. Karl was happy and proud that he had come so far from north German lowlands in just a few years.

'I love to have breakfast at the Ritz, don't you?' he said to Doutreleau one morning when the two of them were sitting together in the hotel on Place Vendôme.[42] She remembers it well: 'Karl ordered a tea and a Coca-Cola,' she says. He then proceeded, quite unashamedly, to spread butter onto his croissant: how very un-French of him! She giggled and pointed out that some people might think it was a bit snobby to eat breakfast at the Ritz. Didn't he agree? 'I don't think it's snobby,' he snapped. 'That's a stupid thing to say about something you like doing.' He almost lost his cool. 'His German accent suddenly became more pronounced,' Doutreleau reports. But she knew that it wasn't some misplaced 'bourgeois French snobbery' that made him do the things he did. She decided to distract him by asking whether it was true that Coco Chanel lived at the Ritz. 'Yes,' he replied. 'I don't know her personally, but at Pierre Balmain rumour has it that she always had a terrible nature.' And he joked: 'I know another woman who isn't easy work either. But, apart from that, you're nothing like her.'[43]

Karl had also met a kindred spirit in the form of fellow designer Yves Saint Laurent. He, too, came from a completely different world. He was born on 1 August 1936 in the Algerian coastal town of Oran,

where his father Charles Saint Laurent owned an insurance company
and a chain of cinemas.[44] The grandparents of both Charles and his
wife Lucienne Andrée had left the Alsace for North Africa during the
Franco-German War of 1870–71, and now the family was comfortably
off. His mother read French fashion magazines and wore tailored clothing. Yves kept himself to himself and drew, he was teased at school,
and he dreamed of a life in Paris – just like Karl in his younger years.
Although he was French, Yves was an outsider in Paris: the French
Algerians, known as *colons* (settlers), were often derogatively referred
to from the 1950s onwards as *pieds noirs* (black feet).

These two outsiders became insiders – through the career that
brought them together. In search of lost time, Yves came up with the
idea of driving out to Deauville on the Normandy coast, just 6 miles
away from Cabourg, where Marcel Proust wrote his six-volume mas-
terpiece *À la recherche du temps perdu*. That summer, in 1957, they set
off in Karl's car with Victoire and kept driving until they reached the
old Hôtel des Roches Noires in Trouville, where Proust had holidayed
with his mother. They spoke at length about the author. Yves was
inspired by his tortured soul and Karl by his linguistic sophistication; Victoire just went along for the ride. The three of them shared
a room and slept soundly together in one bed, much like they did
in Karl's apartment after a long night in the city because Yves was
afraid to be alone at night.[45]

Victoire let the wind blow through her hair every day while they
were away. She had grown to hate the old pinned-back look and was
glad to finally let her hair down. That summer, the tight knots of life
in the 1950s were beginning to come undone. But in July 1957, there
was tension in the air at the seaside resort: a photograph taken on
the wooden decking at a café shows Yves and Victoire deliberately
avoiding eye contact. 'Yves and I had been arguing.' Perhaps it was
because Yves was envious of Karl? Victoire cared about both of
them, after all. 'Yves was like a cicada, all fine-limbed and delicate,'
she said. It was clear that he only had eyes for men, she says. 'But
with Karl, I wasn't exactly sure. I never really understood. He didn't

have a boyfriend. He wasn't just homosexual. Anyway, I had my own thing going on... I loved the two of them as friends.' When they went out together, Karl never pushed himself onto anyone. Unlike Yves, who made it clear that he wanted something from men, Karl didn't seem interested at all. Victoire formed a special relationship with Karl. 'I didn't necessarily tell Anne-Marie every time I went to see him. I loved his German wit, which French people still don't understand to this day.'

Anne-Marie also had a special place in Karl's affections. Her serious expression reminded him of something out of an El Greco painting. When she married José Muñoz, who had fled Spain to escape Franco's regime, Karl remained a close friend and became godfather to their first son, Carlos. The young family often went to see Karl on Sundays. Sometimes the designer would look after the boy and tell him about the world from books about Japanese woodcuts. The group of friends, including designer and artist François-Xavier Lalanne (1927–2008) and his wife Claude (1924–2019), also went on holiday to Saint-Tropez together.[46]

But what did fate have in store for Yves and Karl, who felt that they were destined for better things? They wanted to find out where they were headed, so they went to see a clairvoyant together on a mezzanine at the Rue de Maubeuge. 'She was a fat Turkish woman with the most beautiful turquoise eyes,' Lagerfeld recalled.[47] She predicted great success for Yves but added that it would 'end quite quickly', whereas for Karl things would only really begin when it was all over for the others.[48]

Karl took prophecies like these as gospel. His mother and aunt had been to see the fortune-tellers at the 'Send', a funfair that visits Münster three times a year, and as far as they were concerned, clairvoyance was a serious business. The practice of fortune-telling was commonplace in the state of Münster and even made it into literature in the form of a poem by nineteenth-century German poet, novelist and composer Annette Droste-Hülshoff. Karl often went to visit his aunt Felicitas and his cousin Tita in Münster with his mother. They believed in the gift of second sight, and so would he. When he heard what the fortune-teller told him in Paris, he took her seriously. 'The things she predicted happened,' he said. 'I went to see her every two years after that, and I never made an important decision without her. One day in 1987, the phone rang in my car. Madame said: "I see that you're on your way to sign a contract. A mistake that's going to work against you has crept onto page 7." She was right. A secretary had made a mistake.'[49]

What about the clairvoyant's prediction for the future of these two young designers? Yves was already successful, so why shouldn't the second part of her prophecy come true eventually?

Everything changed in the blink of an eye on 24 October 1957 when Christian Dior died of a heart attack in Montecatini, Italy. He was only fifty-two, and no one saw it coming. But business had to go on, so without further ado the designer's young assistant Yves Saint Laurent was appointed as his successor. Yves and Karl realized the significance of this appointment at the late designer's funeral in Paris: it was practically a national event, with thousands of guests in mourning. Yves had a grave expression on his face at the burial in Callian in the South of France. Then, without further ado, on 30 January 1958, the young couturier made his debut for France's most important fashion house at the tender age of twenty-one. The shy young man was celebrated for his bold 'trapeze line', a more fluid silhouette with narrow shoulders and a wide hem that signalled a move away from his predecessor's signature cinched waist.

This early success led to other changes in Yves Saint Laurent's life. Parisian society paid court to the *petit prince de la mode* who had taken the city by storm. Marie-Louise Bousquet (1885–1975), the Paris editor of *Harper's Bazaar* and an important customer of the Dior fashion house, invited everyone's favourite new designer to her weekly open house on 3 February 1958. She also extended the invitation to the painter Bernard Buffet, whom Yves held in high esteem, and his manager and partner Pierre Bergé, who had also seen Yves's debut show four days earlier. It was a *coup de foudre*: Yves and

Pierre fell in love at first sight.[50] Opposites clearly attract: Yves was a sensitive, self-doubting, vulnerable artist, whereas Pierre was an energetic, strategic, smart businessman. The two men felt an incredibly intense connection, and in time their relationship would set an example for the rest of the world. They showed how to work together successfully as a couple to build a fashion label – with artistic flair and a knack for business.

Yves entered a world of new connections when he embarked on his relationship with this art enthusiast and socialite. They went to the opera to hear Maria Callas sing and were invited to the soirées held by Marie-Laure de Noailles, whose grandmother provided the inspiration for one of Marcel Proust's characters, the Duchess of Guermantes. The two men became friends with the author Françoise Sagan, who was roughly the same age as Yves and had published the international sensation *Bonjour Tristesse* in 1954. They also met director Jean Cocteau, ballet dancer Zizi Jeanmaire, and choreographer Roland Petit, for whom Yves designed costumes later in his career.[51]

None of these people suspected that Yves Saint Laurent would be called to serve in the military on 1 September 1960, or that before long he would be sent to the military hospital because he was suffering from 'nervous depression'. They had no idea that the treatment he would receive on the psychiatric ward would turn him into a nervous wreck – and that he would suddenly lose his job at Dior and be succeeded by Marc Bohan. 'It was so terrible,' Victoire Doutreleau recalls. 'Yves in the military – it's like putting a swan in a cage with shrieking cats.'

But that was all in the future. Right now it was 1958, and things were looking great for Yves. In just one year, he had graduated from assistant to creative director, from loner to lover, from relative unknown to the shining light of Parisian society. Karl lagged behind. He was still a mere assistant, an unknown and a loner – but, as his fortune-teller had told him, time was on his side.

On the Rise

Bored of the work at Pierre Balmain, Karl Lagerfeld made the move to Jean Patou on Rue Saint-Florentin in 1958. Everyone advised him against it, he said, but he was more interested in being in charge there than staying on as an assistant at Balmain.[52] The most important thing was that he would now be the artistic director of a fashion house, like Yves at Dior. But the label created by Jean Patou, who had died in 1936 and was best known for introducing sportswear into haute couture and for perfumes like Amour Amour (1925) and Joy (1930), was not as high-profile or as big as Dior. If anything, it was a little sedate. The brand was directed by Patou's brother-in-law Raymond Barbas, who liked the young man they called 'Monsieur Charles' in the studio. The designer himself initially chose to produce his haute couture collections under the more international-sounding name 'Roland Karl'.[53]

'It was a sensation that such a young designer – and a German one at that – had been given the responsibility of creating the collection there,' says Peter Bermbach, who wrote for lifestyle magazines such as *Schöner Wohnen* and *House and Garden*. Bermbach was planning to do a story on his friend Karl with the photographer Willy Maywald. 'Karl readily agreed to be photographed at work in the studio. He had a very good nose for publicity.'[54] The young fashion designer started purposefully plotting out his career. Even in those days, he was better than everyone else when it came to working the media to his advantage. Karl leaned over the model and draped the heavy taffeta, then paused when Maywald said 'Stop!' and pressed the shutter release. Scenes like this were rare, as Lagerfeld wasn't in the habit of kneeling in front of his models as a fashion designer. He usually left that job to the seamstress, who dealt with the tedious business of draping and adjusting the material while he busied himself with the sketching. Karl would rarely be pictured with the models at fittings for Chloé, Fendi or Chanel. Most of the time, he would sit at the table and ask the assistants and seamstresses to pin something here or apply something there.

Perhaps his first cover: the new guy at Jean Patou
unveils his designs in 1960.

An even more chivalrous-looking Karl adorned the cover of German
weekly magazine *Münchner Illustrierte*. The picture shows the 'new
man at Jean Patou' gesturing as he stands next to the model Kara.
He has a pincushion on his left wrist as a sign of his profession.[55] As
upbeat as he may have seemed in the photograph, the designer soon
realized that he hadn't found happiness at Patou. 'But I told myself,
you're not here as an art critic, you're here to learn something. Zip
it and get on with it. My strategy was simply to work more than the
others and make them surplus to requirements. And it worked.'[56]
But his patience was wearing thin. 'I felt like I was in an old people's
home,' he said later in his career.[57] He only had to design two couture

collections a year, each of which consisted of sixty or seventy outfits. This just wasn't enough for this ambitious young couturier. He was becoming increasingly interested in ready-to-wear clothing, and he wanted to spread his wings. 'Ultimately that's why I became a free-lance designer, which was unusual in the early 1960s,' he said. After his stint at Patou, he was proud to say that he was 'never employed again – by anyone!'[58]

Going freelance also allowed him to keep reinventing himself pro-fessionally. 'I love change,' he said in one of his final interviews. 'Yes, I like change… Tradition may be okay, but you have to be careful not to become a bore… And when designers start to do retrospective[s] and talk about their past and look at their old dresses, it's very danger-ous. It's the beginning of the end.'[59] Of course, he was taking another swipe at Yves Saint Laurent here.

There was a convenient flip-side to the quiet life at Patou: this young designer had a lot of free time on his hands. Unlike the second half of his life, when he worked tirelessly, he found himself living the life of *la jeunesse dorée*. He hadn't yet turned thirty: 'I was very, very, very young. I was lazy, had no taste yet, loved convertibles, the beach, sunbathing, bodybuilding and nightclubs.'[60] There was a fitness club he would go to at least four times a week, for three hours at a time. 'All the elegant gigolos of the time used to meet there in the afternoons. They had to watch their figure in order to please their clients.'[61] One of his assistants at Patou was convinced that Karl must be a gigolo, too, a man whose job it was to please women – or men – profession-ally. After all, he drove such beautiful cars and wore such beautiful clothes, it made perfect sense.[62]

His first car was a fairly modest Volkswagen convertible his father gave him one Christmas. It was green, but he had it sprayed dark blue – because he didn't like the thought of driving around Paris in a green car with a German numberplate.[63] His parents then gave him a Mercedes 190 SL convertible. 'It was the only one of its kind in all of Paris, and I was the one driving it. The convertible made me famous all over town; everyone knew who was coming. That kind of thing would really embarrass me today.'[64] It was a cream-coloured car with red leather seats. In Germany the model was known as the 'Nitribitt Mercedes' because Rosemarie Nitribitt, a high-end escort who was violently murdered in Frankfurt in 1957, had also driven one. The frequent mentions of this name fuelled the rumour in Germany that Lagerfeld drove the very same car, when in fact it was just the same model. What happened to the 'Nitribitt Mercedes' itself is a different story.

Peter Bermbach recalls how Karl often left his 190 SL sitting outside the Deux Magots for hours on end when he went out with the top down. And if it wasn't there, he would be circling the district, taking in Boulevard Saint-Germain, Rue Saint-Benoît and Rue de l'Abbaye before heading back to the Boulevard, the Café de Flore or the Deux Magots. 'One-way streets were rare in those days, and there was no separate lane for buses and taxis yet,' Bermbach says. 'It was still a pleasure to drive around Paris.' Karl was easy-going, cheerful and helpful. Bermbach remembers the time he hired a car and drove out to the countryside with a couple of friends: Charles Simoni, who worked at the Lanvin fashion house and also knew Karl, and another acquaintance from the fashion scene. That Sunday in the early 1960s, their car broke down around 20 miles southwest of Paris, not far from Trappes. With no garage in sight, Bermbach phoned Karl from a bar: 'Could you pick us up, please?' An hour later he was there in the heavyweight Bentley he used to drive around at that time.[65]

When the weather was good, the two friends would often go to the Piscine Deligny, a floating open-air swimming pool moored on the Quai Anatole-France opposite the Place de la Concorde. 'We had membership and would lie there in the sun for hours,' Bermbach recalls. 'Even then, Karl was vain and proud of his well-toned body.' One time at the pool, a rather buff-looking Karl wore an 'all-in-one knit swimsuit that accentuated and enhanced his nether regions', Bermbach says. He remembers feeling embarrassed at the sight of his friend shamelessly strutting around the place in the swimsuit.[66] Karl was simply comfortable in his own body. He was in good shape, his skin was tanned, and his carefully groomed head of hair gleamed in the sun. All the bodybuilding and sunbathing had paid off. People whispered to each other when he strutted past – some smiled indulgently, while others glanced over covetously. Affected though this young man's mannerisms and poses could be, he certainly pulled it off.

More and more people started recognizing Lagerfeld in the neighbourhood. He was often spotted picking up his stack of international newspapers and magazines from the kiosk on the corner of Rue Saint-Benoît, then heading to the Café de Flore to systematically leaf through the pages before getting back into his car to go for a spin. He liked to dine with friends at the Brasserie Lipp across the road. Soon they no longer had to sit with the tourists on the first floor. Miraculously, they always had a table downstairs – like French president François Mitterrand, who later became a regular at the establishment. Karl and his friends would occasionally head to the Montana Bar next to Flore with Françoise Dorléac, the older sister of Catherine Deneuve. 'Karl loved her because she was loud and cheerful,' Bermbach recalls. The actress, who made many films during her short career and worked with François Truffaut, Jean-Paul Belmondo and Roman Polanski, died in a car accident on her way to the airport in Nice in 1967 at the age of twenty-five.

But everything was in upward motion in the 1950s and the 1960s, when political, economic and social developments played right into the hands of fashion designers. The Fourth Republic, and then the Fifth Republic in 1958, laid the groundwork for large-scale modernization in France, establishing fundamental social rights and the modern welfare state.[67] Security and freedom were assured when the country officially joined NATO's western alliance and made peace with its out-of-favour neighbour. A series of social indicators pointed to prosperous development in France. The birth rate had increased steadily since 1942 and was up to almost three children per woman in the 1950s, so the population grew exponentially – from 39.6 million in 1945 to 48.7 million in 1965. As the median age decreased in the *trentes glorieuses* – literally the 'glorious thirty years' between 1945 and 1975

– France benefitted from a younger, more rebellious consumer base with cash to spend. A rapid process of urbanization was underway, the metropolitan area of Paris was growing, and companies in the service sector became the biggest employers in the 1960s. With new motorways, rail routes, seaports and airports, France gained access to global markets and succeeded in doubling its purchasing power from 1949 to 1965. People were more than happy to pay the price for luxury products in this thriving economy.

Karl and his friends reaped the rewards of this new social dynamic. They found themselves right at the heart of the action. 'The Saint-Germain-des-Prés district in Paris served as one of the world's major intellectual hubs from 1945 and was under the undisputed hegemony of Jean-Paul Sartre and Simone de Beauvoir, who epitomized the ideal of the modern intellectual,' writes historian Matthias Waechter.[68] It was a rather happy coincidence that Yves and Karl should often find themselves here at the same time as the existentialists. These young fashionistas would not only have the new wave of consumerism to thank for their futures, but also the general environment of social change. And this social change was perhaps best described by Simone de Beauvoir, who challenged and redefined what it was to be a woman in her 1949 book *The Second Sex*. The gender studies pioneer differentiated between biological gender and cultural imprint, exposed the socially ascribed roles of the mother and carer, and pointed out how men had historically turned women into the 'other' and an 'object'.[69]

Simone de Beauvoir's contribution both accompanied and influenced a fundamental social shift in more ways than one. Women were emancipating themselves from the constraints of society, as more and more were entering into gainful employment, and increasingly open discussions of female sexuality signalled the dawn of a new sexual revolution. From 1965, married women were no longer legally answerable to their husbands and could finally manage their own assets, open a bank account and sign an employment contract without their husband's authorization.[70] With their own self-earned purchasing power, women no longer had to act like shop mannequins for the men in their lives. They were discarding their old roles and their old outfits – and now they needed new clothes to suit their new lives.

Fashion designers were quick to respond to this social development. Yves and Karl were both still working in the elite world of haute couture in the 1950s, producing bespoke tailoring for wealthy clients. In the 1960s, however, the designers conquered ready-to-wear fashion by offering a high-end alternative to haute couture. As well as being available to far more women, this alternative opened up much bigger lines of business for fashion houses. In keeping with the growing freedoms, fashion was becoming more adaptable and there was a renewed thirst for exciting, revolutionary ideas. Couturiers gradually ceased to be mere service providers: now, instead of kneeling in front of models and clients, the designers had women at their feet. A new era was dawning, and new styles were just around the corner. It wouldn't be too much longer until 'Le Smoking' tuxedo for women became a symbol of female self-empowerment, and the miniskirt teamed with a transparent blouse came to stand for female liberation.

Karl knew that he had to move with the times. He also knew that the right contacts would help him along the way. He was on close terms with the actor Anthony Perkins when he starred in the 1961 Françoise Sagan film *Goodbye Again* with Ingrid Bergman and Yves Montand. He also frequently joined Yves Saint Laurent for dinner on his houseboat in Neuilly. 'The two of them were friends for a long time, without there being any jealousy,' says Peter Bermbach. Then Pierre Bergé came on the scene, and Lagerfeld couldn't stand the man. Bermbach realized there was a conflict brewing in the 1970s, when Karl gave him a green angora sweater he had received as a gift from Yves. 'He didn't want anything to remind him of his former friend.'

Lagerfeld's behaviour wasn't to everyone's liking. This young man who was about to become a household name could sometimes be outlandishly arrogant. There was, for example, the time he was invited to dinner by Azzedine Alaïa. The Tunisian couturier was living in the *chambre de bonne* of Comtesse Nicole de Blégiers while working as her housekeeper and tailor. He asked the aristocrat if he could host the dinner while she was away at one of her estates. 'Of course,' she replied, 'as long as you don't go wild.'[71] Though there were no crazy antics at this dinner in 1960, the whole affair left a bitter aftertaste. Anne-Marie Muñoz was probably at the dinner, along with Christoph von Weyhe, who was Alaïa's partner from 1959 until the designer's death in 2017. The German art student found himself sitting across from a designer with a distinctive James Dean quiff. They had never met before, though in fact they could have known each other for years. Weyhe's father, who owned land in the district of Eutin in East Holstein, supplied Glücksklee with milk and was friends with Otto Lagerfeld. 'Otto's son is in Paris too,' his father had told his youngest son Christoph when he moved from Holstein to Paris. 'The two of you should get to know one another.' But that evening, the two men didn't even find out that they came from the same area – because Lagerfeld only ever mentioned his parents' new house in Baden-Baden ... and because he claimed to be of Swedish descent.

Lagerfeld would continue to tell this story for a long time yet.[72] In a French television appearance in 1990, he even claimed that his father was a Swede.[73] His father was a baron, he said, but he wasn't called 'von Lagerfeld' because the prefix 'von' didn't exist in Sweden. He also claimed on several occasions that his father spelled his last name 'Lagerfeldt'.[74] These weren't just ideas he had plucked out of thin air; they were rooted deep in history. The surname Lagerfeld is indeed of Swedish origin; however, it does not come from the term for a field where goods were stored. Nor does it mean 'large field', which is what the journalist André Leon Talley claimed in 1995; he was under the impression that Grand-Champ in Brittany, where Lagerfeld had bought a château in the 1970s, was the French translation of his close friend's Swedish surname.[75] In fact, 'lager' means 'bay' or 'laurel' in Swedish and is used in compound nouns for terms like bay leaf and laurel wreath. Israel Israelson (1610–1648), a Swedish Jew, was ennobled with the surname 'Lagerfäldt' in 1646. The spelling changed over time, and the 'Lagerfeld(t)' coat of arms featured a lush laurel tree with twelve red berries.[76] It is thought that Karl's great-great-great-grandfather Tönnies Lagerfeld(t) moved from Sweden to St Pauli in 1767.[77] This branch of the family tree had dropped the 't' from the end of the surname by the nineteenth century.

But why did the young Karl want to be a Swede? Perhaps he didn't want the French to use the derogatory term *boche* when they spoke about him. And in any case, he liked to embellish his past with his vivid imagination. In the early 1970s, he told American friends he had made through the illustrator Antonio Lopez that he grew up in a castle.[78] He even went so far as to relocate his 'family castle' to the 'Danish border',[79] which is in fact a good 60 miles away from Bad Bramstedt. By altering his date of birth and modifying his heritage, he covered up his roots. This self-assured young man redefined space and time, weaving his own version of events to suit his requirements. He formed the very foundations of his own existence, as in a creation story from the post-metaphysical age.

Karl Lagerfeld hid behind a fictitious identity in order to protect himself. In the field of depth psychology this would be referred to as a persona, a role he adopted to act out socially acceptable behaviour in this anti-German environment – like a 'false self' (C. G. Jung) or the theatrical masks donned in Ancient Greece ('persona') to portray a certain character and disguise the wearer's identity. According to Jung, when a person overly identifies with the persona they present for their public image, they end up neglecting their inner life. This could explain two of the things that best defined this designer: his cult status and his mood swings. The mask he wore allowed him to turn himself into an icon and protect his 'true self', keeping others at arm's length. All the while, the neglected inner world manifested itself in subtle aggressions that could account for his occasional outbursts.

In the decades to come, Karl Lagerfeld and Azzedine Alaïa moved in different circles and hardly ever came into contact. But when Alaïa criticized Lagerfeld's inexorable productivity and lashed out at him for speeding up production rhythms in the fashion industry, there was no holding the latter back. After Alaïa died in 2017, Lagerfeld told *Numéro* magazine that he had lost his two 'best enemies' that year: Azzedine Alaïa and Pierre Bergé. 'I don't criticize him,' he said, referring to Alaïa, 'even if at the end of his career all he did was make ballet slippers for menopausal fashion victims.' He even made a rather cutting remark about the designer 'falling down the stairs', in reference to Alaïa dying of a heart attack in the courtyard of his studio-residence in the Marais.[80] Christoph von Weyhe says he was 'appalled by the impiety'. Almost sixty years after that first dinner, his opinion of this strange Swedish baron had not improved.

Baden-Baden

Elisabeth Lagerfeld got along well with her young neighbour in Baden-Baden. When Marga Ullrich got married in 1965, Mrs Lagerfeld gave her two potholders she had crocheted herself and six small fruit knives with iridescent mother-of-pearl handles. Wedding gifts like these, which clearly tie the bride to the role of housewife, would be frowned upon these days. But despite being a staunch feminist, the old lady who lived at 16a Hahnhofstrasse was also a practical woman with an appreciation for a well-kept home. Marga Ullrich was delighted with the gifts. She has kept the white and blue potholders to this day, and the fruit knives have still never been used.[81]

Otto Lagerfeld had the house in the spa resort of Baden-Baden built in 1959. The place where the Lagerfelds were to spend their retirement, just a few hundred feet from the town centre and Brenners Park Hotel, sounds idyllic: parquet flooring made of prized tropical timber, a large southeast-facing glass façade, and an unimpeded view of the Oos Valley and the Black Forest hillsides across the way. Otto and Elisabeth Lagerfeld moved into the house at the beginning of 1960.

There were plenty of good reasons for the move, not least that Otto Lagerfeld had stepped down as Glücksklee's director in 1957. The architect's drawing, dated 11 March 1959, refers to the project as a 'new residential development' for a certain 'Herr Dir. O. Lagerfeld' – clearly Karl's father wanted to remain a director for life. But in the spring of 1960, Otto was already seventy-eight years old and ripe for retirement after a busy career. Life in Baden-Baden promised to be much more enjoyable than in Hamburg, where the weather was often foul and Elisabeth never really felt at home. The spa town was not destroyed in the war, it was clean, orderly and well-kept, the pace of life was slower, and the climate was very mild by German standards. Otto and Elisabeth would still be more than 300 miles away from their son in Paris, but at least it wasn't as far as the 560-mile drive from Hamburg.

The Lagerfelds proved to be pleasant neighbours. They often popped over to see Marga Ullrich's parents at around 11 am on Sundays. Ullrich remembers Mrs Lagerfeld's Dior perfume lingering in the staircase after they had gone, the scent of lily of the valley. 'She wore a black Persian lamb fur coat and purple stockings, which stood out at that time,' says Ullrich. Otto Lagerfeld, who always wore a suit and tied his tie 'in a thick knot', occasionally brought along some of his son's sketches. Ullrich's father, Josef Weis, worked at the savings bank but was known in Baden-Baden for being an ambitious painter. When Otto asked Weis what he thought about the sketches, his answer was diplomatic: he said that they were completely different in style from his landscape paintings, but that the draughtsmanship was 'self-assured'. Marga Ullrich had the impression that Otto Lagerfeld was proud of his son but also unsure what to make of his art and his career.

Karl visited his parents regularly, sometimes for a couple of days and other times for extended holidays. 'He would drive to Baden-Baden in the summer if there was nothing happening in Paris for a couple of months,' says his friend Peter Bermbach. 'In the letters he wrote, he complained about how terrible things were there. His father annoyed him, but he idolized his mother. Of course, it is often the case that gay men have difficult relationships with their fathers and are very close to their mothers.'[82] The situation was more intense than it had ever been, now that Otto Lagerfeld was at home instead of being away on business all the time. 'There were some serious arguments,' Thoma Schulenburg says. Otto Lagerfeld just didn't understand his son. 'Mule's sexual orientation was a tough blow for him. My mother even drove from Frankfurt to Baden-Baden on several occasions to

With his parents in the 1960s: Karl Lagerfeld
often went to visit his family in Germany.

mediate.' Elisabeth always took her son's side, fighting 'tooth and
nail' for him.[83]

One particular misdemeanour did nothing to improve Karl's
relationship with his father. The house where his parents lived had
in the basement a 'tandem garage', in which two cars could park,
one in front of the other. One day Karl had parked his car – a blue
Jaguar E-Type, if he remembered rightly[84] – above the steep driveway
that led to the garage. 'We were all inside the house when we heard
this dreadful noise,' he later recalled. 'Immediately my mother asked:
where did you leave your car? I told her I had parked it by the door.
But when we looked it was gone. I must have forgotten to put the
handbrake on. And now all of a sudden there were three cars in a
garage made for two.'[85]

It was a real double whammy. The entrance to the garage was at the bottom of a steep, 40-foot slope. 'In Paris you don't have to put the handbrake on,' says Marga Ullrich's son Christian laconically. He and his family have lived in the house since 2005. Between Elisabeth Lagerfeld leaving in spring 1968 and Christian Ullrich moving in, there were only two other interim owners. Very little has changed inside as a result – even the typical bright yellow tiles from the late 1950s can still be found in the kitchen.

Predictably, Karl and Elisabeth took the crash less seriously than the man who had paid for the cars. 'My mother and I died laughing,' Lagerfeld later said. 'My father never forgave us for finding it so very funny. I mean, I had managed to destroy three cars in one fell swoop.'[86] The three cars were squashed like an accordion.[87]

Even though Lagerfeld drove around in some classy cars, he wasn't exactly the best driver. He had passed his driving test 'without issues' at the age of seventeen, but his problem was that he was easily distracted: 'I was always looking out of the window,' he said. 'I wanted to take everything in, instead of keeping my eyes on the road in front the whole time. I just found it too boring. It makes me fall asleep when I have to look straight ahead.'[88] And furthermore: 'That monotonous hum, the mind-numbing noise from the wheels, it makes me tired. Not just in the car either. On the train, on a plane – I fall asleep everywhere.'[89]

He even dozed off at the wheel a couple of times. The first time, his Porsche convertible flipped over at 4 a.m. and he wound up in a ditch in the Ardennes. It was a narrow escape.[90] The next time it happened was in Saverne in the Lower Alsace, when he was en route from Paris to Baden-Baden in his Mercedes 190 SL. Luckily, he somehow managed to hurl himself out of the car when it came off the road and sped full tilt into a tree. But from that point on, the young Karl decided he would never drive again. 'I'm always looking around me – it's better if I don't drive.'[91] Ever a man of his word, he stood by his decision and it worked to his advantage.

As far as his mother was concerned, the car accidents could only mean one thing: 'You'll have to make sure you can always afford a chauffeur.'[92] His father bought him a Bentley 'because he thought it looked safer'.[93] Having sworn off driving, he left it to the chauffeurs to run him around in big, heavy cars like his Rolls-Royce: 'I find them solid and comfortable,' he said.[94] He often opted for Hummer SUVs later in life. His driver, usually Sébastien Jondeau, safely steered monsters like these along the narrow alleys of Saint-Germain-des-Prés and the hairpin bends of Monaco.

Adding to a long list of contradictions in this man's life was his huge fleet of vehicles – it was a strange obsession for someone who no longer drove cars: 'We also have Ferraris and Lamborghinis ... but I don't really care for them. I always feel like a gutter inspector in cars like those. I don't like being so close to the ground. That's why I like my Hummer SUVs. Driving around, you're nice and high above everything.'[95] Mid-range cars definitely weren't his cup of tea. When he invited a few friends to his country estate in Brittany in September 1974, his partner Jacques de Bascher borrowed a Peugeot 504 because the Rolls-Royce had broken down. One of the guests, Thadée Klossowski de Rola, noticed that it wasn't to the host's liking: 'Karl found it tasteless.'[96]

So it would appear that his experience with cars was like everything else in his life: even the misfortunes helped him along the way. Accidents became amusing anecdotes, and there was even something triumphant about his self-imposed exile from the front seat. Pulling up in a chauffeur-driven car made him look the part, much like his father being dropped off at business meetings in his Mercedes. The motoring mishaps in Baden-Baden served a purpose: when Karl Lagerfeld majestically pulled up in his chauffeur-driven Rolls-Royce, it helped boost the reputation he was building for himself.

Chloé

It was Rosemarie Le Gallais's first major interview in Paris. Born in Lüdenscheid in 1937 and raised in Plettenberg, North-Rhine

Westphalia, the young woman had left the scenic Sauerland region for Paris in 1960. She was following in the footsteps of her mother, who had lived there when she was younger and planted the idea of the city in her daughters' heads. When she first arrived, Rosemarie studied French at the Alliance Française, where Karl Lagerfeld, now designing at Chloé, had also studied a few years earlier. She was joined in the city by her sister, whose son Stefan Lubrina, as chance would have it, ended up working closely with the designer many years later – his job as a set designer took him to the big productions at Chanel.[97]

In 1967, Rosemarie heard that one of her favourite fashion houses was looking for an *attaché de presse*. She had loved Chloé ever since she had bought one of the brand's dresses from Boutique Laura on the Avenue du Général Leclerc. The shop on the outskirts of the city was run by Sam Rykiel, whose wife Sonia Rykiel was still relatively unknown at the time. In fact, when Rosemarie bought the Chloé dress from the store in the early 1960s, the knitted maternity wear that Rykiel had been producing since her first pregnancy was still on display without a separate label. Sonia Rykiel rose to international fame with her knitwear when she opened her own store on Rue de Grenelle. She and Lagerfeld had two things in common: a distinctive look and a new creative mindset. With her trademark red hair, Rykiel was the second biggest fashion icon in Saint-Germain-des-Prés after Lagerfeld. And like this German in Paris, she was part of a new cohort of designers who, no longer content with serving the system as couturiers, wanted to be *créateurs* and make their own mark on the fashion world.

Now it was really happening: Rosemarie Le Gallais had been invited for an interview at Chloé. She found herself sitting across from managing director Jacques Lenoir, who had come on board in 1953, a year after the fashion house was founded by Gabrielle ('Gaby') Aghion. He was an intimidating man: tall, serious and good-looking. As Rosemarie sat patiently waiting in the company's head office on Rue Miromesnil, he took a look at her documents and then said: 'Oh, so you're German? My entire family was killed in Auschwitz.'

On a promotional tour in the
US: Karl Lagerfeld travelled to
Los Angeles with Rosemarie
Le Gallais in 1979.

Rosemarie was caught completely off-guard. Her eyes welled up with tears, but she was determined to hold his gaze. Before she knew it, he had already moved onto the next topic as if nothing had happened. She got the job. This was big news: finally, she could prove to her parents in Plettenberg that, at the age of thirty, she could earn a living for herself in Paris. Months down the line, Jacques Lenoir told her: 'Do you know why I decided to give you the job? Because of how you reacted during the interview.'

Rosemarie Le Gallais was joining one of the youngest labels in Paris, where she would work closely with Karl Lagerfeld for the next two decades. He had switched to Chloé in 1964.[98] It was a bold move that involved a certain amount of risk. 'At Balmain, where the focus was still exclusively on haute couture, it was seen as a step in the wrong direction,' says Peter Bermbach. Chloé 'was only doing *prêt-à-porter*, fashion that everyone could wear'.[99] Chloé was the first label that was founded specifically with a view to making affordable ready-to-wear fashion, unlike other brands that started out in haute couture and came to embrace the more accessible ready-to-wear segment over time. But the focus at Chloé was always on luxury ready-to-wear: when Aghion started her fashion house in 1952, she teamed up with tailors from Lucien Lelong, a couture house that had ceased operations.[100]

Another factor that made this move a risk was the fact that Lagerfeld wasn't the only designer at Chloé. Gaby Aghion was always on the lookout for new inspiration and hired plenty of young talent for the brand, including Gérard Pipart, who went on to work at Nina Ricci for over thirty years, and Maxime de la Falaise, whose daughter Loulou would become one of Yves Saint Laurent's muses. Michèle Rosier, the daughter of *Elle* founder Hélène Gordon-Lazareff, also worked at the label as a director before later turning her attention to film. When Karl Lagerfeld joined Chloé, a certain Italian who kept coming back to Paris, Graziella Fontana, was also still on the staff there.

Lagerfeld recalled his early days working under Gaby Aghion: 'We were several designers and she coordinated it all. Every designer was freelancing – a new way of working then – for other companies, often in other countries, me included.'[101] Gaby Aghion came up with a whole new mode of collaboration between fashion houses and their designers. 'In the 1950s, couture assistants still played a supportive role,' says Géraldine-Julie Sommier, who manages the Chloé archives. 'She wanted to give young designers the freedom to unleash their creativity.' This new way of working as a freelance designer was almost tailormade for Lagerfeld. He wanted to work with other labels in Paris and Italy at the same time, and there was no need for direct contact with customers outside of haute couture: 'Everything is anonymous in ready-to-wear clothing; you're working with women you don't know.'[102] His boss was like a mentor to him. In the evenings when they finished work, they would often head back to her house in the fifth arrondissement to continue talking about fabrics, styles and trends in the car. 'She would drop Karl at her house and he would continue home by foot, cutting west across the *quartier latin* back to the Rue de l'Université.'[103] Lagerfeld later wrote that he 'spent the ten happiest, most carefree years' of his life in the apartment at number 35, which he moved into in 1963.[104]

He also fitted in at Chloé because it had a relatively laissez-faire ethos compared to other fashion houses, where etiquette was everything. Gaby Aghion had named her label after a friend, Chloé Huysmans, because she really liked the roundness of the letters. The young fashionista moved in bohemian circles on the Left Bank before starting her own label. She put on her first informal show in the Café de Flore on 29 November 1957, unveiling her styles for the next spring/summer season over a breakfast of coffee and croissants. Aghion's concept revolved around classic, simple, wearable clothing. Lagerfeld was right up Aghion's street with his wit and his unconventional approach to fashion. This label was not concerned with producing pretentious couture for beautiful hangers-on, the kind of women who attached themselves to wealthy men and stood around looking bored at cocktail receptions. It was all about making fashion for emancipated women who went out to the office and earned their own living. At Chloé, the *élégance* of old gave way to modern-day *chic*. With lightweight silk fabrics, knee-length styles and playful additions like ribbons or a quirky hat, this fashion was all about having fun. In the 1950s and early 1960s, Paris had never seen anything like it.

The brand had a strong public image when Lagerfeld joined in 1964, but on the inside everything was still rather modest. 'It was a family business based in an apartment with four rooms,' Rosemarie Le Gallais notes. 'Karl didn't even have a studio of his own. When he came to do the fittings, Jacques Lenoir had to make space for him in his office, where rolls of fabric were propped against the walls.'

As well as being Chloé's press coordinator, Le Gallais also did the fittings with Lagerfeld as she had the right measurements. So now the two Germans were working closely together. Lagerfeld drew the designs, then the seamstresses made the samples in white muslin in the studio. The designs were appraised at a series of fittings: if the garment didn't sit correctly or look good, it was altered until all the proportions and details were just right. Finally, the fabric was chosen and the piece could be made, bringing the stuff of imagination to life.

'Before long he was the number one designer,' says Le Gallais. 'He came to the fittings almost every day; he was incredibly hard-working and versatile.' Graziella Fontana left the company in 1972, frustrated at the indefatigable, industrial spirit of her colleague, who monopolized everything with his boundless energy. Other fashion bosses sometimes had to practically beg their designers for ideas, whereas, if anything, Karl was over-productive and occasionally came up with far more than the customary 220 designs per season. 'Often we just had to shout "Stop!"' says Le Gallais. As a designer, he was in the right place at the right time. He thought haute couture was outmoded. The idea of luxury *prêt-à-porter* fashion, which Gaby Aghion more or less invented, was to create ready-made clothing using sophisticated techniques and the best materials. 'Skirts with a seamless stitch were unexpectedly lightweight. And lingerie dresses in pure silk with lace inserts were reminiscent of delicate porcelain figurines from the eighteenth century.'

Even though Lagerfeld was coming up with designs at breakneck speed, the spirit of haute couture was very much alive behind the scenes. The designer wanted to do more than just make production-line fashion, as shown by the elaborately hand-painted dresses still hanging in the Chloé archives on Rue de la Baume, many of which were inspired by Art Nouveau in the late 1960s. Lagerfeld was a fan of quirky ideas, like when he opted for a playful tie with a tennis motif to go with his expensive Cifonelli suit in 1971. Then there was the 'Interplanétaire' dress for autumn/winter 1970, reminiscent of surrealist fashion designer Elsa Schiaparelli's work with its planet embroideries; and not forgetting the Pop Art dresses he designed for spring/summer 1971, one of which featured a large cat motif. In October 1974, his models even took to the catwalk in sneakers.[105]

'He was completely obsessed with lightness,' says Géraldine-Julie Sommier. The designer loved to act out his romantic side with thin silk georgette, delicate tulle, intricate lace detailing, ruffles, tiered flounces and puffy sleeves. By the end of the 1970s, however, he had started to move away from this ornate style in favour of something more provocative. In a nod to French politics, which he believed was about to swing to the left in 1978, he designed fabric samples featuring motifs from the Russian labour movement, the hammer and sickle and Cyrillic lettering: 'It would be opportunistic if the Left won. If the right won, then it was ironic.' Of course it ended up being ironic.[106]

Lagerfeld also had a pioneering communication strategy, inviting photographers such as Helmut Newton, Deborah Turbeville and Guy Bourdin to stage fashion shoots in his apartment at Place Saint-Sulpice. It worked well for the photographers, as the high ceilings with windows down to the floor provided a wonderful setting for shoots and did away with the need to rent studio space. The designer just so happened to appear in the shot on occasion, for instance in the American issue of *Vogue* from February 1975.[107] This man knew a thing or two about self-promotion. And because he was so warm and welcoming, the models, photographers and journalists didn't hold this against him. Quite the opposite: they were just grateful to have the chance to be part of his ever-expanding universe.

Lagerfeld's designs captured the free spirit of the early 1970s. His fashion shows were a case in point: 'They were incredibly fun and lively,' says former *Vogue* editor Ariel de Ravenel. 'These days the models walk down the catwalk looking moody, whereas back then they danced. It was exhilarating and avant-gardist.'[108] Corey Grant Tippin, who knew Lagerfeld well, was excited by all the different faces on the catwalk: 'Pat Cleveland, Amina Warsuma and Carol LaBrie on the runway: it was so diverse for the time.'[109] And it didn't stop there. Bill Cunningham, the photographer who would soon invent street style photography, tells the story of an unusual last-minute addition to the line-up: Lagerfeld's friend Antonio Lopez was on his way to the Chloé show with several other people when he noticed a woman on the side of the road. He got the taxi to stop, then picked the

Good composition: Karl Lagerfeld was inspired by the composer
Sergei Rachmaninoff for the spring/summer 1973 collection at Chloé.

woman up and asked her if she wanted to model in Lagerfeld's show.
The woman, who turned out to be a prostitute, had no objections to
the idea. Lagerfeld loved surprises like these and dressed her up
for the show; her début for Chloé was 'a sensation'.[110]

This fashion designer was quite the advocate for diversity. One
of the journalists accompanying him on a trip to Los Angeles for a
Chloé show was André Leon Talley, who worked for *Women's Wear
Daily* at the time. There were around ten to twelve people in the
group, and when they went to check in at the Beverly Hills Hotel
they were told: 'I'm afraid we have a problem. This man cannot stay
here.' By 'this man' he was referring to Talley, the only black man
in the group. Lagerfeld's response: 'We'll all leave then.' Eventually
they managed to reach a compromise: Talley was put up in one of
the bungalows, and Lagerfeld's group agreed to stay.[111]

From the early 1970s, Lagerfeld always went out to take a bow when the show was over. As the face of the brand, he was now also working on his own public image. And although Gaby Aghion gave him a completely free rein, she didn't want any other names to be in the limelight. 'Chloé by Karl Lagerfeld' was never on the cards, because the individual designer was not meant to outshine the fashion house itself. But with newspapers and magazines increasingly reporting on the fact that Karl Lagerfeld had designed the collection, the time for polite restraint was over. Eventually, Chloé conceded and credited Lagerfeld as the designer. When Jane Fonda was photographed by Jeanloup Sieff and appeared on the cover of French *Vogue* in February 1970, she was wearing a silk dress by 'Karl Lagerfeld pour Chloé'.[112]

From a small idea, Chloé became a world-famous brand. Clients of the fashion house included Jackie Onassis, Maria Callas and Caroline of Monaco, who would become one of the fashion designer's closest companions over the years. The term 'celebrity marketing' was not in use in those days; people simply worked 'with friends'. Lagerfeld was particularly smitten with Stéphane Audran, who was married to film director Claude Chabrol. He designed her film wardrobes for *Les noces rouges* (Wedding in Blood, 1973), *Folies bourgeoises* (The Twist, 1976) and *Le sang des autres* (The Blood of Others, 1984).[113] In Luis Buñuel's 1972 film *Le Charme discret de la bourgeoisie* (The Discreet Charm of the Bourgeoisie), which was awarded the Oscar for Best Foreign Film in 1973, the actress wears a black dress with large diamond-shaped sections cut out of the back. The Karl Lagerfeld design gained cult status – and yet it still wasn't quite as influential as other outfits from films. The little black Hubert de Givenchy dress that Audrey Hepburn wore in *Breakfast at Tiffany's* (1961) was even more legendary. And when Catherine Deneuve gave her iconic, provocative performance in the 1967 Luis Buñuel film *Belle de Jour*, she wore an even more iconic short black dress with a high neck and a small ivory satin collar – designed by none other than Yves Saint Laurent.

Both designers took inspiration from artists, but some of the art-influenced dresses that Lagerfeld designed for Chloé have not aged well. The prints inspired by Oskar Schlemmer and Aubrey Beardsley, for example, now look terribly nostalgic, whereas Yves Saint Laurent's 1965 'Mondrian' dress was simpler and more effective. It worked because the strict colour and design idiom of Piet Mondrian's 'neo-plasticism' contrasted against the flowing silhouettes of couture with its geometric lines. Although it was really just a shapeless sack dress, it became a symbol of the mutual attraction between art and fashion. And, of course, Yves Saint Laurent had designed it. Karl Lagerfeld was the eternal runner-up. 'Yves Saint Laurent was more successful in the 1970s,' says Ariel de Ravenel. 'Everyone wanted to go there. Chloé was in second place.' But one thing that made Lagerfeld stand out was his sense of humour. Perhaps the best example of this is the midnight-blue Chloé gown that Pat Cleveland wore in the autumn/winter 1979 show. The dress, which is now held in the Palais Galliera collection, is embroidered with pearls and rhinestones in the form of a lightbulb appliqué. It was inspired by Lagerfeld's passion for early German design and serves as a tribute to Peter Behrens, who was arguably the first 'corporate designer'. Behrens became the 'artistic advisor' to the Berlin-based company AEG in 1907 and used the filament bulb motif for his decorative advertising poster. The bulb appliqué on the Chloé gown even has the traditional pointed tip, while the leg-of-mutton sleeves suggest the shape of a rounded bulb. When interior designer Andrée Putman turned up to a party at Le Palace nightclub wearing the dress, the bulb concept came alive as she lit up the room.

Lagerfeld's talent for marketing also played a big part in his success. He frequently flew Concorde to New York to attend 'trunk shows' in US states. These private shows, named after the common practice of transporting the clothes to their destination in trunks, became increasingly widespread during the course of the 1970s. When Lagerfeld arrived in Houston to premiere his autumn collection for Chloé in May 1979, he was greeted with the kind of reception usually reserved 'for a head of state', Rosemarie Le Gallais recalls. A purple carpet was rolled out by the plane, dozens of cheerleaders lined the streets, and a police convoy followed as Lagerfeld, now wearing a cowboy hat, was driven into the city in a car with gigantic longhorn steer horns on the hood. He was treated like a star at the fashion show in the Neiman Marcus department store, and he loved it.

Despite this growing success, there were some undeniable differences between Lagerfeld and Jacques Lenoir. The managing director was understandably mindful of money, whereas his designer was extremely generous. Former Chloé model Renate Zatsch remembers Karl shouting 'Run!' and encouraging the girls to make their getaway, boosting their meagre earnings with the Chloé dress they had worn for the show.[114] The models quickly absconded through the back exit without getting changed.

The designer's growing popularity also added fuel to certain underlying resentments. When the original Chloé fragrance was launched in 1975, Lagerfeld became rich and famous. Lagerfeld and Chloé had formed a new company called Karl Lagerfeld Productions for the perfume deal with Elizabeth Arden, with the shares to be divided three ways. Lagerfeld was given 50 per cent of the shares, and Gaby and Jacques each had 25 per cent. They continued to produce new perfumes even long after Lagerfeld had left. He was the driving force behind the launch, and spent months collaborating with Elizabeth Arden on the product itself and the bottle. The fragrance generated a turnover of 50 million marks in 1977, and Lagerfeld reportedly received 2.5 per cent of the sum.[115] This equated to some 1.2 million marks for that year alone, an extraordinary amount of money for the time, and it only increased as sales of the perfume grew exponentially. He was also extremely well-paid for his work as a fashion designer at Chloé,[116] not to mention his many other jobs.

'There was more tension towards the end; things were no longer pleasant,' says Rosemarie Le Gallais. 'Karl wanted to leave, and he wanted me to go with him.' He finally wanted to use his own name as a brand, and he was going to need her. His appointment as Chanel's creative director in the late summer of 1982 was a brazen statement to his long-term employer. After a year working for both fashion houses side by side, Lagerfeld bade Chloé farewell with a final collection that spoke volumes. The clothes for spring/summer 1984 were embellished with large glittery scissors, pin cushions and cotton reels. Perhaps this was an allusion to haute couture, which Lagerfeld would be returning to in his role at Chanel? Or maybe the scissors were supposed to symbolize the severing of ties? 'Things weren't moving forward,' Lagerfeld said in 1984. 'I was ready to take it to more of an international level. But my business partners couldn't keep up, so I told them: Just go back to sleep, and ciao!'[117]

Gaby Aghion was sixty-two years old when her top designer left at the end of 1983. But she was nowhere near ready for retirement yet, so she kept on going. Lagerfeld's successor, Martine Sitbon, left the fashion house in 1992 after just five years as its creative director. Lagerfeld returned that year, though he was still busy at Chanel, Fendi and his own signature label. Under no circumstances did he want to be reminded of the old days at Chloé. One of the people entrusted with erasing the past was Claudia Bessler, who embarked on an internship in the sales division at the start of 1993. 'Karl said he wanted all his old sketches to be thrown out, so the interns were sent to the warehouse. We put lots of thick folders from the 1960s and 1970s into large blue plastic bags and threw them in the bin.' This crime in fashion history left its mark on the intern, who later went on to become a stylist. 'I thought it was terrible, really brutal. All those wonderful drawings!'[118] And in the short space of five years, it was all over again. This time there was no going back. On the subject of the exhibition celebrating sixty years of Chloé at the Palais de Tokyo in late 2012, Lagerfeld said: 'I looked at it and thought, "That's not bad." But I couldn't imagine that I was the person who had done it. I had no relationship to it.'[119]

After Lagerfeld left Chloé, the fashion house specializing in feminine fashion was headed almost exclusively by female creative directors. In response to the appointment of Paul McCartney's daughter Stella, he said, 'I knew they would take a big name to replace me at Chloé, but I thought it would be in fashion and not in music.'[120] This didn't bother the London designer, who kept her cool and said that her mother Linda had bought a number of Chloé dresses designed by her predecessor in the 1970s. Stella McCartney stayed at Chloé for four years and was succeeded by Phoebe Philo in 2001, then came Paulo Melim Andersson in 2006, Hannah MacGibbon in 2008, Clare Waight Keller in 2011, Natacha Ramsay-Levi in 2017, and Gabriela Hearst in 2020. All these different names show that fashion houses change their designers almost as often as major football teams change managers these days. By constantly bringing new designers on board, the label succeeded in refreshing its image time and time again.

Gaby Aghion sold her shares in the fashion house at the right time, long before she died in 2014 at the age of ninety-three. Her son, Philippe Aghion, became an economist specializing in growth models, always with his mother's growing business in mind. The label remains on good terms with its founder's family; Philippe Aghion's daughter Mikhaela even works there sometimes. Chloé also remains one of the most important names on the ready-to-wear calendar, much to the credit of Karl Lagerfeld. After leading the brand to worldwide fame in the 1970s, he was the designer who stayed at Chloé the longest of all – for a quarter of a century in total.

Fendi

The Fendi sisters were made to wait. When they travelled to Paris in 1964 to get Karl Lagerfeld to sign an agreement on their collaboration, no one answered the doorbell at the apartment. The sisters did the only thing they could: they just sat in the hallway, waiting for him to arrive. And because the hall lights in Paris automatically go off after a minute, they took it in turns to stand up to switch the light back on. 'It's your turn now!' – 'Now you go!' – 'Now your turn!' Their future business partner turned up three hours late. 'My aunts and my mother laughed about it afterwards and retold the story countless times,' says Silvia Fendi. 'He was often late.'[121]

The Roman fashion house, famous for its furs, was in need of an image update after the five Fendi sisters had taken over the label founded by their parents in 1925. Silvia Fendi's mother, Anna, and her sisters Paola, Franca, Alda and Carla were hoping that the collaboration with this young designer from Paris would breathe new life into the brand. It did. Karl Lagerfeld had spent the 1950s getting his bearings and building muscle for the rest of his career, and the 1960s were when he channelled his boundless, feisty enthusiasm into the professional ambition to reinvent multiple labels all at the same time.

Rome was the perfect place for this romantic young German at this point in his career. He could bring his nostalgic longing for Italy to life, following in the footsteps of fellow countrymen Johann Wolfgang von Goethe, whom he regarded highly, and Anselm Feuerbach, a painter he loved. Later on he said to Silvia Fendi: 'Chanel is my French side and Fendi is my Italian side. Better than that, it's my Roman side.'

Lagerfeld spent a lot of time in Rome, particularly during the first few years of his partnership with Fendi. He even had an apartment in the city centre in those days. But when his visits became less frequent after joining Chanel in 1982, he decided to stay at the Hotel Hassler, which was within walking distance of Palazzo Fendi. He worked as the brand's artistic director from 1965 until he died, completing a record fifty-four-year tenure in fashion. He flew out to Rome hundreds of times, and he often travelled to Milan for the Fendi ready-to-wear shows. And because he always wanted to keep business under control, he sent representatives out from Paris to check on how things were going in Rome. One after the other, his confidants Gilles Dufour, Hervé Léger, Vincent Darré, Eric Wright and Amanda Harlech flew out to the Italian capital to make sure that, even though they were in the Eternal City, things weren't taking an eternity. Almost every day, ideas flew back and forth between Rome and Paris by phone and fax.[122]

'For me, he had always been there,' says Silvia Fendi, who was born in 1961, worked alongside Lagerfeld for decades, and has been steering the company's creative fate since he died. 'In the early days, I saw him as some kind of magician. He would sit down, then all you'd see were a couple of lines, and then those lines turned into a complete

Five sisters: the designer is surrounded by (clockwise, from front left)
Carla, Franca, Anna, Paola and Alda Fendi in Rome, 1983.

silhouette, which came to life in the next meeting. I was amazed at how a single idea could be transformed into an entire collection. He became an incredibly important point of reference for me.'[123]

Working long-distance between Rome and Paris was no easy feat. The sketches arrived in parcels, and only in recent years by mobile phone. But there was a lot of trust, and the team knew each other well. The designer wasted no time sounding out his radical ideas on the Fendi sisters. He had the furs cut into strips or pieces, then they were sent to be dyed and embroidered. And because he had learned the importance of a trademark – his father had taught him that much early in life – he knew that the branding had to be recognizable all over the world. So in 1965 he came up with the 'FF' logo, standing for 'Fun Fur'.

Lagerfeld's influence also extended to Fendi bags, even though he wasn't personally responsible for the brand's accessories. Having watched Lagerfeld and her mother at work when she was a young girl, Silvia Fendi took inspiration from their methods. She experimented with bags just as they had done with the furs and dresses, kickstarting the era of the 'It' bag in 1997 with the 'Baguette'. The name of this iconic little handbag was a play on words, combining the French diminutive form '-ette' with the English 'bag'.

The Fendi atelier was more like a laboratory than a design studio. At that time, the accessories team included a young designer with bleached-blond hair who wore thick chains. This designer, whom Lagerfeld nicknamed 'DJ' because he was always playing loud music, was in fact named Alessandro Michele, and he would go on to achieve great success for Gucci as its creative director from 2015. Another two innovators who had a hand in developing the Baguette were Pierpaolo Piccioli and Maria Grazia Chiuri. They both joined Valentino in 2008, taking over the reins as co-creative directors when the old maestro retired. Maria Grazia Chiuri ultimately went on to become the first female creative director at Dior. Michele, Chiuri, Piccioli: three of the most important designers of the early twenty-first century all learned from Karl Lagerfeld how to make ideas become a reality, as well as how to keep their inner freedom despite all the demands they faced in the fashion industry.

In the 1990s, Fendi's success was elevated by its bags, the global 'logomania' trend and the distinctive company signets. The Baguette bag's appearance in the TV show 'Sex and the City' was also a welcome boost. The rapid process of expansion at Fendi was escalated in 1999, when luxury goods conglomerate LVMH started to acquire the company in stages. The head of LVMH, Bernard Arnault, was on good terms with Lagerfeld and would always send him the latest products from Louis Vuitton. Arnault was delighted with the major acquisition because it showed Chanel that he also had a claim to Lagerfeld. In addition, it showed rival corporation Kering, which owned Gucci and Bottega Veneta, that LVMH was also doing well in Italy. Lagerfeld gladly took note of Arnault's rather possessive position. Of course, an individualist like Lagerfeld was hardly going to make for a good trophy, but he wasn't going to rock Arnault's boat either.

The first Fendi *Alta Pellicceria* show on 8 July 2015, during the Paris haute couture fashion week, showed exactly how sophisticated *haute fourrure* (haute fur) could be. Even before the models hit the runway at the Théâtre des Champs-Élysées, one of the coats they were showcasing had already been reserved. The hand-sewn coat, made up of multiple small pieces of mink fur and embroidered with feathers, sold for 270,000 euros.[124] A noisy group of anti-fur activists, among them individuals from the Brigitte Bardot Foundation, had gathered outside the theatre to protest and were carrying banners that read 'Fur: stop torture'. But Lagerfeld never had much sympathy when it came to animal welfare issues: 'Does a butcher apologize for his work?' he once asked. 'I don't have a guilty conscience, and I don't have to feel ashamed of myself for working with fur. I mean, we stopped using panthers in fashion a long time ago. But minks are just like vicious rats.'[125]

When Bernard Arnault came on the scene, Lagerfeld knew he could take things to the next level, just as he had done at Chanel. His ambitions became a reality when in October 2007 Fendi organized a huge, symbolic, ready-to-wear parade at the Great Wall of China, capturing a whole market by showing an appreciation for its culture. Among other elements, many Chinese models graced the catwalk, with outfits in the lucky colour of red to open the show, and the gigantic boundary wall was illuminated to sensational effect.

The show in July 2016 was equally awash with symbolism, as pertaining to Rome: the models walked across the water at the Trevi fountain like Jesus on the Sea of Galilee, albeit on a plane of plexiglass. Then at the beginning of July 2019, the label paid homage to the designer with a major couture show atop the Palatine, one of Rome's seven hills, across from the Colosseum. Amid the Ancient Roman ruins, the label unveiled fifty-four looks – one for each of Lagerfeld's fifty-four years with Fendi. The emperors of Ancient Rome were fond of this view of their city, and no doubt the Emperor of Fashion would have loved it too.

Labelfeld

There are traces of Karl Lagerfeld to be found in the unlikeliest of places. One unexpected trove of this man's work is in Reggio Emilia, between Bologna and Milan in the southern Po Valley. Here, in the refrigerated Max Mara archives, his sketches have been protected from the ravages of time. The sketches look so fresh that it almost seems as if they were drawn yesterday, but in fact they are half a century old. The words 'Max Mara – Eté 72' are written in Lagerfeld's handwriting on a yellow folder that he sent from Paris to the provincial capital in northern Italy in 1971.[126]

Lagerfeld communicated in French with Max Mara's founder, Achille Maramotti (1927–2005). 'Cher Monsieur,' he writes. 'You will find all the explanations on the sketches.' This designer's tough training in the school of haute couture showed through in his drawings for summer 1972, which could not be more detailed. The radius of an unlined circular cape ('cape demi-cercle non doublée') is given as precisely 110 centimetres. A fabric sample is attached to a sketch of a jacket with the note 'en rouge étrusque' to indicate the colour. A pair of two-tone shoes also make an appearance in the sketches, serving as a curious precursor to Lagerfeld's work at Chanel, where Coco Chanel designed her trademark beige pumps with black toe caps in 1957. The instructions for a bolero jacket state that it must be cut to allow for 'toute la liberté du movement'. This requirement, for plenty of freedom of movement, almost sounds like the concept for designing a liberated woman, completely unbound from fashion constraints.

The warehouse-sized archives are managed by Laura Lusuardi, who started working at Max Mara at the age of eighteen in 1964, and

Sketches for Max Mara: Karl Lagerfeld designed clothes
for the label from Reggio Emilia in the early 1970s.

just the following year, as coordinator of the collections, became a
sort of head of design. On the subject of her label's collaboration with
Lagerfeld she says, 'We knew the market and could satisfy our customers' requirements on a commercial level. But we couldn't match
the big names when it came to creativity.' Founded by Maramotti in
1951, the family company was in need of new ideas and inspiration.
Karl knew the young designers Emmanuelle Khanh and Graziella
Fontana from Chloé, where they had collaborated on the 'Pop' concept
in the mid-1960s. He became the first outsider to be involved in Max
Mara's main collection.

Achille Maramotti and his young assistant Laura Lusuardi made
their way to Paris to meet Lagerfeld in the late 1960s. They wanted
to discuss the prospect of working together and to take a look at his
sketches. 'What impressed me most was that he had a fitness room in
his house, full of weights and equipment,' says Lusuardi. 'I had never
seen anything like it before – so modern!' Lagerfeld also impressed

his Italian guests with his work. 'He even did sketches on the paper tablecloths in the Café de Flore.'

Time was clearly of the essence for this prolific designer, who had been working for a virtually endless procession of clients since the early 1960s. After designing budget fashion for Monoprix in 1962, he had quickly added more clients to his portfolio: first Tiziani in Rome from 1963, then Chloé in Paris from 1964, Krizia in Milan from 1964, Curiel in Rome from 1965, and Fendi in Rome from 1965. The list would only grow longer in the years to come. In 1972 a dumb-founded reporter from *Le Monde* newspaper wrote, 'He designs the sweaters at Timwear, the jersey dresses at Helanca de Gadging, the fake furs at Monsieur Z, the shoes at Mario Valentino, and the gloves at Neyret.'[127] The reporter failed to mention that he was also responsible for designing the shoes at Repetto and Charles Jourdan, as well as the sweaters at Ballantyne. The man himself even described his apartment-studio at Place Saint-Sulpice as a 'design bordello': 'The satisfied punters left via the back door as the new tricks came in through the front door.'[128] In 2011 he joked, 'My name is Labelfeld, not Lagerfeld.'[129]

The reputation Lagerfeld was earning for himself as a successful German in Paris also sparked a surge in business in his homeland. In 1969 he embarked on a collaboration with Fritz Ertelt, a fashion entrepreneur from Selm, near Dortmund. Ertelt regularly flew to Paris and sifted through the designer's sketches to find the ones he liked most, then Lagerfeld had the prototypes made up in his atelier and sent on to Ertelt in Selm. 'And that was how Parisian chic made its way into the collection,' says the entrepreneur's daughter, Ulla Ertelt. The company was not allowed to use Lagerfeld's name for advertising purposes, she says, 'but people talked about who was behind the Saint Mignar line behind closed doors, which also contributed to the success'. Ulla Ertelt also came to appreciate Lagerfeld's characteristic blend of positivity and impatience in her time as an intern at Chloé from 1979 to 1981. 'Karl had this boundless creative energy. Working for just one label was never going to be enough for him.

And being the son of a Hamburg businessman, he also knew how to make the most of lucrative licensing arrangements.'[130]

Willebert Boveleth from Mönchengladbach in North Rhine-Westphalia approached Lagerfeld in 1975, hoping to start a partnership that could take his company to the next level. Founded in 1950, Wibor Textilwerke was celebrating its twenty-fifth anniversary and wanted to create a line in collaboration with a big-name designer after a long run of success in premium fashion. Lagerfeld had come recommended by German trade journal *Textilwirtschaft*, so Boveleth looked him up and they entered into a licensing agreement for the 'Karl Lagerfeld Impression' line. The designer drew the collection and flew to Düsseldorf with his assistant Rosemarie Le Gallais every month. They were always picked up from the airport and taken to the office in Mönchengladbach for the fittings, then at midday they would head to the Boveleths' house, where the housekeeper served the *Sauerbraten* (beef pot roast) he so loved. Sometimes after lunch he would go for a nap, then he and Rosemarie would head back to the fittings and catch a flight back to Paris that same evening.

This routine continued for almost ten years. The collections were made exclusively at the Wibor factories in Mönchengladbach, which had their own purchasing managers, dressmakers, patternmakers and a sample studio. It was a common business model at the time, before growing numbers of German companies started using factories in Turkey or the Far East, where production was cheaper than anywhere else. In those days there was no competition from cheap chain stores, and online trade did not yet exist, so clothes were sold by specialist dealers. The Boveleths were delighted with the situation they had created. With Lagerfeld's name, they were able to demand higher prices from customers than they could with their own brand name, Wibor.[131]

Before long, however, Lagerfeld was on his merry way. His fame had reached new heights with the launch of the Chloé fragrance in 1975, and with several new deals on the go, he was away on business in Japan much more frequently. In 1984, two years after joining Chanel, he sold his trademark rights to the Bidermann Group. The American corporation set to work untangling the web of licensing agreements he had woven for himself, and finally the designer parted ways with Wibor. Willebert Boveleth's son Peter, who was now on the board at Wibor, temporarily took over the distribution of the new collection 'KL – Karl Lagerfeld' for the German-speaking world. From 1988, Karl Lagerfeld also worked with Klaus Steilmann, who ran what was then Europe's biggest clothing manufacturing company. From 1996 to 1999, the 'KL – by Karl Lagerfeld' collection was even sold in the German catalogue *Quelle*.

Just how did he manage to do so many things at once? 'He worked incredibly fast,' says Laura Lusuardi. He stayed at Max Mara for three seasons from 1971 to 1972. One of his suggestions involved making coats without a lining. To do this, the fashion house had to develop a special production technique, which it continued to use over the years. 'He was very innovative during his time here.' He also suggested pairing shorts with jackets: 'Also innovative.' He employed unconventional materials for tried-and-tested forms, such as pleated black silk for a cape (his 'cape version soie'). He was also highly skilled at styling, as in putting across the kind of message that went beyond materials, shapes and colours.

'Achille Maramotti was extremely satisfied,' says Lusuardi. 'The house needed to loosen up its classic style.' Buoyed by its positive experiences working with Lagerfeld, the company carried on collaborating with other designers over the years, including Jean-Charles de Castelbajac. Laura Lusuardi also pursued the hunt for emerging talent at the Royal College of Art in London, recruiting more and more young Asian designers with ideas that would allow the brand to compete in an increasingly global market.

Americans

Things were looking good at the start of the 1970s. Karl Lagerfeld had mastered the techniques and the business side of the fashion world. He had established himself at Chloé and was making considerable sums from all his side hustles, not to mention the sizeable inherit-ance he had received when his father passed away. With the sales of the family homes in Baden-Baden and Hamburg complete, Elisabeth Lagerfeld went from being a frequent visitor to a permanent fixture in his large apartment at 35 Rue de l'Université early in 1968. All the professional sovereignty and financial independence he had secured for himself also fed into the designer's personal life. He relaxed and took the time to enjoy his successes, and suddenly this sociable, generous character had lots of new friends. There was an air of social liberation in France following the turbulent events of May 1968, and the atmosphere enriched his life – even if he didn't quite see the point of the protests happening right on his doorstep at the Sorbonne and in the surrounding area.

'The 1970s were great,' he said in 2013. 'It was careless, it was free ... as long as you were young. It had something unpretentious. It was not about money.' He was already a star, but not as much of a star as he would eventually become. Before he turned into the larger-than-life figure the world later knew, he could still move around freely and go to restaurants without drawing crowds. He was left to his own devices and could flip through his newspapers in the Café de Flore without unwanted interruptions. 'There was no red carpet, there were no two hundred bodyguards for famous people. The cool thing was light, young, improvised and fresh.'[132]

One of the main reasons for this new lightness of being was Antonio Lopez, who came to Paris in 1969 and stayed for six years. The illustrator was born in Puerto Rico in 1943 and raised in New York, where his family moved in 1950. He studied design, then started working at *Women's Wear Daily* and the *New York Times* while he was still very young. Lopez completely revolutionized the art of fashion illustration with his radically uninhibited sketches, freeing Paris from the rut it had been stuck in since the heyday of René Gruau in the 1950s. The art form had been starting to look outdated compared to the rapid developments taking place in fashion photography, but Lopez changed all that with his imaginative, psychedelic illustrations.

In the studio at Chloé: Antonio Lopez sketches the model Eija. Juan Ramos (left) and Jacques de Bascher (right) are chatting in the background.

Dripping with excess, and showcasing an incredibly diverse set of ethnic and sub-cultural influences and erotic overtones, his work combined assured strokes with a real lightness of touch.

Lagerfeld was excited by the new arrival. He could sense that change was afoot in the fashion world, with the trend for straight lines and somewhat boxy shapes that had dominated the 1960s gradually moving towards more sensual lines. The whole language of fashion was changing, becoming more fluid. Lagerfeld didn't hesitate to bring Lopez on board at Chloé, engaging him to sketch the latest designs and collaborate on the brand's advertising motifs. 'He came with that New York energy,' says designer Tan Giudicelli, who worked at Chloé during the 1960s. 'His influence was fantastic for the Chloé brand. Karl had snapped him up, and Antonio needed Karl, too.'[133] The generous German provided lodgings for Antonio and his boyfriend, fellow Nuyorican Juan Ramos, in an apartment not far from his own home.

To Karl's mind, Antonio represented all the stylistic liberty of the free artist. But Antonio wasn't his only American alter ego. He also got along well with Juan Ramos, and was fascinated by his systematic approach to collecting new ideas, trends and objects. Karl and Juan often went to La Hune together to buy books about art, design and fashion. Juan would also snap up film posters, graphics, postcards and flea-market finds – anything that he thought might serve as inspiration for whatever project Antonio was working on at the time. He was his boyfriend's art director and a constant source of ideas. His 'magpie-like approach' rubbed off on Karl, who started gathering inspiration for the concept of each new collection as part of his preparations.[134]

One of the young people who could often be found at Antonio and Juan's apartment was Corey Grant Tippin. He had been a regular at Andy Warhol's Factory since 1967 and had dropped out of the Parsons School of Design in New York: 'Why would I keep going when I already knew Andy?' he explains.[135] Many of his friends were called up to serve in the military and got sent to Vietnam. Although Corey was exempted from serving in the army because he had a psychological report confirming that he was homosexual, his mother still advised him to go to Paris to be on the safe side.

He came, he saw – and he was disappointed. 'I was horrified that Paris was so boring, dull, bourgeois and backward-looking,' he says. Life got more interesting when his friend Donna Jordan joined him in the city. He knew Donna from the Factory, and she had already met Antonio at Central Park's Bethesda Fountain during the 'be-ins', the big protests against the Vietnam War, racism and homophobia. In 1970, Donna and Corey met Karl through Antonio and Juan. Karl liked the new clothing, makeup, art and lifestyle trends that were coming out of the US. 'No one really understood what American culture had to offer until then,' Tippin notes. 'For instance, there were very few American designers in Paris. Karl immediately understood pop culture; he could feel the vibe. The prints on his Chloé dresses made that clear pretty soon.'

Three new stars: the American model Donna Jordan, Antonio Lopez and Pat Cleveland were part of Karl Lagerfeld's friendship group in Paris in the early 1970s.

Karl and Antonio sketched together often. 'Oh my God,' Karl once said to Antonio, 'you're so much better than me.' But he didn't let that stop him drawing. 'If you had any ambitions of becoming a fashion illustrator and saw how Antonio could draw, you'd never pick up a pencil again!' jokes Tippin.

As well as letting his friends live in his Paris apartment rent-free, he invited them to dine at La Coupole with him before heading to Rue Sainte-Anne later in the evening. Here, on the street that was to become the epicentre of the Paris gay scene, legendary club owner Fabrice Emaer turned his venue Le Sept into the beating heart of Paris nightlife with the help of resident DJ Guy Cuevas. Everyone who was anyone frequented the club, including the philosopher Roland Barthes and the designer Pierre Cardin. The Americans even stayed so long that they only made it to the Café de Flore for breakfast after midday the following day. 'It was incredible how generous Karl was,' says Tippin. 'He didn't expect anything in return. He disguised his generosity by hastily handing out his presents. He'd just say: Here, I don't want it anymore, you take it!' Pat Cleveland was also flabbergasted by the designer's generosity: not long after she moved to Paris and met him through Antonio, Karl gave her a chiffon dress that he had originally made for Marlene Dietrich.[136]

Karl's friends also met Elisabeth Lagerfeld. 'One evening, I opened a door in Karl's huge apartment – and she was sitting there,' Tippin recalls. 'I said excuse me, then we chatted for a while, and it turned out she knew who I was: "You're Corey, aren't you?"' The elderly lady enjoyed company and was clearly in the know about Karl's social life. In the summer of 1970, the whole group took a trip to Saint-Tropez, where Lagerfeld often went on holiday with Anne-Marie Muñoz and her family. Corey, Donna, Antonio, Juan, Karl and Mrs Lagerfeld all stayed in the beautiful house that Karl had rented. The Americans found it strange to be spending their holiday in the presence of a seventy-three-year-old. 'Our interactions with her were very proper,' says Tippin. 'We were like schoolkids in class, giggling behind the teacher's back. I wish we could have been a bit more mature. When dinner was over, we didn't sit there politely; we jumped up and took off.'

Elisabeth was generous, like her son. Tippin recalls sitting in the buffet car with her on the train to the Côte d'Azur. When the bill came, she slipped him a bank note under the table so that he could save face and be the one to pay. 'She was very discreet. The waiter didn't see a thing.'

Donna was the muse of the group, and the men lavished her with attention. Corey bleached her eyebrows and painted her lips bright red. Karl dressed her. Antonio drew her. 'I had all these sculptors around me,' Donna later said, 'and they were sculpting me, moulding me and making me who I became – the blonde bombshell!'[137] Saint-Tropez had never seen such an unconventionally striking beauty before.

Nor had Paris: when Donna returned from the big trip in 1970, she became one of the most definitive models of her time, a precursor to the It girls and street-style stars of the future.

Antonio brought a different sense of style and physicality with him from Puerto Rico and New York. Another of his muses, Jerry Hall, who was also his girlfriend for a while, remembers the transformation he worked on her. Like any seventeen-year-old girl fresh out of Texas, she used to wear blue eyeshadow and pink makeup for her cheeks and lips. She later recalled that Antonio spent two hours doing her makeup, applying eye liner, false eyelashes and plucking her brows into shape. He helped her say goodbye to her try-hard style. Her awkward poses and outfits had made him laugh. It was all too over the top. She had been running around the whole time looking way too dolled up.[138]

Antonio even got his new friend Karl to loosen up a bit. He had started wearing tunics or silk trousers from Chloé in Saint-Tropez, while his mother remained ever loyal to Sonia Rykiel – after all, she didn't want to flatter her son too much by wearing his designs. Photographs of the group at the beach paint a picture of a completely different man from the rather reserved observer of fashion that people were used to seeing. Rather than using a normal camera, which might have made his subjects nervous, Antonio walked around with a Kodak Instamatic 100 that allowed him to snap spontaneous shots of his friends. His images capture a beau lazing around in the sun; a pretty boy in sunglasses with his elbows resting on a Coca-Cola box like someone from a commercial, holding a bottle in one hand as if he's about to take a sip from the straw; an athlete with impressive biceps and triceps sitting with wet hair at the shore of the Mediterranean Sea in a one-piece bathing suit, pointing at the photographer with a playful expression of annoyance.[139]

Karl only let this openly sensual side show for Antonio. Even in 1976, when Antonio had moved back to New York and Karl visited him there, he was still happy to play along. The photographs from the 'Men in Showers' series show Karl, now a middle-aged man, putting on a playfully sensuous display with the stream of water

Feeling free: Karl Lagerfeld loved his early summers
with the Americans in Saint-Tropez.

coming from the shower. It almost looks as though the water is
coming out of his mouth, like some kind of strange bearded water
fountain. In the last row of photos, he is pictured wearing a large
pair of sunglasses in the shower.[140] Rather than getting involved in
the sadomasochistic and fetishistic aspects of Lopez's Instamatic
series, he manages to keep an ironic distance from any such allusions
in his own contribution. But not everyone was quite so inhibited in
front of the camera. It is astonishing just how many beautiful young
things Lopez catapulted to fame with his art. He also helped to
cultivate the talents of Grace Jones, who was staying at the Hôtel
Crystal with fellow muse Jerry Hall and went on to become a famous
singer, as well as actress Patti D'Arbanville, Cat Stevens's former
girlfriend and the inspiration for his 1970 hit 'Lady D'Arbanville'.
He discovered Jessica Lange, who later starred in *King Kong* and
was awarded Oscars for her roles in *Tootsie* and *Blue Sky*, and Tina

Chow, the fashion icon who married Michael Chow, the founder of the trendy Mr Chow restaurants, in 1972.

The artist, who attracted the attention of men and women and enjoyed sleeping with both, captured the spirit of the times in more than just his sensual drawings. Working simultaneously alongside the likes of Guy Bourdin and Helmut Newton, he created a new, sexually charged form of fashion photography using his humble Instamatic camera – a style that arguably pre-empted the spontaneous aesthetic popularized by Instagram in later years.

This group of creatives, who continued to spend their summers together in Saint-Tropez at Karl's invitation for the next few years, were harbingers of the free love movement. 'Around that time, there was this explosion of sexual freedom in every direction,' says Renate Zatsch. The model, who moved to Paris because Germany was 'too square' for her liking, eventually became part of Karl's clan. 'No one knew about AIDS yet,' she explains. 'There was no tiptoeing around. It was a wonderful time. We just wanted to have fun. We weren't in the slightest bit bothered about money.' This was particularly true for the gay men among the group. 'They completely let themselves go because they suddenly felt so free.'[141]

As values shifted and homosexuality became more socially accepted, gay men moved from the criminalized margins to the centre of enlightened society. Liberated from the age-old stigma, the gay world celebrated unapologetically – and that included Karl's friends. The little apartment on Rue Bonaparte, which Karl had originally bought for his mother before deciding it was too small for her, turned into a sort of mini artist commune, in which the friends enjoyed their new-found freedom. Pat Cleveland joined them in 1971 from New York. She and Donna slept in the bed, while Antonio and Juan slept on the floor in sleeping bags.[142] Later, Karl provided them with a larger apartment at 136 Boulevard Saint-Germain. After the relationship with Karl faltered, Antonio and Juan moved to a flat on Rue de Rennes for their last three years in Paris.

The only one in no hurry to take advantage of 'gay liberation' was Karl. He stayed away from the escapades and kept almost everyone at arm's length. His hesitance was quite understandable: the friends who were constantly getting into sexual exploits were a good decade younger than him, and he also had his fair share of work commitments. The others in the group worked under their own steam and had less responsibility. Ultimately, he was a loner – 'un grand solitaire who was happiest working from home', says Rosemarie Le Gallais.[143] Still, this new-found sensuality started creeping into his fashion, if nothing else.

Karl had to act the part and join in the nightlife, if only to show the scenesters that he had his own clique – like Yves Saint Laurent, who was never to be seen without his entourage. The irresistible pull of these two men and their love of drama went hand in hand with the changing role of the fashion designer. Up to the 1960s, designers had always been service providers who rarely made it into the public eye. But now designers like Yves Saint Laurent, Valentino, Lagerfeld, and Halston in New York were taken seriously by upper-class society. Why? Because they were rich. Perfume deals were the main source of this new-found wealth: they signed their names over to fragrances and reaped rewards beyond their wildest dreams. And all this money bought them grand homes with equally grand interior décor and ever-expanding art collections.

As the self-confidence of these designers reached lofty new heights, their public appearances became increasingly impressive. 'We were like his court,' says Renate Zatsch. 'Le Sept was the destination every night. He would have never gone there alone.' Ever since Pat Cleveland and Finnish model Eija Vehka Aho had gravitated towards the group, their outings had made quite the impression. 'Strong girls: that's what he wanted,' says Zatsch. 'He wanted everything to be youthful.' And that's how it stayed for the rest of his life. Karl was happiest when he was surrounded by young people. He found them infinitely more interesting than older people, and they in turn were more easily seduced by his charismatic charm.

In the 1970s, his 'trial and error' approach occasionally led to some rather bizarre scenes. In the Andy Warhol film *L'Amour*, a tank-top-sporting Karl Lagerfeld only kisses Patti D'Arbanville – but what a kiss! He moves his head from side to side, she grabs hold of his dark mane, and he appears to lick her rather than giving her a proper French kiss. One can only assume that Lagerfeld was a big fan of the director, otherwise why would such a self-contained fashion designer have agreed to make such a remarkable appearance in the film?

Andy Warhol had come to Paris in October 1970, looking for inspiration and with plans to shoot a film. It was going to be an eventful few months for this experimental artist, who found himself caught in the crossfire of two rival clans. There was Yves Saint Laurent and his clique on one side, and on the other there was Karl Lagerfeld, surrounded by all the young beautiful faces Andy already knew from the US. The German designer wanted to make sure the Pop artist was on his side, not in the orbit of Saint Laurent. Perhaps that was part of his motivation for offering up his flat on Rue de l'Université for the film shoot.

Accompanying Warhol from the Factory in New York was his business partner Fred Hughes, who introduced him to Parisian high society when they arrived. They were also joined by Paul Morrissey, a director Warhol had worked with on a number of his avant-garde films since 1965. Their new film, which they were originally planning to call *Gold Diggers '71* or *Les Beautés* or *Les Pissotières de Paris*,[144] was about two American women who had come to Paris in the hope of finding the right wealthy man to get them where they wanted to be. One of these women was Donna Jordan, who had recently appeared on the cover of French *Vogue* in a photograph taken by Guy Bourdin – the cover even makes it into shot in one of the scenes from the film. Her co-star was Jane Forth, who started out as a receptionist at the Factory and had just played the lead in Warhol's film *Trash*. Andy liked Corey Grant Tippin and got him on board as a makeup artist, so he was responsible for their physical transformation in the film.

Karl Lagerfeld was cast as one of the rich, young, heterosexual men: a German aristocrat.

The film was unwatchable: 'There was no script, not much plot, acting ability was thin and there was heavy reliance on improvisation with, at times, disastrous results,' Alicia Drake writes.[145] As the person who has explored this period in Lagerfeld's life most exhaustively, Drake doesn't seem to think too highly of the unscripted arthouse film. But in the end there was no need for performers to be embarrassed by the film: it was released in 1973 and fell into obscurity for four decades until, finally, various excerpts made it onto YouTube. Perhaps hardly anyone had seen the film before because no one made the effort to promote it properly. Or perhaps the film was a flop because the people who made it didn't really believe in it.

'Karl was relaxed during the shoot and thought it was all good fun,' says Corey Grant Tippin, who appeared in the film in addition to doing the makeup. 'He drove the plot forward. Andy needed actors like him because there was no script. Andy's films starred people like Brigid Berlin, who talked a lot and got things going. The rest of us waited for something we could react to when the cameras were rolling. And Karl was never short of something to say. That's why he was so important. That's what made Karl a superstar in this film.'[146]

Lagerfeld was less than complimentary about the whole episode later on. 'It was the most childish moviemaking ever,' he said.[147] Although he could do that kind of thing when he was younger, later in his life he said, 'Nowadays I wouldn't play anyone other than myself.'[148] He made fun of the kissing scene to make it less cringeworthy. But there is another way of looking at it: 'It was such an outrageous scene,' says Tippin. 'I'd never seen Karl kiss anyone before, and now all of a sudden here he was with all this intensity.' The kissing scene also suggests that Karl was only capable of public displays of intimacy if they were artistic, juvenile, or both at once.

The good times with Karl's extended American family could have gone on forever if two Frenchmen hadn't got in the way. Karl had started seeing Jacques de Bascher in 1972, and then there was

his rival Yves Saint Laurent, whose entourage was always collid-
ing with Karl's clique in Paris, almost as if they needed each other
to exist. The Americans gradually started noticing that things
were changing.

Corey Grant Tippin was friends with Clara Saint and Thadée
Klossowski de Rola, who were part of Yves's entourage and lived on
the corner of Rue Jacob. Clara Saint was famed for helping Soviet
ballet star Rudolf Nureyev escape the prospect of returning to Moscow
after meeting him in Paris. At Le Bourget airport on 16 June 1961, she
pushed the dancer into the arms of two *gendarmes* in the terminal
building to keep him out of the clutches of his KGB minders. The
French police officers held him back and stopped the Russian officers taking him back to Moscow with them on the plane. Saint, who
was born in Chile, worked as Yves Saint Laurent's press officer and
was in a relationship with Klossowski de Rola, the son of the painter
Balthus. The couple were part of the designer's innermost circle,
though they did not stay together. Thadée eventually married Yves's
muse Loulou de la Falaise; Clara only found out when she saw the
wedding announcement in *Le Figaro*.[149]

One night when the Americans were having dinner at La Coupole
in Montparnasse without Karl during the filming of *L'Amour*, Yves
Saint Laurent and Pierre Bergé walked into the restaurant.[150] It didn't
take long for fashion's power couple to fall for the Americans' charms:
soon enough, they invited the group – bar Karl – to a party they were
hosting in their apartment at 3 Place Vauban. The guest of honour was
Andy Warhol, whom Loulou de la Falaise and her mother Maxime
already knew from New York. The artist found a kindred spirit in Yves
Saint Laurent, who was also shy but brilliant. Warhol was prolific
in his output and earned a lot of money producing portraits for rich
people. In 1972, he painted a whole series for Yves Saint Laurent, with
his typical sceptical pose, which he sold for 25,000 francs.[151] He even
painted the designer's bulldog Moujik, not necessarily the prettiest
of subjects, in 1986. But not a single Warhol portrait of Karl Lagerfeld
was ever produced.

The evening in Yves Saint Laurent and Pierre Bergé's apartment was a colourful one indeed.[152] The actor Helmut Berger, who had risen to fame in Luchino Visconti's film *The Damned* in 1969, smoked opium with Omar Sharif, star of *Lawrence of Arabia* (1962) and *Doctor Zhivago* (1965). Pornography played on a television screen in one of the rooms. Some of the guests chased Saint Laurent's dog around the apartment, fuelled by drugs and alcohol. The French guests, among them Thadée Klossowski de Rola, thought the Americans were exhilarating. In his diary-like fragments, he wrote: 'Tippin and the women around Antonio Lopez and Karl, a little court / dazzling beauties / not ungraceful / fantastic dancers.'[153]

Donna Jordan and Corey Grant Tippin were getting increasing riled by their friend Patti D'Arbanville, who was sitting next to Berger on the sofa, coming on to him and bragging that he had given her his belt. Corey was high on Mandrax and feeling provocative, so he whispered into his friend's ear, goading her and adding fuel to the fire. Donna was like a loose cannon, ready to blow, and suddenly she sprang for the actress, shattering the glass coffee table and making Patti's hand bleed. 'She had to walk with a cane for the next few days; it was a good look,' says Tippin. 'But it was all soon forgotten. At the time Donna and I were living in a hotel together with Patti and Jay Johnson, the twin brother of Andy's partner Jed Johnson.'

Another incident involved Jay and Corey: 'Yves and Pierre invited us to Chez Minou with them. Jay had taken too many pills, and suddenly he passed out and collapsed at the table. Yves and Pierre were afraid of making a scene, so they got up right away and took us home. I'm sure that from then on they must have thought, they're a bit dangerous for us.' But these little scandalous episodes only served to make the Americans even more exciting. 'Pierre and Yves liked how I did Donna and Jane Forth's makeup,' says Corey. This prompted them to hire Corey as a consultant for the cosmetics and perfumes they were producing with US-based company Charles of the Ritz. 'For example, they sent me to the head office of Charles of the Ritz in New York to explain the latest looks. Pierre and Yves wanted things to be more international ... more skin colours, more diversity.' This was an important assignment for Tippin. Yves Saint Laurent's haute couture business was in deficit, and the profits from the beauty products and fragrances were making up for the losses, so it was a big responsibility. Yves was clearly satisfied with his work, and he even got the handsome Corey on board to model in the first show for his new menswear collection.

Saint Laurent was always the centre of attention. When Coco Chanel died in 1971, followed by Cristóbal Balenciaga in 1972 and Elsa Schiaparelli in 1973, he became the face of Parisian fashion. The new duplex apartment he and his partner had been living in at 55 Rue de Babylone since 1972 boasted a huge garden, and was a home fit for a head of state. Of course Karl Lagerfeld didn't show that he was bothered by any of this, even though he could tell that his eternal rival was reaching a whole new level. And the closer his American friends gravitated towards Saint Laurent's universe, the further they drifted from their German friend in Paris.

By this stage, Jacques de Bascher had entered Karl's life and was making his presence known to everyone around him. 'He came to Saint-Tropez one day in the summer of 1972,' says Corey Grant Tippin. 'He was very young and still finding his feet in Karl's world. He was annoying and got a lot of attention from Karl. Jacques was not cool. He dressed conservatively, like someone from an elite boarding school or a member of a fraternity.' Even his style looked foreign to them. The Frenchman was clearly proud of his aristocratic roots and was always talking about his family background. 'He observed how we dressed, and he copied us.' The Americans didn't even find him attractive. So what was it about Jacques, who had turned twenty-one years old that summer, that appealed particularly to older Frenchmen? 'As gay men, they felt less guilty being with Jacques: he came from a good background, and he wasn't just some gigolo you could pick up at a urinal,' says Tippin. 'Jacques was like a new project for Karl. He was educated, he was young, he looked good, he was the kind of person you could take along to any dinner party.'

Lagerfeld's friendship with the Americans gradually fizzled out in the heat of Saint-Tropez. Juan Ramos started seeing the painter Paul Caranicas in 1972, and Karl couldn't stand his new partner. 'He was jealous of my relationship with Juan, and he was angry that Juan and Antonio were slowly drifting away from him,' says Caranicas. He, in turn, thought the designer was superficial and obnoxious: 'Karl was very insecure and jealous of other people's talents. When we spoke about my work, for example, he only had disparaging things to say.'[154]

The Americans made it easy for Lagerfeld to go off them. 'Antonio and Juan, for example, stopped taking his calls,' Caranicas recalls. 'And we all made fun of his ridiculous ways of speaking and his mannerisms.' It all came to a head in Saint-Tropez after the pettiest of arguments in the summer of 1972. The boys were all intoxicated and wreaking havoc, and somehow Elisabeth Lagerfeld's aluminium chair ended up at the bottom of the swimming pool. 'She was furious, and Karl blamed Paul,' says Corey Grant Tippin. But according to Caranicas, it was actually Jacques who had thrown the chair into the water. Had Jacques passed the blame onto Paul in a bid to drive an even greater wedge between Karl and the Americans? Whoever was responsible for the pool incident, that was the last summer Karl spent with the Americans in Saint-Tropez. Because to add insult to injury, Juan and Paul gossiped about Karl the next day when they were in the bath, and outside one could hear every word ... and Karl happened to be outside. He lost his temper and kicked them out of the house. 'He never forgot about what happened,' says Tippin, 'not even at the end.'

Paloma Picasso – the illegitimate daughter of Pablo Picasso, who had died a few months earlier on 8 April 1973 – was another reason for the growing centrifugal forces at play. Karl took the jewelry designer with him to Plage de Tahiti in summer 1973, and she quickly became one of 'Antonio's People'.[155] With her dark, swept-back hair, her Frida Kahlo look, and her beautiful name, Paloma became a muse for Karl and his friend Helmut Newton. But he would have to share her, too, because of course Yves Saint Laurent was already working with her.

The Americans still went out a lot, albeit in different constellations. There was no way they were going to miss Karl's thirty-fifth (i.e., his fortieth) birthday in La Coupole, or Andy Warhol's vernissage on 22 February 1974, or the cocktail party in his honour at Rue de Babylone three days after the opening. Paloma, Yves, Pierre, Clara Saint, Jacques, Thadée and Karl were all photographed at the event together. In one of the pictures taken by Philippe Heurtault, Yves has his arm around Karl's shoulder. But even amicable displays like this had to be treated with suspicion; as far as Lagerfeld was concerned, they signalled a degree of condescension. 'The main problem was that Yves and Pierre had no respect for Karl's fashion,' says Ariel de Ravenel, who was friendly with both cliques. 'And Karl could sense it.'[156]

Le Sept became the stage for this friendship-cum-rivalry. Yves dined upstairs with his muses Loulou de la Falaise and Betty Catroux, not forgetting the rather sour-faced Pierre Bergé, whereas Karl's clan made some legendary appearances in the nightclub, often making a beeline for the dancefloor. Renate Zatsch, the slender beauty from the Rhine, was enjoying her new-found freedom; Donna Jordan, the pale star with a gap between her teeth, danced naked on the table; and Karl Lagerfeld, the voyeur, took it all in. Antonio Lopez worked his charms on the latest arrival: a long-legged Texan with flowing blonde locks. Jerry Hall fell head over heels, and he turned her into the model of the moment. The couple got engaged in Jamaica in 1975, during a fashion shoot for British *Vogue* with photographer Norman Parkinson and stylist Grace Coddington. But it didn't last long, and soon Jerry Hall moved on: first to Bryan Ferry, then to Mick Jagger.

Slowly but surely, the group was falling apart. Donna and Corey disappeared as swiftly as they had appeared. Antonio and Juan returned to New York at the end of 1975, and though they did see Karl occasionally over the years, it all ended on a sour note. Antonio was diagnosed with AIDS in the early 1980s, and he was trying to raise the money he needed for his treatment. He approached Karl in the hope that he could give him some paid illustration work, but Karl turned him down. Antonio's friend Bill Cunningham remembered the designer's response to his request: 'Well, my dear, supposing you get sick in the middle of the campaign and can't finish it?'[157] Paul Caranicas overheard the telephone call: 'Antonio just sat there on the floor, devastated.' And when in the early 1980s Lagerfeld arrived at The Pierre hotel on Fifth Avenue, where he was staying with his Chloé assistant Rosemarie Le Gallais, there was a letter waiting for him. He gave the letter to Le Gallais to read. It was from Antonio, and he was asking Karl for money. Le Gallais told him: 'Come on, you have to help him.' But Lagerfeld simply put the letter to one side.[158] Antonio waited in vain for a response and finally turned to the New York designer Oscar de la Renta instead. Bill Cunningham tells the story: 'Antonio went up to Oscar de la Renta and said, "Look, can we do a campaign for you?" And he said, "We may not be able to finish it." And they said "Do whatever you can."'[159] Was Karl being completely callous? Was this his way of exacting revenge on the Americans who had poked fun at him so often in the past? Or was he trying to drown out the reality of sickness and death again? 'Engaging with Antonio would have forced him to face up to Jacques's illness,' says Karl's former assistant Eric Wright. 'He already knew Jacques had contracted AIDS, and dealing with Antonio would only have made the illness a reality for him'[160] That was one truth he did not want to acknowledge. Antonio Lopez died of complications related to AIDS on 17 March 1987, aged forty-four.

Andy Warhol died in New York on 22 February 1987, just a few weeks before Antonio. His death was caused by complications following a routine gall bladder operation. Lagerfeld had learned from Warhol that a distinctive look can turn an individual into an icon, and that artist collectives could generate wonderful ideas. Wolfgang Joop met his fellow countryman in the mid-1970s: 'Karl Lagerfeld reminded me of Andy Warhol,' he writes. 'Isn't it true that they both surrounded themselves with a group of people who could experience all the excesses of life for them, while they kept themselves safe, like their own bodyguards? Sobriety was key to their creativity. Their art earned adulation and respect for the visible, the superficial, even the "impersonal".[161] Lagerfeld always brushed off any comparisons to the Pop artist. He wanted to be an original. 'First of all, I'm better groomed,' he said in 2007. 'And also he pushed people. I never push people.'[162]

Jacques

The first time he saw Karl Lagerfeld was at La Coupole in the early 1970s. The young Frenchman was sitting in the brasserie in Montparnasse when the fashion designer walked in with a group of friends including Antonio, Juan, Donna, Pat, Eija and Kenzo, the young designer from Japan who quickly became a star on the Paris fashion scene. Jacques later recalled the 'divine silence' that spread through the whole of La Coupole as the group made their entrance.[163] Karl was the central attraction. Even then, he oozed self-confidence. 'In that suspended moment,' writes Alicia Drake, 'Jacques saw a group of people living the life he yearned for.'

Soon enough, this dandy from the French aristocracy became Karl's partner – and he, too, was living a life many others yearned for. Lagerfeld liked the young man because he found him 'amusing': 'I was amazed by his nonchalance and his almost cynical lack of professional ambition. He never bothered studying. "I'm going to die young," he told me. "Why should I go to all that effort?"'[164] Opposites attract, clearly: 'We couldn't have been more different,' Lagerfeld said. So, in a strange twist of fate, this decadent Frenchman was the perfect match for the German workaholic. 'It just clicked,' Lagerfeld said.[165]

Jacques de Bascher liked the fact that his family had been ennobled by Louis XVIII in 1818 for their role in the brief restoration of the monarchy. He enjoyed flirting with the narrative that his family had fought against the troops of the First French Republic (1793–96) in the bloody uprising headed by the counter-revolutionary Royalist and Catholic army in the Vendée region. He also indulged his snobbery by making an addition to his surname: he called himself Jacques de Bascher de Beaumarchais, unlike the rest of his family, who were simply 'de Bascher'.[166] The surname was later cause for amusement in the upper echelons of Parisian society. People started to misappropriate the name and call him *de pas cher de bon marché*, a play on words meaning 'not expensive [but] cheap'.[167]

Jacques de Bascher was born on 8 July 1951 in Saigon (Ho Chi Minh City), where his father was working as the administrator of a Vietnamese province. Antony de Bascher left his governmental role in 1953 when he secured a job at Shell in Cambodia. At that point, Jacques's parents sent his three older siblings – Gonzalve (b. 1943), Elisabeth (b. 1944) and Anne (b. 1946) – to boarding school in France, while they stayed on in Cambodia with the younger children, Jacques and his brother Xavier. It was another two years before Antony and Armelle de Bascher followed them back to France: in 1955, they moved into the upmarket Parisian suburb of Neuilly-sur-Seine, where they lived on Boulevard du Commandant Charcot, on the edge of the Bois de Boulogne park. Antony de Bascher worked as the managing director of Shell's insurance department, while his wife Armelle raised their five children. They spent summers together at Château de la Berrière near Nantes. This family holiday home was less than 60 miles from Grand-Champ, where Lagerfeld would buy his own château in the mid-1970s.

Jacques wasn't fond of school. He transferred from the Lycée Pasteur in Neuilly to the Lycée Janson de Sailly in Paris's sixteenth arrondissement. He then attended the Lycée Charlemagne in the Marais, where writers such as Honoré de Balzac and Victor Hugo had gone before him. The teachers had trouble with him in various subjects. History: 'He draws attention to himself, but sadly not through his work.' German: his behaviour is 'unacceptable'. Mathematics: 'disrespectful and idle'.[168]

What he lacked in academic and professional ambition, he made up for in charm. Jacques was a beguiling young man – a good-looking daydreamer who dressed like a dandy. He was in a relationship with his English teacher at the Lycée Janson de Sailly, and he even managed

to 'convert' his fair share of sailors in the Navy.[169] After serving on
the high seas, he worked in the French Naval Ministry before briefly
testing the waters as a law student in 1971. But he was always more
concerned with his quest for sexual gratification, whether he was
relentlessly pursuing his next conquest at the Café de Flore, party-
ing at Le Sept, or having clandestine encounters in the Jardin du
Carrousel, between the Louvre and the Tuileries, where men have
been meeting in secret since the eighteenth century.

Jacques's reckless pursuit of pleasure prompted his younger brother
Xavier to write him an angry letter in November 1971, calling him
out for his narcissistic ways.[170] Did it make any difference? It's hard
to say. But one thing is for sure: Jacques de Bascher did try to hold
down a regular job in 1972 – for the first and last time in his life. He
worked as an air steward for Air France, but only for a short while.

This upper-class family was also rocked by the changes that
were taking hold in society following the actions of the *soixante-
huitards* who had propelled civil unrest in 1968. Jacques's sister,
Anne de Bascher, was one of the 343 feminists who signed Simone de
Beauvoir's 'Manifesto of the 343', which was published in the French
weekly news magazine *Le Nouvel Observateur* on 5 April 1971.[171] The
women who signed the petition, including Catherine Deneuve and
Jeanne Moreau, all admitted to past abortions and were now campaigning for more liberal legislation in France. They accomplished
their mission in 1975. The *Loi Veil* (Veil Law), named after health
minister Simone Veil, was finally introduced and abolished the
penalty for early abortions. The magazine headline inspired Alice
Schwarzer's campaign entitled *Wir haben abgetrieben!* (We've had
abortions!), which was published in *Stern* magazine on 6 June 1971
and sparked an acrimonious debate around paragraph 218 of the
German Criminal Code.

Anne de Bascher's brother was not particularly interested in
emancipatory movements like these, much to her disappointment.
Jacques was more concerned with tending to his own personal style
– a mix that was as original as it was daring. 'He borrowed from film

In honour of Andy Warhol: Jacques de Bascher, Karl Lagerfeld, Clara Saint and Fred Hughes are guests at a reception in Yves Saint Laurent's apartment on Rue de Babylone in February 1974.

stars of the 1930s and the decadent French dandies of the Belle Époque, but he also took cues from the rather eccentric Ludwig II of Bavaria, whom Helmut Berger portrayed in a peerless performance in Visconti's film,' writes historian Günter Erbe.[172] Jacques was fascinating in his own unique way: he was provocatively louche, curiously old-fashioned, and 'slightly diabolical', says Wolfgang Joop.[173] These traits appealed to Lagerfeld, who by now had gradually grown weary of the Americans' popular modern style.

The two men met by chance. It was 1972, and they were both out at Nuage, a small club owned by impresario Gérald Nanty, whom Lagerfeld knew through the fashion designer Valentino Garavani. The man behind the decks was Guy Cuevas, the Cuban DJ who would go on to gain legendary status at Le Sept. Jacques approached Karl and started talking. The twenty-one-year-old man about town was wearing traditional Tyrolean dress that night; no doubt this reminded the thirty-seven-year-old designer of his younger years, when he used to don lederhosen and Tyrolean hats. The pair stayed up talking until five in the morning.[174]

From then on, this bon vivant's lifestyle began to change dramatically. Lagerfeld took him along to his favourite tailors, Cifonelli and Caraceni, and ordered made-to-measure suits and shirts for him. 'We wanted to wear clothes that no one else had, shirts printed with my designs,' the designer said later on.[175] And instead of driving around in his family's Citroën 2CV, Jacques now cruised the streets in Lagerfeld's Rolls-Royce or his Bentley. Thadée Klossowski de Rola started referring to them in the plural: he calls them 'les Lagerfeld' in his diary.[176] The relationship, which would continue for around seventeen years, is unfathomably strange: the two men went out together and loved the free, easy-going conversation, regaling each other with ideas, anecdotes and rumours, but they didn't consummate the relationship.

Lagerfeld claimed that he never had sex with his life partner.[177] When Karin Joop-Metz asked him if Jacques was his lover, he said: 'Boys are fun, but if they want sex I tell them, go stand outside the barracks! If you let boys get too close, they'll ruin you.'[178] And when his old friend Victoire Doutreleau asked him if he slept with Jacques, he said: 'Are you mad? Never! Never with a man. I'm not fussed about it.'[179] Then again he also claimed, 'I've tried my fair share of both' in an interview in 1978.[180] As far as he was concerned, love and sex were not compatible. When asked on a German talk show if it was true that he said he wouldn't sleep with someone he loved, he said, 'That's the best thing you can do, really.'[181]

But perhaps this was all part of an attempt to protect his private life and sustain his aloof image. And perhaps he didn't want to besmirch the divine young Jacques with base physicality, bringing him down to earth with the rest of humanity. After all, this was a man who surrounded himself with beautiful male models such as Baptiste Giabiconi and Brad Kroenig in later years, men he viewed first and foremost as aesthetic ideals. Lagerfeld's long-time friend Patricia Riekel has a polite way of putting it. 'He was fine by himself.'[182]

The two men never lived together. Lagerfeld needed his space to read and be productive, while his young man about town needed the time to keep pursuing his conquests. Jacques lived in a 320 ft² apartment on Rue de Dragon, just around the corner from Boulevard Saint-Germain, a street full of cafés and brasseries that brought the promise of a meal and something for dessert. With such a generous partner looking after him, Jacques wanted for nothing. Occasionally he would even treat himself to a line of cocaine and a double Scotch before midday.[183] And he thought nothing of introducing his young friend Marc Rioufol to hard drugs in the mid-1970s: 'Hash is for poor people,' he said.[184] Rioufol developed a serious habit and cracked under the weight of his addictions. Decades later, despite returning to therapy repeatedly over the years, he took his own life.

Karl turned a blind eye to a lot of Jacques's exploits, or at least that was the impression he gave. 'He took things in his stride and loved that naughty child,' says Wolfgang Joop. 'He thought it was fantastic having someone "impossible", as he put it, around.'[185] It didn't seem to bother the designer that his boyfriend slept with other men. But it was a different story when Jacques and a female friend drove around Paris in his Rolls-Royce and started pulling up outside schools, inviting boys to join them in the back of the car and seducing them with champagne and more. De Bascher's friend Philippe Heurtault recalls how Lagerfeld reacted when he found out: 'I'm not paying anymore.'[186] They could be very harsh with one another – Jacques once called Karl a *sale boche* (filthy German) – but they were also affectionate. 'Jacques loved the money, but it was like living in a gilded cage,' says Heurtault. 'And he only got what Karl let him have, which wasn't always necessarily what he wanted.'[187]

Karl didn't like it when Jacques seduced women, either. But this Don Juan, who enjoyed the conquest at least as much as the act itself, broke down all boundaries of gender, age and shame. It was like a drug for him. Things became even more complicated when Yves Saint

Laurent came on the scene. By this point, the fashion designer had been professionally and personally involved with Pierre Bergé for so long that the relationship was beginning to lose its lustre. And when Jeanloup Sieff photographed him nude for 'Pour Homme', his first eau de toilette for men, Saint Laurent gained the status of an idol on the gay scene. Now this timid-looking but exceptionally tenacious designer had his sights set on the young aristocratic dandy who was already with Lagerfeld. Perhaps that was part of the attraction...

Clara Saint, who was friends with both groups, invited Jacques to a fashion show in the atelier on Rue Spontini in April 1973. Yves was smitten and kept sending the young man bouquets from Lachaume. Philippe Heurtault remembers that eventually there were so many flowers that they practically blocked the apartment entrance. The two men embarked on an affair that was dangerous in more ways than one: in their BDSM sex games, the fashion designer with a penchant for masochism let his young lover humiliate him, lock him in the wardrobe, and almost choke him to death, all in the name of sexual gratification.[188]

'It wasn't Jacques who suggested the games; Yves was the one who wanted it,' says Heurtault. He was Jacques's best heterosexual friend and knew him from their time in the Navy. 'You can't even imagine what he asked of me,' Jacques once told him. 'Eventually I did what he wanted.' Yves Saint Laurent was almost twice his age. 'That was his choice,' says Heurtault, 'but he was just crazy for Jacques.' Heurtault listened in on many of their conversations on Jacques's second handset, and even recorded some of them. He remembers one day when Yves called up the apartment sounding desperate. 'I'm losing my mind,' he said. 'The collection needs to be ready in three weeks but I can't do a thing.' Karin Joop-Metz remembers speaking to Jacques and him saying: 'I really loved Saint Laurent. I could have saved him.'[189] With all this going on, it makes complete sense to Wolfgang Joop that Karl Lagerfeld should have held his competitor in such low esteem: 'Karl bitched about Yves like a housekeeper.'

Sensing that his partner was drifting away from him, Pierre Bergé warned Saint Laurent and his friends to stop spending time in Jacques's company. On a night out at Le Sept, Bergé took Lagerfeld to one side and snapped: 'Keep your little whore away!' An indignant Lagerfeld replied, 'Yves is not your property!'[190] Heurtault remembers Bergé calling the apartment on Rue de Dragon one autumn day in 1975: 'If you don't end things with him, there's nothing I won't do,' he told Jacques. 'Really?' Jacques asked. 'Nothing at all?' Bergé's response: 'Nothing.'[191] Jacques was terrified. His cocaine habit was already making him paranoid, and Bergé's threat only made things worse.

Before long, Jacques was living like a king in Karl's old apartment at 6 Place Saint-Sulpice. The tall windows of the eighteenth-century building looked out onto Saint-Sulpice Church, which had been designed by the same architect. Lagerfeld had moved to the beautiful square because his mother was unhappy in the apartment on Rue de l'Université. He wasn't overly keen on it either: he was convinced it was under some kind of curse – not because of Andy Warhol's ill-fated film, but because of an apparition. Karl told his cousin Tita's daughter that the ghost of a lady who used to live there kept appearing. Apparently she would either be walking along the corridor or sitting at the end of the corridor in the kitchen.[192] 'Everyone who lived there after me died in mysterious circumstances,' he later wrote.[193]

The sprawling apartment in Place Saint-Sulpice, on the other hand, didn't seem to be haunted. Lagerfeld had even more freedom to indulge his passion for Art Nouveau here, and from 1973 he proceeded to fill the house with art and furniture from the 1920s. But before long he was done with this obsession, too, and his love for the eighteenth century took him back to Rue de l'Université. This time he moved into Pozzo di Borgo, the town house at number 51. Now Jacques used the apartment in Place Saint-Sulpice for some rather shady activities. In 1976, he hosted a party in honour of former Foreign Legionnaire and French National Front member Jean-Claude Poulet-Dachary. In the middle of the room was a Harley Davidson Sportster 1200. The designer had bought it for Jacques but banned him from

Glazed stare: Yves Saint Laurent only has eyes for Jacques de Bascher.
Artist David Hockney and Andy Warhol muse Nicky Weymouth look more relaxed.

riding it following an accident.[194] With nowhere to go, the Harley became a practical piece of furniture: Jacques turned the mirrors so they were pointing upwards, then he piled cocaine on top and left some razorblades and straws on the glass so that guests could help themselves.[195]

With over 3,750 ft² of real estate to play with, there was more than enough space for Philippe Heurtault to set up a small darkroom and develop his photographs in the apartment. One evening the doorbell rang; it was Yves Saint Laurent. Jacques wasn't going to let him in, but the designer wore him down by ringing the bell and making a racket. Through a crack in the door Heurtault could see him kneeling in front of Jacques in the next room: 'Please, please! Do whatever you want! I love you!' But Jacques replied: 'Please go, go, go! I don't want to die!' He threw Yves out, but by that point the residents had complained and the police had turned up, so Yves was forced to spend the night down at the station.

Despite the drama, the two clans tried their best to keep their cool in public. On 25 February 1974, the whole pack – Lagerfeld, de Bascher, Saint Laurent, Bergé – were seen out together at a party on Rue de Babylone. The men were all in good spirits, or at least they were putting on a good show. Just one of the photographs Philippe Heurtault took that night tells a different story. It shows a rather unsuspecting David Hockney on the left, listening dutifully to the young man whose portrait he was soon to draw in day-long sittings. While Jacques chats away, glass in hand, Yves stares at him intently, almost menacingly. That evening the designer was so inebriated that he kept rambling that he was a pariah and an outcast.[196] He also broke one of the narwhal tusks in the entrance to the apartment when he collapsed in a drunken stupor.[197]

Whether it was down to Pierre Bergé's relentless anger, Yves Saint Laurent's submissive behaviour, Jacques de Bascher's thirst for adventure or Karl Lagerfeld's intervention, Yves and Jacques ended their affair in 1975.

Jacques had an interest in the arts and he enjoyed watching films. He had also seen how the everyday could be transformed into art in the work of Andy Warhol. When Lagerfeld came up with the idea to shoot a promotional film for Fendi's first ready-to-wear collection in 1977, it was as if this was what he was always supposed to do. Jacques wrote the script and directed *Histoire d'Eau* (The Story of Water), the first fashion film in history. The film follows Suzy, a young American woman in Rome, as she writes to her mother in New York, all the while pretending that she is in Baden-Baden, Germany. In the postcards, she complains about the weather and says that she wishes she had brought more furs, she loves the spas, and she has bought herself a lovely cat named Karl. In actual fact, she is bathing in Rome's fountains, taking photographs and heading to Fendi to try on furs. At the end of the film, when the word 'END' appears on the screen, a letter 'F' floats over from the left and an 'I' joins from the right, spelling out the word 'FENDI'. Many years after his partner had passed away, Lagerfeld revisited the idea behind this playfully directed film and its many witty references: in 2013 he published *The Glory of Water*, a book of his own photographs of Rome's fountains. *Histoire d'Eau* is a play on the title of Anne Desclos's 1954 erotic novel, *Histoire d'O* (The Story of O), one of the best-known examples of sadomasochism in literature. Water, submission, dominance, eroticism: the title is full of connotations. Ultimately, the woman in the film is surrendering to the pull of consumerism. 'It must have been gruelling to film,' said Lagerfeld.[198] Jacques reportedly worked on the film for seventeen or eighteen hours a day. With finance from Fendi, and the assistance of one of Federico Fellini's cameramen, he had invented the concept of the fashion film, a genre that would inspire thousands of other works and imitators. Jacques was lucky enough to have a partner who could open any door for him, but he simply wasn't cut out for work and he chose to live a life of decadence instead. No doubt that didn't bother Lagerfeld; indeed, he preferred him that way.

Ultimately, Jacques well and truly surrendered to this life of decadence, celebrating gay liberation until there were no more boundaries left to push. Things had changed a lot from the comparatively innocent nights at Le Sept on Rue Saint-Anne. On 24 October 1977, he and Kenzo's partner, Xavier de Castella, took things to a much darker place when they hosted a party at La Main Bleue. The night was held 'in honour of Karl Lagerfeld', but apparently he wasn't the only one they were celebrating: 'Even before it started the party was a scandal, as word spread that Jacques had planned the night as an homage to Andreas Baader.' The Red Army Faction terrorist had killed himself in his cell at Stammheim, a maximum security prison in Stuttgart, a few days earlier on 18 October 1977.[199] But there were no visible tributes to the Baader–Meinhof leader on this dark night, just men in leather masks and military uniforms, fetish gear and sex acts on the open stage: '*très* hard', Kenzo later said.[200] Lagerfeld paid for everything and was delighted to have the chance to flirt with danger.

The designer's own 'Venetian Ball' on 12 April 1978, inspired by Truman Capote's Venetian parties, was positively mild by comparison.

The only one not in fancy dress is Andy Warhol: Karl Lagerfeld (centre, wearing a tricorn) hosts a Venetian ball with a Truman Capote theme at Le Palace in 1978. Paloma Picasso (in strapless dress) is among the guests.

He invited guests to join him for the event at Le Palace, which Fabrice Emaer had founded as the Parisian answer to New York's legendary Studio 54. The club had opened six weeks earlier and was instantly immortalized in Amanda Lear's disco hit 'Fashion Pack': 'In Paris you got to be seen at Maxim's / The Palace / The 7 and then go Chez Regine / Champagne / Caviar / Haute-[couture] / Expensive cars / Saint Laurent and Loulou / Rich ladies with a few bijoux.' The masked ball was quite a civilized affair in contrast to the debauched nights that were yet to come: Jacques de Bascher turned up dressed as the Rialto Bridge, *Vogue* editor Anna Piaggi wore a tray with a fish on it for a hat, and Paloma Picasso had the letters V, E, N, I, S, E sticking out of her hair. Lagerfeld wore a tricorn, and Andy Warhol donned ... a wig.

Paris and New York were the ultimate destinations for those in search of complete freedom in the 1970s. Whenever Karl and Jacques flew to New York, their first stop was Studio 54. The designer would head back to The Pierre hotel on Fifth Avenue early, while Jacques kept the party going in various shady clubs. Rosemarie Le Gallais recalls leaving her suite to dash off to the first meeting of the day with Lagerfeld, then bumping into Jacques on his way back from one such nocturnal adventure.[201]

There would be a price to pay for all the affairs, gang bangs and sadomasochism: an early grave. In 1981, a mysterious new immunodeficiency syndrome was identified in the United States. Then in 1982 growing reports of the disease followed from Europe, charting the spread of what was shockingly referred to as the 'gay plague'. Researchers at the Institut Pasteur in Paris isolated the virus in May 1983, and in the same year Klaus Nomi died after contracting the disease. The German countertenor, who was a friend of Antonio Lopez and had provided ambient music for Chloé's fashion shows, was one of the first celebrities to die of this new illness. AIDS mercilessly struck one victim after another: Michel Foucault died in 1984, then Antonio Lopez in 1987, Xavier de Castella in 1990, Halston in 1990, Tina Chow in 1992, Rudolf Nureyev in 1993, and Juan Ramos in 1995. All these people had socialized in the same clubs.

Even when everyone was talking about how deadly dangerous it all was, and even when old acquaintances stopped frequenting Le Palace, Jacques de Bascher and certain other friends continued to pretend that nothing had changed.[202] 'It was no longer a lifestyle. They were just hooked on sex and drugs,' his friend Ariel de Ravenel recalls.[203] 'When you've gone so far, so very far, too far, it's hard to turn back – sometimes impossible,' Lagerfeld reflected, many years down the line. He wrote that it was heartbreaking that his friends from the 1970s 'had so little time to live in this feverish, almost scary euphoria'.[204]

Jacques de Bascher received the fatal diagnosis in 1984. At first he only told his partner about it, but soon it was impossible to ignore how weak he had become. He retreated and put up with the treatments. Karl was with his partner much of the time, despite his intolerance for diseases, drawn-out illnesses and death. In 1985, the designer bought a house known as Le Mée, in Le Mée-sur-Seine, near Fontainebleau. This was where Jacques was to recover, and Karl, too. But in 1988, Jacques was taken to the Raymond-Poincaré hospital in Garches, to the west of Paris.[205] 'Karl visited him every day,' his assistant Eric Wright says.[206] Lagerfeld spent the last four nights of his partner's life sleeping on a spare bed in his hospital room. When Jacques de Bascher died on 3 September 1989, Karl was right by his side.

Even in those difficult days he managed to stay strong. 'It didn't take him long to get back into the office,' says Lagerfeld's long-time assistant Caroline Lebar. 'He was very disciplined. The reason he didn't show emotions wasn't that he had none; he just chose not to show them out of respect for others.'[207] Jacques was cremated. In accordance with his last will and testament, the ashes were divided up: one of the urns went to his mother, and the other was given to his life partner. Decades later, Lagerfeld said he was keeping it in a secret location along with his mother's ashes. 'One day my ashes will go in there, too.'[208]

Lagerfeld once described his relationship with Jacques as the kind of chance encounter that only happens 'once in a lifetime'. He wasn't looking for a 'second-rate replacement' after Jacques was gone. 'The same thing can never exist again, nor should it.'[209]

Germans

In 1973, two friends found themselves standing in the elevator of the building at number 12 of the upmarket shopping street Avenue Montaigne, opposite the Hôtel Plaza Athénée. They were Karl Lagerfeld and Helmut Newton, and by this point they had known each other for a long time. Both men were funny, razor-witted and cheeky – unusual traits for people from the fashion world to have. They cracked jokes in German and laughed, knowing that no one else could understand them.

Lagerfeld and Newton were on their way to a mini adventure. Newton was finally going to be introduced to Marlene Dietrich, a fellow Berliner. Their mutual Hamburg-born friend loved bringing the people in his life together, and he was eager to introduce the entrepreneurial photographer to Germany's biggest diva. 'He was like an excited schoolboy in the elevator that took us to Marlene's apartment,' Lagerfeld said. Apparently the actress had played quite the role in Newton's sexual awakening as a youngster in Berlin.[210] And now here she was, in person, opening the door to her guests. Lagerfeld thought she looked terrific. The summit of these three famous Germans was about to commence; it was just a pity it had to fail so spectacularly.

Three stars from the worlds of film, photography and fashion, all of them from Germany. It beggared belief. Just what was it that Germany had to offer in those popular artforms? The British interviewer Andrew O'Hagan was equally surprised when he interviewed the fashion designer in 2015: 'Lagerfeld spoke much more about Germany than I had expected.'[211] This was quite a typical reaction from British, American and French interviewers. For some reason, they just couldn't believe that this man – who came from Germany – never stopped being German, had lots of dealings with Germans, and often travelled to Germany on business. Of course he spoke about Germany a lot. Was he supposed to talk about England instead?

Rarely has one human being absorbed German culture with such intensity. Karl Lagerfeld was an avid reader of German literature and watched many German films, particularly the old ones. He was obsessed with designers and architects such as Peter Behrens and Konstantin Grcic, and he listened to all kinds of German music, from Richard Strauss to Lotte Lenya and Kraftwerk. He could often be found flipping through German magazines and newspapers, and he published whole books on German literature, cultural history and photography. He shot photographs for such magazines as *Stern* and German *Vogue*; he did illustrations for newspapers; he was acquainted with artistic directors, museum directors and editors; and, of course, he knew lots of actresses, including Veronica Ferres, Marie Bäumer and Diane Kruger.

When it came to German history, he was particularly fond of the first quarter of the twentieth century, before Nazism decimated the many cultural movements that were shaped by Jewish artists. 'My idea of Germany does not necessarily match up with the reality,' he once said. 'What I'm thinking of is the civilized Germany of Walther Rathenau, *Simplicissimus*, and the German avant-garde of Bruno Paul and Harry Graf Kessler. That's what my idea of Germany would be.'[212] He claimed he 'would never have gone to France' if post-war Germany had been anything like it was in the 1920s.[213] The vision of Germany he kept alive in his mind centred on the Berlin where Elisabeth Lagerfeld, Helmut Newton and Marlene Dietrich had all grown up, amid the fragile freedoms of the Weimar Republic.

Paris was where he came to know who he was as a German. He had left his homeland behind him while he was still very young. And like many young people who venture out into the world to work or study, he had no great longing for home when he was still finding his feet in his new life. In the 1950s he was busy getting settled in France, and then in the 1960s he was carving out a career for himself. But the older he got, the more he became aware of his roots. 'I am completely German,' he once said.[214] And he was no longer ashamed of it: when *Vogue* editor-in-chief Carine Roitfeld told him that her father liked Hildegard Knef, he immediately sent her a stack of CDs by the singer.[215] Familiarity breeds self-assurance. Lagerfeld regularly worked with Germans, and he loved every aspect of German culture, even the brash side: yes, he did pose next to a Christmas tree dripping with silver tinsel in the 1980s.

Marlene Dietrich embodied many of the designer's German obsessions. The actress, born in 1901 in Berlin, had risen to international fame after starring in *The Blue Angel* (1930), becoming one of the few German stars in Hollywood. Though her glamour faded a little over the years, Dietrich's effortless Berlin wit, incisive sharpness and relaxed style still appealed to Lagerfeld: 'She only ever wears jeans and men's shirts,' he said in 1973, 'but sometimes I bring her an old pyjama-style mock-up from Chloé.'[216]

Even then, Dietrich was in her own world. The apartment she was living in looked out onto the exclusive avenue, but later she was forced to move into a cheaper apartment with views at the back instead.[217] Still, she had a lot in common with the two men standing in front of her. 'Things were the same for Karl Lagerfeld as they were for Marlene Dietrich: they had both outgrown Germany,' says Princess Gloria von Thurn und Taxis, who could clearly empathize with this predicament. 'Germany was too small for them.'[218] Now even Paris was getting too small for this diva. When French *Vogue* decided to publish a special issue dedicated to her in December 1973, Lagerfeld was asked to step in. He showed her a series of pictures by each of the photographers being considered by *Vogue*. The magazine was asking for new images, so it was up to Dietrich to decide who she wanted to take the photographs. Dietrich chose Helmut Newton over Guy Bourdin and told Lagerfeld, 'I'd like to meet him.' Lagerfeld agreed and said he'd be happy to bring him over sometime.[219]

Helmut Newton was excited. The son of a Jewish button-factory owner, he was born in Berlin in 1920 and forced to emigrate in 1938, eventually ending up in Australia. Now, in his early fifties, he was looking forward to reminiscing about pre-war times in Berlin, when he worked as an apprentice for the German photographer Yva. The encounter got off to a rather unspectacular start, however. Newton was suffering from heart problems, so medical matters dominated the conversation. But then all of a sudden things got a bit more interesting. Dietrich wanted Lagerfeld to tell her if the trousers that fashion designer André Courrèges had sent suited her. 'That day, Marlene was wearing a body stocking made from Lycra jersey and nothing but a leather wraparound skirt on top, whose snap buttons she suddenly ripped open,' Lagerfeld recalled. All of a sudden she was exposed from the waist down. Newton's impulsive reaction: 'The legs are still great!' This comment backfired on the photographer: the seventy-one-year-old diva threw him out.[220]

The sole encounter between the photographer and the film star was a complete flop. The new pictures for Paris *Vogue* never materialized, so the magazine had to rely on old material. The cover for the December 1973 issue was black, with the words 'Par Marlene Dietrich' written in gold. The photographs inside had all been taken in her heyday.

It was all too much for the hapless go-between Karl Lagerfeld, who decided he wanted very little to do with Dietrich from that point on. All the same, he continued to wear the gift she had once given him: a gold Cartier pin from 1937.[221] 'Karl only had bad things to say about her,' says Peter Bermbach. 'He broke off contact with her.'[222] At that stage, he could no longer see her as the sophisticated woman she once was. This lady talked too much about the geraniums outside her window and the pigeons she was always trying to chase away with a water pistol. Soon she became a complete recluse. The former actress, now suffering from muscle atrophy, was always at home and refused to let anyone look at her in the final years of her life. Her existence was shrouded in mystery: nothing from this woman's private life entered the public domain. Her parting gift to Lagerfeld before she passed away in 1992 was an important lesson. She taught him that discretion was close to myth, and he was rather taken with the idea.

When Helmut Newton died on 23 January 2004, he ended up strangely close to the woman he had dreamed of in his younger years. By the strangest of coincidences, the photographer's grave is just a few feet from Marlene Dietrich's resting place in the graveyard at Friedhof Stubenrauchstrasse, a small cemetery in Berlin-Friedenau. Lagerfeld was surprised to discover that his old friend had been buried there of all places in 2004. The two of them hadn't got along while they were alive, and now they were going to be forced to spend eternity side by side. He was scandalized, arguing that his friend had been buried in the wrong plot.[223]

His reaction was, not for the first time, a bit over the top. The photographer's widow, June Newton, had nothing against the two famous Germans being buried so close together. Especially since the house at 24 Innsbrucker Strasse, where the young Helmut Neustädter was born and raised before he emigrated and became Helmut Newton, was roughly half a mile away.

These three German legends just couldn't seem to escape each other, even in the afterlife. Lagerfeld became close to the German diva again in his own way: through fashion. When his last ready-to-wear collection was unveiled in March 2019, after his death, many of the models took to the runway wearing Marlene trousers.

Château

Wolfgang Joop and his wife Karin were in town for Haute Couture Week in July 1975. They had already worked on collections in Germany, but here in Paris they were on assignment for the national Sunday newspaper *Welt am Sonntag*: he did the illustrations, and she wrote the content. As far as they were concerned, Yves Saint Laurent was god. Still, that didn't make them any less excited to run into Karl Lagerfeld and his entourage on the street one day. The Joops were around thirty years old, and they looked striking, wearing – by German standards – outlandish clothes. Lagerfeld asked who they were; they began to talk, and they instantly hit it off. Lagerfeld, a man of fast decisions, invited them to spend the weekend at the château he had just bought in Brittany.

The already established designer and the younger couple had a lot in common, particularly when it came to their love of old Prussia. Lagerfeld sketched his guests as they sat across from him at the dinner table in the château. He looked at Wolfgang and said: 'I'm drawing a Prussian squire with a cigarette.' In these aristocratic surroundings, Lagerfeld talked about Menzel's *Round Table* and how he had longed to own the painting as a boy. What a coincidence: as a child, the little Wolfgang had often wandered around the large park at Sanssouci Palace on visits to his Aunt Ulla in the Potsdam borough of Bornstedt.[224]

Château de Penhoët was like a small-scale Sanssouci, and could easily pass for the residence of a noble Breton family. By owning it, Lagerfeld was edging closer to his ideal of courtly life. A long driveway leads up to the large iron gate, providing a rather deceptive view of the château from the front. The imposing scale and depth of the

His mini Sanssouci: Château de Penhoët in Grand-Champ, Brittany,
became Karl Lagerfeld's weekend retreat in the mid-1970s.

property are only revealed from the left-hand side, over the high wall
that Lagerfeld had built after he bought the property. With dozens
of rooms, there was plenty of space for weekend visitors.

Back in Paris, Lagerfeld had moved into a 10,750 ft² apartment at
51 Rue de l'Université. In the building that formerly housed the Pozzo
di Borgo hotel on the Left Bank, and here in his new country château,
he was free to indulge his passion for the eighteenth century. He saw
the exuberance of pre-revolutionary France as a welcome contrast
to the vile modernism that was dominating the worlds of art and
architecture in the 1970s. It was also perfect for Jacques de Bascher,
who encapsulated the era with his counter-revolutionary bloodline
and his anachronistic attire.

Eager to delve deeper into the eighteenth century, Lagerfeld must
have been happy that the château was in dire need of renovation.
The outbuilding was dilapidated, the garden was overgrown, and the

château itself was in serious disrepair. The designer set to work on his new project, reading historical literature, sifting through auction catalogues, consulting experts, and drawing up plans. His friend Patrick Hourcade says that the Hôtel de Crozat on Rue de Richelieu in Paris, whose bed chamber and gallery hall had been immortalized in one of the famous snuffboxes by Louis-Nicolas Van Blarenberghe in around 1770, was a major source of inspiration. Lagerfeld adored the miniature painting, just as he adored the eighteenth century. Echoing his earlier obsession with Art Nouveau, he proceeded to immerse himself in the era for the best part of twenty-five years, until the turn of the new millennium, when he decided to leave the past behind him and live only in the future.

Patrick Hourcade, who had studied art history, helped Lagerfeld to create the desired interior effect. He went on a hunt for suitable pieces at auctions and antique shops, and came away with a treasure trove of furniture, porcelain, bronze sculptures, vases, tapestries and paintings. The haul included Louis XV chairs by Nicolas Heurtault, Jean-Baptiste Tilliard and Louis Delanois, vases by Rouillé de Boissy, and bronze wall lamps by Jacques Caffieri, as well as paintings by Jacques de Lajoüe, Jean-Marc Nattier, Jean-Honoré Fragonard and Philippe de Champaigne. To recreate the setting of a baroque garden, Lagerfeld also had orange trees and decorative boxwood planted outside.[225]

Jacques de Bascher spent a lot of time at the château. He had time to kill, so why not do it there? Lagerfeld rarely stayed for long: he would take the train to Vannes, then hop in a taxi or get Jacques to pick him up and take him to the château. When he arrived, he would check on the progress of the construction work and consult with the architects, gardeners and various tradespeople, then the next day he was off again. The locals were charmed by the new owner of the Grand-Champ estate when he donated 50,000 francs to build a new library. The 'Golden Book' of Grand-Champ contains a picture he drew of the town hall to mark the occasion of a 'wonderful soirée on 18 September 1987'. He also supplemented the tradesmen's wages with bottles of Chloé perfume, though not all of them had a use for the gift.[226]

Lagerfeld succeeded in bringing the château back to life. The whole place was quite literally blossoming. One of the frequent visitors was *Vogue* contributor Anna Piaggi, who became one of Lagerfeld's muses with her eccentric style and distinctive hats adorned with flowers. The Italian fashion writer took hours getting ready before emerging in the most outrageous of outfits, which, of course, Lagerfeld just had to sketch. The locals couldn't quite believe their eyes when Lagerfeld's friends were in town; for example, when Jacques went out for coffee in Grand-Champ wearing a white suit and a Panama hat, or when walkers spotted several guests wandering around the local park in vintage silk coats. Sometimes they even mistook the lord of the manor for the popular Greek singer Demis Roussos, who, like Lagerfeld, had a thick head of hair and a dark beard.[227]

When Karin and Wolfgang Joop accepted Lagerfeld's offer and joined him at the château for the weekend, there was something they couldn't quite get their heads around. While they were there, they met a man named José, whom Lagerfeld had appointed to look after the accounts at the château. Jacques referred to the man as his 'cousin', and had altered his name to make him sound aristocratic: José-Maria Bazquez-Sarasola became José Basquez de Sarasola.[228] José's parents, who were in fact middle-class, originally came from Spain and had moved to the Nantes area, so José had grown up fairly close to the château that was owned by the Bascher family. Karin and Wolfgang joined Jacques and José on the beach, while Karl stayed at the house and continued to work on his sketches. 'José wanted to be close to us, that much was clear,' says Karin Joop-Metz. 'He kept following me around all the time. I found it very strange.'[229] Did he want to tell them a secret? Had he fallen in love with one of them? Was he in dire straits?

If they thought the mild-mannered young man with dark hair was odd, then his 'cousin' Jacques was positively sinister by comparison. He waxed lyrical to Karin about Baron Gilles de Rais, one of the worst serial killers in history. During the fifteenth century, the notorious baron tortured and murdered more than a hundred children in Machecoul, Brittany, just 60 miles from Grand-Champ. As if the topic of conversation weren't creepy enough, he then summoned the two visitors into his room and proceeded to pull a trunk out from under his bed. The trunk was full of newspaper and magazine cuttings showing young men in tight jeans. Only the middle sections of the photographs remained: Jacques had snipped off the heads, arms and legs. 'It was his special collection, I guess,' says Karin Joop-Metz. Wolfgang Joop also recognized photos he had seen in a report about a paraplegic in *Stern* magazine. He believed the bizarre demonstration could only mean one thing: 'He wanted to give us a glimpse into his sexual fantasies.'

The Joops took the train back to Paris with Lagerfeld on the Sunday, and said goodbye to their new friend at the station. Lagerfeld had to get back to keep working on his Chloé collection before the holiday season began in August, so he couldn't hang around for long.[230] Within a few short weeks, tragedy struck in Brittany. Some money went missing from Grand-Champ, and the finger was pointed at José as the one responsible for the accounts. The twenty-eight-year-old tried to deny it, but there was no convincing Lagerfeld.[231] On 26 August 1975, José threw himself under a train close to Vannes. The locals believed that the train that killed him was the one that Karl and Jacques had boarded at Vannes on their way back to Paris. In fact, the young man had thrown himself under the train travelling in the opposite direction.[232]

The Joops were baffled by their new friend Karl's behaviour later that year, in the autumn. They were shocked when they heard about the suicide. Karl just dropped it into conversation after the Chloé show and was very offhand about the whole thing, almost as if he found it amusing. 'Jacques had to identify him, and the only way of doing it was with a toenail,' he said. They thought the way he talked about it was cold and brutal – repulsive, even. 'He sent me a gorgeous scarf afterwards,' says Karin Joop-Metz, 'but it was like a switch had gone off and I lost all admiration for him.'

They stayed loosely in touch for a while. The next time Wolfgang was in Bornstedt, he bought all the East German books he could find about Potsdam and sent them over to Lagerfeld. But eventually their friendship petered out. The encounter between Germany's foremost male fashion designers would last only a fleeting moment in fashion history. Both men had turned their backs on the ugly post-war era in their homeland, choosing instead to abscond into the realm of fantasy known as Prussia. Both had sought salvation from the devastation wrought by Nazism by immersing themselves in a bygone era. But now that chapter was finally over, as was their friendship.

Joop and Lagerfeld exchanged biting remarks and vicious criticism in the media over the decades. In an interview in 2011, Lagerfeld had a few final disparaging things he wanted to say about Joop: 'His drama is that he's not me. No one knows him internationally. He can imitate everything well enough, but he has no style of his own.'[233] It was an interesting theory, but it wasn't true. Joop had created his own signature style long before, through his Wunderkind label, and he, too, was in no small way inspired by Prussia.

The legend of Prussia lived on at Château de Penhoët, especially when Elisabeth moved in. Having left Germany for Paris to be with her son in the spring of 1968, she was perhaps closer to him now than ever before. Nannies often looked after the children in Bissenmoor and Hamburg, but after moving to France Elisabeth didn't stray far from Karl's side. She was the only person Karl ever lived with. Apparently Antonio Lopez found her so fascinating to look at that he felt compelled to sketch her as she sat on the sofa reading the German press.[234] It was an intimate mother–son relationship. Karl affectionately referred to her as *Wollmaus* (wool mouse) because she had once worn a thick woollen coat, and the Americans thought the word sounded funny.[235] Despite the sarcastic tone, Elisabeth's pride in her son shines through in a letter to her sister in 1972: 'The crazy boy has only gone and grown himself a beard. Imagine! Well, the hair grows very fast on him. You would think Grandpa had climbed out of the picture frame.'[236]

Karl was a busy man and didn't have time to look after his mother himself. 'He is irrepressible when it comes to work, like his father,' Elisabeth wrote in a letter to her sister in the summer of 1969.[237] She was stuck at home with one of the staff in the daytime and hardly knew a soul in Paris, so who was she supposed to turn to for company? The model Renate Zatsch, who occasionally worked for Karl, popped round for a chat: 'She was happy when I came to visit, because I was German like her.'[238] Peter Bermbach also visited the old lady a couple of times at Lagerfeld's request. 'I talked to her about her son, about the weather, or about Germany.'[239] But he avoided going out in public with her at all costs: 'She wore a turban and dressed like a circus princess.' Her attire was a step too far for the cultural journalist. 'When the hairdressers were away at war, German women used to wear turbans to cover up their hair. But in the 1960s no one would be seen dead walking through Paris with a turban on at four in the afternoon. To do so made people think of the disgraced actress Arletty, who had fallen out of favour after the war and was branded a *collaboratrice* following her relationship with an officer from the German air force during the occupation.'

Elisabeth no longer had the Americans for company, now that their joint holidays in Saint-Tropez were a thing of the past. In a letter to her sister in April 1974, Elisabeth wrote: 'Mule & I have no great desire to go to Saint-Tropez.' Evidently the pet name from Karl's childhood had stayed with him into adulthood. 'The crowd isn't what it used to be these days. He's thinking of selling the apartment and buying something in Brittany instead. Just like his father: always buying and selling. It makes me laugh.'[240]

Brittany was also starting to look like a sensible prospect for this increasingly frail old lady, who had been complaining about health issues more and more in recent years. In a letter from 1972, she says that Karl is the one struggling: 'Mule has lower back pain, which he gets every couple of years.'[241] Then, in 1974, her own health was the problem: 'This darned high blood pressure is most unpleasant... Walking is even harder than it used to be: my legs are like lead.'[242]

There is also a letter to her sister dated April 1976, which she sent from the hospital after suffering a stroke. In her spidery script, she writes that her left leg and her left arm are 'unfit for work', and Karl has 'visited every day'.[243] When Karl had to travel to Italy for the Fendi show and couldn't visit his mother at the American Hospital in Neuilly, he sent Rosemarie Le Gallais in his place. The assistant told Elisabeth that she had just spoken to her son, and apparently the show had been a great success. A rather nonplussed Mrs Lagerfeld simply said, 'What's new?'[244] Rosemarie was not impressed by the flippant response.

Eventually Elisabeth retreated to the château in Brittany, where she spent most of her days reclining on the sofa in her own private quarters. Jacques was often at Grand-Champ with her, and they got along well. But whenever her son turned up in the company of Anna Piaggi or other guests, Elisabeth failed to make an appearance. Pilar and Rafaël, the Spanish couple entrusted with her caretaking duties, were always around to attend to her needs.[245] 'She would ring the bell if she so much as dropped her handkerchief – and she had been doing that for eighty years,' her son once said. That explains why the home help were allegedly paid three times their usual salary.[246] There was nothing for Elisabeth Lagerfeld to miss about Paris. She had hardly made any friends there, and she never went to her son's fashion shows. It was nothing new; she had never visited his father in his office, either.[247]

In the late summer of 1978, a good two years after the stroke that had seriously affected her health, Elisabeth found herself bothered by a persistent cold. She made an appointment for her hairdresser to come to the château on the morning of Thursday 14 September, before the doctor was due to visit to prescribe medication for the cold. The freshly groomed eighty-one-year-old died that same day, just as the doctor arrived.

Karl had turned forty-five just four days before his mother passed away. That Thursday he was at Wibor in Mönchengladbach, where he was attending the fittings for his Karl Lagerfeld Impression line.

He was sitting next to his assistant Rosemarie Le Gallais when he was summoned to the telephone. Le Gallais was already expecting the worst when he left the room. 'When he came back in, he sat down next to me and took my hand and squeezed it. Then I knew for sure.' He took the news incredibly calmly. He scribbled a note on a slip of paper: 'Let's just keep going. I don't want anyone to find out about this.'

When they flew back to Paris from Düsseldorf that evening, Le Gallais offered her support: 'I can go with you to Brittany tomorrow if you like.' But Lagerfeld didn't take her up on her offer: 'You don't have to do that. I'm not going either.' Apparently his mother had said that not even her son should attend her funeral.[248] He also claimed, at a later date, that she had left a note saying she didn't want her son to see her dead.[249] Lagerfeld did what he was told, and he stayed away – just as he had done eleven years earlier, when his father passed on.

The only people to attend the cremation were Pilar and Rafaël. According to Lagerfeld, his mother was buried in the private chapel at the château, but locals claim that her ashes were scattered in the forest behind the building. Either way, Elisabeth Lagerfeld's final resting place was in the town of Grand-Champ in the department of Morbihan, some 685 miles as the crow flies from her late husband, who was buried in the Lutheran Nienstedten Cemetery on the Elbchaussee.

Château de Penhoët lost its meaning for Lagerfeld when Jacques passed away in 1989. The designer even claimed that he never went back, even though he held on to the château for at least ten years.[250] He did return for one last special occasion in June 1990, when he opened the doors of his mini Sanssouci to welcome a royal visitor from England. The lord of the manor and his guest of honour, the Queen Mother, drank tea together in the garden, stood next to a table with a huge pyramid of colourful macarons atop a white tablecloth, and marvelled at the beautiful flowers on display. But this would be almost a farewell visit. Lagerfeld sold the château in the 1990s and had much of the furniture moved to Pozzo di Borgo and his retreat in Le Mée-sur-Seine. And with the money he made from what had been his favourite pastime in the 1970s, he paid off the tax debts he had accumulated over the years.

Interiors

Matteo Thun was busy designing a hairdryer for Wella in his studio in Milan one morning in 1981 when he heard a voice call out to him from the showroom: 'There's a German here. Could you come over?' The young designer was in for a shock when he walked into the showroom: standing there was none other than Karl Lagerfeld. One of Thun's friends from Milan, Anna Piaggi, had told Lagerfeld that he should drop in on the Memphis design collective while he was in the area. Lagerfeld asked Thun which item of furniture he would recommend. 'We still hadn't sold a single thing at that point,' says Thun. 'So with a courage born out of desperation I said, just buy it all!'[251]

The Memphis Group had been founded in December 1980 by Ettore Sottsass, Matteo Thun, Michele De Lucchi and various other designers. The collective took its name from the capital city of Ancient Egypt and Elvis Presley's birthplace in Tennessee; and, like the late Elvis, these designers were intent on shaking things up. Form ceased to follow function in these designs, with their erratic lines, abstract shapes, and colours bright enough to bring tears to the eyes of a Bauhaus fan like Karl Lagerfeld.

Always ahead of the curve, Lagerfeld was excited by what he saw. No doubt he could see the dawn of a new post-modern era on the horizon, or at least a shift away from minimalism in the 1980s. The designer was also happy to have found the perfect furniture for his new apartment in Monte Carlo. He had never lived in a modern building before and hadn't the slightest idea how to furnish it, he later said. Memphis was just what he was looking for, and he did indeed want it all.[252]

Lagerfeld turned to Matteo Thun and told him: 'Package it all up and send it on to me in Monte Carlo.' Thun couldn't believe what he was hearing. 'It was our salvation; it was incredible.' The movement

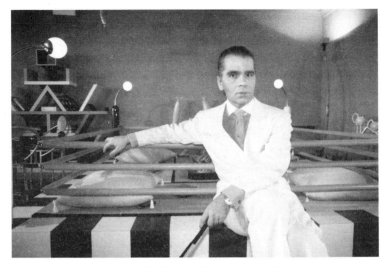

In the style of the times: Karl Lagerfeld decorated his Monaco apartment
with Memphis Group furniture in the early 1980s.

had been attracting a lot of interest, but nothing had sold until
Lagerfeld came along. Sottsass and Thun were still spending their
days working for industry clients and had to save their Memphis
designs for the evenings. 'I pre-financed all the ceramics,' Thun says.
So as well as providing an all-important morale boost, the Paris-
based designer's spending spree also gave them the financial support
they so desperately needed. He spent 65 million lire on Memphis
products, roughly the equivalent of £30,000 (US$42,500). 'Ridiculous,
when you think about it,' Thun says. 'But that was a huge amount
of money in 1982.'

Matteo Thun and interior designer Andrée Putman helped
Lagerfeld to furnish his apartment in Le Millefiori, one of the tallest
buildings in Monaco. The black floors, grey walls and black-and-white
Helmut Newton photographs were practically begging for a bold
injection of colour in the form of several key pieces: the Suvretta

shelf by Sottsass, Riviera chairs by Michele De Lucchi, Marco Zanini's Dublin sofa and George James Sowden's Unknown table. Lagerfeld chose not to stay in the apartment and kept it as a kind of show-home. He posed for photographs in his shrine to Memphis, which helped to promote the design collective while also boosting his image as a design connoisseur.

It was a short-lived affair, not as enduring as his passion for Art Nouveau or eighteenth-century furniture. He decided to auction off his collection through Sotheby's in October 1991, parting with more than a hundred items of furniture and ornaments. An unusual display cabinet in wood and plastic by Ettore Sottsass went under the hammer for 120,000 francs, while Helmut Newton paid 48,000 francs for one of the designer's totemic Carlton room dividers. Lagerfeld had succeeding in sniffing out a trend early on, then distancing himself as soon as everyone else had caught on and was paying top dollar for the pieces. Net earnings from the auction: 1.593 million francs (some £220,000/$US310,000).[253]

Lagerfeld also took advantage of the 1991 Sotheby's auction to sell various items of furniture and objets d'art from his Art Deco collection. With a bid of 550,000 francs, a Japanese buyer paid the highest price for a *Vase de tristesse* (c. 1900) by ceramic artist Émile Gallé. The Centre Pompidou secured seven important pieces of furniture by Eileen Gray from her E-1027 house in Roquebrune – including a Transat chair in wood and synthetic leather (c. 1929) – for 340,000 francs. A private German museum offered 160,000 francs for the E-1027 table, which had been estimated to sell for a maximum of 60,000 francs.[254]

Karl Lagerfeld was a man who acted on impulse and made radical decisions. This also extended to his choice of furnishings and interior design. 'I'm a fashion person,' he explained. 'I change clothes, furniture, houses, collections. Life is about change. There is a moment when things cannot become any better; then you change.' This was no great sacrifice for him: 'I have no sense of possession.'[255] The designer was always looking for new projects and ditching old ideas,

At Rue de l'Université: Karl Lagerfeld recreated the feel of the
eighteenth century in his town house (1983).

and he adopted the same approach to his interior furnishings. There
would be no rest for his assistants, or for the removal firms, furniture
packers and warehouse workers. Even when Lagerfeld found a style
he liked, he had the pieces shunted back and forth between Paris,
Grand-Champ, Monaco, Le Mée, Hamburg, Biarritz and warehouses
until the picture was finally complete ... and began to bore him.

Lagerfeld took his passion for the eighteenth century to a whole
new level in Paris. His love for the era, which was ignited when he
set eyes on the Menzel painting as a boy, was now reflected in a vast
collection that continued to grow. He recalled his first investment
– a pair of gilded French Régence chairs, re-upholstered in yellow

suede – taking pride of place by the windows of the ground-floor apartment he lived in on the Quai Voltaire in the early 1960s, along with a Louis XVI chest of drawers between the windows.[256] His old friend Peter Bermbach has no recollection of any Régence chairs in the apartment, however, so it is quite possible that Lagerfeld didn't acquire them until later on. Perhaps the designer just projected the chairs back into the apartment in his mind. In any case, it is clear just how important furniture like this was to him.

Though Louis XIV furniture was popular among collectors, Lagerfeld preferred the more refined Louis XV style and the transition to Neoclassicism. As far as he was concerned, the later designs achieved a level of 'comfort, elegance and a way of life that remains unsurpassed to this day'.[257] The generously proportioned town house on Rue de l'Université, built in the era of Louis XV, was the perfect place to retreat into the past. Its nearly 15-foot-high ceilings, magnificent wall panellings, intricate chased brass door fittings and stunning ceiling frescoes were an extraordinary setting in which to display all the antique treasures he had amassed.[258] Lagerfeld had in his possession probably the most extensive collection of paintings by Jacques de Lajoüe. The rococo artist's imaginative garden scenes had served as the inspiration for the renovation work in the gardens at Grand-Champ. With his unusual painted scenes, this master of the *genre pittoresque* was a fellow aficionado of the *fête galante*. Lagerfeld was a glutton for Lajoüe's pastoral scenes and allegorical depictions. He repeatedly returned to the style in his own work, recreating the atmosphere of an idyllic rendezvous for his fashion shows and echoing the antique style in the *mise-en-scènes* for his photography series.[259]

Pozzo di Borgo was regal in character, like a mini château in central Paris. The large hall was a wonderful venue for private dance lessons and large gatherings. Journalist Godfrey Deeny remembers one of the dances the designer hosted there in the mid-1990s. The event was attended by many famous faces from the fashion world, including Gianni Versace and German supermodel Nadja Auermann. 'It was a wonderful evening with lots of Latin American music, which he loved,' says Deeny. 'Karl danced a lively rumba with Kate Moss, even though he was still carrying extra weight at that time.'[260]

The urban mansion and the château in the country were like playgrounds for expensive furniture, and so the designer amassed a great deal over the decades. When the auction catalogue was issued in April and May 2000 in Monaco and New York, it spanned almost a thousand pages and three separate volumes. It was an astounding range of collector's items, with one hundred and fifty paintings and four hundred pieces of furniture and fixtures. Among the lots for sale were the designer's Louis XV tulipwood dressing table, bronze Louis XVI candelabras, and an ornately decorated knotted-pile carpet from the Savonnerie manufactory. Left with an empty house when the auction ended, Lagerfeld prepared to face the future with white sofas and flat-screen monitors.

One of the advantages to having so many homes was the scope for metamorphosis. New apartments offered new backdrops for fashion shoots, interviews and film shoots. Andy Warhol had used the first apartment on Rue de l'Université for his film *L'Amour*. A commercial for Chloé perfume starring Stéphane Audran was shot in Lagerfeld's property in Place Saint-Sulpice, and Anouk Aimée also made an appearance there in the 1978 film *Mon premier amour*.[261] The historic Monte Carlo villa known simply as La Vigie (meaning 'the lookout tower') in Monaco was the best setting of all for photo shoots. Originally built for British publishing tycoon William Ingram in 1902, this three-storey cuboidal mansion is perched on the top of a hill and boasts a vast terrace with panoramic views. The property had long stood empty when one of Lagerfeld's friends, Prince Rainier III, offered it to him on the condition that he restore it. Lagerfeld agreed, reportedly investing US$14 million in the project. The villa was renovated and furnished, and the reception hall on the ground floor turned into a dancefloor and a photography studio. Lagerfeld chose the top floor for his private quarters, where one of the bathrooms had a western aspect that looked out onto Monte Carlo by night, and the other faced east for views of the Mediterranean in the morning light. Shoots, parties and product launches were all held at La Vigie over the space of a decade. In the end there were no opportunities left to explore, and the villa had served its purpose.

The designer still had his penthouse in Monaco, plus he had been busy with Villa Jako in Hamburg since 1991. Then there was his new retreat in Biarritz, Villa Elhorria, which he had been decking out with furniture, light fittings and porcelain from the 1920s and 1930s. The sheer volume of modernist items he had collected over the years for his properties in Biarritz and Monaco was revealed when he auctioned them off through Sotheby's in Paris on 15 May 2003. More than two hundred lots were listed, the most notable being the fifty or so items of furniture by French designer Jean-Michel Frank. Lagerfeld's impeccable taste was also evident in the selection of pieces by Pierre Legrain, Marcel Coard, Eileen Gray and Paul Dupré-Lafon. Henri Simmen ceramics, Maison Desny lighting, a chrome inkwell by Jacques-Émile Ruhlmann and an opulent mirror by Dagobert Peche were among the Art Deco works from the 1920s and 1930s. Funds raised: almost 7 million euros.

This all sounds like quite the hotchpotch of furnishings. But perhaps it ought to be expected – after all, this was a man who completely threw himself into his interior design projects, just like everything else in his life. Lagerfeld acquainted himself with every home, taking in its ambience, location, lighting conditions and size before choosing his next aesthetic obsession. He knew that eighteenth-century French furniture would never work in his 2,150 ft² apartment in Gramercy Park in Manhattan, for example, so he came up with a more minimalist concept there instead. He intended to decorate the New York apartment in the style of the Deutscher Werkbund, a movement that had been producing modernist art and designing in Germany since 1907, before World War I and before the dawn of Bauhaus. The walls were home to various German posters from 1905 to 1915, which Lagerfeld had collected almost manically. 'Something almost like Pop Art was happening with graphic art in Germany at that time. It was distinctly German and not yet influenced by the

French or other traditions.'[262] Many of the posters in his collection depicted technical objects, such as electrical appliances from AEG. Others reflected the tense, foreboding atmosphere in the lead-up to World War I, such as Walter Schnackenberg's 'Erry & Merry' and Thomas Theodor Heine's 'Die 11 Scharfrichter'. The latter references the political cabaret of the same name (meaning 'The 11 Executioners') in Munich, which was constantly at loggerheads with the censorship authorities and famously denounced the morality clause in the Imperial Penal Code shortly after the turn of the century. Posters like these were more suited to New York than Paris, so that was where they stayed – at least until 2011, when Lagerfeld sold the apartment.

The house he purchased in 2008, on an island in Lake Champlain, appears to have been a bit of an impulse buy. Perhaps he saw this property in Vermont as an opportunity to act out his internal contradictions in matters of taste, contrasting with the futuristic environment of his new apartment on the Quai Voltaire. As well as being a fan of progress, this designer had a fondness for the idealistic portrayal of American life in Norman Rockwell's paintings and the naivete of Grandma Moses's art. So without a second thought, he spent half a million dollars on the Vermont house. He never lived there and only visited briefly, but the investment paid off all the same: it provided the backdrop for the Chanel advertising campaign of spring 2009 and ultimately made a rather generous present for one of his favourite models, Brad Kroenig.

'Suddenly you are confronted with a past that can no longer be your present or become your future,' he wrote on the occasion of his major auction in April and May 2000. 'There are strict limits to your dreams. You don't outgrow them – you only have to walk in another direction,' he wrote in the introduction to the three-volume auction catalogue. 'Lives, like novels, have chapters.'[263] However, this designer never fancied himself as a museum curator: 'I didn't want to go all quiet and gentle,' he said.[264] With the turn of the new millennium came a new lightness of being: the auction was done and dusted, and on 1 November 2000 the designer embarked on the diet that would completely transform him in the space of just a year.

Lagerfeld also stuck to the bare essentials when it came to his interiors. He had closed the chapter on the twentieth century. Very little remained of his enormous collection of eighteenth-century treasures. The eight-room apartment at 17 Quai Voltaire was turned into an ultramodern space, in which the rooms were divided by glass panels instead of walls, and the library was located behind two sets of twenty-five retractable glass doors on either side. One push of the button, and the doors simultaneously opened to reveal Lagerfeld's vast collection of reading books on one side and art books on the other.[265] When he moved into this apartment in 2005, life was all about looking to the future. He wanted no reminders of the twentieth century here – apart from himself and all the books, of course.

The Quai Voltaire apartment was home to a glossy chrome chair designed by Marc Newson and a curved futuristic-looking white sofa by Amanda Levete. Martin Szekely was commissioned to make two tables in white Corian with metal stripes, one of them for writing and the other for sketching. Both tables were nearly 10 feet long and faced each other in the space Lagerfeld had made from three rooms, which measured over 65 feet in length overall. For Lagerfeld, the apartment was 'like a flawless spaceship flying over Paris', because of the big windows at the end that looked out onto the Seine, the boats and the Louvre. He wanted to be completely alone there. The kitchen was barely used: 'I hate the smell of cooking,' he said.[266]

The designer would eat in a different apartment, one of the many he owned and rented in the area and frequented for lunch, to read the newspaper or to accommodate guests. He kept the furnishings from his childhood room, even though he didn't use them because the pieces were 'too tiny' for him. There was a beautiful set of Biedermeier furniture. The desk was where he had learned to write and sketch as a boy, and there were paintings that his mother had hung on the wall in his room 'because they weren't good enough for her'. Despite referring to these German Romantic paintings as his mother's 'leftovers', he never put them up for auction.[267]

Karl Lagerfeld in Paris, 1984

1983 to 1999

Lagerfeld

He could have started his own fashion label long ago. Yves Saint Laurent and Pierre Bergé had been enjoying phenomenal success under the French designer's name since 1961. He could have followed hot on their heels, but in a dig at his rival Karl Lagerfeld once said, 'In Hamburg, unlike in Oran, nothing is less elegant than having your name over the door. You can be an industrialist, a banker, but not a shopkeeper.'[1] In 1987 he explained that his parents would not have been in any hurry to lend their name to a fashion house: 'I can still remember the sarcastic remarks they used to make about Hamburg merchants who ran businesses.'[2] He wasn't overly keen on the responsibility either. 'Placing orders, costing materials, dealing with staff: who wants that?'[3] He preferred to work for other labels – that way, it wouldn't be his problem if something went wrong. And as his former colleague Rosemarie Le Gallais explains, 'A fashion designer who doesn't have to deal with the business side of things is freer and possibly a better designer as a result.'[4]

But this was the early 1980s, and a few things had changed since the early days of Lagerfeld's career. About a decade after his father died, he lost his beloved mother too. Chloé was getting in the way of his urge for worldwide recognition, and he wanted to make sure the prospects were good for the employees who left Gaby Aghion's label with him. Things were getting serious again in the fashion world, even though Lagerfeld never took his eye off the ball; unlike his contemporaries, he didn't get swept up in the endless nights of the 1970s. He kept a safe distance from all the excess and debauchery, and when everyone else was intoxicated he was already back home. 'I did everything and saw everything,' he told his assistant Eric Wright. 'And I'm not one for repetition.'[5]

Work was his drug of choice. It saved him from the darker sides of those wild years. 'AIDS, *gauche caviar* and a progressive paralysis of the spirit' had changed the free way of life forever, he wrote in 2009.[6] The reference to the 'caviar left' was shorthand for the people in the circles around the first socialist president of the Fifth Republic, François Mitterrand, who was elected on 10 May 1981. Politicians like Laurent Fabius, Dominique Strauss-Kahn and Ségolène Royal became figureheads of the *gauche caviar*: their heart was on the left (*le cœur à gauche*) but their wallet was on the right (*le portefeuille à droite*).

Lagerfeld despised hypocrisy, a trait he ascribed to France's two socialist presidents, François Mitterrand (1981–95) and François Hollande (2012–17). The presidents he admired were the neo-Gaullist Jacques Chirac (1995–2002); the republican Nicolas Sarkozy (2007–12); and Emmanuel Macron (elected 2017), who managed to circumvent the left–right model in his politics. Lagerfeld's respect for these presidents was evidenced by his good relationships with their respective wives. He dressed Bernadette Chirac, and she always attended his fashion shows. He knew Carla Bruni-Sarkozy well from her modelling days, and she could often be spotted in the front row at his Chanel shows. Small group dinners gave him the chance to get better acquainted with the Macrons, and he didn't hold it against Brigitte Macron that she mostly wore Louis Vuitton.

In the spring of 1981, the threat of socialism had the beautifully rich people and the rich beauties of Paris quaking in their boots. They were worried about their assets, their prosperity and France's future political alignment in the Cold War, concerned that a government under Mitterrand would make France turn to the East. Many of these individuals took their money out of the banks and sold their shares, causing stocks to plummet by 30 per cent.[7] Helmut Newton moved to Monaco, fearing that taxes were going to be hit, and he advised his friend Karl to follow suit. Lagerfeld knew the royal family and already had two apartments on the twenty-first floor of the Millefiori skyscraper – one for Jacques de Bascher, one for himself – so in the summer of 1981 he registered as a resident of the principality. He flew to Monaco frequently in the beginning, spending whole weekends there, and remained an official resident until his death. But not even this was enough to keep the Parisian tax authorities at bay in the long run.

A new era was dawning in the designer's career. After taking up the post at Chanel in 1982, he turned his attention to starting his eponymous label in 1983. The French industrialist Maurice Bidermann, whose company held licences for brands including Yves Saint Laurent and Ralph Lauren, had acquired the rights to the Lagerfeld name. With so much international expertise at the helm, Lagerfeld had his sights set on a new global challenge. Work on the new label got off to a running start in 1983, when the team moved into the office at 144 Champs-Élysées, near the Arc de Triomphe. The first fashion show was held in March 1984, to the music of Cliff Richard: 'It's so funny how we don't talk anymore.' A farewell to Chloé, perhaps?

Antonia Hilke, something of a fashion authority on German television, delivered an encouraging, albeit lukewarm, verdict: 'Not exactly a fashion revelation, just very good, coherent fashion.'[8] Lagerfeld's signature fashion line was accompanied by a range of perfumes. In the summer of 1982, the company had launched the KL fragrance across various locations, including Hamburg.[9] The men's fragrance, KL Homme, was also launched in Hamburg three years later, the day before Lagerfeld was awarded the Officer's Cross of the Order of Merit of the Federal Republic of Germany in the city hall by First Mayor Klaus von Dohnanyi.[10]

Caroline Lebar started interning at the fashion house in September 1985, when she was nineteen years old. 'The 1980s were a successful decade for us,' she recalls.[11] The label was still new at the time, and she soon became part of the family, along with managing director Ralph Toledano, 'Directrice de collection' Céline Engel (later Toledano's wife), atelier director ('Première') Anita Briey, accessories designer Eric Wright, and 'Directrice' Rosemarie Le Gallais, who left in 1987 (after twenty years working alongside Lagerfeld, she turned her attention to designing a line of fashionable accessories for the Tyrolean crystal manufacturer Swarovski).[12]

The whole scene was becoming increasingly professionalized. Designers and entrepreneurs were realizing that there was a lot of money to be made, particularly where perfume deals were concerned. Giorgio Armani, Gianni Versace and Gianfranco Ferré had started their own labels in Italy in the 1970s, and by now they were so successful that Milan Fashion Week was threatening to steal the thunder of its Parisian counterpart. The unstoppable growth these designers were experiencing was contagious, spilling over to other Italian innovators. Franco Moschino brought alternative style to the mainstream from 1983, then Domenico Dolce and Stefano Gabbana founded Dolce & Gabbana in 1985. Jil Sander started to show her collections in Milan, and Miuccia Prada turned her family's leather goods company into one of the most important fashion labels in the world from 1988 with the help of her husband Patrizio Bertelli.

Suddenly things were heating up on the ready-to-wear schedule for Paris Fashion Week. Christian Lacroix, Thierry Mugler, Claude Montana and Jean Paul Gaultier were all having their heyday. And following in the footsteps of the Japanese trailblazer Kenzo were Issey Miyake, Yohji Yamamoto and his girlfriend Rei Kawakubo (founder of Comme des Garçons), who fascinated Lagerfeld with their moody designs. One young entrepreneur saw an opportunity and grabbed it with both hands. Bernard Arnault, who had joined his father's construction company after studying engineering, purchased the ailing textile company Boussac Saint-Frères, which owned Christian Dior, in 1985. Two years later, the businessman invested in Christian Lacroix. Then, in 1989, he became the majority shareholder of the French conglomerate LVMH (Louis Vuitton – Moët Hennessy). As well as Louis Vuitton bags, Moët Chandon champagne and Hennessy cognac, LVMH was already home to a whole host of luxury products, including perfumes, cosmetics, watches, and other wines and spirits. Even more big names would be added to the list in the years to come. Arnault's empire, where the sun never sets, would soon welcome a long line of fashion houses into the fold: Givenchy, Céline, Berluti, Kenzo, Loewe, Fendi, Emilio Pucci and Loro Piana. His rival, François-Henri Pinault, was also quick to recognize the potential for fashion in the luxury goods sector in the 1990s. He invested in the burgeoning market by purchasing fashion houses such as Gucci, Yves Saint Laurent and Bottega Veneta for his company, which was renamed Kering in 2013.

With the groundwork set for rapid expansion in the luxury sector in the 1980s, the business of fashion went from strength to strength. The growth was driven by new markets such as Russia, China and the Middle East, with an additional boost from online trading from the turn of the new millennium. The global trade in fashion only suffered occasional setbacks along the way: 9/11, the SARS pandemic of 2002–3, the Iraq War in 2003, the global financial crisis of 2007–8 and, most recently, the coronavirus pandemic. But generally speaking the only way was up for the major labels of Paris, Milan and New York. Luxury goods entrepreneurs became billionaires, models became supermodels, designers became stars. Karl Lagerfeld was everywhere: he was a friend of the Arnault family, a renaissance man who worked in multiple fields, one of the founding fathers of the supermodel era, and last but not least a star among fashion designers.

Now he was causing a buzz under his own name. 'Karl wasn't world-famous at that time, but he was a very charismatic person,' says Caroline Lebar, who always wanted to be an 'attachée de presse' and would become one of the most important people in Lagerfeld's life over the decades. She worked on fashion shows, organized interviews, and kept track of his countless deadlines (and any delays). 'Karl was always bringing people together, that was his way of showing affection,' she says. 'I mean, we were practically still kids!' It sounds as if she is also thinking of Lagerfeld here: the man-child who approached all the challenges of running a prospering fashion house with positively playful ease. He would spend his mornings at home sketching and reading before taking a car to the Chanel head office on Rue Cambon in the afternoon. Then when evening came around he went to take care of his own business at the Karl Lagerfeld headquarters, which relocated from the Champs-Élysées to 14 Boulevard de la Madeleine in 1992.

Sometimes he also had to venture beyond Paris. Bidermann's ambitions for Lagerfeld's eponymous label took him all the way to New York, where he opened an atelier in Manhattan. Here, the fashion designer chose the youngest candidate, Eric Wright, as his studio director. Wright would play a major role in Lagerfeld's business affairs over the years. The American stylist and designer was a font of ideas and inspiration, a liaison for licences in Germany, and Lagerfeld's right-hand man at Fendi. 'Karl was like a father to me,' says Wright. 'I was twenty-four years old when I started working for him in 1983.' He stayed with the designer for twenty-three years – first in New York, then in Paris, and eventually in Rome.

Lagerfeld was no stranger to the States, having visited regularly during his time at Chloé. His perfume deal was with Elizabeth Arden in the US, and that was where the biggest sales were. Jacques also liked to fly to New York, and now they had one more reason to make the trip. Lagerfeld frequently flew Concorde, usually in the company of Rosemarie Le Gallais and sometimes with his partner, but always with over a dozen suitcases in tow. The flight took little more than three hours. This supersonic aircraft was the perfect symbol for a supersonic designer. Still, that didn't mean he always got there on time: 'One time we were all on the plane with the engine running,' Rosemarie Le Gallais recalls, 'and we had to wait another quarter of an hour for him to turn up.'

In the end, the ambitious New York plans went awry. Eric Wright was supposed to be focusing on fashionable sportswear with the label's American arm of the brand, but of course Ralph Lauren and Calvin Klein had already cornered that market. The venture was a flop, and the licensing agreement with Bidermann Industries was terminated as a result in 1987. Wright was summoned to Paris, where there was plenty of work to be done. He was also sent to Lagerfeld's homeland: 'No one in Paris knew that we were working in Germany as well.'

The designer had been working on the 'KL – by Karl Lagerfeld' line since 1988, collaborating with Klaus Steilmann from Wattenscheid, Europe's biggest clothing manufacturer at the time. By now Wright, the New Yorker who lived in Paris, was a frequent visitor to Wattenscheid. 'It was a completely different world,' he says. Wright was fascinated by Germany and took photographs of everything from paved streets to manhole covers. The motifs he photographed made their way onto jewelry pieces at the Karl Lagerfeld label.

'Karl juggled his jobs,' says Caroline Lebar. 'He had several different departments in his head. If he decided to do something, he did it properly. When we asked him how the fittings at Chanel had gone, he could barely even remember them happening. There were thick walls between the different sections of his mind.' He was so intensely focused on the task at hand that he forgot about everything else, including time. Compartmentalizing helped to sharpen his concentration. The three desks in his apartment were a case in point: one was for letters in French, another was for letters in German, and the other was for writing in English.[13]

The eponymous label was a place of experimentation, a kind of testing ground for Chanel. The ideas flew back and forth through Paris. Lagerfeld also gathered plenty of inspiration from his side gigs, like the time he worked on the costumes for the production of Hugo von Hofmannsthal's play *Der Schwierige* (The Difficult Gentleman) at the Salzburg Festival in summer 1991. While sourcing materials for the costumes, Eric Wright came across a transparent skin-coloured stretch fabric at the Munich fabric trade fair. He and Lagerfeld liked it so much that they used a slightly altered version for the Karl Lagerfeld collection.

It was also the perfect place to test the waters with new employees and suppliers. When they were working in the atelier at 144 Champs-Élysées, Lagerfeld and Wright used to frequent an independent record shop called Champs Disques. They would pick up a large Diet Coke from McDonald's on their way down the avenue (then another on the way back) and head to the record store to find out all about the latest music from the young record seller Michel Gaubert. Most fashion houses just used one DJ for their runway music up to this point, but now, in the late 1980s, Wright wanted a change. He and Lagerfeld found a new DJ in the underground music department at Champs Disques, and before long Michel Gaubert had revolutionized runway music. His eclectic mix of old and new, Stravinsky and Daft Punk, raised the bar – first at Lagerfeld, then at Chanel, and eventually at other major fashion labels.

'We were made for each other,' says Gaubert, who already knew Lagerfeld from Le Palace. 'He was often at the shop, he knew a lot about music and had a crazy record habit. He bought all the new stuff. He already knew the old stuff, so he was curious about what else was out there.' The fashion designer invited Gaubert to his office in the autumn of 1989, handed him a copy of Malcolm McLaren's latest record 'House of the Blue Danube', and asked him if he could do something with it. Without further ado, Gaubert joined forces with DJ Dimitri from Paris and set to work. They created a continuous soundtrack, rather than lining up new tracks one after the other: 'We mixed soul with house, Bizet with soul, and Pavarotti with house. It was a wild mix of styles.' And when the fashion show ended, the guests were all asking who did the music.[14]

This eclectic designer was so successful because he was open to new ideas and new people. 'He recognized people's talents faster than they did,' says Caroline Lebar. 'Karl saw Michel as the music producer of the future for fashion shows.' According to Eric Wright, he was a man who had no preconceptions. 'He took people as they were.' Lagerfeld didn't care that his assistant was black, for example. 'He was inclusive on a professional and a private level, more so than anyone else,' says Wright. 'No one else did what he did for me as a black man.' Obsessed with social status and cachet, the fashion scene hardly welcomed this young New Yorker with open arms. 'There were some people who didn't want me in Paris,' he says.

Lagerfeld's generosity extended to his faith in other people. His employees found this attitude extremely motivating, and trusting other people enabled him to delegate effectively. His father before him had managed hundreds of employees across several locations, and now Karl too was taking advantage of a model based on division of labour. This approach required a delicate balance of trust and supervision. Freeing himself up to focus on his sketches meant relinquishing control and leaving the fittings in the capable hands of Eric Wright, Virginie Viard and his most loyal director of atelier, Anita Briey. While he was at home drawing up sketches for a completely different collection, they would be in the atelier for the morning fittings. The specialized nature of modern working life suited Lagerfeld, who was good at surrounding himself with the right people for the right tasks. He was an incredibly strong communicator who provided in-depth instructions, and he had a vast capacity for work and very little patience for discussions, gripes and meetings.

Every single one of Lagerfeld's employees knew that it could all be over in a heartbeat. 'You need a sword of Damocles hanging over a relationship. Then things work,' he once said.[15] If the people around him got too demanding or weren't giving enough, the balance tipped and the split was drastic. Céline Toledano experienced this first-hand in the autumn of 1993. After ten years, the collection manager's enthusiasm for Lagerfeld's fashion was waning, and he could sense it. Toledano knew that he was aware she had gone off his designs because he was showering her with gifts. Now, rather than once a week, he was sending her books, flowers and CDs of classic music he loved every day.

One day in September 1993, the Lagerfeld team were in the studio on Place de la Madeleine for the fittings, just a few hundred feet away from Place de la Concorde, the site of Marie Antoinette's execution on 16 October 1793. The team were working on a collection in the style of the former queen of France. Lagerfeld took a pad of paper and drew portraits of all the people in attendance, each of them wearing a Marie Antoinette wig. When Céline Toledano's turn came, he drew a hand holding her severed head by her shock of hair. In true eighteenth-century style, the sword of Damocles had struck.[16]

'He could forgive a lot of things,' says his long-time assistant and press attaché Sophie de Langlade. 'But when it was over, it was over.'[17] She first met Lagerfeld in 1975, when she was still a young *Vogue* editor, then she followed him to Chanel in 1983 and joined him at his own label from 1986 after a stint at Dior. As cheerful, charming and pleasant as Lagerfeld could be, he didn't hesitate to cut people out of his life if they failed to live up to his expectations: 'They know the score, they know my criteria,' he said. 'It's up to them to play the part or take the risk.'[18] When he spotted Céline Toledano in the distance after their split, he crossed the street to avoid her.

'Different people influenced him at different points of his life,' says Eric Wright. 'He switched people out because he always had to be moving. He always knew exactly what he wanted.' Wright knew he would be the next one to go in 2005. 'I already knew that it would end at some point,' he says. 'I had already seen him cut ties with plenty of people, like Inès de la Fressange, Claudia Schiffer, Céline Toledano and Gilles Dufour at Chanel. I didn't want to leave him because I didn't want to be thought of as disloyal, but there was a tension in the air. He offered me a role that I couldn't accept, so I didn't sign the contract.' Wright parted ways with Lagerfeld and moved into menswear in order to avoid comparisons with his old boss. He later worked for Trussardi, Roberto Cavalli, and Mafalda von Hessen, the former Giorgio Armani muse who ran a fashion label in Rome for a few years.

Bidermann Industries sold the Lagerfeld line to the French luxury goods group Cora-Revillon in 1987. Business went well under the new ownership, and the fashion house had complete autonomy. Ralph Toledano, who had joined as managing director in 1985, succeeded in channelling Lagerfeld's energy with the help of his tight-knit team, providing the kind of strong commercial management the designer had known at Chloé and Chanel. By 1989 the fashion house was breaking even, and in 1990 it started to turn over a profit.[19] But before long the business changed hands again: the British luxury goods company Dunhill bought the rights in 1992 before merging to form the Vendôme Luxury Group, which was later dissolved by the Richemont group. When Dunhill bought the rights to the Lagerfeld line, the company had its reasons for wanting to do the designer a favour. Chloé, one of its brands, was no longer performing particularly well, and Dunhill wanted Lagerfeld to help restore the fashion house to its former glory. So in 1992 the designer returned to Chloé, and in the five years that followed he was more prolific than ever. Each ready-to-wear season from 1992 to 1997, he simultaneously worked on the collections for four major shows: Chanel, Chloé and Karl Lagerfeld in Paris, and Fendi in Milan.

The sheer extent of his output was unprecedented in the fashion world. On a practical level, things were getting more and more confusing. It was hard to keep track of where this busy designer was at any one time. Lagerfeld's former assistant Arnaud Maillard remembers the phone calls between Chloé, Chanel and the Lagerfeld label: 'Is he with you?' – 'No, we thought he was still with you.' – 'Call us as soon as he gets there.' – 'What about Chloé?' – 'Too late. He already left. Speak soon…'[20]

Things were getting even more complicated at the Karl Lagerfeld line. With so many jobs to juggle, the designer was unable to focus on his own business with the same intensity. His managing director, Ralph Toledano, was feeling relegated because he now had to report to the CEO of Chloé, Mounir Moufarrige. Eventually a dissatisfied Toledano followed in the footsteps of his wife Céline, who had left the label a year earlier. The fashion house ran at a loss from 1996. When Lagerfeld's contract at Chloé came to an end in 1997, Richemont gave him back the trademark rights to his eponymous label. But the Swiss group, founded by Johann Rupert, decided to hang on to Chloé.

Now Lagerfeld tried going it alone with a new concept, launching a smaller collection called Lagerfeld Gallery in 1998. The Lagerfeld Gallery boutiques, on Rue de Seine in Paris and in Monaco, were a kind of concept store offering a mixed bag of fashion, books and photography. Lagerfeld Gallery was often on the runway schedule, but most of the critics found the style unconvincing. Compared to the Lagerfeld they knew from Chanel, and despite the original ideas he was coming up with, this Lagerfeld had less of an air of exclusivity. The clothes seemed somehow cheaper and less tasteful. His one-time employee Pascal Brault says he didn't seem to care about the things he was putting out under his own name. 'He was just a good mercenary,' says Brault.[21]

The gallery concept never really caught on either. By the 1990s, the main attraction in the boutiques was the Fendi Baguette bag, whereas Lagerfeld's own designs were confined to the basement and fell into insignificance. He quickly lost interest when things didn't work. By now he was already working on a new business venture – 7L, a bookstore and photography studio he was planning to open at 7 Rue de Lille. He was also busy getting ready for a major auction of his artworks and furniture in 1999. With so many things taking up his time, there had to be some casualties along the way.

However, it wouldn't stay that way for ever, and eventually things started looking up for the Lagerfeld name. The designer himself became an icon after his strict diet and weight loss in 2001, and his collaboration with H&M in 2004 made him a household name the world over. Then along came Tommy Hilfiger, who helped Lagerfeld realize the true potential of his name.[22] Hilfiger's fashion corporation bought the rights in 2005: with a few detours along the way, the Lagerfeld brand had made its way back into the hands of professional shareholders.[23] Lagerfeld himself still held a zero per cent share in the Lagerfeld name. So now, even at his own label, he was just a mercenary. Lagerfeld was happy with this situation: it meant he was free, but still earning good money.

One reason for the company's success in later years was Pier Paolo Righi, who was appointed to the helm of the Karl Lagerfeld International B.V. headquarters in Amsterdam in 2011. The half-German and half-Italian CEO spoke to Lagerfeld in German, and he was trusted. Business was looking good for the brand in 2019, with 150 stores (roughly half of them franchise stores), 450 employees, and annual sales of half a billion euros, not to mention licences for shoes, glasses, watches, jewelry, perfumes and menswear.[24] In the years leading up to Lagerfeld's death, and in the year that followed, the company posted steady revenue growth of 30 per cent or more. Lagerfeld and his investors doubled their business in the last three years of his life – a late triumph. Work commenced on the luxurious new headquarters in a seventeenth-century former bank in Amsterdam. When the designer visited the premises at 182 Herengracht in 2018, it was still very much a work in progress.[25]

Up to this point Yves Saint Laurent and Pierre Bergé, Tom Ford and Domenico De Sole, Marc Jacobs and Robert Duffy, Alessandro Michele and Marco Bizzarri had served as paradigms of successful collaborations between fashion designers and their managers. And now Lagerfeld was able to join their ranks. After a successful run in the 1980s with Ralph Toledano, he had finally found the right managing director once again: 'We have a huge collection here,' says Righi. 'It's a unique repository for us. All the designs produced since 2006 have been photographed, archived and safely stored away.' Design director Hun Kim, who joined Karl Lagerfeld in 2015, knows his fashion codes. 'Our logo is a silhouette,' he says. 'Other labels have a polo player or a crocodile, but there is nowhere else that uses the silhouette of a head as its trademark.'[26]

Karl Lagerfeld lives on through his brand, much like Coco Chanel, Christian Dior or Yves Saint Laurent. But unlike luxury ready-to-wear or haute couture collections, the prices here are far from astronomical: this brand is much younger and much more affordable, with more logos and less prestige. The profit margins are lower at Karl Lagerfeld, where a biker jacket costs 795 euros, a trench coat 495 euros, a pinstripe tunic 195 euros, and a T-shirt 89 euros. With plentiful followers on social media and customers aged between twenty-five and thirty-five, the products and brand image are aimed at a younger audience than the rest of the luxury market. The former editor-in-chief of French *Vogue*, Carine Roitfeld, and Lagerfeld's bodyguard and confidante, Sébastien Jondeau, are all set to keep breathing new life into the name as brand ambassadors.

As if he might walk back in at any minute: months after his death,
all the fashion designer's materials were still there waiting for him
at the Paris headquarters of the Karl Lagerfeld label.

The Paris branch of the company on Rue Saint-Guillaume is full of reminders of Lagerfeld. Months after his death, his tools were still exactly as he left them on his desk in mid-January 2019 after the last fittings of his career: waterproof wax pastels from Caran d'Ache, wax-based Prismacolor professional colouring pencils, a set of twenty Akashiya Sai Aquarell brush pens, a pad of blank sheets of paper, scissors, a thimble, staples, needles, and a milky white crystal glass from his collection for Swedish glass manufacturer Orrefors. The wall was still lined with sketches for the autumn/winter 2019 collection, complete with notes that attest to his characteristic style: 'chemise à poches' for a white shirt with pockets, 'partie detachée' for a removable element, and 'col haut' for a high collar.

Chanel

Headhunting Karl Lagerfeld was like a secret mission. Kitty D'Alessio, the head of Chanel's US operation, had been following the designer for a long time. She liked his Chloé collections and admired his virtuosity. When Lagerfeld stayed at The Pierre in New York, she made sure there were flowers and gifts from her waiting for him. 'She did everything she could to lure him,' says Rosemarie Le Gallais.[27] And it worked: her mission was successful.

By now Lagerfeld knew his worth and was not going to be an easy catch. The secret negotiations commenced; everything had to happen on the quiet as Lagerfeld couldn't risk being seen waltzing into the Chanel headquarters in Paris.[28] In 1982, he received an invitation to a dinner with Alain Wertheimer in London. Kitty D'Alessio flew in from New York, and Rosemarie Le Gallais accompanied the designer from Paris. Wertheimer and Lagerfeld instantly hit it off. 'Despite their wealth, Alain and his brother Gérard Wertheimer are also pleasant and down to earth,' says Le Gallais. 'They were a good match for Karl.'

In September 1982, Chanel made an announcement: Lagerfeld would be unveiling his first haute couture collection for the label in January 1983. The revelation took the fashion scene by surprise. A German working at a Parisian fashion house with Jewish owners?

For a label whose founder had been involved with the German occupying forces? An haute couture designer who was only known for ready-to-wear? 'Everyone thought it was a mistake,' said Alain Wertheimer, 'except the ones who made the decision.'[29] Chloé boss Gaby Aghion felt betrayed by designers who had learned the trade with her and succumbed to the 'siren call of couture'.[30]

Lagerfeld was attracted by the challenge, rather than the prospect of creating haute couture. He saw himself as a trailblazer, and he was excited to become Chanel's creative director. He was ahead of the curve: this was a time when Parisian labels were still headed by French designers – a tradition which, as he once pointed out, is no longer the norm.[31] This trend for foreign talent at the helm of French fashion houses only gained ground in the 1990s, with designers such as Gianfranco Ferré and John Galliano at Dior, Alexander McQueen at Givenchy, Marc Jacobs at Louis Vuitton, Michael Kors at Céline, and Stella McCartney at Chloé. In the foreword to his first coffee-table book of Coco Chanel photographs, Lagerfeld tells of how the Chanel name was the first brand to be reborn. 'Many others followed,' he wrote.[32]

Although Chanel had done brilliantly in the past, the fashion house had been struggling to perform in recent years. The time had come to drag the classic styles into the present. The designer and icon Gabrielle Chanel, who later simplified her name as she did her fashion, made life easier for modern women. Born into poverty in 1883, Gabrielle had to become independent while she was still very young. She was just twelve years old in 1895 when her mother died and she was sent to an orphanage with her older sister. It was there, with the nuns at Aubazine Abbey in the department of Corrèze, that Gabrielle learned to sew. The strict lines of Romanesque art characterized her own style, where form and function would form a happy partnership.

Quite the libertarian, Gabrielle rejected the styles of the Belle Époque, with its wide-brimmed hats and corseted dresses. She left the orphanage when she was eighteen and moved on to the Notre Dame boarding school in Moulins in the Auvergne region. Then at the age of twenty, she started working in a shop selling gifts and baby products – first as a shop assistant, then also as a seamstress.[33] She also performed in café-concerts at the Pavillon de la Rotonde in Moulins. Legend has it that she liked to sing the songs 'Qui qu'a vu Coco?' and 'Ko Ko Ri Ko', which is what prompted the soldiers from the garrison town to start calling her by the nickname Coco.

In 1906, the ambitious young woman met Étienne Balsan, a former officer and the wealthy heir to a textile dynasty. She became Balsan's mistress and moved to Royallieu, his estate near Paris, where she prepared herself for her future career dressing the upper echelons of society. Brushing shoulders with the rich and the beautiful, she learned to ride horses, played sports, and discovered a new style of clothing that suited the lifestyle. In what would become the basic principle of her artform, she incorporated elements of menswear into a style that women could wear.[34]

Karl Lagerfeld's short film *Once Upon a Time...*, a celebration of Chanel's 100th anniversary, looks back at the designer's early love affair with hats. The black-and-white film shows two young maids walking past 'Gabrielle Chanel', a hat shop that has recently opened in Deauville: 'How awful!' – 'Who is this Gabrielle Chanel?' – 'No idea, but she has no taste!' At the beginning of the film, Gabrielle, played by Keira Knightley, waits in vain for customers to arrive. In the meantime, she flirts with her young English suitor Arthur ('Boy') Capel, who also supports her in her business.

Even though Coco was already running an atelier – on Rue Cambon, no less, at number 21 – the Chanel brand was only truly born when she opened the boutique in Deauville.[35] Her fresh look and forward-looking approach appealed to women, making her label a success. Though Madeleine Vionnet and Paul Poiret may have done away with the corset before her, Coco was the one who made this new, wearable style even better known with her loose-fitting jersey dresses. In Lagerfeld's film, she even exclaims, 'I hate Poiret!'

Coco Chanel appealed to Karl Lagerfeld as more than just a fashion revolutionary. To him, she was an icon because she was an independent woman with a loose tongue and she wouldn't let men push her around. No doubt he was reminded of his mother when he started to study the designer's life and work in depth from 1982. Elisabeth Bahlmann – who had died just a few years earlier – was also from the countryside and had set off for the big city as a young woman. And, like Coco, she had campaigned for women's rights and worked in the fashion houses of the 1920s. Working at Chanel was almost like fulfilling some kind of biographical mission for Lagerfeld. Elisabeth, who was fourteen years younger than Coco Chanel, had abandoned her career as a manageress in Berlin. And now here her son was, working in the name of a legend who resembled her as much as one Chanel suit does the next. With her short haircut, cynical expression, acerbic wit and formidable feminist drive, Lagerfeld's mother had a lot in common with the legendary designer.

The young Elisabeth Bahlmann would have made for a good customer in the early days of Coco's fashion house. The modern Chanel woman stepped out in comfortable skirts, wide-legged trousers and nautical styles, quite revolutionary for the 1910s and 1920s. 'Mademoiselle', as she continued to be known in the later years of her life, could take credit for having single-handedly liberated women – at least where clothes were concerned. She came to embody the ideal of a modern, independent, self-confident woman.[36] Between the two world wars, she quickly made a name for herself with her iconic designs: the canotier (a straw hat with a flat top), the two-tone pumps (beige sling-backs with a mid-height heel and black toe), the Little Black Dress (a modern cocktail dress made from silk), quilted leather bags, and various items of reasonably priced fashion jewelry. Further down the line, she took inspiration from men's attire to create a tailored jacket with a contrasting trim and patch pockets. The jacket was paired with a slightly flared below-the-knee skirt, and a fashion classic was born: the Chanel suit.

The young Karl used to make fun of this older woman's conservative approach to clothing. One day in the late 1950s over breakfast at the Ritz with his friend Victoire Doutreleau, Coco Chanel came up in conversation. The Ritz was conveniently close to the Chanel headquarters, and the designer lived in one of the suites there until she died. 'She must hate the word sexy, mustn't she?' Lagerfeld scoffed.[37] His spiteful remark reflected the general consensus at the time. Coco Chanel had fallen out of favour with the public over her refusal to move with the times: she despised jeans and miniskirts, and her fashion no longer exactly embodied youthfulness. As Lagerfeld later wrote in the introduction to a book of photographs by Douglas Kirkland, this put her 'in the position of the has-been oracle of style and fashion' and would make the years to come 'clouded for her by gloom and bitterness'.[38]

The blot on her reputation was even more damaging than her outdated style. The people of France struggled to condone the designer's former relationship with Baron Hans Günther von Dincklage, special commissioner of the Reich Security Head Office in France. Coco had met the German intelligence officer in 1940, when the officers were garrisoned at the Ritz, and proceeded to collaborate with the German occupying forces. According to the American author Hal Vaughan, she even planned 'Operation Fashion Hat' in 1944 with General Walter Schellenberg, Chief of SS intelligence.[39] The story goes that Coco had been acquainted with Winston Churchill through the Duke of Westminster, who was her lover in the late 1920s. As part of a secret mission, she was to meet with the British prime minister and persuade him to negotiate with the Germans. The plan failed, and when the German occupation was over in September 1944 she was arrested at the Ritz for being a collaborator. She was released a few hours later.

This wasn't the only thing that made Coco Chanel a hated figure among the people of France. There was also the matter of her antisemitism. Pierre Wertheimer had acquired the majority share in Chanel in 1924, but was forced to flee to the United States in 1940. Coco Chanel used Wertheimer's exile and the fact that he was Jewish to try and strip him of the 'Parfums Chanel' division under the Nazi 'Aryanization' laws. Fortunately, Wertheimer had been shrewd enough to transfer his shares to a friend, the industrialist Félix Amiot, who returned the shares to him when the war was over.[40] It is hardly surprising that the fashion designer consequently decided to spend the next eight years in Lausanne, Switzerland. She left France as soon as the occupation ended and only made her comeback in 1954, bringing her boxy style to Paris as an alternative concept to Christian Dior's wasp waist.

The fashion house was managed rather poorly when Coco Chanel died in 1971. Two of the designer's former assistants, Yvonne Dudel and Jean Cazaubon, took over the couture collections. 'But they croaked under the pressure,' says Marietta Andreae, who served as director of public relations for Germany and Austria at the brand from 1976.[41] Around this time, most of the revenues came from perfumes, particularly Chanel No 5 – probably the most famous perfume in the world. The guests at the shows on Rue Cambon remained firmly seated in their gilded chairs. Andreae recalls the Chanel suit being produced in dark blue with a burgundy trim one time, then in burgundy with a dark blue trim another time. Sophie de Langlade was a junior editor at French *Vogue* in the 1970s and remembers the lack of enthusiasm for the brand among her colleagues in the editorial office. Every season the question would be: 'Who's going to Chanel?' To which the writers would unanimously reply: 'Moi non!'[42]

Alain Wertheimer said it himself: 'Chanel was dead. Nothing was happening.'[43] The businessman and his brother, born in 1948 and 1950 respectively, were young enough to take a chance on the brand their grandfather Pierre had co-founded. Entrusting such a self-assured designer with the creative direction was a risky business. They would have to grant him a great deal of artistic licence, not to mention the hefty fee he was demanding. He is reported to have received $1 million a year, plus dresses to the value of a $100,000, which he gave to editors and friends such as Ira von Fürstenberg and Jacqueline Brynner, who was married to the actor Yul Brynner.[44]

The two owners had to give Lagerfeld free rein to do his thing. Over the three and a half decades of their working relationship, they shrewdly maintained a low profile and stayed out of the spotlight.

They usually sat towards the back of the audience at Chanel fashion shows, often in the fourth or fifth row, out of the focus of the society photographers. Then at the end of the show, they would quickly make their way through the backstage door to congratulate Lagerfeld before making a swift exit. Lagerfeld felt at ease with the Wertheimer brothers: 'There is only one deity in the entire world of fashion,' he once said, 'and it's Alain Wertheimer.'[45]

Lagerfeld's mission to bring Chanel up to date began on 25 January 1983. Isabelle Adjani, Paloma Picasso, Claude Pompidou, Andrée Putman and the rest of the guests gathered at the fashion house to feast their eyes on his new collection, his first as the brand's creative director. The models stepped out in modern, well-tailored dresses with dramatic proportions and full, low pleats. The beiges and pastels of old gave way to contrasts, with lots of black, white, navy and red. Similar to Coco's return in 1954, Lagerfeld's first haute couture collection for Chanel provoked a lukewarm response. Things were soon looking up, however: 'The success started with my second season,' he admitted.[46]

Lagerfeld's mastery reached new heights. The ideas were practically spilling out of him, he was very experienced but still full of ambition, and his versatility expressed itself in a diverse range of styles. He delegated effectively, organized the ateliers, made deals with his clients, and succeeded in piquing his customers' curiosity. The fashion world had not seen anything like it since Yves Saint Laurent's debut at Dior in 1958. Here Lagerfeld was, subverting the founder's trademark style with completely different elements. This kind of trickery, satirizing and venerating the tradition all at once, required extraordinary confidence.

The models stepped out in everything from flared skirts to fringed tweeds and suits paired with cropped tops or high-necked shirts. They wore white heels or went barefoot, and accessorized with long pearl necklaces or thick gold chains like rappers. 'It was exhilarating,' says Lagerfeld's former confidante, Marietta Andreae. 'The transformation was palpable, and the shows were drawing bigger and bigger crowds.' Inès de la Fressange was also instrumental in bringing about this

Free to do as he pleased: Karl Lagerfeld interpreted Chanel so freely that
he was full of surprises, like the over-the-knee boots in March 2006.

transformation when she signed exclusively to Chanel. Fressange
was an aristocrat, like so many models in the post-war era, which
meant she represented tradition. But at the same time, the new face
of Chanel had a spontaneity, wit, charm and effortless beauty that
also helped to breathe new life into the brand.

Lagerfeld concentrated on haute couture when he first joined the
fashion house. His contract with Chloé stipulated that he was not
allowed to design ready-to-wear for any other label in France until
1984, so initially he entrusted that side of the business to Hervé Léger,
his assistant at Fendi. At least, that was the official version of the story.
In fact, Lagerfeld was ubiquitous: 'Late in the evening, when he had
finished working at the Karl Lagerfeld brand, he would come back
to Chanel under the cover of darkness,' says Eva Campocasso, who
was responsible for ready-to-wear accessories at the time. 'He would
bring fresh sushi with him, and then finally we could have dinner
and start the secret fittings.'[47]

Things did not get off to an easy start, mainly due to friction between the long-standing Chanel employees and the Lagerfeld camp. The established members of the team were annoyed that the designer was making references to the 1920s and 1930s with his first couture collection and sidestepping the latter part of Coco Chanel's career. Many of the regulars had been part of the comeback in the 1950s and were not happy with the decision. Eva Campocasso recalls one Chanel employee watching aghast as she snipped the ends of the fingers off a pair of leather gloves for one of the first collections. Such a sacrilegious act! Now even Chanel was being influenced by the punk movement that had made its way over to Paris from London. The more conservative faction also disapproved of the bags with the CC logo that heralded the dawn of logomania in the 1980s.

Lagerfeld was also rubbing people up the wrong way with his recruitment policy. He brought his former assistants Hervé Léger and Eva Campocasso with him, as well as the suit maker Paquito Sala, whom he knew from his time at Balmain, and former model Mercedes Robirosa. 'I'm working like the Communist party,' Lagerfeld joked in an interview with *Women's Wear Daily* before his first show, 'bringing in my own people and placing them everywhere.'[48]

Some of the conflicts at Chanel dragged on for decades. Alain Wertheimer wanted his two most senior creatives, Karl Lagerfeld and Jacques Helleu, to work together at the brand. The artistic director – son of the artist Jean Helleu, who was a friend of Coco Chanel – was in charge of orchestrating the image of the fragrances, cosmetics, watches and fine jewelry. But Wertheimer's plan never materialized. Helleu was jealous of his colleague's success, apparently. Lagerfeld's publisher Gerhard Steidl recalls the designer telling him that the rift between the perfume and the fashion divisions at Chanel was like the Berlin Wall, only bigger.[49] Lagerfeld also thought that Chanel's accessories designer, Frances Stein, had to be put in her place. He gave her one of his witty trademark nicknames, a wordplay on Frances Stein: 'Frankenstein'.[50]

In the midst of contract negotiations in October 1985, Lagerfeld refused to come out to greet the audience after his latest ready-to-wear show. Instead of the million dollars a year he was already earning, Lagerfeld was reportedly demanding a million per collection from Alain Wertheimer. It was a shrewd tactic. Alicia Drake describes how it worked: 'When Karl refused to come out at the end of a ready-to-wear show to take his bow, rumours flew that he would leave the house. Chanel issued a denial and Karl got his money.'[51]

As business went from strength to strength over the decades, Lagerfeld was able to command higher and higher rates. In 2011, when asked for his opinion on the $10 million a year Marc Jacobs had reportedly negotiated for his move to Dior, his response said it all. Did he think it was excessive? 'It depends,' he said. 'There are more expensive [designers]. But they bring in even more [money].'[52] Experts calculate that in the final years of his life Lagerfeld must have been earning more than 20 million euros a year from Chanel alone, as well as around 10 million from Fendi and a more modest figure in the millions from his own label. He might have inherited his fashion sense from his mother, but he had his father – the Hamburg merchant – to thank for his tough negotiation skills.

Lagerfeld had extraordinarily high expectations of himself and his colleagues. If someone failed to make the grade, he was quick to react and exact his revenge. Madame Colette was one such individual who fell victim to his sensitivities. As head seamstress of the haute couture *flou* atelier, she was responsible for soft fabrics, drapery and dresses.[53] While working on the haute couture show in July 1990, she made a serious blunder involving Christy Turlington and Linda Evangelista, two of the models that would dominate the modelling scene for the next decade after appearing on Peter Lindbergh's legendary British *Vogue* cover with Naomi Campbell, Tatjana Patitz and Cindy Crawford in January 1990. When Christy and Linda hit the runway, the flaps at the front of their redingotes had been left undone, exposing more than just their matching thigh-high boots. The whole audience could see the models' underwear. 'Karl was fit to be tied,' writes Natasha Fraser-Cavassoni, who was his assistant at the time.[54] Others, including Lagerfeld's friend Caroline of Monaco, were amused by the sight. But the designer showed no mercy: Madame Colette would have to go, right away.

The rest of the world heard nothing of the incident, and the fashion house succeeded in keeping up appearances. Haute couture was a status symbol in the 1980s, the epitome of sophistication and elite society. One of Lagerfeld's clients at the time was Gloria von Thurn und Taxis from Regensburg, who had married one of Germany's richest men, Johannes von Thurn und Taxis, in 1980. There were very few German clients in the world of haute couture in those days. 'But haute couture was a must for anyone who wanted to play in a certain league,' she notes. She travelled to Paris in search of attire befitting of her place in high society, and her search took her to Lagerfeld. 'I liked that he was very funny and direct. And he was even that bit more gregarious back then, before the weight loss.'[55] André Leon Talley, Lagerfeld's friend from American *Vogue*, could often be found at the Rue Cambon salon during haute couture week. 'It was a nice place to go,' says Gloria von Thurn und Taxis, who amassed an extensive collection of couture pieces over the years. 'The ladies were always pleased and bought a lot when André was there.' The man behind the designs rarely made an appearance on Rue Cambon: 'I also used to buy clothes from Christian Lacroix and Hubert de Givenchy, but Karl didn't deal directly with the customers like they did. He left that job to the women in the salon.'

This designer wasn't trying to change the world; he just wanted to interpret things differently. The German fashion journalist Antonia Hilke praised Lagerfeld's chameleon-like ability to adapt to the Chanel style and make it work for him.[56] This was a man who immersed himself in Coco Chanel's world and breathed new life into her style, becoming a kind of reincarnation of her spirit.[57] He also embellished certain parts of his life story, like Coco Chanel when she turned the poverty of her early years into a sheltered childhood.

But Lagerfeld kept adapting and moving with the times. When designers such as Thierry Mugler and Gianni Versace started making explicitly sexual references in their fashion in the 1990s, Lagerfeld didn't let the trend pass him by. For spring/summer 1994 he dressed Naomi Campbell in a miniskirt so short it was barely there, and for the autumn/winter 1995 show he had Stella Tennant appearing in a micro-bikini whose top consisted of two tiny black pads with CC logos covering her nipples and just a strap holding them in place. But not all Lagerfeld's provocative looks hit the right note. A media storm broke out when Claudia Schiffer hit the runway for the spring/summer 1994 show wearing an haute couture dress with a tight-fitting bustier that had verses from the Qur'an embroidered on it. Lagerfeld had taken the text from a book about the Taj Mahal, assuming it was a love poem from India.

Long-standing Chanel devotees were left gasping, while the younger generation breathed a sigh of relief. Now they could finally wear Chanel without fear of looking more outdated than they would in Dior, Givenchy or Yves Saint Laurent. With the old reputation out of the window, the brand succeeded in keeping the public on the edge of their seats. Lagerfeld's constantly changing fashions sparked curiosity, rumours, excitement and debate, providing endless material for photographs and reports. 'He was incredibly brave. He just followed his instincts,' says Eric Wright.[58] Wolfgang Joop admired him from afar, marvelling at the nerve it took to make such bold, controversial statements: 'What a gamble!'[59]

The whole enterprise was a great success. Now Chanel was generating higher revenues and had more stores and an even bigger workforce. Of course, this wasn't all down to Lagerfeld's fashion. The growth was also driven by the brand's extremely popular fragrances, which were not part of his remit at Chanel. More scents followed over the years, including Coco in 1984, Égoïste in 1990 (for men), Allure in 1996, Coco Mademoiselle in 2001, Bleu de Chanel in 2010 (for men), and Gabrielle in 2017. Perfume and accessories generally account for a higher share of turnover than clothing at most fashion houses. Take the 2.55 handbag, for instance, which Coco Chanel launched in February 1955, and which Lagerfeld proceeded to reinvent in a whole series of design variants: this iconic quilted leather bag has an enormous profit margin.

Even Lagerfeld thought the growth in the luxury goods market was staggering: 'There are so many new markets, and in China there are so many new stores. The US market is looking almost small these days.'[60] Chanel started using its impressive earnings to invest in specialist workshops such as shoemakers and jewelers.[61] By 2019, Chanel's Paraffection subsidiary was home to twenty-seven artisanal businesses, known as *maisons* or *ateliers d'art*.[62] Chanel steps in when workshop owners are getting older or the threat of closure is looming over the business: 'We have to safeguard their savoir-faire,' says Bruno Pavlovsky, managing director of Chanel's fashion division, who worked alongside Lagerfeld for almost three decades. Most of the *maisons* are located in or near Paris, making their survival even more important. 'We have six weeks for a collection, so we can't wait long for deliveries. We need our suppliers close by – and we have to be able to keep working [with them] in twenty years' time.'[63]

The artisanal workshops gave Lagerfeld the inspiration for his Métiers d'Art concept in 2012. Taking advantage of a gap in the fashion calendar before Christmas, Chanel started unveiling a new, intricately crafted line of clothing in a different part of the world each year to celebrate the *maisons* and their work. Even before the new show was added to his list of commitments, Lagerfeld was already juggling two ready-to-wear shows and the accompanying pre-collections, as well as two haute couture shows. From 1990 he also had the Chanel Cruise collection to present in May, for customers who set off for warmer climes over Christmas. The final addition came in 2018, when Lagerfeld launched Coco Beach (a line of swimsuits, beach bags, espadrilles and other products for boutiques in seaside locations like Saint-Tropez) and Coco Neige (a collection of down jackets, ski pants and boots for skiing holidays). Eventually there were ten annual collections to organize at Chanel alone. And he came up with all the ideas for them.

Lagerfeld's assistant came to play an increasingly important role in managing this ever-expanding workload. Virginie Viard (see p. 338), whose maternal grandparents had been silk manufacturers in Lyon, started out as an intern at Chanel in 1987 and worked for Lagerfeld at Chloé from 1992 to 1997. The French designer worked exclusively on haute couture upon her return to Chanel, before eventually adding ready-to-wear to her remit in 2000. In her role as studio director, she was responsible for interpreting and explaining Lagerfeld's sketches to the head seamstresses in the ateliers, known as *premières*. The team would spend all day working on the designs until Lagerfeld arrived in the late afternoon or evening for two hours of fittings. It was a streamlined, efficient operation. There was no place for flat hierarchy in the studio. As open as he was, his working method was not up for debate. 'I can do what I want, how I want,' he said. 'I work directly with the president [of Chanel], but he doesn't tell me to do this or do that. It's not up for discussion.'[64] With statements like this, he was making his intentions clear. In a way that no other designer would ever dare in the new millennium, he was confining the fashion house's management to the side lines. And because Bruno Pavlovsky always had the nous to maintain a low profile, it worked out well: even ideas that may well have come from the president were attributed to the famous creative director.

'Design, image, advertising, storefront: I do it all,' Lagerfeld said. 'At Fendi it's less straightforward. There are lots of small bosses in large corporations. I told Fendi's owner, Bernard Arnault, that I could make it more like Chanel – but then they would have to put up with my almost fascist methods. There are no contradictions with me, because I stop and think before I speak. That's not to say I can't change my opinion. But generally speaking, I don't change my mind very often.'[65]

The fashion division was constantly expanding, and this growth in turn benefitted the brand's perfumes, cosmetics, watches and jewelry. With all the fashion shows, campaigns, promotional films and store openings, Chanel was becoming more and more visible.

Lagerfeld's fame also helped raise the label's profile, but with so many other roles to play on different stages, this leading actor was careful not to overshadow the fashion house itself. For all that he loved working at the label, Lagerfeld still insisted on keeping a safe distance.

On 17 June 2019, Chanel reported that its group sales were up 12.5 per cent to 9.88 billion euros, while net profits had increased by 16.4 per cent to 1.9 billion euros. The company had made its operating figures public for the first time in 2018. When Patricia Riekel wrote her eulogy to Lagerfeld, she revealed that he had his own theory about what would happen to Chanel when he was gone: 'Chanel will probably be sold to the Chinese,' he surmised.[66] This prediction didn't go down well in Paris, where Chanel had more or less become part of the national cultural heritage.

The Wertheimer brothers continue to invest the profits from their business in new companies.[67] Perhaps these acquisitions hint that they are on the defensive, afraid of the prospect of being usurped by their rivals. Authority is the key to invulnerability, after all. LVMH boss Bernard Arnault's aggressive pursuit of Hermès struck fear and anxiety into other luxury brands. The best defence to such threats lies in sheer scale, growth and self-confidence. A group photograph taken at the 'Karl For Ever' tribute in the Grand Palais on 20 June 2019 symbolizes the delicate balance of power: François-Henri Pinault, the CEO of luxury group Kering, stands between Chanel's president Bruno Pavlovsky and Sidney Toledano, the chairman and CEO of LVMH. It almost looks as though Pinault is trying to keep LVMH at arm's length from Chanel.

Peace reigned over the tribute: any cravings for takeovers were quelled by the commemorative spirit of the evening. But how long would Bernard Arnault be able to hold himself back from this tantalizing prospect? Just a few months before the tribute, he became the third-richest man in the world, and a year afterwards he acquired the American jewelry brand Tiffany & Co. for about $16 billion. This man's resources don't stop there, and the Wertheimers are fully aware of that. Karl Lagerfeld imbued Chanel with the myth of unassailability – and they will have to keep the myth alive for a while yet.

Photography

Lacklustre photographs for a Chanel press kit were how it all started. It was impossible to attract major photographers for assignments like these in the 1980s, so inevitably the quality suffered. Lagerfeld complained about it to Eric Pfrunder, Chanel's image director, who dared him to see if he could do any better: 'OK, now you do it,' Pfrunder challenged. Lagerfeld didn't need to be asked twice. Starting with the spring/summer haute couture collection for 1987, he took it upon himself to do all the photography for Chanel's press kits. He then shot the haute couture collection for autumn/winter 1987, and soon he was taking all the photographs for Chanel's fashion campaigns.

'Doing photos, doing advertising, you meet with other people. You are not isolated,' Lagerfeld once said in an interview.[68] His new role gave him a different perspective on models, makeup, accessories and styling. 'The collection also changed as a result,' says Eric Wright. 'Until then we had thrown outfits, earrings, belts, sunglasses and hats together. And we wanted to get it all into the shot.' But working on the photographs taught them how important it is to make the styling sharper. 'We started paring things down for the shows, too. There had to be a clear message that everyone could understand.'[69]

Lagerfeld's side gig became increasingly important. Before long, his photography progressed beyond consumer snaps and advertising campaigns, venturing into the realms of abstract photography, fashion shoots and portraits. He published books, exhibited his work and became a photographic artist over the years. Of course, he never reached the same dizzy heights as a photographer as he had as a fashion designer. But he made up for this with his love of composition, a lot of hard effort, and his relentless quest for perfection. Gerhard Steidl describes the occasionally fraught experience of being on a shoot with Lagerfeld: 'He started taking photographs at nine in the evening,' he says, 'and at three in the morning, he got

At home with his new hobby: Karl Lagerfeld shared his favourite
photographs ahead of an exhibition in 1991.

it into his head that he needed to make more changes.'[70] Model Julia
Stegner still remembers the gruelling night-time sessions in Rome,
when they kept working 'until the stylist eventually said she had no
more outfits'. When she and Lagerfeld were looking at the results
together on the screen, he told her: 'Come here, Julia, sit on my lap!'
It would have sounded odd coming from anyone else, but not from
Lagerfeld. 'He had this really paternal way about him,' says Stegner.[71]

Many different elements have to come together for a major photo
shoot to be a success. This much is clear in the *Modern Mythology*
series, in which Lagerfeld sought to recreate the atmosphere of
Longus' Ancient Greek romance *Daphnis and Chloe* in an incredibly
elaborate production. He had discovered the classic pastoral novel

in an edition from 1935, featuring illustrations by the German artist Renée Sintenis. Lagerfeld started by copying the drawings, and then he incorporated stage directions: 'It was an exact script, and he spent weeks preparing it,' says Steidl, who was also involved in the photo shoots.

It didn't take Lagerfeld long to decide who should play the foundlings in the story: he cast Baptiste Giabiconi and Bianca Balti, his go-to models at the time. The setting for the romance was swiftly relocated from Ancient Greece to the South of France, and filming began in Saint-Tropez in 2013. That summer, Lagerfeld headed the convoy with the models in his Rolls-Royce, followed by several black vans transporting the makeup artists, hairdressers, stylists and photography team. Hot on their heels were two vans with food and drink, then came the livestock trucks with goats, sheep, horses and a cow. Last but not least came the furniture vans with sculptures that were deposited throughout the woods, as if at random. The whole exercise took three days to complete. There were even a couple of cooks, a butler and waiting staff on the shoot. They set up collapsible tables in the woods and covered them with white tablecloths, and in the afternoon there was coffee and cake.

There was little room for error when it came to processing the photographs. Lagerfeld had the contact sheets made up after the shoots, then he cut out the photographs he liked, stuck them on sheets of paper and instructed Steidl to process the images. After decades of working together in this way – with Lagerfeld behind the camera, Eric overseeing the work, and Gerhard processing the photographs – they were all familiar with the German terms for their roles. Even the Frenchman Eric Pfrunder, who was involved in the preparations for the *Modern Mythology* series, knew the terms *Heimarbeit, Vorarbeit, Ausarbeit* and *Zusammenarbeit* (homework, groundwork, elaboration and cooperation).[72]

The series, commissioned by a London-based art collector whose Mayfair dining room the works now adorn, was typical for this stage in Lagerfeld's career. German art historian Hubertus Gassner describes the photographs of Baptiste Giabiconi as an appropriation with the camera lens.[73] The attempt to capture the fleeting moment was taken to extremes in pictures of this beautiful young model. 'Every image is a farewell,' Lagerfeld once wrote. 'A faithful witness to evanescence. This fragile, melancholic power which binds me to photography.'[74]

Lagerfeld's interest in pastiche and illusionistic techniques shone through in his work, in which he created a *tableau vivant* reminiscent of trompe l'œil paintings.[75] His treatment of the story of Daphnis and Chloe goes beyond what meets the eye, reflecting his love of *fête-galante* paintings in pastoral scenes typical of the rococo and baroque periods. The choice of subject reveals a more personal aspect: as well as recognizing his younger self in Baptiste Giabiconi, Lagerfeld was captivated by the young man's erotic magnetism. The deeper meaning and different levels of his work only become apparent when these elements are taken into account.[76]

Not all Lagerfeld's photography series have these layers of meaning. The more superficial commissioned works *Room Service* (2006) and *Visions and a Decision* (2007), a series of photographs featuring Brad Kroenig and Claudia Schiffer in various scenes in his apartment on Rue de l'Université, are pleasing commissions with a dash of humour.[77] The autumn/winter 2010 advertising campaign for Fendi, which he photographed in the style of Edward Hopper, is more impressive from an artistic perspective. Lagerfeld even breathed new life into classic design in *Cassina as seen by Karl*, his book of photography for the Milanese brand Cassina. In one of the images, several of Gerrit Thomas Rietveld's Zig Zag chairs (1934) are positioned against a black background to create a precarious sculpture. In another, he moves two Auckland chairs (2005) by Jean-Marie Massaud closer together, almost making it look as though they are locked in an intimate embrace. Gio Ponti's Superleggera chairs (1957) are arranged to form an absurd installation that resembles something out of Eugène Ionesco's *The Chairs*.[78]

Reinterpreting historical materials was Lagerfeld's forte. His *Hommage à Feuerbach* was created in the spirit of the German painter

Anselm Feuerbach, who devoted himself to the art of antiquity in late nineteenth-century Rome. Lagerfeld used the medium of art to elevate and inspire his photography, particularly on assignment for German *Vogue*. When he photographed Toni Garrn and Baptiste Giabiconi on the German island of Rügen in 2008, for example, he viewed his subjects through the eyes of the German Romantic painter Caspar David Friedrich. He was interested in creating 'a more poetic form of reality' in his work. The same applied to his portraits of Brad Kroenig: 'I'm not a urologist,' he once said, explaining the lack of full-frontal nudity in his photography.[79]

Sometimes photographs alone were not enough for Lagerfeld. As part of preparations for a major Chanel exhibition at New York's Metropolitan Museum in 2005, various garments from the history of Chanel were photographed on mannequins for inclusion in the exhibition catalogue. 'The dresses didn't hang right,' recalls Gerhard Steidl, who was working with Lagerfeld on the project. 'He didn't like how they looked at all.' Lagerfeld got Steidl to make large-format prints of the original photographs, then he cut out the items of clothing and rearranged them into collages. Steidl then made another print of those images, and Lagerfeld coloured in the black-and-white photographs with lipstick. He scoured fashion magazines from the 1920s for suitable images, then he cut out the heads, superimposed them on the bodies and had another print made. Finally, a special technique was used to turn the layered designs into a series of algraphy prints. The outlay for the 'Chanel Then Now' project was staggering, but the result was a work of art.[80]

Of course, fashion shoots were what Lagerfeld worked on most often, including editorials for *Numéro*, *V*, *Vogue* and *Harper's Bazaar*. Forced poses and unnatural staging are a common sight in this kind of studio photography, and the heavily retouched images certainly aren't as captivating as his fashion designs. But the most important thing to Lagerfeld was the process, rather than the artistic result. Being such an authority in the fashion world allowed him to incorporate other brands like Dior or Valentino into his shoots. These flirtations with different labels, much like his casual references to Diesel jeans, Dior suits and Hilditch & Key shirts, were a way of quietly letting Chanel know that he was independent and above it all. And this attitude only served to extend the reach of his power.

Lagerfeld also curated photography towards the end of his life. His selection for the 2017 'Paris Photo' exhibition attests to his familiarity with the abstract architectural work of Mathieu Bernard-Reymond, the stylized nature photographs of Mat Hennek, and classic photographers such as André Kertész and Lee Friedlander. The collection also included two pieces by Arnold Odermatt, a Swiss police photographer who spent decades documenting accidents. This choice is interesting from a biographical standpoint: in a scene that echoes Lagerfeld's own experience in the 1960s, one of the images shows a Mercedes that appears to have wrapped itself around a pole after a crash.[81]

Lagerfeld's love of photography also led him to film. He started making short films on photo shoots, first with a handheld camera and later on his iPhone. Then came his serious film projects, most notably *The Return*, a short film from 2013, starring Geraldine Chaplin as Coco Chanel returning to Paris in 1954. The 2014 short *Reincarnation* was probably the peak of his cinematic creativity. It stars Cara Delevingne as Sisi and Pharrell Williams as both Franz Joseph I and the elevator boy who provides the inspiration for the iconic Chanel jacket. Coco Chanel, played once again by Geraldine Chaplin, notices the elevator attendant's uniform while holidaying in Salzburg and is inspired to use the idea of the jacket for women's fashion. Only Karl Lagerfeld could come up with such an idea. Or Coco Chanel. Or both.

Models

When Eric Wright first started working at the Karl Lagerfeld label in the early 1980s, he noticed a young woman sitting in the foyer. The tall, slim, pretty brunette might have looked familiar, but he didn't know who she was. 'Wait here,' the young assistant told the woman, then rushed over to his boss, excited: 'Karl, you have to see this model outside! She's so amazing!' Lagerfeld replied: 'Then show her in!'

Wright fetched the young woman and walked her over to the studio. The designer and Inès de la Fressange couldn't help but laugh out loud; they had already been working together for a while.[82]

Lagerfeld was quicker off the mark than most when it came to discovering models. He had a particularly close and successful relationship with Inès de la Fressange, who was born in 1957 and signed an exclusive contract with Chanel in 1983. The model, known simply as 'Inès' in France, was instrumental in raising the brand's profile. According to German fashion journalist Antonia Hilke, the face of Chanel was earning 650,000 marks a year from the very start.[83] But as well as earning a high sum for herself, she generated a lot of revenue for the company. She was a brand ambassador before the job description even existed, and she was a supermodel before the term was coined.

It was all going well – until 1989, when Inès posed for the bust of Marianne, a symbol of the French Republic. Lagerfeld was not impressed. He thought the whole thing was bourgeois, distasteful and parochial. 'I do not dress monuments,' he protested. And with that, Inès parted ways with Chanel.[84] It all happened quickly: as early as the haute couture in July 1989, she was missing from the line-up on the runway.[85] Their split was a scandal that had tongues wagging in France for weeks. The true reason for the fallout never came to light, although Lagerfeld did offer another explanation later on: 'One day she embarrassed M. Wertheimer by asking for more money in front of other people. So he told me, "Invent something to get rid of her." Marianne was an excuse, a total invention – I couldn't care less.'[86]

Inès had her own theory. She believed that the rift had something to do with her relationship with Luigi d'Urso, whom she married in 1990. When Lagerfeld died, she described how he had a kind of sixth sense and nothing got past him. 'He saw everything,' she wrote. 'Like the day I tried to justify a delay by telling him I'd had a dip in blood pressure, when actually I was with my fiancé. I thought I was very convincing, but he didn't believe me.' She says despite everything that happened, they always stayed in touch. He supported her when she

With his favourite model: Karl Lagerfeld and Inès de la Fressange
work on a ready-to-wear collection in March 1987.

was starting up her own label, he let her daughter Violette d'Urso do
an internship at Chanel, and he used her as a model again later on.[87]

The truth about the split is probably much simpler than all this.
'He never stayed still; he just had to keep moving,' notes Eric Wright.
'And that's why Inès had to go. That's the only way to stay one step
ahead in the fashion scene.'[88] Lagerfeld had internalized fashion's
unforgiving obsession with youth and regeneration, so as far as
he was concerned, Inès was past her prime. 'Her high days on the
runway were over – now the girls are between fifteen and twenty
and she was already in her early thirties,' he said.[89] Still, Lagerfeld
was more loyal to his fit models than most other designers. As well
as enduring long fittings in the studio, some of his in-house models
also made it onto the runway. One such woman is Amanda Sanchez,
who modelled for Lagerfeld behind the scenes at Chanel from 2001
to 2019 and has also graced the big stage.

With Claudia Schiffer as 'bride': Karl Lagerfeld receives his
applause after the haute couture show in January 1995.

By 1988, a new era had already dawned in Lagerfeld's career. He
had recently discovered a new muse: a sensual young German named
Claudia Schiffer, who was totally different from Inès. He invited the
young blonde to the studio on Rue Cambon. 'No sooner had I arrived
than I was already being dressed in a look from the new collection.
The next day we drove to Deauville, where Karl photographed my first
Chanel campaign,' says Schiffer, who was eighteen at the time and
had been spotted a year earlier in Düsseldorf. 'He had this incredible
energy. And it was contagious. I was full of adrenaline whenever I
worked with him.'[90] Even when everyone else on the set was tired,
the two of them just kept going. Apparently he joked, 'We're the only
ones who are disciplined, live healthy lives, and don't drink alcohol.'

Schiffer and Lagerfeld were more productive in the 1990s than any
other designer–model partnership the world has seen before or since.
Schiffer clocked her fair share of miles on the runway for Chanel, she

has appeared in more Chanel advertising campaigns than anyone else to date, and she regularly flew Concorde to New York with Lagerfeld to accompany him at events. Lagerfeld published books about Schiffer and photographed dozens of the magazine covers she appeared on over the years, of which there have been more than a thousand. His portraits of her made it onto the cover of *Vogue* as well as trend magazines such as *Self Service*. 'Karl was a wizard,' says Schiffer. 'He transformed me from this shy German girl into a supermodel. He taught me everything about fashion and style – and how to survive in this business.' Described as the reincarnation of a young Brigitte Bardot, she even appealed to the French. And with her pristine image, she helped to conquer completely new markets for Chanel. 'Even the style changed with Claudia,' says Sophie de Langlade, who was working at Chanel at the time. 'She was sexy, and her sexiness was reflected in the collections.'[91]

Schiffer was more than just a replacement for Inès. She also had a lot in common with Lagerfeld. Like him, she was German and could effortlessly switch back and forth between German, English and French around other people. 'We loved the shoots in Berlin, Munich and Vienna,' says Schiffer. 'We got to eat traditional dishes like *Knödel* and *Kaiserschmarrn*. The rest of the team weren't exactly impressed.' They liked to exchange quirky little sayings, too, such as 'Morgenstund hat Gold im Mund' (the early bird gets the worm). And indeed the early hours of the morning did prove productive: 'Some of the photo shoots went on until sunrise.' Lagerfeld always had so many ideas, it was easy to get carried away. Despite this intensity, Schiffer says that working with him was incredibly easy. She remembers one time when they were shooting an advertising campaign in Monaco: 'Frédéric the butler, who was part of the family, served us a picnic on the beach at lunchtime.'

Schiffer, who was always on set on time and didn't have an attitude, unlike some other supermodels, was very much influenced by her creative director. 'He loved work the way other people love going on holiday, so he didn't actually need holidays.' Her Calvinist work ethic, her unwavering commitment to quality, her insistence on strict control over the creative process – these are all things she learned from Lagerfeld. 'He was a genius like Mozart. Incredible skills came naturally to him.'

Nevertheless, their working relationship temporarily came to an end in the late 1990s. 'It was only natural,' says Schiffer. 'In fashion, everything has to be reinvented all the time, so I understood. I just started working more for labels like Versace, Yves Saint Laurent and Valentino. Then in 2006, we were both at a dinner in Spain and we picked up where we left off – with advertising campaigns, magazine shoots and fashion events.'

Lagerfeld was also powerful when it came to getting the models he wanted. As the creative director of three, sometimes four fashion houses, he knew how to use his influence to his advantage. If an agency was declining to provide a model for one of the Karl Lagerfeld shows – for instance, if another label had first refusal – he issued a veiled threat: 'Ah, what a shame, then she won't be able to model at Chanel or Fendi either.' By wielding his influence in this way, he made sure that he always got his hands on the models of the moment. 'And it wasn't just the models,' says Eric Wright. 'He also did the same thing with fabric manufacturers.'[92]

Lagerfeld's models, who were also ambassadors for the brand, opened up whole new worlds for the designer. Inès de la Fressange, Claudia Schiffer, Vanessa Paradis, Stella Tennant, Kristen McMenamy, Devon Aoki, Cara Delevingne, Vanessa Paradis's daughter Lily-Rose Depp, and Cindy Crawford's daughter Kaia Gerber: with their family backgrounds, their social milieu and their refreshing style, these models helped to cultivate a space in which Lagerfeld could realize his grand ambitions. And, in turn, he made them so famous that eventually they could go without their surnames. With Inès, Claudia, Cara, Kaia and the rest of his girls, he succeeded in constantly rejuvenating the brand without ever having to get any younger himself.

Hamburg

He couldn't resist this house. A cobbled footpath leads steeply down to an archway, where a blue gate marks the entrance. The sprawling grounds are lined with spiked metal fencing for protection. A woodpecker can be heard chiselling into the beech trees. Were it not for the din of the children at the local high school during breaktime, it would be easy to forget that this is still in a major city. Set amid the lush greenery behind the gate to 17 Wilmans Park is a Neoclassical villa. The name 'Villa Jako' was once spelled out by letters in the little holes above the entrance.

As far as Karl Lagerfeld was concerned, 4,765 ft^2 of living space was not excessive. A gallery above the atrium provided ample space for bookshelves, while the living room boasted 20-foot-high coffered ceilings painted with gold leaf as well as three huge arched windows that perfectly framed the view of the meandering River Elbe and the ships sailing in and out of Hamburg harbour. 'Karl was fascinated,' says Marietta Andreae, who joined him at the first viewing. 'He wanted to know how it felt to go back to his roots.'[93] It was supposed to be a kind of homecoming ... but in the end, he turned his back on 'back home'.

The house in Blankenese was a fantastic idea. It was just over half a mile as the crow flies from Baurs Park, where he spent the first year of his life. And, like his first home, it was nestled on a hillside overlooking the river. The villa, built in the 1920s, also harked back to his favourite era. The opportunity couldn't have come at a better time: Lagerfeld had lost his life partner, known lovingly as 'Jako', two years before, and now he was eager to throw himself into new projects. He bought the property in 1991 and called it Villa Jako.

Whenever Lagerfeld arrived in Hamburg, his first port of call would be the Felix Jud bookstore, where he bought dozens of books which manager Wilfried Weber had set aside for him. From there, it was onward to Blankenese, where the contractors were ready and waiting for him at the house. 'It was incredible how much energy he put into the villa,' says Matthias Prinz. As Lagerfeld's lawyer, he was responsible for preparing the various agreements for work on the project.

'The meetings with the contractors really made an impression on me. They were completely chaotic; he was just bursting with ideas.'[94] The lawyer and his wife Alexandra von Rehlingen were in the process of doing up their own house in Harvestehude at the time, and Lagerfeld was more than happy to take a look at their plans. He recommended painting the sitting room a light green. So that's what they did, and the colour served the room well for decades.

'He was obsessed with his new house,' says Alexandra von Rehlingen. She and her husband witnessed the full extent of this obsession when Lagerfeld invited them over for dinner one summer evening. They were wowed by the view across the terraced baroque garden and onto the Elbe. But they were puzzled by what was going on in the host's imagination. 'Can you hear the voices?' he asked. 'I can hear my mother's voice.'[95] What his guests didn't know was that Lagerfeld was 'a very spiritual person'. His old acquaintance Gloria von Thurn und Taxis remembers him telling her he had seen a lady in the mirror in Monte Carlo. Apparently he and Caroline of Monaco had had an intense discussion on the subject.[96] The designer confessed to a whole array of superstitions in conversation with Paul Sahner: 'You mustn't break a mirror, put a hat on the bed or put shoes on the table; you can laugh about it all you want, but that doesn't change the fact that there are people who believe these things.'[97]

Lagerfeld felt close to his childhood at Villa Jako. Still, his visits were usually short and he only stayed the night on rare occasions. All the restoration work, tidying up and organizing took months to complete. The rooms were given names: one was named after the Swiss Neoclassical painter Angelika Kauffmann, then there was the Klinger bathroom, and he called the study the Werkbund room. The antiquated house, which had a gloomy feel about it in places, stimulated his imagination. It became the subject of his book *Ein deutsches Haus* (A German House), published in 1997, which was dedicated to the interior of the house and its trappings. He held fashion shoots in the villa and unveiled his men's fragrance, Jako, to around two hundred journalists there in August 1997. But like so many times before, he was more in love with the idea than the reality. In the autumn of 1997, having exhausted its possibilities, he sold the property to the music publisher Michael Haentjes. 'He got bored,' says Matthias Prinz. 'As soon as something was finished, he already had another five ideas lined up.' It was clear to Marietta Andreae that he had lost interest in the villa when he opened it up to the public. 'Anyway, in the long term it wasn't compatible with his workload or his international commitments.' His former assistant Eric Wright thinks there was another reason. 'Karl wasn't overly keen on Germans because he thought they were mundane.'[98]

The designer moved on, and yet in a manner of speaking he made his way back to the villa. The floor lamp that stands on the left in the sitting room today is a unique early twentieth-century piece designed by the Wiener Werkstätte artist Dagobert Peche. The current owner, Michael Haentjes, is a fan of Peche's work. He bought the lamp at Sotheby's in Paris in 2006, and it was only later on that he realized it had taken pride of place in the villa once before. He recognized it in one of the pictures from the book *Ein deutsches Haus*. There it was: the exact same lamp, with its artfully gilded cockatoos. Lagerfeld had sold the lamp at an auction at Sotheby's in 1998, but the new owner gave it back to the auction house, prompting Haentjes to snap it up. With a couple of detours along the way, the lamp had made it back to the home that Lagerfeld had originally intended for it. A coincidence indeed. Haentjes takes this extraordinary story as proof 'that certain objects have a soul'.[99]

As Lagerfeld moved onto pastures new, he also bade farewell to Marietta Andreae. They had worked together for years at Chanel, where she served as director of public relations for Germany and Austria until 2000. She then left to focus on her own PR agency, but continued to collaborate with Lagerfeld on various projects and photography exhibitions. Andreae had seen the designer cut ties with several close colleagues over the many years of their relationship, so she was prepared for what was to come. Everything suddenly went quiet in November 2007. He sent her a giant basket of amaryllis and roses for Christmas, but that would be the last time.

Though Lagerfeld had moved on, he wouldn't stay away from Hamburg forever. The next time Marietta Andreae saw him was at the Elbphilharmonie on 6 December 2017. He was going back to his Hanseatic roots for his latest Métiers d'Art show. When a journalist asked whether the audience could expect to see all the familiar Chanel fashion codes at the show, he replied, 'This time they're my codes.'[100] He described Hamburg as part of his own personal background. 'It's like wallpaper inside my brain,' he said.[101]

The orchestra played 'La Paloma' as the first of the models made their way through the long walkways in the auditorium. Nautical styles were everywhere, from horizontal stripes to *Elbsegler* sailor caps and 'shipping container' bags. The male models took to the stage holding long smoking pipes in their mouths. At the end, when Lagerfeld came out to take his bow with his nine-year-old godson Hudson, the orchestra started playing 'La Paloma' again. It was a song Lagerfeld had listened to countless times as a young man, in the Hans Albers version from 1944.

Was Lagerfeld suffering from a touch of homesickness? On the evening of the show, he talked to *Die Welt* journalist Inga Griese about the island of Sylt, where he had spent many a childhood holiday with his family. 'I would so love to go back to the Sansibar,' he told the journalist. She offered to organize a trip to the famous restaurant on the dunes, but he politely declined: 'Somehow I don't think that will be possible in my lifetime.'[102] She understood that he was too busy with all his other commitments, but the designer may well have been alluding to the end of his life with this response: by this point he had been living with his cancer diagnosis for over two years.

Hamburg's historic fish market, the Fischauktionshalle, was transformed into a harbour tavern for the evening event. In true Hamburg style, there was salmon and eel soup on the menu. The champagne flowed, as did the beer. Was this all Chanel's doing? No, there was more to it than that. An uncharacteristically withdrawn Karl Lagerfeld said very little all evening. But when the a-cappella shanty choir sang 'Das ist die Liebe der Matrosen' (That's the Sailors' Love), he was spotted gently swaying from side to side with Lily-Rose Depp and Kristen Stewart, who were sitting next to him at his table.

The prodigal son had come back home for the last time. And the next day he was off again.

Flowers

The lead-up to the fashion shows is high season for Caroline Cnocquaert and her sister Stéphanie Primet, who work at the florist's shop at 103 Rue du Faubourg Saint-Honoré. The rest of the time business ticks over at hourly intervals, but now every ten minutes another huge bouquet leaves the shop wrapped in delicate paper. Loyal customers have been frequenting Lachaume for over a century and a half now. Marcel Proust would call at the shop – 'maître fleuriste depuis 1845' – every morning to buy a Cattleya orchid to slip inside his buttonhole. Another former regular was Christian Dior, who lived in the same building when the shop was based at 10 Rue Royale. And in recent decades, one very special, high-profile customer really helped the business to blossom.

Caroline Cnocquaert and Stéphanie Primet's grandmother took over the shop in 1971. Legend has it that Karl Lagerfeld was the first customer she served on her first day in May 1971, when he popped in to buy a long-stemmed white rose. That same afternoon, the new owner's daughter served Yves Saint Laurent, who also asked for a long-stemmed white rose. It was a strange coincidence. Were they exchanging gifts? Were they trying to woo the same man? The florists say they don't know the truth. Then again, perhaps they choose to keep the secret of the rose close to their chests. By their own admission, florists have to be 'très discret'.[103]

Lagerfeld used to frequent the shop in person in his early years in Paris. Eventually this was no longer possible and he started faxing his orders to Cnocquaert instead. Then he got an iPhone. 'He would call almost every day,' she says. 'Particularly when fashion week was coming up.' All the most important British, American, Italian and German fashion editors found a huge bouquet of flowers waiting for them when they checked into their hotels, along with a hand-written card from Chanel's creative director: 'Welcome to Paris! Karl'.

It was a perfectly coordinated operation. Before the shows, Chanel would contact sixty or so important fashion editors to ask when they were arriving and where they would be staying. Lagerfeld then proceeded to order a particular bouquet for each of the editors (very few of whom were men), and made sure that it got to the hotel on time for their arrival. 'He knew everything,' says Caroline Cnocquaert. 'One person would get white roses, another would get purple roses.' Then he sat down, wrote the card, and slipped it inside the envelope with the hotel's address hand-written on it. His drivers dropped the cards off at the shop, and the florists attached the envelopes when the flowers were ready. Finally, one of the shop's drivers would pick up the magnificent bouquets and transport them to each hotel. Other fashion labels greeted fashion editors in a similar way – but not usually with a personal greeting from the designer, and rarely with such lavish bouquets.

Lagerfeld's generous nature had a lot to do with gifts like these. When Alexandra von Rehlingen stopped by at Chanel with her husband in the mid-1990s, he said, 'Alexandra, why don't you pick out a couple of suits to take with you?' She was pregnant at the time, so as grateful as she was for the offer, she politely declined. 'Then at least take a couple of bags,' he insisted, then pressed a blue bag and a black bag into her hand. Lagerfeld later confided in her husband, 'Other lawyers' wives always take ten suits and then sell them on.'[104] André Leon Talley was invited to interview the designer at the Plaza Hotel in 1975, while he was still at *Interview* magazine. No sooner had he walked through the door than Lagerfeld started lavishing him with shirts from Hilditch & Key. Later, when Talley turned fifty, Lagerfeld gave him $50,000.[105] Such generosity positively dwarfs his gift to German journalist Alice Schwarzer, who says they had a 'casual friendship' from the 1980s. 'The black overcoat he gave me is still hanging in my wardrobe,' she says.[106] Every year before Christmas, Lagerfeld invited Caroline Cnocquaert to choose a handbag from Chanel, Karl Lagerfeld or Fendi. The other mothers were surprised to see the florist always toting the latest style when she went to pick up her children from school.

Can fashion editors really remain impartial when they have just received a bouquet of their favourite flowers worth hundreds of euros? Of course, the ugly words 'bribery' and 'corruption' are not part of the vocabulary in the world of fashion, where instead there are only 'friends'. But Lagerfeld's generosity wasn't born out of love alone. Many a time he spoke openly to Baptiste Giabiconi about the benefits of having his own 'white army', i.e. Lachaume flowers, fighting on his side. 'It's crazy what you can achieve with an orchid,' he told his young friend.[107] He was probably right about that. For all the orchids they were sent over the years, the editors let it rain red roses for their friend Karl in their magazines.

The designer also knew how to keep his head seamstresses sweet, making sure they received their bouquets as soon as the Chanel shows were over. And for the man himself, there would always be a bouquet of lilies of the valley waiting at home when he returned from the Grand Palais. The florists work with a grower who cultivates the springtime flowers all year round, so it was never too much to ask. Lilies of the valley were one of Lagerfeld's favourite flowers – along with orchids, white roses and pink carnations, which perhaps reminded him of the branding on the tins of evaporated milk his father used to sell. 'He rarely bought flowers for himself,' says Cnocquaert, 'because he got so many from other people.'

Lagerfeld knew exactly what he wanted, which made him their easiest customer. He also called the shop up plenty of times outside the official fashion calendar, often to order bouquets for Caroline Lebar, Carine Roitfeld and Virginie Viard ('my Virginie', as he called her when speaking to the florists). Sonia Rykiel also received a bouquet before each of her shows. 'It was a lot of work, so much work,' says Cnocquaert. She has kept all the old faxes she exchanged with the designer, who accounted for roughly 20 per cent of the turnover at this sizeable shop in central Paris. Not bad, considering that Lachaume also supplies fashion houses such as Balenciaga, Alexandre Vauthier and occasionally Dior. For all the extra work he created, Lagerfeld was also entertaining. 'We laughed so much with him,' Cnocquaert recalls. And he was always curious, wanting to know all the latest news: 'What are your children doing these days? How old are they now? Which school do they go to? Send me photos! Ah, how wonderful! You must be happy!'

One day Lagerfeld sent the two sisters an iPhone each as a gift. When Stéphanie Primet called to thank him, he asked, 'Do you know how to take photos on them?' She didn't, so the designer gave the florist a quick explanation. He was pushing eighty at the time, and she was half his age: 'You need to go to portrait mode and press "studio light", then you'll get the best pictures.' The two florists have been a hit with their photographs on Instagram ever since.

Journalists

Karl Lagerfeld had a close relationship with the press. Other fashion designers stick to the script, with very little to say about the collections and no thoughts to share about life in general. The only ones with a distinctive communication style are usually the entrepreneurs – designers such as Jean Paul Gaultier, Christian Lacroix, Marc Jacobs and Wolfgang Joop, who have built their own brands. But of all the creatives who worked for major labels and could hold a conversation, Lagerfeld was perhaps the only big-name designer with absolutely no inhibitions. He would merrily ramble on and speak his mind freely, not making any allowances for the companies who paid him.

'He was approachable and spoke to everyone. He was polite, pleasant and disciplined,' says Marietta Andreae. 'Important people didn't impress him in the slightest. But he was extremely courteous with humble employees, waiting staff and other people – journalists, for example.' Even when the appointments were piling up over the course of the day, cancelling an interview was never an option. 'He did get bored quickly when he kept hearing the same trite questions, though,' says Andreae.[108] He was the perfect guest for radio, television and newspaper interviews. 'Quick-witted, multilingual and multifaceted. Educated but not academic. Funny but not corny,' Andreae notes. 'He had a lot of fun [being interviewed].' He was a favourite on German television, often gracing the couch on Thomas Gottschalk's talk show 'Wetten, dass..?' (Wanna Bet..?) and frequently appearing in the line-up for the 'NDR Talk Show'. German hosts Alfred Biolek, Sandra Maischberger, Johannes B. Kerner, Reinhold Beckmann and Markus Lanz liked to invite him for one-on-ones on their shows. He could easily talk for forty-five or sixty minutes, so he was a popular choice.

Whatever the medium, he adapted to make it work. *Women's Wear Daily* (*WWD*), the most important trade journal in fashion, published an eagerly awaited sneak preview of the collection for industry insiders on the morning of each major show. 'I needed quotes and photos for my pre-event reports,' says Godfrey Deeny, who was Paris bureau chief of *WWD* in the early 1990s. Time was of the essence. The layout needed to be finalized. The photographs, which were either sent in a roll of film or had already been developed, had to be rushed off by motorbike and taken to the Concorde that was due to leave Charles de Gaulle for Kennedy airport in New York, then make their way from there to the *WWD* headquarters in Manhattan. Deeny sent the text over by fax. *WWD* is also printed in Paris, so issues of the journal could be distributed the next day before the show. 'It was always complicated with Yves Saint Laurent,' says Deeny, 'whereas Karl was a consummate professional. He personally made sure that we had good pictures on time. And of course, he then wanted to be on the cover.'[109]

Lagerfeld was also a good point of contact for Deeny and his successors Miles Socha and Joëlle Diderich because he was friends with *WWD*'s legendary publisher, John Fairchild, and the then editor-in-chief Patrick McCarthy. The designer worked hard on his relationship with the media behind the scenes. He was on good terms with Samuel

Irving ('Si') and his cousin Jonathan Newhouse from Condé Nast in New York (*Vogue, GQ, Vanity Fair*), Friede Springer from Springer (*Bild* and *Welt* newspapers), and German publishers Aenne and her son Hubert Burda (*Elle, Bunte, Burda Moden, Instyle*). In an almost unbelievable turn of events, he attended Aenne Burda's funeral on 10 November 2005 in Offenburg, where he threw a little soil over the coffin in the grave and said, 'We have lost a great woman and a good friend.'[110]

Lagerfeld was always up for fun in his interviews. In a witty play on the words 'man' and 'pute' (French for 'whore'), he told Godfrey Deeny that he thought the androgynous-looking interior designer Andrée Putman was 'more man than pute'. Many of the comments he made in his interviews became popular catchphrases: 'Sweatpants are a sign of defeat. You lost control of your life, so you bought some sweatpants.'[111] 'Nowadays, sexuality is just a kind of sport.'[112] 'I can't cook. I can barely open the freezer door.'[113] 'The modelling profession is based on certain injustices. You could be considered beautiful today, then barely even wanted for cleaning work tomorrow.'[114] 'Don't dress to kill, dress to survive.'[115] And on model Heidi Klum: 'I don't know Heidi Klum. She was never known in Paris. Claudia Schiffer also doesn't know who she is.'[116]

The designer also used one-on-ones as an opportunity to mine his interviewers for information. 'He wanted to know the latest gossip,' says Godfrey Deeny. Lagerfeld was also more than happy to provide soundbites for Austrian journalists, who weren't part of the most influential inner circle of the media world. He spoke to everyone, including television channels as diverse as Arte and RTL. If the critics' reports turned out to be favourable, there would be flowers and a crate of wine in the editorial office at Christmas – from Château Rauzan-Ségla, a Bordeaux winery owned by Chanel. Lagerfeld also impressed editors with his connections. In 1994, for example, he introduced Deeny to various high-profile figures, including Helmut Newton and Princess Caroline, at the Sun Moon Stars perfume launch at Villa Vigie in Monaco.

The product launch was hosted by Lagerfeld's business partner Elizabeth Arden, and the beauty company invited fashion editors from all over the world to join. The tradition of financing journalists' flights, accommodation and pampering packages escalated over the following decades. Now major labels were inviting editors to join them on trips lasting several days, taking them everywhere from Havana to Hamburg, Rio de Janeiro, Tokyo, Marrakesh and Palm Springs. These 'destination shows' were all about the new mid-season collections, of course, but they also provided a welcome boost. Marketing spectacles like these are even more effective than a bouquet when it comes to creating a good mood, keeping important media players sweet, and putting a positive spin on editorial content.

Lagerfeld became schooled in the art of seduction early on in his career. 'He often came by the office to stay in touch,' says Ariel de Ravenel, who contributed to French *Vogue* from 1967, mostly writing about accessories. 'It was usually early in the evening, and he would have a bottle of champagne for us. He also came by out of curiosity and because he wanted to know what was happening [at the magazine]. He'd take a look at the layout and make a couple of suggestions because he had a good eye.' In this way, he would be one of the first outsiders to know what was coming up in the next issue. Not one to waste an opportunity, he also drew the editors' portraits. 'He gave us the originals,' says de Ravenel. 'I loved how he did that.'[117]

One of Lagerfeld's many friends was Francine Crescent, who, with her unapologetically bold imagery, made the French edition the global *Vogue* leader under her editorship from 1968 to 1987. She published Helmut Newton photographs that 'no other fashion magazine would have dared to print at that time', Lagerfeld wrote in 1982. 'She often risked her job' for him, he noted.[118] He generally cared about his relationships with the various *Vogue* editors-in-chief over the years, including Anna Wintour (US edition), Carine Roitfeld (France), Franca Sozzani (Italy) and Christiane Arp (Germany). He was always trying to get close to the new players on the scene. Although he was not thrilled when Roitfeld left French *Vogue* at the end of January 2011, he was immediately anxious to get on good terms with her successor Emmanuelle Alt. He also had a standing dinner date with Wintour for the first Sunday of every Paris fashion week: 'The hours I spent with him at the table make me feel luckier than any stroke of fortune I've had at my editing desk.'[119]

He even stepped out of his usual role and started working as a journalist for French *Vogue* when Francine Crescent was at the helm. He wrote reviews of new books for the magazine, adopting the rather quirky pseudonym of Minouflet de Vermenou, which he chose because he liked how it sounded. The title of his column was 'Ex libris' and the first piece was published in February 1979. In it, the new critic wrote about the importance of staying on top of the latest developments in the world of books, an activity he referred to as 'a great pleasure'. He also shared his well-informed opinions about books, mostly in the fields of international art, film and fashion.[120]

Lagerfeld felt so comfortable with the press that he didn't even want to put up a fight when *Bild* newspaper published an article alleging that he had had a disabled man thrown out of first class on a plane in 1990. His lawyer Matthias Prinz virtually had to convince him to take legal action. Prinz asked him: 'So, is it true that something happened with a disabled man?' The designer simply replied: 'I haven't flown with a commercial airline for years.'[121] Prinz successfully filed for compensation but had to sign a non-disclosure agreement, so has never revealed the sum. *Bild* printed an apology on page one.

Prinz also represented Lagerfeld in the dispute over the 1994 film *Prêt-à-Porter* (released in the US as *Ready to Wear*). In Robert Altman's satire on the fashion industry, one of the characters calls Lagerfeld a 'voleur', a thief. 'He couldn't stand that,' says Prinz. He obtained a temporary injunction in March 1995, blocking distribution of the film in Germany as long as Lagerfeld was referred to as a thief or, in German, 'Dieb'. The film company found a clever workaround: they played a beep over the top of the offending line. So from then on, one of the designers in the film says 'if I were Lacroix or that – beep

– Lagerfeld...'. Prinz saw the film at a cinema in Paris. 'It was like at the *Rocky Horror Picture Show*, with people waiting for a certain scene so they can clap and cheer.'

Being an avid reader of newspapers and magazines also helped Lagerfeld in his dealings with journalists. Every morning, his driver stopped by the kiosk on Boulevard Saint-Germain to pick up reading material for him hot off the press – everything from *Vanity Fair* to *Figaro* and the *International Herald Tribune*. Despite discovering a love for iPhones and iPads later in his life, he still preferred print media to screens. Suzy Menkes was chatting to Lagerfeld before a dinner in 2011: 'For the first time ever, my review was only posted online today instead of appearing in the paper,' she told him. The only mention of her column on page one of the *International Herald Tribune* was to direct readers straight to the website. Lagerfeld said, 'But I prefer reading on paper.' 'So do I,' Menkes agreed.

Sketches

He started early. As soon as the little Karl Otto could hold a crayon at the age of two or three, he called out to his nanny to ask for paper. He wanted clean, blank paper; nothing else would do. According to his former nanny's niece, Martha Bünz was astonished at how accurately he could draw her and his mother Elisabeth when he was only four or five.[122] Sadly the world would never get to see these early drawings. 'I never kept anything,' he said in 2015. 'I always drew for the sake of drawing. Even before I started school. It's what I've done my whole life.' And what did he find so thrilling about it? 'Imagining a world that was completely different from the environment of Schleswig-Holstein.' So the attraction was that he wanted to dream his way out of this small world? 'Exactly.'[123]

He found plenty of inspiration at home. He copied the illustrations from his father's favourite book, Leo Tolstoy's *War and Peace*. His mother was always bringing new magazines back with her from Hamburg, though in fact the colourful pages didn't offer him much in the way of prospects back then: 'I didn't yet know it was possible to make a career out of fashion,' he said in 2015. 'So I decided I wanted to design costumes for the theatre. Of course I eventually did that, too, for the Burgtheater and the Scala. But I don't have time for that these days.' He no longer had the desire for it, either. 'I'm not used to being told what to do.' He was happiest when he was the one running the show. 'Like in my films. I do everything: I direct and write the dialogue. It wouldn't interest me otherwise.'

No one bothered him when he was busy drawing; he was in complete control. His art teacher, Heinz-Helmut Schulz, encouraged him to pursue his hobby, then in Paris he set about honing his skills and sharpening his eye. Working in the couture ateliers at Pierre Balmain and Jean Patou, he learned how to turn abstract ideas into reality. It must be an almost godlike feeling: you have this idea, you put it down on paper, and then it comes to life. 'Even today, it never fails to surprise me.' Lagerfeld created a new world every morning. 'I often have a vision before I go to sleep or when I wake up.' The multitasker said he needed 'a clear head' so that he could put his nocturnal inspiration straight onto paper. Alcohol was off limits, and he didn't want to take sleeping pills because he was afraid they might make his head fuzzy. Many of his ideas came to him in dreams – like the vision for the spring couture show in January 2015, which he immediately put onto paper exactly as he had pictured it. The set, full of bright, artificial flowers, was the perfect backdrop for the new collection. Baptiste Giabiconi came out at the start of the show to water the plants, and soon they began to blossom, powered by mini engines. The bride stepped out at the end of the show wearing a gown with an elaborate floral train that had taken fifteen Chanel employees three weeks to complete.

Lagerfeld called this kind of nocturnal vision an 'electronic flash'. And just in case inspiration struck, he made sure he kept a sketchpad by his bed. 'Otherwise you just forget it when you fall back asleep.' First thing in the morning, he would throw on a long white smock shirt from Hilditch & Key. 'Everything gets dirty when you work with pastels and other colours.' The shirts, the bed linen and everything else had to be washed every day. 'I like everything to be fresh and white,' he said. 'There's nothing I hate more than when it smells fusty. Unkempt bachelor? No, thank you very much! I shave and take a bath once the dirty work's done. Then it's worth it.'

Lagerfeld needed his peace in the mornings. Unsolicited calls could make him snap. 'I want to be alone with Choupette and to draw in peace without constantly checking the time. I only schedule appointments for afternoons, otherwise I won't make it.' This time at home was his favourite part of the day. Not all his morning sketches instantly became masterpieces, however. 'I throw a lot of them away,' he said. There were large wastepaper baskets all over the place. His apartment was 'basically a studio' and looked like something out of the École des Beaux-Arts, the art school just a few hundred feet away. 'Angled windows for the light! I've almost run out of space on my four drawing tables, there's so much stuff on them.'

Sketching the designs had two advantages. For one thing, it saved him time as it allowed him to leave the seamstresses to deal with the painstaking task of bringing his ideas to life. It also meant he didn't have to work on live models. Draping wasn't his thing: 'I have a totally abstract method. I have this conceptual vision and I put it onto paper in 3D, with all the technical specifications. I don't have to make that many changes when I see the design made up in fabric.' This was what also set his work apart from technical fashion illustrations. 'Computer-generated designs all look the same to me, whereas my sketches are like handwriting.'

Most of the designs that started out in these sketches went into mass production. Lagerfeld's 'handwriting', however, clearly identified him as the man behind the idea. He put a lot of thought into the materials he used for his signature style. Pencils were so important to him that he even became an ambassador for Faber-Castell's Albrecht Dürer watercolour pencils. The 'Karl Box', a set of three hundred and fifty pencils and paintbrushes created in collaboration with the German manufacturer, came out in 2016. The designer also admitted to spending 'a ridiculous amount of money' on paper from his local art supplies specialist, Sennelier.[124]

Light touch: the designer sketches
designs for Chloé in 1979.

This draughtsman – who didn't call himself an 'artist' because he thought it sounded 'too pretentious' – kept the artistic side of the craft alive at a time when everything else was polished to a shine. It was quite the contradiction: a solitary man in a long white shirt, his hair in a loosely tied ponytail, spent his mornings sitting at a table, working away under his own steam ... maximizing profits for his clients at major fashion houses and fuelling their turbo-capitalism in the process. The Fendi archive in Rome is home to more than fifty thousand of the sketches he produced over half a century. Prolific is one way of putting it.

Drawing was like an exercise in meditation for Lagerfeld. Whatever the subject – fashion designs, his pet cat Choupette, invitation cards or caricatures – it was always the same: 'Sketching is like breathing, I don't have to think about it. My whole life I've done nothing but draw.' Lagerfeld's former associate Caroline Lebar says that what she remembers most of all when she thinks about him is 'the sound of the pencils and the rustling of crumpled-up pieces of paper ending up in the bin'.[125] He never stopped. 'He even sat and sketched while he was discussing contracts with lawyers,' says Rosemarie Le Gallais. 'But that didn't mean that he wasn't listening.'[126] He had an extraordinarily vivid imagination. The staff at his Karl Lagerfeld label saw it with their own eyes in 1989, the night before Gianfranco Ferré was due to unveil his first collection for Dior. One of the team asked Lagerfeld what he expected to see at the launch, and with rapid strokes he sketched his prediction for the new Dior look. The others chimed in and threw further names at him, so he also sketched the 'future collections' he envisaged for Sonia Rykiel, Ralph Lauren and other fashion designers. 'You didn't know whether to laugh or be amazed,' said Ralph Toledano, his managing director at the time.[127]

Lagerfeld revisited an episode from his childhood in his later years. When the *Frankfurter Allgemeine Magazin* published his 'Karlikaturen' between 2013 and 2019, this renaissance man became a caricaturist after all. The old tomes of *Simplicissimus* were ready and waiting on his drawing table. He found himself turning to Thomas Theodor Heine and Olaf Gulbransson for inspiration once again, studying the mischievously barbed remarks and grotesque exaggerations in their satirical magazine. Now he was making a political statement, too, attacking empty political rituals, calling out obvious abuses of power, and casting aspersions on right-wing politicians. He brought the spirit of *Simplicissimus* back to life in his caricature of one particular French politician. Inspired by Heine's emblematic canine, he drew a bulldog with the face of Jean-Marie Le Pen, the former National Front leader who threatened to start a new party to hurt his daughter. The cartoon is accompanied by a mini warning: 'I'll bite my daughter Marine in the leg with my new party.'[128] Lagerfeld's decision to become politically active in his later years would attract its fair share of criticism.

Books

The journey to Karl Lagerfeld's world of books led through his bookstore at 7 Rue de Lille. Before heading into his photography studio in the afternoon, he would hover by the tables in his 7L store to check out what was on display. His two booksellers, Hervé Le Masson and Catherine Kujawski, were always adding new releases to the collection. There were books on everything from photography, art, design and architecture to film, theatre, dance, craft, gardening, and even a little bit of fashion. 'Yes to this one, yes to that one, no to that one,' he said, tapping the books. Lagerfeld liked this little luxury: he bought his books from his own bookstore, with a 5 per cent discount.[129]

This wasn't the only bookstore where he was the best customer. For decades he had been frequenting Galignani on Rue de Rivoli, where he claimed his purchases accounted for 11 per cent of the store's considerable sales revenues. In New York he shopped at Rizzoli on Broadway; in Berlin it was the Bücherbogen at Savignyplatz; and in Hamburg he was a regular at Felix Jud on the Neuer Wall shopping street. For decades he bought between one and two dozen books a day. Even he described his habit as 'some kind of strange bulimia'.[130]

Lagerfeld had known Hervé Le Masson and Catherine Kujawski since the early 1980s, when they used to reserve books for him at La Hune on Boulevard Saint-Germain. He built his photo studio in the former courtyard on Rue de Lille in 1999 and was left with a spare 860 ft^2 of space at the front, complete with large display windows facing onto the street. Le Masson was at a training course in Nantes when he received a long letter from Lagerfeld: 'Would you be interested? We could open a bookstore together, completely free and independent.' They arranged to meet on Rue de Lille. Lagerfeld, who was photographing Carole Bouquet for *Egoïste* magazine in the studio that day, took Masson by the hand and showed him around the building. They celebrated the opening party on 7 December 1999 with just one book, *Iwao Yamawaki*, about the Japanese photographer who had trained at the Bauhaus in Dessau from 1930 to 1932. It was the first volume from the new 7L photo-book series that Lagerfeld had recently founded in collaboration with his publisher Gerhard Steidl.

It was the beginning of a new era for these two booksellers. 'It all went so quickly, it was all so new to us,' says Le Masson. 'Things were always fun and exciting when he was around,' recalls Kujawski. 'Even when we first met him in 1981, he was formidable but also completely open and friendly.' Conversation with him was spirited: 'There was a lot of back and forth, like a game of ping pong.' He even cloaked his disapproval of book choices in charming irony: 'Ah, Hervé, you like *this* book?!' Or: 'Well, I guess you won't be ordering that book. We're not a provincial bookshop now, are we?' When the two booksellers – who were soon joined by a new assistant, Vincent Puente – ordered a book on Yves Saint Laurent for the shop, they tucked it away right at the back of the store or hid it in a drawer underneath a table. Despite their best efforts, the boss still stepped in on occasion. 'If I see things I don't like, I just buy them all and throw them away.'[131]

Lagerfeld was proud of his bookshop. 'A man stumbled upon the shop once and ended up ordering 56,000 euros worth of books,' he recounted. Some wealthy customers ordered books by the metre for their homes 'to appear cultured'.[132] Occasionally Lagerfeld could be seen standing outside the main door like a proud shopkeeper, sparking up conversation with passers-by. 'He was good at approaching people directly; it came naturally to him,' says Caroline Lebar. People were always delighted to see him: 'Hello, Karl! Hello!'[133]

The route that snaked around the tables of books eventually led down a corridor to another room where the butler, Frédéric Gouby – always wearing a white jacket – served fresh food and drink to all

A library in the photography studio: only about a quarter of Karl Lagerfeld's
book collection was stored in the studio at 7 Rue de Lille.

the models, stylists, interviewers and colleagues who were made to wait for hours for an appointment with Lagerfeld. After this was another space with a table where the designer would sit to draw and give interviews. An awe-inspiring sight awaited on the other side, through a partition: the walls of the huge studio stretched more than 20 feet from floor to ceiling and were covered with books. Most of them were stacked sideways on the shelves. Lagerfeld gave two reasons for this: it prevented warping, and it meant he didn't have to turn his head to read the title on the spine.

The collection adorning the walls on Rue de Lille was only about a quarter of the books he owned. He also had thousands in his apartment on Rue de Saint-Père, at his Monaco residence and at his house outside Paris, not to mention the many books stored away in a warehouse, which he paid a librarian to manage. He even had supplies for the summer holidays in a villa he rented at La Réserve Ramatuelle in Saint-Tropez. 'The villa was overflowing with books,' says Gerhard Steidl. 'Emmanuel, who ran the warehouse, carted the books there at the start of the holidays.'[134]

It would have been easy for anyone else to lose track with all the comings and goings, but thankfully Lagerfeld had a fantastic memory. Sometimes he organized the books by subject, as at home, where he grouped all the dictionaries together. But most of the time he didn't need to arrange the books alphabetically or by genre. He knew where they were 'in the context of the room'.[135] 'I often go to my bookshelves and visually commit the location of the books to memory. And if I need something specific, I can call and say, "It's on the bookshelf, fifth row up", etc.'[136]

Lagerfeld's favourite bookstore haunt in Germany was Felix Jud on Neuer Wall in Hamburg. The shop was owned by Wilfried Weber, whom Lagerfeld had met through Florentine Pabst in the 1980s. The two men hit it off, and Lagerfeld became Felix Jud's best customer over the years. The designer would place his orders by fax, then the staff would parcel the books up and send them on to Paris. When Weber died in 2016, bookseller Marina Krauth took charge of catering for Lagerfeld's bibliophile needs. 'His interests were tremendously varied,' she recalls.[137] His orders included books by the greats of philosophy such as Johann Gottlieb Fichte, Friedrich Nietzsche and Walter Benjamin, literary classics by Joseph von Eichendorff, Hans Christian Andersen and Rainer Maria Rilke, serialized Franz Kafka collections, and complete editions of Thomas Mann's work. He bought books on architects Peter Behrens and Bruno Taut, anything to do with the Bauhaus movement, the history of the aristocracy from Metternich to Queen Louise of Prussia, and literature on early film, including books about Fritz Lang's *Metropolis* and actresses Adele Sandrock, Asta Nielsen and Eleonora Duse. According to Krauth, he was really tuned into pioneers of graphic art: illustrators such as Henry van de Velde, Kay Nielsen, Léon Bakst and Walter Schnackenberg fascinated him. Likewise, he thought women's art was truly revolutionary, particularly with respect to the Bauhaus.

Few people were better acquainted than Lagerfeld with Cranach-Presse, the publishing house founded by Harry Graf Kessler in Weimar in 1913. Lagerfeld studied Kessler's life and work widely; he even owned a first edition of his Walther Rathenau biography. Everything he needed to know about Art Nouveau and the Vienna Secession he found in issues of *Ver Sacrum* magazine. And when a collector was selling off all his old copies of the Dutch art and architecture magazine *Wendingen*, which was published from 1918 to 1932, the booksellers bought the whole lot for Lagerfeld. 'He was excited. It was a real treasure trove for him,' recalls Krauth. As part of preparations for the Métiers d'Art show in December 2017, the bookseller dug up everything she could find on the history and architecture of Lagerfeld's hometown. She sent him 'at least forty books', including a volume of photographs of Hamburg by Albert Renger-Patzsch, which she could only get hold of in England. And for the Métiers d'Art show in Salzburg in December 2014, the research was all about fabrics, costumes and waltzes.

'Even if you had only spoken to him briefly, you would feel inspired for the rest of the day,' says Krauth, whom Lagerfeld referred to as

'Madame Krauth'. She was also an art dealer, so whenever she came across particularly well-crafted antique crockery, silverware, chairs and lamps, she would bear him in mind. Provided the wares were historically significant and, if possible, still in working order, she would offer them to Lagerfeld. 'What interested him, again, was the mind of the person behind the work.' Someone he admired for his versatility was legendary designer Henry van de Velde, a kindred spirit who worked on a *Gesamtkunstwerk*, a synthesis of the arts, which included books, ceramics and interior design. Lagerfeld saw himself in this fellow multitasker.

Early in 2017, a number of Aubrey Beardsley vignettes were being put up for sale at a small New York auction house. Knowing that Lagerfeld loved Art Nouveau illustrations, Krauth was sure to let him know. 'Oh, I'd love to have those,' he said. So on the spur of the moment, she flew over to New York and bagged three vignettes at the auction. He called her right away when he received the news. 'Excellent! What? You flew out just to get them? Send me all your receipts.'

Not content with being an illustrator, publisher and author, Lagerfeld also got a taste for the art of bookmaking. After discovering a children's book published by Münster-based Coppenrath-Verlag, he invited the publishing house's founder and managing director Wolfgang Hölker to visit him in Paris. Hölker was struck by the impressive surroundings at Lagerfeld's home on Rue de l'Université. 'It was eleven o'clock in the morning. He had the curtains drawn, candles burning and everything prepared, like at some kind of reception.' Lagerfeld also impressed the publisher with his knowledge of Münster. Much to Hölker's surprise, he knew that the Coppenrath bookstore was on the corner of the historic main marketplace, the Prinzipalmarkt.[138] Lagerfeld was proposing that they publish a version of *The Emperor's New Clothes* featuring his own illustrations. Hans Christian Andersen's folktale had fascinated him as a child, he said. The pair went straight into discussing the layout, format and paper. Hölker was sold: 'I had never worked with an illustrator who was so generally well informed and truly interested in everything.' The book, complete with forty illustrations, was launched at a book fair in 1992.[139] It was a hit. 'But that didn't interest him at all,' says Hölker.

Much of the time he was more concerned with the language, style, layout, format and paper than the subject matter itself. He loved Proust for his distinctive style, not the content. His go-to purchases were coffee-table books about fashion, art and design. He had to be able to hold them in his hands: 'Paper has a smell that no screen can ever replace. I'm sorry, I love iPads, but books are better,' he told Roger Willemsen. 'I want to flip through and touch and smell the paper.'[140] This passion for paper was something he shared with Göttingen-based publisher Gerhard Steidl. As a screen-printing specialist with his own in-house printing department, Steidl is an expert in different varieties of paper and printing techniques. He and Lagerfeld met in the early 1990s. The designer once referred to him as 'the best printer in the world', and was inspired to come up with a lot of new ideas through working with him. Lagerfeld published dozens of photography collections with the publishing house, starting with *Off the Record* in 1994. They joined forces in 2000 to establish L.S.D. (Lagerfeld, Steidl, Druckerei Verlag), an imprint specializing in literary titles and non-fiction books. Its publications include the memoirs of Hélène Mercier Arnault (wife of Bernard Arnault), new writing on Nietzsche, and Justine Picardie's Chanel biography. Lagerfeld was overflowing with ideas for new titles for the publishing house. So much so that, even after his death, there were still twenty more books to come.

Being such an avid reader, Lagerfeld could also be very demanding of his friends. He was always giving Steidl new reading recommendations, like the time he sent to Göttingen a copy of William H. Gass's *Reading Rilke: Reflections on the Problems of Translation*. The study from 1999 completely fascinated Lagerfeld. 'You must read it,' he said. 'It's extremely interesting.' A week later he was back again asking, 'Have you read it?' Steidl hummed and hawed. He wasn't overly interested in the challenges of translating Rilke poems into English. 'Go on, make the effort,' said Lagerfeld. 'You have to read it, otherwise we won't be able to talk about it.' The next time Lagerfeld called, Steidl was forced to admit that he had only made it to page thirty of the book. Lagerfeld lost his temper. 'Let me just say one thing: if I recommend literature to you, then please read it because I'd like to talk to you about it. If you don't want to do it, then we can just call the whole thing off.' So Steidl read and read. He kept reading … and they continued to work together.

Reviewing a Lagerfeld collection, 2010

2000 to 2019

Diet

This saddle of venison was one to be remembered. Werner Thiele
certainly knew how to cook meat. He had spent many years as the
chef and driver to the aristocratic Bismarck family, serving the grandson of Germany's Iron Chancellor Otto von Bismarck. When Prince
Otto died in 1975, Thiele continued to work for his widow, Ann-Mari,
Princess of Bismarck (1907–1999). Ann-Mari, who liked to shop at
Chanel and was friends with Karl Lagerfeld, invited him to dinners
when he was in Monaco. On the menu this particular evening was a
beautiful roe deer that a gamekeeper had caught in the vast wood-
lands by the Bismarcks' residence in Hamburg. Werner Thiele had
smuggled the meat to Monaco in his suitcase so that he could prepare
it especially for the meal at Ann-Mari's house. Lagerfeld, quite the
epicurean at that time, was delighted.

'Cher Monsieur,' he wrote on 21 April 1990 from Le Mée, his house
outside of Paris, 'I never got round to calling because I'm always
afraid that someone from the B family will pick up and recognize
my voice.' He makes his attempt to poach the Bismarcks' personal
chef for his new home in Hamburg sound like a top-secret mission.
At the end of the letter, which he wrote on a stationery set from Le
Mée, he makes his intentions clear: 'Anyway, I would be very interested to know if you would consider coming to work for me.' Sadly
for Lagerfeld, it didn't work out. As far as Thiele was concerned, the
villa that the fashion designer had bought in Blankenese in 1991 was
'creepy'. And because the building was listed, permission was never
granted to build the garage with an apartment above it for Thiele
and his wife to live in. 'We then heard that whenever he moved, he
took his people with him. We decided we would prefer to stay with
the prince.'[1] Perhaps Lagerfeld would never eat such a delicious

saddle of venison again in his life. Still, he found ways to indulge his insatiable appetite. The waiters at Café de Flore served his usual whenever he was there: frankfurters with a glass of fresh blood orange juice, then cheese for dessert.[2] He also loved his junk food, with plenty of mayonnaise.[3] One particular journalist was shocked to witness the designer's eating habits in the Chloé atelier: 'He guzzles chocolate.'[4]

If that wasn't bad enough, things got even worse when Jacques de Bascher died in 1989. Lagerfeld was filled with grief and started binge-eating to help him cope. Eventually, he had the baroque figure to match his artistic predilections. As expensive as they were, the suits from Comme des Garçons or Yohji Yamamoto could no longer hide the extra weight. While his favourite models – Stella Tennant et al. – were getting thinner and thinner, he kept piling on the pounds 'without realizing it'. He subsequently talked about this in his book *The Karl Lagerfeld Diet*, describing the tempting delights on offer at the Café de Flore: 'The wonderful cold meats, the slices of black bread thickly spread with delicious salted butter. And the wonderful pastries, *pains au chocolat*, croissants, and brioches; the cookies, the shortbread, and the famous *Kaiserschmarrn*.'[5]

There were many reasons for the designer's healthy appetite. Although his parents were well-to-do, he was fed like the children of simple folk who had to go out and do physical labour. 'Despite the fact that I grew up during the war, our cook used to make big, creamy, sweet, German cakes. Indeed, milk, butter, and cream exist in unlimited quantities in northern Germany.' In fact, he said he 'wasn't too fond of that type of cake, which was certainly nice but rather over the top'. Apparently, there was always plenty to eat at home.[6]

'I didn't really start to put on weight until I was about forty, under the combined influence of dinners out (which I continued to enjoy) and the fact that I had given up bodybuilding.' The extra weight only bothered him later: 'At first I didn't care; later I began to get annoyed.'[7] In an interview on German television, he said he let himself go and put on the weight 'out of carelessness'.[8] Stress can also contribute

to weight gain. As well as grieving for Jacques, he had all his different jobs and the houses he had bought recently, not to mention
the photography, which was becoming more and more absorbing.
He had plenty of reasons not to listen to his body or notice what
was happening.

The turn of the millennium was the perfect time to make a change.
'Farewell to my magnificent 18th-century furniture, which had been
auctioned off. Farewell to my Japanese clothes after ten years of
faithful service. Farewell to the extra pounds. Hello to modern furniture and minimalist décor. Hello to serenity and dealing calmly
with problems.'[9] Aware that the extra weight could cause him problems in the long term, Lagerfeld made a decision: 'Vanity is good
for the health.'[10] On 1 November 2000, he started a radical diet and
would never look back. 'He had made up his mind, and now it was
happening,' says Caroline Lebar. He completely changed his attitude
to food, cutting out everything that was bad for him. 'He only had to
think of sugar and it made him feel queasy,' says Lebar.[11] And in
the space of just thirteen months, he had already lost 92 pounds
in weight. 'Nowadays my ambitions are bound to the superficial,'
he told one German television presenter.[12]

Hedi Slimane's fashion revolution was getting underway at exactly
the right time. Hired by Bernard Arnault in 2000, this young designer
put the Dior menswear collection on a diet, creating a skinny silhouette that completely rewrote the rule-book for men's fashion. Before
long, Lagerfeld was able to wear the jackets Slimane was designing:
'As long as I can fit into a size 48 at Dior, then everything's fine.'[13]
And soon he was wearing the same A.P.C. trousers as his bodyguard
Sébastien Jondeau: 'I wear the same size jeans as Sébastien!'[14]

The yoyo effect was never an issue for this designer: when he made
a decision, he stuck to his guns. Conveniently, the new diet suited
the later stage he had reached in his life. He didn't enjoy going out
in the evenings as much as he had done, so it was easier to fast. But
even when he did attend big dinners, he was still strict with himself.
On the evening of the Métiers d'Art show in Salzburg in December

A new man: Karl Lagerfeld looking very slim in October 2001,
eleven months after starting his diet.

2014, for example, he headed to the St Peter Stiftskeller restaurant
with journalists Christiane Arp and Patricia Riekel, and friends
including Iris Berben and Geraldine Chaplin. While the rest of the
group were served Austrian specialities such as *Tafelspitz* (fillet of
boiled beef), *Kaiserschmarrn* (fluffy torn pancakes with rum-soaked

raisins), *Salzburger Nockerln* (dessert soufflé) and wine, he opted for a meal of steamed fish and vegetables instead.

This strict self-control made him even more formidable. Now anyone who had previously made fun of his corpulence was forced to marvel at his inner strength. He used to try and cover himself up, but now he could put himself out there. The diet gave him prestige, strength and power. It also helped him to turn himself into a kind of logo.

Logo

The weight loss gave Karl Lagerfeld a new lease of life. Standing in front of the mirror at home, he would study his reflection from every angle. 'I really like what I see,' he said. 'It's like I've become my own clothes hanger. When I stand there undressed, the mirror tells me the person opposite sort of reminds him of the skeletons in the anatomy room for medical students.'[15] He was enjoying the new lighter way of life. The camouflage had to go: no more waving a fan to distract the gaze of onlookers. As his waist continued to shrink, so too did his pant size. He also needed new shirts, so he took to the shops. 'He could spend tens of thousands on one of his sprees,' says Sébastien Jondeau. 'He always ended up buying twenty jackets, twelve suits, and jeans from Dior (under Hedi Slimane), Saint Laurent, Givenchy (under Riccardo Tisci) or Colette. Not only for himself, though – a lot of the time half of it was for me.'[16]

Even when he was much younger, he always attached great importance to appearances. 'I think I was born wearing a tie,' he once joked.[17] His ties, like his hair, remained an important element of his signature style. All the other trends were just passing. In the early 1970s he opted for the full-bearded look: 'I need over an hour to get it just how I want it,' he once said. His hairdresser at the Carita salon would wash and blow-dry his facial hair then coif it into shape with a round brush, adding some brilliantine for gloss and a spritz of perfume to finish. In those days, he wore a rimless monocle on his right eye, like his mother had after the war. With his reinforced stand-up collar, cravat and Art Deco accessories, he was quite the dandy. The German journalist Florentine Pabst, a firm friend of Lagerfeld's since that era, justifiably called him 'the most immaculate luxury dandy in Paris'.[18]

His style aged well. The idea of the ponytail came to him in 1976, initially as a way of taming his curly locks. His mother said this hair made him look like 'an old terrine' with its handle sticking out. 'But I didn't want to cut it because people always said it doesn't grow back if you do.' So he chose the most convenient solution: 'All I have to do is brush it, put an elastic band around it, and then it's done.' He didn't even wear his hair down when he was at leisure at home. 'I just tie the band lower so it isn't so tight, even when I'm sleeping.' And because he felt like his hair was thinning as he got older, he kept the ponytail loose instead of scraping it back. Hair was also important when it came to his fashion shows. 'The fashion, the makeup, the hair, the shoes and the girl must come together to form a complete look. There's nothing worse than working with talentless hairdressers and makeup artists. I'd go mad.'[19]

Lagerfeld's hairstyle, which the French referred to as his *catogan*, became a trademark over the years. And from the turn of the new millennium, the addition of white powder made the look even more distinguished, almost presidential. 'My mother's hair was black like the wings of a raven, and it eventually turned pure white. My hair was the colour of Coca-Cola and would resemble an old cow's tail today.' His hair colour reminded his mother of 'an old chest of drawers'. The designer remembered seeing a photograph of his mother at a masked ball. The photograph was taken 'around 1927' and she had white hair, which he thought was exquisite. 'And now my white hair is powdered, eighteenth-century style.'[20] It was a ritual: 'I use dry shampoo every morning to make it white, then I apply a bit of lacquer so that it holds. Then in the evening I brush it out again.'[21] He used 'a special powder room' for the dry shampoo because it made such a terrible mess and went everywhere. His hairdresser, who had been doing his hair for decades, only visited him at home about once a month, when he washed his hair. 'I can't get my hair to dry right when I do it myself – it goes curly when I wash it.'[22]

However, it would take more than just a hairstyle to turn the look into a logo, a kind of silhouette that was recognized all over the world. Lagerfeld claimed that the whole thing came about naturally, but in fact it took a series of small steps to turn the designer from the slightly aimless dandy he once was into the icon he eventually became. One of the key elements was his distinctive high collar. Even when he was a boy, he liked the idea of wearing a stiff shirt collar buttoned onto a collarless shirt. He took a nod from his godfather and uncle Conrad Ramstedt with the style, which had its first heyday in the Biedermeier era. He was also inspired by two men his mother regarded as good role models for her son: the politician Walther Rathenau and the writer Harry Graf Kessler.

Lagerfeld also took after his father, at least when it came to style. Whenever Otto Lagerfeld was in London or Paris, he made it his business to visit the bespoke shirtmakers at Hilditch & Key. The Parisian branch, which opened its doors on Rue de Rivoli in 1907, used to specialize exclusively in tailored shirts. Lagerfeld had been shopping there since he was a young man. Then, in the mid-1970s, the company started selling high-collared, wide-cuffed shirts in its shops.[23] As time went on, Lagerfeld designed new shirts and collars for himself to wear. He would give his driver the sketches to drop off at the shop, so that Hilditch & Key could get the designs made up for him in a studio outside of Paris. All in all, Lagerfeld estimated that he commissioned the company to produce shirts in 'more than three hundred different shapes and designs' for him.[24]

The collars and cuffs on these shirts are detachable, as they were in the old days. Lagerfeld would also order shirts that buttoned at the back. 'Many of his ties – most of which were navy blue or black – were very thin, so it would have been easy to see the button-facing on a normal shirt,' says Philippe Zubrzycki, head of the Paris boutique. 'A slim-cut shirt gives the wearer a certain bearing, and the high collar is good for disguising creases in the neck.'[25] Not that that really concerned Lagerfeld: he looked after himself and rarely went out in the sun in the second half of his life. 'I don't want to look like an old tortoise,' he said in 2015. 'Hence my beautiful skin.' He was proud of how he was ageing. 'Not so bad, right? Without retouching!'[26]

Most of the shirts he bought were made of poplin from Egyptian and Sea Island cotton. Another of his custom requests was for the smock shirts he wore for sketching. As Hilditch & Key's best customer, he often ordered more than the loyal politicians or managers who bought forty or fifty tailored shirts per year. The boutique was also a favourite port of call for gifts. One of the recipients was Eric Pfrunder, his friend at Chanel: every year Lagerfeld sent him twenty shirts for his birthday. Lagerfeld exceeded the minimum price of some 700 euros (£600/US$850) for a tailored shirt because of all his custom orders, which occasionally included an extra forty cuffs or twenty collars.

Although they looked like something from a bygone era, the high collars were in increasingly high demand owing to Lagerfeld's growing popularity. 'We get lots of calls from people asking if they can have a collar like Karl Lagerfeld,' says Philippe Zubrzycki. 'The answer has always been "no" – this collar was meant for him alone, even after his death. The only exceptions are requests from Chanel or the people at Karl Lagerfeld.'

The black-and-white look harked back to how his grandfather, the Prussian district administrator Karl Bahlmann, dressed in his day. It was also surprisingly versatile. He might pair a black shirt and a white collar with an anthracite suit, or a white shirt and a black tie with a silver jacket. Sometimes he would wear a monochrome outfit with a pair of jeans, preferably white in the summer on the Côte d'Azur. He could also jazz it up for special occasions, such as the fashion show in Havana in May 2016, when he stepped out in a jacket covered in colourful sequins (see p. 313). He more or less stuck to the Chanel rule of thumb: one classic look, endless variations. 'You cannot compete or compare yourself to what you were before,' he said in 2013, 'so you better change.'[27]

The monochrome base was like a canvas for this artist in self-stylization, allowing him to pep up his look with ties and jewelry. He overcame gender stereotypes, opting to accessorize with brooches, stone necklaces or diamond lapel pins more typically worn by women. His choices for a public appearance in 2017 included a brooch by Suzanne Belperron with a portrait of his cat Choupette, and two small earphones dangling on a chain around his neck. The earphones were in fact diamond-studded jewelry designed by Nadine Ghosn, the daughter of the then Nissan-Renault boss Carlos Ghosn.[28]

Lagerfeld wore fingerless gloves to avoid skin contact when shaking hands. 'Because the world is polluted and dirty,' he explained. The fact that they were fingerless meant he didn't have to take them off to greet people.[29] The gloves also helped to disguise his fingers, which his mother thought were too fat, as well as the skin on his hands, which was beginning to develop age spots. He got them from the Chanel-owned glovemakers Causse (Gantier) in Millau, close to Roquefort, where the famous sheep's milk blue cheese is made. The region is home to lots of lambs, whose leather provides soft, lightweight material for Causse's products. Lagerfeld ordered gloves from the French manufacturer each season: in lamb's leather or eel leather, in silver, grey or black, and either studded or with chains.[30]

Despite choosing to keep his hands mostly covered, he always wore Chrome Hearts rings. The sheer extent of his collection is demonstrated at the beginning of the film *Lagerfeld Confidential* (2007), when he grabs a bowl and tips all the rings he could possibly need on a short trip to Monaco into a zipper bag. It was as if he was trying to make up for what all the other men were missing. Sometimes he even wore more than twenty at a time, not forgetting his mother's signet ring.[31] His parents' wedding rings could also frequently be seen dangling around his neck on a chain.[32]

The addition of glasses finished the look. He wore slightly tinted lenses from the late 1970s, moving on to black lenses later in his life. 'My eyes are for private use only, not for the public,' he explained. He liked how sunglasses helped him observe the people around him because no one could tell where he was looking. He also thought they made him look ten years younger.[33] Glasses were Lagerfeld's 'burka': 'I'm a little shortsighted, and people, when they're shortsighted, they remove their glasses and then they look like cute little dogs who want to be adopted.'[34] He even made fun of how hard he worked on his image. 'Each morning I have my little fifteen-minute styling session, then I start pulling the strings and directing the puppet.' A professional quirk, he called it – *déformation professionelle*.[35] He was openly proud of how the puppetry had worked out for him, image-wise.[36]

The use of irony helped him conceal the fact that he had modelled himself as a kind of logo. God did not create this man; he created himself. But the style Lagerfeld chose for his iconic look was strangely paradoxical. The German sociologist Tilman Allert has explored the 'tremendous discipline' underpinning Lagerfeld's eccentricity, which he says 'took on a life of its own' and became 'a habit of grandiose self-expression'.[37] Dandies are not exactly known for being hardworking, but this Prussian in dandy garb never stopped working. Then there was the psychological paradox: Lagerfeld – this friendly, outgoing designer – dressed in a way that made him appear unapproachable. It was a kind of armour, protecting him against the kinds of wounds that had been inflicted on him as a child and a young man. The mask stopped the trauma happening again, because fictional characters feel no pain.

Or was he deluding himself if he thought he was protecting himself? Was he, in fact, a prisoner of his own image? The trademark look he had cultivated over the years was practically made for Instagram. As surprisingly old-fashioned as it made him look, his unmistakable appearance also made him stand out in a sea of influencers and football stars. 'He became more and more recognizable when everyone started carrying smartphones around with them,' says his confidant Sébastien Jondeau.[38] Lagerfeld was amazed at how, 'even in the most forgotten suburbs', people knew who he was.[39] Slowly but surely, he grew tired of the passers-by vying for his attention. They were becoming increasingly intrusive, coming up to talk to him and asking for autographs or selfies. 'We're German, too,' some tourists once said to him. 'Yes,' he replied. 'There are eighty million of us.'[40]

Even when he was tucked away in his apartment at 17 Quai Voltaire, where he spent entire weekends whiling away the hours in his own company, he was never completely alone. Occasionally he would hear a voice blasting over the loudspeaker from the *bateaux mouches*, the tourist boats sailing along the Seine below him: 'Up there is where Karl Lagerfeld lives!' Gloria von Thurn und Taxis recalls an anecdote he once told her, about a tourist on the Quai who thought he had seen him. 'That's Karl Lagerfeld,' he said. One of the others chimed in to tell him that couldn't be right: 'That's nonsense, he doesn't go out on the street anymore because of all the people.'[41]

He tried on many different guises throughout his life. It all came together over the decades, and what emerged in the end was a clear, unambiguous image of someone who was somehow completely current yet also remained completely detached. He straddled both sides of the timeline, occupying the past and the present in a way that suited him. Though he outwardly referenced Goethe's era, the German Empire and Bauhaus, he looked to the future with his work. His antiquated style was a response to the fickle nature of his industry. The fashion scene constantly seeks the present, whereas he was playing the long game. He thought along longer historical lines than those who follow trends, and everyone could see that.

Still, there's a fine line between logo and caricature. Karl Lagerfeld was one of the most popular choices for Halloween costumes the year he passed away. On 31 October 2019 thousands of doppelgängers confirmed the power of his silhouette using the hashtag #karllagerfeld on Instagram. And the legend lived on through the 'Grosses Têtes' at Nice Carnival on 15 February 2020, when a colossal Coco Chanel appeared pushing a stroller with a familiar face inside. It was a larger-than-life Karl Lagerfeld, complete with trademark high collar, dark sunglasses and white ponytail – and a pacifier in his mouth. History repeats itself – in this case not as tragedy, but as farce.

H&M

It was another swift decision from Karl Lagerfeld. Donald Schneider, former art director at French *Vogue*, had a creative agency based in Paris and regularly provided consulting services for H&M. In 2014, he came up with the idea for a new campaign for the Swedish clothing company: mixing high with low, haute couture with fast fashion. It was a big idea that called for a big name. In a meeting with the brand, he suggested they try Karl Lagerfeld. Would he even consider it? Schneider had to know, so he called him. 'Karl, have you heard of H&M?' he asked. 'Of course! My assistants shop there too,' Lagerfeld replied. 'So how would you feel about designing a little collection for them?' Schneider asked. 'Great idea! In the future there will only be "high" and "low" fashion anyway; the rest is already getting dull. The "high" fashion's already taken care of at Chanel,' he said. So there was still a gap to fill. 'Wonderful. We'll set up a meeting then,' Schneider said. 'Wait! One more question, Donald: did you ask any other designer before you came to me?' Lagerfeld asked. 'No, you're the first,' Schneider replied. That was enough for Lagerfeld to get on board. 'Good, then let's do it.'[42]

And that's how it all began. It was a bold move, one that was not without its risks. When the collection had been designed and Lagerfeld had long since finished shooting the advertising campaign in his studio on Rue de Lille, when the billboards were up and the stores had received the deliveries, Lagerfeld got cold feet. Everything was good to go, but the night before the big launch in November Lagerfeld called Schneider in New York: 'Donald, I can't get a wink of sleep. What if it's a flop? What if no one comes? What will we do then?' Schneider reassured him: 'It'll work, you'll see.' Although he knew the marketing power of the Swedish company, even he was nervous. This was the first project of its kind, so they were in uncharted waters.

The cheapest piece in the collection, a T-shirt with a graphic print of Karl Lagerfeld's image, was just 14.90 euros (£13/US$18). Previously most consumers could rarely afford to buy more than a lipstick or a perfume from a famous fashion designer, but now Lagerfeld was opening himself up to the masses. The collection, consisting of fifty or so designs for men and women, was available in five hundred branches of H&M across Europe and North America. Even though the pieces were more expensive than the rest of the range, they were still far more affordable than high-end designer wear. The clothes were designed by Lagerfeld and his team, of course, but they were produced in large volumes and didn't cost much to make. Most of the items were black – a favourite for H&M's customers and Lagerfeld himself – teamed with white contrasts to reflect the designer's individual style.

Lagerfeld's communications director Caroline Lebar recalls the morning of the launch on 12 November. She was standing inside the H&M store on Rue de Rivoli with a journalist who was reporting on the collection. When the doors opened, there was pandemonium. The masses of people who had been queuing up on the street suddenly made a dash towards Lebar and the journalist. The pair had to run for cover so as not to be trampled. 'It was madness,' says Lebar. 'People were fighting over T-shirts. The first items in the collection sold out within five minutes.' She called Lagerfeld right away to tell him the news. 'He was surprised and delighted,' she says.[43]

The staff at Chanel and Fendi were confused as to why their creative director was farming out his services to the fast fashion brand. 'How can you do haute couture *and* H&M?' they were asking.[44] The Swedish company had been posing a growing threat to the traditional fashion industry ever since the 1990s. This was particularly the case in Germany, which was H&M's biggest market and already home to 269 stores in 2004. As a 'vertically integrated' company, H&M controls the entire value-added chain, from design to purchasing and logistics through to sales. This means the company has the capacity to bring new products onto the market in the space of weeks, all the while keeping prices low and putting increasing strain on long-established fashion labels and stores.

'It was very smart of Chanel to accept the collaboration,' says Carine Roitfeld, who was Lagerfeld's advisor and did the styling for the advertising campaign. 'Ultimately it did Chanel good, because now suddenly there were all these new people discovering the brand.'[45] The ever-adaptable fashion scene was thrilled with the success of the campaign. Confirmation came in January 2005 when the scenesters gathered for the haute couture shows. Eric Wright remembers seeing several Chanel clients at the Ritz sporting bouclé jackets, pearl necklaces and diamonds. They then opened their jackets to reveal a T-shirt emblazoned with Lagerfeld's face, clearly proud to have bagged one of the sought-after H&M pieces.

'Twelfth of November 2004 was a game changer,' says Caroline Lebar. 'Up to then he was just a famous designer, but now suddenly he was this superstar.'[46] Young people knew who he was now, too, even if they only recognized him from the advertising campaign he starred in with American model Erin Wasson. 'People found him so relatable that they came to the Karl Lagerfeld stores when they wanted to have a piece from the H&M collection altered,' says Sophie de Langlade.[47] Lagerfeld was also amazed that so many people knew who he was. 'They all think I'm their friend,' he said to Carine Roitfeld, 'even though I've never met them.'

H&M's success was measured by the edge the campaign gave them over competitors such as Zara and C&A, not to mention the added turnover. In 2004, sales went up by 11 per cent to 53.7 billion Swedish krona (more than 5 billion euros). And in the fourth quarter, when Lagerfeld's collection was released, the company experienced a 14 per cent surge in sales. A new model for success was officially born. Elio Fiorucci, Stella McCartney, Viktor & Rolf, Roberto Cavalli, Lanvin, Versace and others followed where Lagerfeld had led, designing collections for the brand. Even names like Comme des Garçons, Marni and Matthew Williamson, who were previously only known among fashion devotees, had their big moment at H&M.

The collaboration made Lagerfeld a star, but he still wasn't happy. 'They didn't produce large enough quantities, and the clothes were sold in less than half of the shops,' he told *Stern* magazine soon after the success story in 2004. 'I don't think that's very nice of

Larger than life in Berlin, too:
the designer poses with the
American model Erin Wasson
on a billboard for his
H&M collection.

them, particularly for people who live in small towns and Eastern European countries.' He accused the company of 'snobbery' within what was supposed to be 'anti-snobbery'. He wasn't convinced by the limited-edition concept, which fuelled demand and made the clothes less obtainable. He was also under the impression that H&M had made small clothing sizes bigger, which didn't go down well.[48] As time went on, Lagerfeld stopped complaining and only had good things to say about the collaboration. He even approached H&M about doing another collection further down the line, but by that point the company had moved on. As well as working with other designers, the company had managed to recruit major celebrities such as Madonna, Kylie Minogue and David Beckham. For all the collaborations that followed, it was 'Karl Lagerfeld for H&M' that set the mould.

Advertising

He arrived into Düsseldorf on a private jet from Paris on 14 April 2011 and headed to the Dorint Hotel to freshen up. Over at the 'Lightbox' in Graf-Adolf-Platz, more than a hundred guests were waiting for him to make an appearance … and for the dinner to begin. Schwarzkopf, the haircare brand owned by the local consumer goods company Henkel, was doing a pop-up in the cubic pavilion on the south side of Düsseldorf's Königsallee for the month leading up to the Eurovision Song Contest in mid-May. The event was being sponsored by Schwarzkopf, and Germany was hosting following Lena Meyer-Landrut's win in 2010. The singer returned to defend her title but finished in tenth place on the night – not as good as the last time, but still pretty outstanding by German standards.[49]

Lagerfeld's black silhouette was instantly recognizable against the backlit cube, and the weary fashion metropolis was bustling in anticipation of his arrival. 'Düsseldorf is a young, hip city,' said mayor Dirk Elbers. 'So this event is perfect for us.' Hans Van Bylen, who was chairman of the board at the time and later became Henkel's CEO, was delighted with the result of the design collaboration between Lagerfeld and Schwarzkopf. It was a major coup for the company, not to mention for the city. Local fashion retailer Evelyn Hammerström was not the only woman who wore a bouclé jacket from Chanel in honour of the designer that night.

Lagerfeld arrived with his muse of the moment, Baptiste Giabiconi, and completely lived up to the expectations of his advertising partners and fans. The designer had a smile or even a few words for everyone at the 'Lightbox' opening event. When a reporter asked him if he also had 'bad hair days', he didn't understand what she said. She repeated the question and he still didn't understand, so he just said: 'I don't know this woman.' He even managed to get out of embarrassing situations in a way that had everyone laughing in

A finger in many pies: Karl Lagerfeld also advertised for Diet Coke in 2011,
although he mostly drank the rival product Pepsi Max at the time.

the end. Lagerfeld seemed to have time for everyone, and he really
did – this advertising icon was booked more than almost any other
celebrity. Lagerfeld was an old hand at marketing, and he was more
influential than ever in 2010. At this point in his career he was famous
all over the world and still had a healthy appetite for high-paid gigs.
He would lose this appetite a little in the years that followed, but for
now he was at the peak of his public impact.

Lagerfeld often endorsed different brands at the same time, appearing in television commercials, advertising campaigns and posters for
Sky TV, Magnum ice cream, Coca-Cola, Volkswagen and of course
Schwarzkopf. But, strictly speaking, he didn't always identify with
what he was selling. He hadn't been behind the wheel of a car for
almost half a century, he rarely watched television,[50] he didn't use
Schwarzkopf on his hair,[51] he no longer ate ice cream, and he didn't
drink Coca-Cola. The Lalique glass his butler Frédéric Gouby would

discreetly serve him on a silver tray during television interviews, fashion shows or fashion shoots actually contained the low-calorie alternative, Pepsi Max.[52]

All these commitments in the form of press events, premieres and meetings with VIPs didn't seem to tire him out in the slightest. If anything, they energized him and gave him the chance to set the ball rolling for other projects. When he met Veronica Ferres in Düsseldorf, he asked her if she would be able to join him in Paris for a photo shoot. 'And of course,' said Ferres, 'when Karl asks you can't say no.' Didn't it all get a bit much for him at times? Apparently not. 'It keeps me entertained, I do it alongside fashion and photography. You have to fight against routine. Being too busy is better than sitting all alone in an ivory tower. I don't find that creative.' Fresh insights were important to him: 'Curiosity is what drives me: the new models, the new look, the new spirit, the new attitude. Lots of the things that come along won't survive as long as I will. I can keep moving, you see. Often people get stuck in a generation or a style, or they become outdated. That's – how to put it? – a cruel affair.'[53]

There was more to this seventy-seven-year-old's success than his distinctive image and his razor-sharp wit. Good, hard effort was also part of the secret. Hamburg model Charlott Cordes, whose silhouette was among the backlit motifs on the Düsseldorf 'Lightbox', can attest to this after working on the photo shoot with Lagerfeld until well into the night. And there was no doubting his stamina just a week earlier, when he started working at five in the morning and only stopped in the early hours of the next day: he wanted to catch the right light for a promotional film he was shooting for Chanel at the casino in Monaco, then he was off on a visit to the palace until the afternoon, before heading to the Coca-Cola event in the evening. Baptiste Giabiconi was long gone when Lagerfeld was still giving interviews at two in the morning.

Lagerfeld was always being approached by potential advertising partners, most of whom he hastily turned down. If the idea was inspired and he hadn't done anything like it before, he usually accepted the offer – but only if the money was right. Often it was car manufacturers whose proposals appealed the most. He designed three BMW E38 7-series, the first of which was unveiled in 1992 and featured a built-in fax machine and a pen holder in the glove compartment. It even had a tissue holder inside the door, for art-smudged hands. He photographed the 2006 calendar for the VW Phaeton model in the constructivist style and published the book *Factory Constructivism* around the same time. Then, in 2012, he was invited to Rolls-Royce's Goodwood facility near Portsmouth to take photographs in the style of the 1920s – each of the edition of seven comprised fourteen photos and cost 90,000 euros (some £75,000/US$110,000). Lagerfeld also did his bit for road safety, donning a high-vis vest for a national French campaign in 2008: 'It's yellow, it's ugly, it doesn't go with anything, but it could save your life' was the slogan of the awareness-raising effort by Sécurité Routière, the French authority for road safety. In 2010 and 2011, his Diet Coke designs made him famous in a completely different area. Other designers and labels used their iconic fashions for their designs, whereas Lagerfeld used his persona, opting for a black silhouette of himself to contrast with the aluminium bottles. Even when he was selling products, he was advertising himself.

'He was an exciting prospect for Schwarzkopf because he was also a strong German brand,' says Tina Müller, former head of marketing at Henkel.[54] In 2009, the company was celebrating its 111th anniversary. At the launch for *We Love Hair*, the book accompanying the anniversary campaign, Lagerfeld was reconciled with Gabriele Henkel, the widow of the company's former chief executive. In true style, he was late to the reception at the NRW Forum.

Public appearances like these – photo shoots, interviews and evening receptions – cost his business associates astronomical amounts of money. 'He wouldn't leave the house for less than a million euros,' says Tina Müller. 'Then there was the fee for his entourage and his flight by private jet.' But it was worth it. 'He gave the brand a touch of glamour, and that was exactly what it needed,' says Müller, who later joined Opel, and then became the CEO of Douglas. The designer also used commitments like these to gain insights into new sectors. In his brief address on the evening of April 2011, Lagerfeld said, 'Were I not in fashion, I would have an advertising agency.'

Market researchers were puzzled by Lagerfeld's successes in advertising. The 'Promimeter' is a test used by the experts at the IMAS Institute in Munich to determine celebrities' potential for endorsing brands and products. According to the survey, almost everyone in Germany knew who Karl Lagerfeld was around this time, but only 11 per cent thought he was likeable and 29 per cent found him unlikeable. He scored highest when endorsing clothing and cosmetics, but he wasn't necessarily the best advertisement for TV programmes or cars. The industry started to fear what was referred to in German as the 'Verona Pooth effect': when celebrities promote too many brands at once and their credibility is called into question. When this happens, the celebrity is the only one who stands to benefit, rather than the brand itself.

That evening in Düsseldorf, Lagerfeld left behind much more than the memory of a dinner of asparagus-tip vinaigrette, crayfish and stuffed poussin. The designer lived up to his advertising role – by dancing to his own tune, rather than aiming to please. When a reporter asked if he was getting excited about the Eurovision Song Contest, he replied, 'I have no connection whatsoever to things that have nothing to do with me.' And how did he feel, being in Düsseldorf? 'I'm supposed to have feelings now, too?' he quipped. Clearly he had no strong feelings about it, because by eleven in the evening he had vanished again. When the last guests were still clinking champagne glasses, he was already high above the clouds on his way back to Paris.

Enemies

They all came to the funeral service for Yves Saint Laurent at the Saint-Roch church in Paris on 5 June 2008: President Nicolas Sarkozy and his wife Carla Bruni, designers Christian Lacroix, Sonia Rykiel, Valentino Garavani, Vivienne Westwood and John Galliano, the mayor of Paris Bertrand Delanoë, philosopher Bernard-Henri Lévy, actress

Catherine Deneuve, model Claudia Schiffer, his old friend Victoire Doutreleau, his muse Loulou de la Falaise – and his mother, Lucienne Andrée Mathieu-Saint-Laurent, who passed away two years after him at the age of ninety-five. Everyone came to pay their respects to the designer, who had died from brain cancer on 1 June 2008. The only one who didn't join them was his old friend Karl Lagerfeld.

The two legendary designers hadn't seen eye to eye for a very long time. The nights in the 1950s with Victoire Doutreleau and Anne-Marie Muñoz were a thing of the past, as were their lively discussions about Marcel Proust. The many similarities between the two men had given way to even bigger differences over time, and any friends they had in common made sure they kept their relationships strictly separate. There was too much resentment: too many lines had been crossed and lies told; too much had been said, both out loud and in whispers.

The scars from the 1970s ran particularly deep. Around that time, Yves Saint Laurent was hurt because Jacques de Bascher had ended their affair, and Pierre Bergé was angry because the *amour fou* had made things even more difficult with his life partner and business associate. Their relationship was in such bad shape that Bergé ended up leaving the apartment on Rue de Babylone. He took a room at the Hôtel Plaza Athénée on 3 March 1976, then he moved into an apartment on Rue Bonaparte.[55] Lagerfeld only added fuel to the fire with his provocative ways, publicly accusing Bergé of being in love with Jacques himself. Bergé fought back via Alicia Drake: 'I do not fall into that trap,' he said. However, he proceeded to get angry and his tongue ran away with him – so he did fall into a trap, just a different one.[56]

The one woman who succeeded in bringing them all together again was Paloma Picasso. The artist's daughter was friends with both factions and refused to get involved in their conflict. So when Paloma married the Argentinian writer Rafael Lopez Sanchez on 10 May 1978, she extended this impartiality to her wardrobe: she wore a white spencer jacket with a ruffled red blouse and a black wraparound skirt from Yves Saint Laurent for the ceremony, then for the evening soirée at Lagerfeld's townhouse on Rue de l'Université she wore a romantic puff-sleeved red dress designed by her host. The dinner reminded Lagerfeld of the scene from the court of Frederick the Great in Menzel's painting. Anna Piaggi's feathered hat catching fire on one of the candles on a silver candelabra wasn't the only sensation of the evening: after years of silence, Yves Saint Laurent and Karl Lagerfeld found themselves sitting next to one another, engaged in spirited conversation. They complemented one another on the outfits they had designed for Paloma. Even Bergé and Lagerfeld spoke for a while. 'What is this love affair?' Loulou de la Falaise asked ironically. 'This marriage is not only a union of Paloma and Rafael, but it brings together good friends. I only hope it will last.' The party went on until dawn, as the guests rolled into Le Palace, where Lagerfeld and Saint Laurent even briefly danced flamenco together.[57] But this would be their last dance. In the decades to come, the rift became wider and the resentments only grew. Swords were drawn when Saint Laurent told journalist Janie Samet about a dream he had involving Coco Chanel: while walking through Paris together, they stopped to look in the window at Chanel on Rue Cambon and both cried at the sight.[58] Lagerfeld was sharpening his knives, too. When one interviewer asked his opinion about Saint Laurent's departure from ready-to-wear, he simply said, 'I don't care.' But at the same time, he made a point of praising Tom Ford, who designed ready-to-wear at Yves Saint Laurent from 2002 to 2004: 'He did some really great things [there].'[59]

The rivalry had taken on a life of its own. The two major designers repelled each other like magnets of the same pole. 'Lagerfeld never asked about Saint Laurent in my interviews,' says Godfrey Deeny. 'But he wanted to know everything about him.' Joan Juliet Buck hosted a reception to celebrate her appointment as editor-in-chief of French *Vogue* in 1994. Lagerfeld was one of the many designers invited to attend the event, and Deeny later asked him how it had gone. 'I had one of the most disgusting moments of my life,' he said. 'Yves Saint Laurent came over to me and kissed me on the cheek. I had to wash it off.'[60]

Enemies for life: even when the mood was festive, as here at the wedding of Paloma Picasso in 1978, the tensions between Karl Lagerfeld and Yves Saint Laurent were palpable.

But he felt even more strongly about Pierre Bergé, the man who did all the talking for Saint Laurent. He couldn't stand the man, calling him a 'poison dwarf', and accusing him of being status-hungry and controlling. The difference between Saint Laurent and Lagerfeld: 'I don't need to put up with Pierre Bergé every day.'[61] Lagerfeld also despised Bergé because he supported the socialists who were causing him a headache over taxes at the time. When Saint Laurent had already fallen ill in 2007, Lagerfeld said the designer was 'okay' in his day but had since 'dozed off'. Not without a hint of pity, he accused Bergé of neglecting Saint Laurent, saying what he did was basically criminal: 'He was supposed to be looking after him. That's his duty. Yves was great when he was younger. Pierre Bergé's job was to keep him above water.'[62]

By this Lagerfeld was alluding to Saint Laurent's addiction to drugs, alcohol and painkillers, as well as his bouts of depression, which often resulted in him being admitted to the psychiatric ward of the American Hospital in Neuilly for weeks at a time. Saint Laurent's first stint at rehab was when his relationship with Jacques ended in 1975.[63] 'I have grappled with anguish and I have been through sheer hell,' he said when he announced his retirement on 7 January 2002. 'I have known those fair-weather friends we call tranquillizers and drugs. I have known the prison of depression and the confinement of a hospital.'[64]

As if to have the last word on the conflict when Saint Laurent had passed away, Pierre Bergé made his opinions clear in his *Lettres à Yves*, some of the pages of which read more like 'Lettres à Karl' than letters to his late partner. 'Pierre Bergé hated Lagerfeld because he criticized him for his mediocrity,' says fashion historian Peter Kempe.[65] Bergé took the opportunity to fight back in the book, where he pointedly named his late partner and Coco Chanel as the two most important designers of the twentieth century: 'Chanel in the first half, you in the second.'[66] Of course, he had every intention of provoking Lagerfeld with this sense of pretentious entitlement – putting Saint Laurent above even Christian Dior, the man who had paved the way for his career in fashion. A few years before she died, Coco Chanel did say that she could picture Saint Laurent as her successor, but Bergé went so far as to claim that he had to console her with a bouquet of flowers because Saint Laurent was more interested in continuing to focus on his own fashion house.[67]

Even Jacques de Bascher, who had passed away long before, was drawn into the battle. 'I never understood how you could fall in love with an effeminate seducer,' Bergé writes, clearly disappointed in his late partner for being weak and succumbing to Jacques's charms. He said it had become clear to him that Yves's greatest wish was 'to play

with the devil'.[68] Lagerfeld, for his part, was amused by Bergé's sug-
gestion that he had orchestrated the whole thing, setting Jacques
onto Yves in order to sabotage his relationship with the designer and
destroy the business they had built together.

Bergé had some interesting material to support his theory.
He writes about how 'K...' had called him one day to tell him about
how he had found some letters from Yves to 'J. de B'. Apparently the
letters were so vulgar, obscene and full of sexual violence that he had
been tempted to burn them. But instead he decided to keep them,
partly as a threat and partly as blackmail. Supposedly Bergé told
Lagerfeld the letters didn't bother him.[69] Jacques had given Karl the
vast collection of letters from Yves, complete with explicit sketches,
in the 1970s. No doubt he was afraid that Bergé would come round to
his apartment, as he had threatened to do previously, and find them
while he was there. 'I have all the love letters in the vault,' Lagerfeld
told Wolfgang Joop and his wife in the mid-1970s. 'It's enough to make
you blush, honestly!'[70] Presumably he also had Philippe Heurtault's
recordings of Saint Laurent's calls in safekeeping.[71]

This material had all the potential to cause a scandal, and yet
Lagerfeld chose to keep it to himself. There were plenty of opportunities to take it to the press over the years, especially in his startlingly
frank conversation with Jacques de Bascher's biographer Marie Ottavi
in 2017. He wanted to put the record straight and talk about his life
with Jacques from his own perspective, so this was his chance. But
as bitter and as vicious as he could be at times, putting the boot in
was not his style. Presumably he had also moved on from all those
past alliances and misalliances after Saint Laurent's death.

Lagerfeld had always finished in second place, but now he was
the last man standing. He was head and shoulders above the competition, and no one could match him for status and charisma. Saint
Laurent had repeated himself a few too many times in the 1980s and
the 1990s, and his classics – the see-through blouse, the 'Mondrian'
dress, the tuxedo for women, and the safari jacket – were fit for a
museum. And that was where they ended up, in the two Yves Saint

Laurent museums, in Paris and Marrakesh, which opened in 2017. He quit ready-to-wear in 1998 to concentrate exclusively on haute couture. From then on he was the guardian of his own past until finally he retired in 2002.

Lagerfeld was energized by Saint Laurent's departure from the fashion world. Clearly the clairvoyant had been right when she predicted that his rival would bloom early and he would enjoy fame later in life. Over the next seventeen years, he could finally step out from his former friend's shadow and steal the limelight. He moved with the times, successfully adapting to the rise of affordable fashion, the acceleration of fashion cycles, the growing numbers of fashion shows, globalization, online marketing, social media ... and haute couture.

Yes, haute couture was on the rise in the new millennium. The market was performing incredibly well, with new markets such as Russia, China and the Middle East experiencing a surge in demand for bespoke dressmaking and tailoring. A single haute couture item often costs in excess of 20,000 euros (£17,000/US$24,000), with some items fetching more than 100,000 euros. These prices are justified, however, because so much expensive craftsmanship goes into making the clothes. In fact, the profit margins are low for companies because the clothes cost so much to produce. This classic tailoring is an important marketing tool, as the images are circulated around the world, boosting sales of licensed products such as perfumes and sunglasses.

A number of fashion houses have now returned to haute couture following a long hiatus, including Givenchy in 2015, Balmain in 2019 and Balenciaga in 2021. But the fashion houses that still dominate in this small but sophisticated market are Chanel and Dior. Despite competition from designers John Galliano, Raf Simons and Maria Grazia Chiuri at Dior, and for all the impressive qualities of brands such as Valentino and Giambattista Valli, the indefatigable Karl Lagerfeld reigned supreme. He was the master of haute couture in the new millennium. After half a century working in the industry, he knew the system inside out. No one else could boast such a broad stylistic repertoire, with designs ranging from elegant to deconstructed to sexy. And no one else had such an incredible pool of resources in the form of the *petites mains* of Chanel, the in-house dressmakers, the decorative feather makers, the pleaters and all the other artisans at the fashion house.

All this was most satisfying for Lagerfeld. Other designers weren't so fortunate: Christian Lacroix quit for financial reasons in 2009, Jean Paul Gaultier abandoned couture in 2020, and John Galliano cracked under the pressure in 2011, when he was forced to leave Dior following a drunken rant in a bar. Karl Lagerfeld, on the other hand, had everything under control, even himself. He stuck it out in haute couture, proving Pierre Bergé wrong once again. In 1991, the Frenchman had claimed that couture was dead because even wealthy women preferred ready-to-wear. He also claimed that the only real couturiers left were Hubert de Givenchy and Yves Saint Laurent. Lagerfeld called this rather gloomy prophecy 'ridiculous'[72] at the time. Now, finally, he was triumphant. But it was a Pyrrhic victory: even in the later years of his career, he was still unable to design the kinds of fashion classics that made it into the history books, as Yves Saint Laurent had done.

Lagerfeld was busy on 11 June 2008 when the ashes of the man they called 'the last couturier' were scattered in the rose garden of the Jardin Majorelle at his villa in Marrakesh. 'It will begin for you when it ends for the others,' the clairvoyant had told him. The fact that he had met Baptiste Giabiconi a few days earlier, on 8 June 2008, was a sign that this prophecy was about to come true.[73] The final phase of his life was going to be extremely productive.

Baptiste

Fashion designer meets unknown eighteen-year-old and turns him into the world's most famous male model. It was the perfect story. Baptiste Giabiconi had been working at Eurocopter, a helicopter plant in Marignane, Marseille, when he met Lagerfeld. The designer, recognizing his younger self in Baptiste, helped this somewhat aimless young man in any way he could. He put him up in his empty apartment

Guests at Dior: Baptiste Giabiconi (left), Karl Lagerfeld and Sébastien Jondeau (right) visit the menswear show hosted by the rival label in 2010.

on Rue de l'Université in the summer of 2008, then let him stay in the studio on Rue de Lille, and before long he would be spending half the weekend in his company in his apartment, a privilege that was off limits to most people. Lagerfeld also booked him for a series of racy private shoots there.[74]

Lagerfeld immortalized the young French model in countless campaigns for labels such as Chanel, Fendi, Hogan and Dior. He also cast him in multiple fashion shoots and photographed him for several books. Baptiste is one of the very few men to have graced the catwalk at womenswear label Chanel. Even in 2008, he was already a hit with the paparazzi. That summer, Lagerfeld was spending the holidays in the villa he rented at La Réserve Ramatuelle. Sébastien Jondeau and British model Jake Davies stayed at number 19, while Baptiste stayed at number 16 with the designer. Karl enjoyed spending time in Baptiste's company when he wasn't working or reading, at least when the three younger men weren't driving to a nightclub in Saint-Tropez in the Lamborghini from his impressive fleet. 'They were young and liked to talk about new films, new music and the latest trends,' says Gerhard Steidl. They were therefore his connection to the rest of the world.[75]

Karl also got a kick out of provoking the paparazzi with his male companions. He liked it when Sébastien drove him from Ramatuelle to Saint-Tropez: they would sit by the harbour under the awning of Café Sénéquier, order a Pepsi Max, and let the passers-by gawp. In the summer of 2008, he would also be spotted strolling along the promenade with Baptiste for the first time. His new friend stood out from the crowd with his bold quiff, colourful shirt and teeny shorts. The press lapped it up. When Karl and Baptiste returned to the harbour in Karl's open-top Rolls-Royce a few days later, they basked in the outcome of their little stroll. The press had gone into raptures over 'la musa', the 'friend of the summer', Karl's 'toy boy'.[76] According to Baptiste, newspaper coverage like this played a big role in 'putting a planetary icon in a good mood'. The designer was now embarking on 'his greatest years' – his final, most joyful reign as 'Kaiser Karl'.[77]

When Baptiste turned twenty, his mother hosted a party near Marseille and invited all his friends to come along. Lagerfeld hadn't confirmed, which made it all the more surprising when he turned up, unannounced, having flown in by private jet. He stayed at the party for a long time and took photographs of all the guests – every relative, friend and neighbour. Afterwards he sent Baptiste all the prints, each of them with a personal dedication. Karl's gift was even more touching: it was the watch that his father Otto had given to him on his eighteenth birthday.[78]

Baptiste recalls standing with his mentor in the pristine, chrome-laden kitchen of the Quai Voltaire apartment one day. 'Did you know, Baptiste, that you broke down a barrier today?' Lagerfeld said. 'You're the first [to do that] since Jacques. Do you realize that?' Baptiste was taken aback. His friend was usually so loath to show his feelings, and here he was putting his heart on his sleeve. Without thinking, almost like a reflex, Baptiste hugged his mentor tightly, kissed him on the cheek, and held the embrace for a long time. He was surprised by the response from his fatherly friend, who was clearly moved by the display of warmth. 'He was shaking. I can still see him in front of me, lost for words, as if he hadn't experienced feelings like those for years. Time stood still.'[79] It was probably the first time in years that Lagerfeld had experienced real tenderness. Perhaps it was also the last.

Moments like these cannot last forever. Everything started changing as Baptiste became more independent. In the autumn of 2011, the model joined the line-up for *Dance avec les stars*, the French version of *Strictly Come Dancing*, or *Dancing with the Stars*. Karl, not normally one for television, religiously followed the series on TF1 and begged everyone he knew to vote for Baptiste. Karl wouldn't miss an episode for anything. Even when he was invited to the studio with Marie-Louise de Clermont-Tonnerre's friends and family to celebrate Chanel's legendary head of press winning an award, he didn't hang around too long. 'Excuse me, my dear Marie-Louise, but I have to go and watch Baptiste dance,' he said, then promptly disappeared.[80] He was outraged when his protégé lost in the final, claiming that the vote had been fixed.

Making the most of his growing popularity, Baptiste decided to embark on a career as a singer. By this stage he was successful in his own right, and not just thanks to his mentor. Karl was afraid of losing him and became increasingly controlling. When Baptiste went out in the evenings, Karl would do some detective work to find out who else was there, what he had been drinking, and what time he had gone home.[81] Soon Baptiste felt as if he was living in a cage. 'I heard you did cocaine yesterday,' Lagerfeld accused him over the phone

one day.[82] Baptiste, who claims he has never taken cocaine in his life, felt like he was under surveillance. He kept seeing Karl's employees casually cycling past the window of his apartment, checking up on him. 'There are five or six of you sleeping in the apartment,' Lagerfeld said. 'Have you told them they can stay with you? Who's living there with you?' Finally, he summoned him to the Chanel studio and gave him a dressing down for his 'moods', for 'being impossible', and for keeping 'bad company'.[83] Karl wanted to completely possess the friend he had made famous or have nothing to do with him at all. But both these things were impossible.

Hudson

There were two major appearances at the Chanel show on 5 October 2010. Inès de la Fressange was back on the runway for the label for the first time in over twenty years, modelling the ready-to-wear collection for spring/summer 2011 to rapturous applause. It was also the debut of Karl's favourite godchild, Hudson. Holding his father Brad Kroenig's hand and wearing perhaps the smallest Chanel jacket ever made, the two-year-old starlet walked through the baroque garden created especially for the set.

A long backstory led up to this toddler's big performance. Brad Kroenig, born in St Louis in 1979, had been one of Lagerfeld's favourite models since 2003. Besides working on fashion shoots, advertising campaigns and the runway, he was also part of the designer's entourage in Paris and Saint-Tropez. Lagerfeld was fascinated by this 'All-American Boy' and photographed him repeatedly. In a series of the coming-of-age photographs entitled *Metamorphoses of an American: A Cycle of Youth*, Lagerfeld's Midwestern muse posed as Lawrence of Arabia, Truman Capote, Elvis Presley, James Dean, and even as himself. The images mounted up to a four-volume book devoted entirely to Kroenig.[84]

Lagerfeld already had various godchildren, including Carlos (whose mother was his friend Anne-Marie Muñoz), Jacob Karl (the son of his friend Florentine Pabst) and Cosima (whose mother is the model Nadja Auermann), but he became a godfather again when Brad Kroenig's son Hudson was born in 2008. Being a godfather suited Lagerfeld down to the ground. The designer counted Johann Wolfgang von Goethe's *Wahlverwandtschaften* (Kindred by Choice) among his favourite books,[85] if only for the title. He had created his own substitute family, complete with substitute offspring. Having children was out of the question for him: 'There are certain people who shouldn't have children, and I'm one of them,' he once said. 'I don't belong to any generation and I'm not part of any milieu; I don't belong anywhere and I fit in everywhere.'[86] He got past age barriers easily and was good with kids. But a two-year-old on the runway? Brad Kroenig had no objections, though his wife thought it was a strange idea. 'At the beginning I thought Brad was nuts for thinking he could do it,' says Hudson's mother Nicole, daughter of tennis coach Nick Bollettieri who trained, among others, Andre Agassi and the Williams sisters. 'I was in the audience and my heart was beating so fast.'[87]

Soon enough, Hudson was a regular on the runway. Sometimes he would step onto the catwalk holding a model's hand; other times he would go it alone. Sometimes his father hadn't been invited on stage and had to watch from the front row instead. Hudson started accompanying Lagerfeld when he came out to take his bow at the end of the show. It was a clever move by the designer, who knew a thing or two about how to accessorize. As well as gaining the sympathy and respect of the audience, he took the focus away from his increasingly frail appearance and gait. But above all, Lagerfeld just liked having his little friend around. He could see the young Karl Otto reflected in his godson, and the crowd saw Hudson as a portrait of the artist as a young man.

Nothing – apart from Choupette, of course – gave Lagerfeld as much pleasure in his later years as this little boy's astonishing self-confidence. One of the anecdotes that tickled Lagerfeld originated when Hudson was three years old and had to go to nursery. Apparently he hit the other boys and said: 'I have nothing to do with you. I am a supermodel.'[88] Another time, the nine-year-old Hudson was in an

Havana, May 2016: Karl Lagerfeld flew his godson Hudson Kroenig
in from New York for the Chanel Cruise show.

elevator in New York, carrying a special Louis Vuitton bag he had
been given as a gift. A man asked him where he got his fantastic bag
from, and Hudson replied, 'You've got to know the right people.' And
when Hudson was sitting in the front row of a Chanel show next
to Anna Wintour from *Vogue*, the little one told the most powerful
woman in fashion, 'I'd prefer to be sitting next to Pharrell Williams.'
Lagerfeld was amused by statements like these, especially coming
from his mini-me: 'He's hilarious!'[89]

Hudson's godfather showed his affection with gifts, so of course
the boy's wardrobe was full of custom-made Chanel clothes.[90] The
last of the outfits he received was for the show at the Metropolitan
Museum on 4 December 2018, for what would be Lagerfeld's last public
appearance. The Dendur Temple provided an evocative backdrop for
the image of this ten-year-old boy, who lapped up the applause as he

stood beside Lagerfeld and his assistant Virginie Viard. Gold trousers, gold boots, gold hat and a top with Egyptian motifs: Hudson looked like a little pharaoh.

Shows

Supermarkets were not his natural habitat. At this point in his life, Karl Lagerfeld got most of what he needed from his trusted bookshops, the hip Colette boutique in Paris, and the menswear department at Givenchy. 'I work,' he said smugly after the show on 4 March 2014. 'I don't go shopping.' But for many of the guests at this Chanel show, it was a different story. As soon as the models had paraded past in the autumn and winter trends, the ugly side of capitalism manifested itself in many of the beautiful faces at the event. Gripped by the competitive spirit of consumerism, the fashion editors made a dash for the shelves of the giant supermarket Lagerfeld had had built in the Grand Palais. The stylist and street-style star Anna Dello Russo almost tripped over her high heels as she charged in the direction of the doormats printed with the words 'Mademoiselle privé'.[91]

Mademoiselle Chanel would have been happy with the big idea from her successor. Lagerfeld surprised around 2,700 guests with a whopping 100,000 carefully arranged products – from bottled water labelled 'Eau de Chanel' to 'Jambon Cambon', ham named after the street that is home to Chanel's head office. More than just fodder for the dawning age of Instagram, this was also a commentary on the unbridled consumer habits of 'fashion victims'. Guests revealed their primitive urges in the race for doormats and feather dusters.

It was a rare occurrence in the grand scheme of fashion history: a show that was both self-reflective and engaged with its wider context. Perhaps there were similar moments of self-awareness when John Galliano created a sense of alienation in the audience by stepping onto the stage at the end of the Dior shows dressed as a pirate, a dandy or an astronaut. Or at Jean Paul Gaultier in October 2011, when the backstage area was exposed on stage and the spectators

Supermarket set: Karl Lagerfeld does one last lap of the set with model
Cara Delevingne after the Chanel show in March 2014.

were invited to follow the making of the show in real time. Or at
Odeeh in January 2019, where the label had guests sitting on the
stage in the Haus der Berliner Festspiele while the models stood in
the auditorium, employing the change of perspective used as a theatrical device in such plays as Peter Handke's *Publikumsbeschimpfung*
(Offending the Audience).

Fashion shows are all about presenting the latest designs in their
best possible light, and these were all perfectly good attempts to
take this concept to the next level. But Lagerfeld was the first in his
field to fuse content, grandeur and self-reflection in such an innovative way in the shows he masterminded from 2005 to 2019. Just like
Richard Wagner's *Gesamtkunstwerke*, in which the individual arts are
subordinated to a common purpose, Lagerfeld created total works
of art for Chanel – albeit artworks that venerated capitalist interests
rather than some kind of social utopia.

In a way, all the advertising displays also served as mini anti-capitalist declarations. At Chanel's supermarket show, Lagerfeld was lifting the lid on aspirations and addictions, undermining the same insatiable consumer habits that fuel the success of any fashion label. Still, his show was by no means a Communist manifesto – the fashion designer had too much fun with the production, especially with the healthy dose of wordplay in names such as 'Coco Cookies' and 'Lait Coco'. The 'Brie Gabrielle' was a nod to Coco Chanel's birth name Gabrielle; the 'Signorina Farfalle' translated 'Mademoiselle' into Italian; and the gold shade of wall paint 'Doré St. Honoré' was named after Rue Saint-Honoré.

This was a bold attempt to liberate fashion shows from the narrow mindset of the post-war era, when journalists, customers and buyers used to sit on gilded chairs at exclusive showings inside the fashion houses. The post-war history of fashion commenced at 10.30 a.m. on 12 February 1947, when Christian Dior unveiled an extravagant new collection to a tightly packed audience at his company's head office at 30 Avenue Montaigne. Through the medium of fashion, the designer declared that the war was well and truly over. Even after the untimely death of the maestro, the show had to go on regardless. The best-known photographs of Yves Saint Laurent after his premiere for Dior on 30 January 1958 were taken on the balcony of the head office; presumably Dior's eternally anxious successor was in desperate need of a breath of fresh air. Finally the photographers had a different perspective on this twenty-one-year-old designer, catching him on camera somewhere other than the narrow corridors and stairwells of the company headquarters. It was perhaps the most beautiful moment in fashion history: even the people on Avenue Montaigne cheered for this bashful young genius.

When Coco Chanel stood at the top of the staircase in her apartment on Rue Cambon after making her fashion comeback in 1954, the wall of mirrors gave her a prime view of the audience and allowed her to gauge almost everyone's reactions. And Hubert de Givenchy's white smock, which he even wore on the runway at his final show in October 1995, was a symbol of his commitment to craftsmanship over showmanship.

Coco Chanel, Cristóbal Balenciaga, Christian Dior, Yves Saint Laurent and Hubert de Givenchy all made a name for themselves in a small setting. Now Karl Lagerfeld wanted to shake things up and give the system an overhaul. It was all very intimate at Chloé in those days. 'We used to host shows at the Brasserie Lipp,' says Rosemarie Le Gallais. 'The press representatives were served breakfast. We dressed the girls upstairs, and then they walked down the staircase. It was a pleasant atmosphere, all quite personal and unconventional.'[92] Then Lagerfeld took things to the next level. When he started out at Chanel in 1983, the shows were still a small, cramped affair on Rue Cambon. The label branched out in the 1990s, taking the collections to the Carrousel du Louvre, but soon that wasn't enough for him either – this fashion designer with self-confidence by the bucketload had his sights set on the big stage. The turn of the millennium was the perfect opportunity for Lagerfeld to finally realize his grand ambitions. The growing market for luxury goods called for extravagant productions. Events culture was becoming an increasingly important part of modern life. Audiences wanted more excitement; people were no longer content with watching the continuous loop of Yves Saint Laurent shows at the Hotel Intercontinental towards the end of his career. Asian customers, accustomed to things being done on a completely different scale with their huge shopping temples, wanted bigger, more glamorous spectacles. Finally, the launch of Instagram in 2010 gave rise to a crucial marketing tool, feeding into the image-hungry fashion scene and creating a demand for striking background motifs.

Dolce & Gabbana, Gucci and Louis Vuitton were adapting to this scenario by staging increasingly spectacular fashion shows. John Galliano's theatrical productions for Dior and Alexander McQueen's existential experiments for his signature label must have inspired Lagerfeld to some extent. But only the most powerful designer could turn night-time inspiration into twenty-minute-long *Gesamtkunstwerke* costing 7 million euros and, in many cases, more than 10 million euros (£8.5 million/US$12 million). And it took real intellect to play on the meta-level with trompe l'œil effects, effectively telling audiences that what they were seeing – perhaps even the fashion itself – was all wishful thinking. And even if most people missed the point, then that, too, was a trick of his self-reflective, illusionary art.

In 2005, Chanel secured an exclusive collaboration with the Grand Palais for its couture shows in January and July and its ready-to-wear shows in March and October. The exhibition hall was off-limits to other labels from that point forward, becoming a giant playground for the designer with his first show on 7 October 2005. 'The space gave him the freedom to fully express himself,' says his former assistant Eric Wright.[93] The sheer scale was extraordinary. The shows at Michael Kors, a speed record holder among fashion designers, only last eight or nine minutes, whereas at Chanel it takes a single model more than three minutes to circle the runway. Usually there are more than eighty models, and because of the 'one model, one look' principle, there is no need for a quick outfit change backstage during the show. With so many models walking around at the same time, the stage is like a scene from a super-sized 'hidden picture' book.

Every detail was meticulously planned. The major fashion editors had received their bouquet in their hotel room days before the event. The invitation cards had been printed on premium paper by Gerhard Steidl in Göttingen. A calligrapher had written the guests' addresses on the envelopes, which were then taken to the hotel or the editorial department by courier. Nine days before the show, set designer Stefan Lubrina was in the Grand Palais with his team, ready to build the giant set. 'The hypermarket was his idea, of course,' says Lubrina.[94] Presumably the response from Chanel would have been lukewarm. It was hardly the most luxurious concept, after all – but who was going to try and get in the way of Lagerfeld and his ideas?

Set designer Stefan Lubrina worked with Chanel from 1994. He started out designing stores for the brand before moving on to work on its fashion shows. He was usually only given three months to prepare for a show, so sometimes he had to work on several sets at a time. Lagerfeld would explain his idea to him, then Lubrina would make a mock-up of the space. They discussed the design some more, and then Lubrina started work on the set in his workshop before finally completing the project in the Grand Palais. 'It would have been too risky to develop the concept six months before [the show],' says Lubrina. 'He had so many ideas that we would have been forced to keep making changes.'

First of all, the space had to be filled. 'It was like coming up with the soundtrack to a film or composing music for a play,' says sound designer Michel Gaubert. 'The space is huge. You can't play punk or intimate music there. The music has to be well-produced, it has to sound polished and full.'[95] Lagerfeld understood the space, says Stefan Lubrina. 'You have to play with the scale of the hall.' No single show could be like another; the team had to create a whole new atmosphere every time. The models' walkways and the seating were always different. The audience were assimilated into the set, forming part of the scenery as in modern theatre productions. Judging by the shows Chanel has hosted since Lagerfeld died, everything will be done on a smaller scale in the future. 'Nowadays it's not so easy,' notes Lubrina. 'For example, all the decorations have to be recyclable, so we can no longer use as many materials.'

At his prime, Lagerfeld produced sets on a bigger scale than anyone else. The Fendi show at the Great Wall of China in October 2007, the Fendi couture show at the Trevi fountain in July 2016, the Chanel Cruise show in Havana in May 2016, the supermarket show in the Grand Palais in March 2014, and the show with the giant rocket in March 2017 were some of the most spectacular shows in fashion history. Lagerfeld liked to describe himself as a story-teller. Each time he put on one of these extravagant spectacles, they sparked a media frenzy that generated the equivalent of several times the original outlay. It would have cost the label far more to reach an audience of this size through advertisements in magazines or on websites.[96]

Lubrina and his extensive team built a launchpad and a 120-foot-tall Saturn V rocket for the show in March 2017. With the 'Centre de Lancement N° 5', the collection evoked the original space age with glitter boots, silver foil coats, planet embroideries, astronaut prints, safety glasses and crewneck dresses. Karl Lagerfeld and Hudson Kroenig pressed the button together, the launchpad scaffolding opened up, and the countdown began. Sparks flew and the engines roared as the rocket appeared to lift off 30 feet into the air in a cloud of smoke.

'Great, no?' Lagerfeld asked after the show. The smoke from the dry ice tricked the audience into thinking that the rocket had actually lifted off. In fact, the middle section had just risen inside the top part, making it look as if the rocket had launched and bust through the dome at a height of 145 feet. The music helped the illusion along nicely. Michel Gaubert played Kraftwerk's ambient track 'Radioactivity' first, followed by Serge Gainsbourg's playful 'Contact!', then Daft Punk picked up the pace. For the climax, he played Elton John's 'Rocket Man'. 'The idea was for it to end like a really corny sci-fi film,' says Gaubert. 'And it worked.' The stars in the front row, including Anna Wintour, Pharrell Williams and Cara Delevingne, looked transported as they applauded the spectacular display.

Lagerfeld was familiar with trompe l'œil techniques from art and often used optical tricks like these in his shows. There was the 43,000 ft^2 beach in October 2018, the deceptively realistic forest panorama complete with real oak trees in March 2018, and the feminist protest ('History is Her Story') in September 2014, where the models marched along a faux boulevard lined with convincing-looking Haussmann building façades. Everything built up to the finale, where all the different elements came together for everyone to see: the elite models, the entire collection, and the coordinated hairdos, which the Scottish hairdresser Sam McKnight was responsible for from 2010 onwards. Finally came the epiphany when the maestro took his bow.

Giddy on excitement and champagne, the guests were more than happy to play along. And of course, the master of ceremonies made sure the mood stayed high. 'Help yourselves to fruit and sweets,' he shouted after the supermarket show in March 2014, with the kind of cheery disposition one could only wish for in many a supermarket manager. 'They're free!' By that point most of the guests had already vanished with their spoils. But many of them didn't get far: apart from the fruit and the sweets, they had to hand everything over when they reached the exit. In a capitalist world, nothing comes for free.

Criticism

This man was better than almost anyone else when it came to using publicity to his advantage, but he couldn't bear it when the public invaded his private life. Alicia Drake experienced this first-hand when she published an exposé of the love–hate relationship between Karl Lagerfeld and Yves Saint Laurent in her 2006 book *The Beautiful Fall*. Lagerfeld particularly objected to Drake's portrayal of his childhood in the countryside, which she painted in shades of grey rather than the brilliant colours he preferred for his back story. He was also furious that his cousin Kurt Lagerfeld had revealed his true birth year, as had Karl Wagner and various other friends from his younger days. Lagerfeld took Drake to court on the basis of Article 9 of the French Civil Code, which states that every citizen has the right to respect for his or her private life. As well as attempting to block distribution of the book in France, he tried to impose a fine of 10,000 euros for every book sold after the proposed ban had been enforced. He was pushing for Drake to pay 100,000 euros in damages, and for the court's decision to be published in five publications of his choice at Drake's expense. On 15 January 2007, after two hearings without Lagerfeld in attendance, the court dismissed the charges and Lagerfeld was ordered to cough up 6,000 euros in costs.[97] Lagerfeld called the well-researched book *Schundliteratur*: trash.[98]

The designer had a similarly harsh reaction when Arnaud Maillard released a book divulging details of everyday life working as his assistant.[99] When Maillard called Lagerfeld one day in 2005 to announce that he wanted to quit and go to another label, Lagerfeld told him,

'It's over. Don't ever call me again. You'll see where that gets you.'[100]
When the German television host Johannes B. Kerner asked the
designer whether he was disappointed in his former employee, he
jibed, 'The poor boy is a nobody; it's impossible to be disappointed.
He's a barman in Spain now, so he can't have been all that talented.'
And what did he think about the book? 'Quite frankly, I feel sorry for
all the trees that were felled to print such garbage.'[101]

Lagerfeld was quick-witted, brilliant and generous, but he could
also be thin-skinned, prickly and resentful. He was both stylish and
elitist, quality-conscious and snobby, sociable and narcissistic, hard-
working and overambitious. For all these reasons and more, people
either loved him or they hated him. There were a lot of people with
bad things to say about the designer in his native Germany, where
dandyism is quickly equated with snootiness. Author Sibel Schick
took to Twitter[102] on the day of his death to declare that no one should
be mourning 'a racist, sexist, classist individual like Karl Lagerfeld'.
This judgment, as harsh as it was wrong, sums up the kind of criticism that had been mounting up against Lagerfeld, particularly in
the final years of his life.

Generally speaking, he remained politically neutral until 2015. The
student uprising, the new social movements of the 1970s, the Greens
and Socialism more or less passed him by in France. 'I've never voted
yet. I don't have any affiliations,' he claimed in 2013.[103] He rarely spoke
about German politics either. Chancellor Angela Merkel became a
popular subject for his caricatures, but for years his tone remained
relatively benign and tongue-in-cheek. For instance, he poked fun at
the politician's almost masculine grip on power in 2014, drawing her
in a trouser suit with the caption: 'I wear the trousers around here!'[104]

This neutrality shifted towards the end of his life. The designer
became increasingly politicized following the Islamist attack on
Charlie Hebdo magazine in Paris on 7 January 2015, the influx of
refugees to Europe from the summer of 2015 onwards, the terrorist
attacks in Paris on 13 November 2015, and the string of sexual assaults
on women on New Year's Eve 2015 in Cologne, where the majority of

the assailants were reported to be of North African or Arab origin. The tone of his 'Karlikaturs' in the *Frankfurter Allgemeine Zeitung* became more pointed and controversial. In the cartoon published on 13 February 2016, he drew the German Chancellor wearing a black headscarf with the caption: 'Mrs Merkel's new migrant-friendly look'.[105] It was a bold statement from a man who always used to observe German politics from a safe distance: he was establishing a direct link between the preponderance of Muslim immigrants, the increase in antisemitism and the rise of right-wing populism. The nationalist Alternative for Germany (AfD) party was gaining ground in Germany, as was the National Front (now: National Rally) in France, the Freedom Party of Austria (FPÖ) and Geert Wilders's 'Party for Freedom' in the Netherlands.

Lagerfeld's critique became more extreme in two of his later political cartoons. At the German federal election on 24 September 2017, the AfD won 94 seats in the Bundestag after experiencing an upswing of 7.9 percentage points and securing 12.6 per cent of the votes. Lagerfeld responded to this development in his 'Karlikatur' on 14 October, which shows Merkel in the foreground, holding her hands over her mouth in horror, while Hitler hovers in the background: 'What have I done?' she gasps. The caption above is the response from the ghost of Hitler: 'Thank you very much for inadvertently allowing my descendants to be represented in parliament.' Lagerfeld said he hoped that 'something like this would never happen again in my life' and that he was 'ashamed for Germany'.[106] It was a provocative statement: he was directly accusing Merkel of fuelling support for right-wing populists with her liberal 'welcome' policy. However, his accusation is in fact supported by various analyses of the voting shift: around one million people who had voted for Merkel's CDU centre-right party in 2013 had switched to the nationalist party by 2017.

Lagerfeld upped the ante with his critique when he appeared as a guest on Thierry Ardisson's talk show 'Salut les terriens!' (Hello Earthlings!) on the French television channel C8 on 11 November 2017. 'One cannot – even if there are decades between them – kill millions

Growing criticism of Angela Merkel:
Karl Lagerfeld published a 'Karlikatur'
of the German chancellor wearing a
'pro-migrant' black headscarf in the
Frankfurter Allgemeine Magazin
in February 2016.

of Jews and then let millions of their worst enemies into the country,'
he said. The French media regulator was immediately inundated
with complaints from hundreds of viewers. But his comments on
antisemitism weren't completely unfounded, as the coming weeks
would show. The Central Council of Jews in Germany complained
about the hatred against Jewish people in Germany, claiming that
the insults 'from Muslims' were the loudest of all, and on 18 January
2018 the Bundestag resolved to establish a new antisemitism commissioner post in the federal government.

Lagerfeld went a step further in his 'Karlikatur' of 13 January 2018,
depicting Angela Merkel in a hijab with a halo of crescent moons
around her head. The caption: 'Immaculate Conception'. Lagerfeld,
tongue firmly in cheek, was comparing the German Chancellor to
the Virgin Mother, saying she welcomed the migrants with open
arms and that she likes to think she is immaculate.[107] His criticism
of Merkel was even harsher in an interview with *Le Point* magazine
in May that year: 'Did she have to say it was necessary to welcome
a million migrants? We must remember our past in Germany. I hate
Mrs Merkel for forgetting that.'[108] On 11 May 2018, the front page of

Bild newspaper summarized his statement with the headline: 'I hate Madame Merkel.'

The growing climate of antisemitism was bound to anger him. He had a great passion for Jewish culture from the pre-war era, plus many of his friends – and clients – in modern-day Paris were Jewish. But this was different. Now something fundamental had come to light: 'He became increasingly conservative, almost reactionary,' says Gloria von Thurn und Taxis. 'It wasn't the migrants per se that bothered him; it was the uncontrolled migration. He was a control freak and he couldn't bear that kind of chaos.'[109] Ironically, this control freak had now lost control of himself. Political statements from a fashion designer can be dangerous for the people around him. He had never shown much consideration for the labels he worked with, but now any inhibitions he might have had went right out of the window. 'Eventually his self-restraint just slipped away,' says Wolfgang Joop.[110] The man who liked to look as if he had everything under control was letting it all hang out.

His caricature of Harvey Weinstein caused outrage when it was published on 11 November 2017. In it, the disgraced film producer is depicted as a pig and referred to by the name 'Harvey Schweinstein'. *Die Welt* accused Lagerfeld of digging 'deep into the chest of [old] antisemitic clichés'. According to the German newspaper, he was engaging with an age-old pictorial tradition of portraying Jews as pigs, a practice that started with sculptures in medieval times and was still rife in the Nazi era, when Jews were similarly debased in caricatures, photographs and films.[111] Lagerfeld, of all people, antisemitic? In his defence, he said he was inspired by the #BalanceTonPorc initiative, the French equivalent of the #metoo movement, literally meaning #OutYourPig. 'I only translated what everyone was saying,' he claimed.[112] The eighty-four-year-old made no allowances for diplomatic sensitivities, and it didn't bother him when the applause came from the wrong side.

If anything, it seemed he always strove to be politically incorrect. This much is clear from his contribution to the debate about skinny models. 'Strangely, people make a lot more fuss about anorexics than fat people these days.'[113] 'There are less than 1 per cent of anorexic girls, but there are over – in France, I don't know [about] England – over 30 per cent of girls who are big, big, overweight,' he said in another interview. 'And this is much more dangerous and very bad for the health.'[114] He described the pop star Adele as being 'a little too fat'. Lagerfeld was partly responsible for the preponderance of skinny models on the runway. But as attitudes began to change, his views on body image gradually became outmoded. Older models and normal-weight models have been seen on runways more and more in recent years, including at Chanel since 2019.

Lagerfeld was generally opposed to political correctness, state interventions and moralistic rules. This son of an entrepreneur was in favour of an open market and didn't take kindly to obstacles impeding market forces. He enjoyed spending lots of money, he helped people in need, and he backed various initiatives, such as 'Sauver la vie', a programme promoting the training of medical students and medical research at the Paris Descartes University, which he supported from 2015.[115] Taxes, however, were a bugbear. His final dispute with the French tax authorities came to light at the beginning of 2016. By setting up a series of companies to funnel cash to the British Virgin Islands, the US state of Delaware, Ireland and other tax havens, Lagerfeld had reportedly succeeded in withholding more than 20 million euros in earnings from the French authorities over six years.[116] He stated for the record that he paid 'several millions of euros in taxes every year' in France. It would be another case for his trusted financial advisor, Lucien Frydlender, who knew how to handle disagreements like this discreetly. Lagerfeld jokingly called the old man who looked after his money 'ma nounou' (my nanny).[117]

A report in *Le Monde* also caused ripples in September 2000. Lagerfeld was embroiled in a tax scandal when the French newspaper published the transcript of a video showing property developer Jean-Claude Méry openly talking about illegal party financing that took place while Jacques Chirac was mayor of Paris. The newspaper reported that the tax lawyer Alain Belot had given the video to the then-finance minister Dominique Strauss-Kahn in 1999.[118] Apparently, in exchange for the video, Strauss-Kahn had used his influence to reduce Lagerfeld's tax liabilities from 300 million francs (£39 million/ US$54 million) to roughly 50 million francs. Strauss-Kahn put the record straight, stating that Lagerfeld's tax arrears from 1992 to 1997, which amounted to roughly 80 million francs, had been reduced to 46 million. The former minister of economy, finance and industry offered assurance that he had been following advice from the tax authorities.[119]

Le Monde reported that Lagerfeld had stopped paying taxes in France in 1982, as he was registered in Monaco and 'more than half of his income' came from abroad. The designer had already had an initial bill for back taxes from 1989 to 1991 reduced from around 60 million to 10 million francs in 1995, before Strauss-Kahn's time as minister.[120] Evidently the authorities had always been rather generous with this tardy taxpayer.

Following the revelations in *Le Monde*, however, the tax office seemed to be making a concerted effort to do better. Lagerfeld's former assistant Arnaud Maillard remembers the day they got the call from Virginie Viard in the Chanel atelier: apparently the people from the tax authorities were in the building and they were planning to drive to Lagerfeld's residence on Rue de l'Université. The designer and his assistant immediately rushed home, packed up a lot of documents, and threw the suitcases in the BMW in the courtyard because they were too heavy to carry. They then dashed onto the street and hailed a cab. As they were driving away, they saw an unmarked police car pulling up outside the building with the blue light flashing.[121]

For Lagerfeld, public concerns came second to private interests. He was not particularly interested in the threat that financial freedom can pose to the balance of nature. He came from a different time, belonging to the grandparents' generation of the 'Fridays for Future' movement established in the year before his death. In this respect, it was only understandable that the climate crisis protests failed to make a mark on him. Still, the sheer extent of this designer's personal contribution to global warming and littering is staggering. His H&M collection, which is often praised for its role in the 'democratization' of style, was instrumental in making cheap fashion even more popular. More than most other designers, he boosted the damaging trend for fast fashion, an industry known for draining energy and resources and contributing to the long-term global waste problem. All sorts of chemicals are used in manufacturing processes in fast fashion, the transport routes are long, and polyester is used on a huge scale even though it is not biodegradable. Moreover, cheap products are more disposable than their expensive counterparts, so the environmental impact is even greater.

Lagerfeld's carbon footprint was nothing to be proud of. He frequently flew on a private jet, and once claimed that he had visited Rome more than four hundred times in his life. He also repeatedly flew to New York, Monaco, Milan, Hamburg, Berlin, Tokyo, London and many other international cities over the decades. Up until the 1970s he flew with commercial airlines, then when he started earning more money at Chanel in the 1980s, he started leasing a private jet. Concorde was his preferred mode of transport to New York. This kind of thing was completely normal for the super-wealthy. In times of climate crisis, however, the way people think about air travel is beginning to change.

Generally speaking, attitudes towards shows of wealth are shifting. Nowadays, the relentless quest for status, insistence upon privileges, mass consumption of luxury products and extravagant set design all seem a little outdated. The private jet, the Rolls-Royce, the maid for his cat and the butler with his silver tray – all these luxuries seem like relics of a bygone era. 'These big shows are also anachronistic, with all the trees being felled and the iceberg being imported [from Sweden],' says Wolfgang Joop. 'People have had their fill of wastefulness and excess. They don't want calfskin leather bags either.'[122] When Karl Lagerfeld died, so too did the brave old world of luxury and fashion, in which consumerism without remorse was still possible.

Choupette

She wasn't really Karl's cat. Choupette was born on 19 August 2011 and belonged to Baptiste Giabiconi, whose brother had given the kitten to him as a birthday present in November. The model was planning to spend the Christmas holidays in Marseille, so he asked Karl if he would mind looking after his little Birman cat while he was out of town. 'For how long?' Karl hesitated. 'Just over a week, then I'll take her back... But send me messages to keep me updated,' said Baptiste. Karl was concerned about hygiene and pests, but Baptiste assured him that Choupette was quite clean. 'She's had all her vaccinations!'[123]

Karl took better care of the cat than anyone could have imagined. Initially he stuck to his word and sent his friend in the South impromptu updates, sounding increasingly besotted: 'Elle est belle', 'Elle est exquise', 'Elle est fabuleuse'.[124] Then he went silent and there were no more photos, no more messages. 'When I got home, he didn't want to give her back,' recalls Baptiste. 'He had completely fallen for her.'[125] Karl started to become confrontational when Baptiste returned to collect Choupette from his apartment on the Quai Voltaire on 2 January 2012. 'You have no idea how to look after her properly,' said Karl. 'It's much better for her here, she'll live a life of luxury.'[126] Baptiste took her away with him regardless. But he soon realized that the separation was making his friend miserable, and so a few days later he brought Choupette back. This time she would be staying for good. 'There's no greater gift,' Lagerfeld said, overwhelmed. 'I've never received anything so wonderful before.'[127]

The Birman kitten moved in with her new keeper when she was less than a year old. In the beginning, Lagerfeld didn't like her cutesy name (which roughly translates as 'sweetie' or 'pumpkin'); in fact, in 2012 he said he thought it was 'dreadful'. But over time he got used to it. 'Now I almost find it comical,' he later said. In an appearance on a German talk show, the designer explained that 'houpette' means 'powder puff' in French, and the cat's name had to start with a 'C' because of the breeding line, so 'Choupette' seemed just right.[128] Giabiconi also pointed out that Choupette works in every language,

'Kind of Greta Garbo': Karl Lagerfeld even turned
his cat Choupette into a star.

which sounded perfectly acceptable to Lagerfeld. And yet, cats will be cats: 'You talk to her, "Choupette", she's not answering. She answers only when you say, "Chou-pi-nette".'[129]

No doubt one of the many reasons Lagerfeld loved his furry friend was her typically feline independent spirit. She was his pride and joy, and now every time he met up with friends he would pull his iPhone out of his pocket, push his glasses up onto his forehead and start scouring his phone for recent snaps of Choupette. When he found a picture he liked, he would pass his phone around so that everyone could coo over his Birman cat with the beautiful sapphire eyes. Then his friend, editor-in-chief of *V* magazine Stephen Gan, tweeted a photo with the caption 'Meet Choupette' in mid-January 2012, and the rest was history. Lagerfeld even managed to make his pet famous, as he had done with so many of the people around him. Choupette's career break in 2012 was very timely: this was the year when Grumpy Cat went viral and 'Petfluencers' arrived on the scene.

These new online influencers kept the cute content coming, making social media users smile and raking in the cash for their owners through advertising deals.

Ashley Tschudin, a social media specialist from the New York fashion industry, recognized Choupette's market potential early on. A cat that has a maid and flies on a private jet? 'Goodness,' she thought, 'you could build a whole persona around that.' And so she did, confident that the story of this luxury cat's life would resonate with the fashion world. She started on Twitter in 2012 and then became a hit on Instagram with 'Choupettesdiary'. Tschudin, granddaughter of Hollywood actor Rod Steiger, essentially wrote a script for the Instagram age. She reposted photos from other people's Instagram accounts and created a 'playful personality' for the cat, indulging in a spot of wordplay and sharing funny little anecdotes. She even hired an illustrator to help transform the kitty into a diva, and soon even pop stars like Fergie and Katy Perry became fans. 'We had good, loyal followers,' says Tschudin. Lots of social media users would send her pictures and messages about their own cats, as if she was their friend.[130]

And so the feline starlet reached dizzying new heights of fame. Lagerfeld made sure she kept the best company on her photo shoots: Choupette outside the Eiffel Tower at night with Laetitia Casta in *V* magazine (September 2012); Choupette with Linda Evangelista on the cover of German *Vogue* (July 2013); Choupette with Gisele Bündchen on the cover of Brazilian *Vogue* (December 2014). Only the most sought-after models would do for this beautiful animal. The first book, *Choupette: The Private Life of a High-Flying Fashion Cat*, was published by Thames & Hudson in 2014. A second volume, *Choupette by Karl Lagerfeld*, which consisted of Lagerfeld's personal iPhone photos from 2018 and was originally intended as a Christmas gift for his friends, came out posthumously with Steidl in 2019. In the foreword to the collection, Lagerfeld reveals that he didn't really think of himself as all that famous: 'Now, Choupette really is famous. She has become the most famous cat in the world.'[131]

The designer was projecting his decadent image onto his cat. He boasted that she had 'two personal maids' who played with her and took care of her 'beautiful white hair' and 'the beauty treatments for her eyes'. He said she was 'kind of Greta Garbo'.[132] She loved private jets and was only interested in beautiful things and seducing people.[133] 'I am not the most important person in my house,' he noted, adding: 'I think Choupette made me a better person – less selfish.'[134] He also named her as one of the heirs to his fortune.[135] Choupette allowed him to indulge his imagination – after all, she couldn't speak, so she couldn't answer back. Who knows, she may not even have wanted to if she could.

With fame came the advertising jobs. Any offers to endorse pet food were immediately dismissed. 'I'm commercial. She's not. She's completely pampered.'[136] But there were two pitches he simply couldn't turn down. First, Lagerfeld's favourite cosmetics brand Shu Uemura brought out a makeup collection called Shupette. Then there was the offer from Opel, which appealed to Karl because his mother used to drive an Opel convertible – 'ridiculously luxurious, but during the war it just sat in the garage without any tyres'.[137] It was an advertising gig for the fifth-generation Corsa, which is more popular with women than men. Steffi Graf and Claudia Schiffer had advertised the model previously, and now Lagerfeld was photographing his pet on the bonnet of this small car. 'Normally there wouldn't be any claws on the paintwork during an advert,' says Tina Müller, who was the head of marketing at the car manufacturer at the time. 'That alone made the concept original.' The campaign gave Opel 'a touch of humour', she added.[138]

Lagerfeld even opened a bank account for his beloved cat. In 2014, these advertising appearances alone netted her a total of 3 million euros.[139] Lagerfeld was proud that Choupette was as well-known as the TV dolphin Flipper and Cheeta, the chimpanzee from the Tarzan films, only 'a higher earner'.[140]

When Lagerfeld died, there was a battle to control the rights to Choupette's online presence. Ashley Tschudin had been selling a range of products (the 'Daddy Collection') via an online shop, but the Karl Lagerfeld brand wasn't going to tolerate that kind of business. On 15 August 2019, the Lagerfeld camp created a separate account for Choupette, 'Choupetteofficiel', managed by a French social media agency. 'That was a real blow for me,' says Tschudin. She was the one who had made the cat a hit on Instagram, and now her followers were asking: 'Where's Choupette? Why aren't you posting any new photos?' The answer was very simple: the new competitor account had watermarked its images, and now Tschudin could no longer use the photos.

Choupette continued to be a pampered puss, even after her owner passed away. Her main minder, Françoise Caçote, moved into Lagerfeld's house outside Paris with her. The pair were occasionally visited by someone from the social media agency coming to take pictures for the 'Choupetteofficiel' Instagram account. But these were almost the only interruptions to an otherwise tranquil existence. Rarely has a cat enjoyed a more pleasant sunset phase in its life.

The End

Sébastien Jondeau can clearly remember the beginning of the end. It was 5 June 2015, in Saint-Tropez. Karl Lagerfeld had stayed in his villa in Ramatuelle to work, while Jondeau headed out to the beach with a friend. He was sitting in the sun when a text message appeared on his phone from his boss. He immediately called to see what was the matter: 'I have a problem,' Lagerfeld said. 'I can't pee.'[141] Apparently he had been having trouble urinating for a while. 'I took it very seriously straight away,' Jondeau said in 2019, after the designer had passed away. He phoned Yves Dahan, one of Lagerfeld's long-time acquaintances, who was well connected in the medical world thanks to the work he did with his foundation 'Sauvons l'hôpital'. 'Five minutes later I had two of the most important professors of urology in Paris on the other end of the line.' They recommended that Lagerfeld get it looked at right away, but he protested: 'Ah, non! No nurses!'

At around 8 p.m. Jondeau was zooming along the winding streets to take a urine sample to the hospital in Gassin, just a few miles away from Ramatuelle. The results of the lab tests came back at 4 a.m.; by that point Lagerfeld still hadn't slept a wink, and neither had Jondeau. 'The results were alarming.' The pair went back to Paris together. 'I had never seen him in such a state before, looking so distraught.' For the next four years, and even after his death, only a handful of people knew that he was suffering from prostate cancer – not pancreatic cancer, as was originally assumed after he died. 'A lot of people are now saying that they knew,' says Jondeau. 'But in truth, no one knew.'[142]

Everything changed that day in June 2015. Even then, Jondeau had barely had a day off since he started working for Lagerfeld. He could rarely make dinner plans with friends, as the designer would contact him every couple of hours to ask him to pick something up, drop something off, or set something up for him. And in these last years of service, he was to be put to an even more gruelling test. 'His illness made life harder for him,' says Jondeau. 'He was completely different in the last months of his life. His energy was gradually dwindling. But he didn't complain. And he spoke to no one about his illness.'

Jondeau had become Lagerfeld's closest confidant over the years. It was this bond that kept him going – not to mention a good helping of grit. Born in Paris in 1975, Jondeau didn't have the easiest childhood. His parents split up when he was still at nursery, and he spent his early years in the notoriously rough neighbourhood of Aubervilliers, as well as with his grandmother in the modest southeastern suburb of Ivry-sur-Seine and with his stepfather in Gonesse in the north of Paris.[143]

While helping at his stepfather's removals company in the summer of 1990, the fifteen-year-old Sébastien found himself waiting outside the house at 51 Rue de l'Université for Lagerfeld to make an appearance. The fashion designer was four hours late when he finally turned up. 'You're very young,' he said to Sébastien. 'Shouldn't you still be at school?' Sébastien told him, 'Yes, but it's the holidays and I have to earn money to buy myself things.' The generous designer tipped the workers 500 francs, much to Sébastien's surprise. It would be another eight years before he saw Lagerfeld again.

When Sébastien left school, he got a job transporting medical devices such as CT scanners and X-ray machines to disposal points, becoming a specialist in recycling sheet metal, iron, aluminium, rubber and plastics. He only went back to work for his stepfather when he was twenty-one and had served in the Army. He had a side gig in a security firm, and also sold sandwiches at the Stade de France because he wanted more money. 'Three jobs! I slaved like a madman. I wanted to finally earn some money and gain some independence.'

In October 1998, the furniture movers were on location working at Villa Elhorria, Lagerfeld's large summer retreat in Biarritz. The job lasted over a year, there was so much to do. Sébastien saw an opportunity and finally mustered up the courage to ask, 'Could I come and work for you?' Lagerfeld was surprised. 'Don't you want to work for your stepfather anymore?' he asked. 'No, I want to learn things that I can only learn from you.' That was that. Lagerfeld took him under his wing, and finally Sébastien had found someone who could answer all his questions – someone who even had answers to questions that had never occurred to him.

The bond they formed that day would only grow stronger over the years. Now this boy from the suburbs was suddenly inhabiting the same milieu as some of the world's richest, most powerful and most beautiful people. Presidents like Emmanuel Macron, CEOs like Bernard Arnault, actresses like Diane Kruger, singers like Katy Perry – he was rubbing shoulders with all of them. Now he had a real job and a higher calling. No more feeling out of place as he had done at school, no more selling sandwiches at football matches, no more standing around bored while working security at the Cartier shop on Rue de la Paix. Sébastien called his mother and told her about his new job; he was so happy, he started crying.[144]

Colleagues were dubious about the young man, but Lagerfeld, who had a knack for spotting talent, liked him. The designer was amused by this tanned young thing who wore baggy jeans and was always turning up for work covered in scratches and plasters. Lagerfeld loved public life – and now he had someone who could be his eyes and ears, keeping him informed about what was happening in the real world while he stayed safely indoors. When they drove to Le Bourget airport to catch Lagerfeld's private jet, Sébastien steered the car through the suburbs where he had grown up. And as the plane took off and Sébastien looked down, he saw the places where he had sped around on his BMX bike as a boy.

In the last years of Lagerfeld's life, being so irreplaceable to this fashion god also became a burden. According to Caroline Lebar, there was no one Lagerfeld trusted more than his faithful bodyguard and driver around this time. 'Seb', as he was known to the Lagerfeld family, had to be there for Lagerfeld at all times. He could no longer move around freely and even had to give up boxing, which had been his favourite hobby. Lagerfeld wanted him to be at his beck and call, and couldn't bear it when he was away. He asked after him and controlled him. They spoke about Lagerfeld's illness every day. 'It was like a battlefield inside of me,' Sébastien later said, with the same candour that the designer had always admired in him.[145]

Sometimes the medical tests gave glimmers of hope, but at other times the results were devastating. Lagerfeld's health was the only thing that mattered now. He asked Sébastien to work exclusively for him and to give up any other engagements. In a playful nod to Sébastien's blossoming career as a fashion designer, he occasionally asked others: 'Can my colleague come too?'[146]

The subject of Sébastien's future was off limits. 'You'll never work for anyone after me, don't you worry,' Lagerfeld told him. By now their bond was so strong that Sébastien could even imagine dying at the same time as his boss.[147] Even in Lagerfeld's most intimate circle, no one else knew that the designer was living with a terminal diagnosis. Perhaps the butler cottoned on when Lagerfeld swapped Pepsi Max for still water in 2016. From then on, Frédéric Gouby found himself trailing a full glass of water around with him on his silver tray more and more of the time. The glass was never empty, even though he kept encouraging Lagerfeld to drink. 'He wasn't drinking enough at all,' Gouby said, after his boss passed away. 'And it's important for old people to make sure they get plenty of fluids.'[148]

Lagerfeld was gradually getting weaker. His tottering on the runway could be attributed to his sciatica; he was getting treatment from acupuncturist Nadia Volf after years of sitting in an unhealthy posture while sketching. He was also becoming more cautious after the time he fell on the famous mirrored staircase at Chanel because the carpet had gathered and tripped him up.[149] Rumours of possible health problems started to fly after the Chanel haute couture show in the Grand Palais in July 2015. The palace had been transformed into a casino for the event, with models and stars like Kristen Stewart, Julianne Moore and Rita Ora seated at roulette tables for the spectacle. This time, however, Lagerfeld did not do his usual lap of the runway. Barely leaving the backstage area, he merely ventured a few steps to the banister that separated him from the audience. From then on, he only ever walked short distances on the runway. He emerged very briefly at the end of the show in 2017, when the set had been transformed into a waterfall, and again in 2018, when iconic *bouquiniste* bookseller stalls lined the catwalk. He simply stepped forward for a moment and waved at *Vogue* editor-in-chief Anna Wintour, having located her in the audience beforehand. Then he swiftly disappeared into the wings once more.

Lagerfeld started appearing with his assistant Virginie Viard when he came out to take his bow in the very last seasons of his career. She first accompanied him at the Cruise show on 3 May 2018, standing with him on the bulwark of *La Pausa*, the replica ship named after Coco Chanel's villa in Roquebrune-Cap-Martin on the Côte d'Azur. She also joined him on the boardwalk at the artificial beach in the Grand Palais on 2 October 2018. The seaside scene was the beach at Sylt: he called it 'the beach of my childhood', the 'least polluted place in the world'.[150] For his last ever ready-to-wear show he decided to take one final trip down memory lane.

Both his assistant and his godson held him by the hand for what would be his last appearance on a runway, at the Métiers d'Art show

With his assistant: the designer came out to take his bow with Virginie Viard again in October 2018, lining her up as his natural successor.

in New York's Metropolitan Museum in December 2018. Confronted with his own mortality, he was already lining up Virginie Viard as his successor. It was his way of thanking his assistant, whom he referred to as 'my right and my left hand', rewarding her for over three decades of faithful service. It also allowed him to reign supreme as the most important Chanel designer, even after he was gone. If the fashion house were to recruit a major talent from outside the company – like Nicolas Ghesquière or Hedi Slimane – there was every possibility that his legend would quickly be overshadowed. The Wertheimers saw no problem with his choice, announcing Viard as Lagerfeld's successor just hours after he had passed away.

Things were also starting to change dramatically backstage from 2015. Until around the turn of the millennium, the designer had always mingled with the models, stylists, makeup artists, hairdressers, assistants, journalists, photographers and camera crew who turned the backstage area into a chaotic hub of activity at Chanel in Paris and Fendi in Milan. He enjoyed switching back and forth between French, English and German as he fielded all the questions that came his way, often going into so much detail that he completely lost track of time. Patricia Riekel from the German magazine *Bunte* and her Paris correspondent Brita von Maydell regularly made lunch plans with him after the shows, and he would leave them waiting for him while he chatted to everyone and anyone. 'He existed in the here and now,' says the former editor-in-chief. 'He had his own sense of time.'[151]

Then at some point the walls came down and the designer was no longer so present. Security guards cordoned off the backstage area, and eventually Lagerfeld had his own separate space in the Grand Palais, with only a few people invited to enter. This allowed him to stay seated when he welcomed the American singer Pharrell Williams, the French actress Vanessa Paradis, or Christiane Arp, the editor-in-chief of German *Vogue*. The list of backstage guests became shorter and shorter. It seemed as if the designer was slowly retreating from the public eye. He no longer set foot out of his door without getting straight into a car; he even had Sébastien Jondeau drive him the few hundred feet from his apartment at 17 Quai Voltaire to the photography studio at 7 Rue de Lille.

Lagerfeld started to avoid receptions and parties. He made a swift exit when he attended the private viewing of his own photography exhibition at the Palazzo Pitti in Florence in June 2016 and the opening of a new Rimowa store on Rue du Faubourg Saint-Honoré in March 2017. Now he only went out on rare occasions, and when he did he was very selective about where he went. He only visited establishments he had known for a long time, like the Maison du Caviar, or he only accepted invitations to private meals – at Bernard Arnault's house, for instance. People who weren't around him every day were more likely to notice his subtle demise. In 2016, when Baptiste Giabiconi asked his friend why his face looked puffy, Lagerfeld made some excuse about receiving cortisone treatment for a stubborn cold. When pushed, he admitted that it was more serious, that he had the best doctors at the American Hospital, and that he had already been subjected to CT and MRI scans.[152]

Later, in the final phase of his life, his deteriorating health was increasingly obvious. The faxes to Gerhard Steidl had reduced to just two or three pages from the usual fifteen or twenty. From 2015, his instructions weren't as meticulously detailed as they had been. He was also getting into the habit of taking longer than expected to send his sketches over to Steidl.[153]

His attitude was becoming increasingly hostile, too. He became obsessed with rampant Islamism and the spread of right-wing populism. As his worldview grew darker, he became more intolerant and bitter. 'Towards the end he suddenly had this indescribable hatred,' says Patricia Riekel. 'He could get really scathing at times.'[154] His workaholic ways served as a distraction, of course, but now he was unmistakably in poor health. 'In autumn 2018 his face had suddenly gone puffy and blotchy,' says Riekel. Not even the beard he started growing earlier that year could hide visible signs like these. On 22 November 2018 he made a public appearance with mayor Anne Hidalgo to turn on the Christmas lights on the Champs-Élysées. When he opened his mouth to laugh, he revealed unsightly gaps in his teeth, leaving the tabloids to speculate over the cause of this physical deterioration. In this case, however, the tooth stumps were just a sign that he was undergoing dental treatment and the crowns hadn't been fitted yet.

Lagerfeld's visit to New York for the Métiers d'Art show at the Metropolitan Museum at the beginning of December 2018 was his last big trip. After that, he stayed in Paris over Christmas to get ready for the upcoming collections. There were two haute couture shows scheduled for Tuesday 22 January: one at 10.30 a.m. and another at 12 p.m. Two days before the shows were due to happen, Lagerfeld was sitting in the studio with music guru Michel Gaubert, Chanel director Bruno Pavlovsky, and Chanel co-owner Alain Wertheimer, checking to see how the clothes, hair and accessories were all coming together at the fittings. In a short Instagram video posted by fashion journalist Suzy Menkes, Lagerfeld appears strangely distant. His eyes also look tired; he is wearing glasses without tinted lenses, as he had been doing in recent months, which made it more obvious. Miles Socha, editor-in-chief of *Women's Wear Daily*, saw Lagerfeld the same evening and thought he was looking frail: 'But because his mind was still sharp, you blocked out the fact that that his body was getting weaker.'[155]

Virginie Viard made a very brief appearance after the first of the shows on the Tuesday morning, this time without Karl. The guests looked around in disbelief. Michel Gaubert announced over the loudspeaker that Lagerfeld would be joining them at the end of the second show. But he still didn't emerge, which only served to make the whole thing more puzzling. Chanel issued a statement saying that he felt 'tired'. He called his florist Caroline Cnocquaert that afternoon. 'I'm going through a bit of a rough patch,' he told her. 'I'm having problems with my stomach. I couldn't go out there in the state I was in.' She took that as a bad sign.[156] That day, many fashion journalists started to write obituaries for Lagerfeld as a precautionary measure. Being so frail must have made him feel distraught. His whole life long, he had wanted nothing to do with illness, suffering or death. In 2011, the German talk-show host Markus Lanz had asked him a probing question: what would he do if he realized he couldn't carry on anymore? As an advocate of assisted suicide, he confessed, 'I'm not against disappearing.' When the presenter repeatedly asked him whether he wanted to decide when it was time to go, he said, 'I'm not against it. I mean, I wouldn't want to be a burden to others. That's a horrendous situation, even if you're paying for it.' Of course the designer could afford it if he wanted. 'Well, there are some things you don't want to have to pay for,' he said. 'I'm in favour of letting the other person off the hook if you can tell that there's no hope left and there's nothing else for it.' The studio audience cheered.[157]

Despite his ill health, Lagerfeld kept looking to the future. There were more ready-to-wear shows just around the corner – for Fendi in late February, and Chanel in early March. The designer was taken to the American Hospital mid-February. He ordered flowers from

Caroline Cnocquaert over the phone on 13 February: 'No card,' he said, his voice cracking. 'You can write the card.' This had never happened to her before. After she hung up, she told her husband, 'It's all over.' Then she called her sister and burst into tears: 'Stéphanie, he's not going to be with us for much longer.'[158] The last bouquets he ordered were for Caroline of Monaco, Bernard Arnault and Françoise Dumas, an old friend who organizes private events.

Baptiste Giabiconi could also hear that his fatherly friend was ailing during their last phone call. 'They had pumped water out of his lungs.' He tried to cheer him up, saying he was sure he'd be better next week. 'Baptiste,' Lagerfeld said, 'next week it'll only be worse.'[159] Baptiste tried to get through to his elderly friend several times over the next few days. Then on 13 February he received a short text message that would also be the last: 'Ferme les yeux... Tu me verras' (Close your eyes [and] you'll see me).[160]

Sébastien Jondeau spent the last three nights sleeping in the room next door to Lagerfeld's in the hospital. His duties were non-stop. They kept working and calling colleagues, even though Lagerfeld's voice was getting more and more faint. They even discussed the details of the next show over the phone with Silvia Fendi. Lagerfeld didn't want to believe that anything could stop him. 'Shouldn't they be letting us out today?' He even made Sébastien book the private jet so that they could fly to Italy for the Fendi show on 21 February. 'Of course I knew that it was the end. But right to the last minute I believed he would survive, that he was immortal.'

At 10.20 a.m. on 19 February 2019, Karl Lagerfeld passed away with Sébastien Jondeau holding his hand.[161] One of the first people Sébastien called was Baptiste Giabiconi. 'Il est parti. C'est fini,' he told him: 'He's gone. It's over.'[162]

Karl Lagerfeld's death certificate mentions the prestigious *décoration* awarded to him by President Nicolas Sarkozy in 2010: France's highest civil merit of Commander of the Legion of Honour. The address on the certificate states '1, allée des Genêts, Monaco', his penthouse apartment in the Millefiori complex. It all happened quickly:

the certificate was issued at 11.06 a.m. and signed by the registrar Anne-Marie Foubert.[163] Then at 1.05 p.m. the German branch of the French news agency AFP made the announcement: 'Fashion designer Karl Lagerfeld: dead at 85.' Two minutes later, at 1.07 p.m., Chanel's German press office issued the 'official statement from Paris regarding the passing of Mr Lagerfeld' and the appointment of Virginie Viard as his successor.

The media coverage of Lagerfeld's death eclipsed most of the other news stories of the year. Only major political developments received more attention than the passing of this German in Paris: Boris Johnson's appointment as British prime minister and the confusion surrounding Brexit, Greta Thunberg's public appearances and the climate crisis, US President Donald Trump and his many critics, the European elections on 24 May and the new President of the European Commission Ursula von der Leyen, the Hong Kong protests, the war in Syria and the fire at Notre Dame. Hannelore Elsner, Doris Day, Niki Lauda, Toni Morrison, Peter Fonda, Ferdinand Piëch and Robert Mugabe all died in 2019, as did Lagerfeld's photographer friend Peter Lindbergh and his former neighbour Jacques Chirac. But none of these deaths prompted such a torrent of tributes, obituaries, TV specials and special editions all over the world.

That very evening, the most discreet tribute of all happened on German television. When the news show 'Heute Journal' was broadcast on the ZDF channel at 9.45 p.m., the host Claus Kleber began the programme wearing a grey suit and a white shirt with a white-spotted burgundy tie. But when Gundula Gause had finished reading out the news and the camera spun back around to Kleber, he was wearing a black tie in honour of the designer. The last news item of the day, of course, was the obituary notice for Karl Lagerfeld.[164]

His final collection: Chanel, ready-to-wear, 5 March 2019

Legacy

People were in mourning all over the world. President Emmanuel Macron declared that fashion had lost 'its most famous ambassador'. Melania Trump, the then-US First Lady, called Lagerfeld 'a creative genius'. But Germany's top politicians remained quiet. Chancellor Angela Merkel was perhaps under no obligation to praise Lagerfeld after all the criticism she had endured from him. But there was also silence from Federal President Frank-Walter Steinmeier, who only days earlier had praised the late Swiss actor Bruno Ganz for his role in portraying 'the highest highs and the lowest lows of German history'. At least First Mayor of Hamburg Peter Tschentscher had something to say, referring to the late designer as 'an extraordinary Hanseatic citizen and ambassador of Hamburg'. Michael Roth, Minister of State for Europe at the German Federal Foreign Office, said that the late Mr Lagerfeld had 'probably done more for German–French relationships than many politicians'.

The Fendi show in Milan went ahead as planned, two days after Lagerfeld's death. Michel Gaubert's song choices for the show included David Bowie's 'Heroes' and Lou Reed and John Cale's 'Small Town', about a boy from a small town who wants to get out and make his way in the world. When Silvia Fendi stepped onto the runway alone to take her bow, the audience gave her a standing ovation. The show closed with a video recorded in 2013: Karl Lagerfeld sketching himself as he appeared on his first day at Fendi in 1965, capturing every single detail from his Cerruti hat to his Norfolk jacket made of Scottish tweed.

The people who were closest to Lagerfeld attended the cremation in the Parisian suburb of Nanterre the following day. Caroline of Monaco was there with her daughter Charlotte and her son Andrea Casiraghi. Bernard Arnault arrived with his wife Hélène Mercier and his sons Alexandre and Antoine. Anna Wintour, Inès de la Fressange and Gerhard Steidl were all there. Representing Chanel were Alain and Gérard Wertheimer, Virginie Viard, Bruno Pavlovsky and Eric Pfrunder. Then there was Karl's substitute family: Sébastien Jondeau, Caroline Lebar, Pier Paolo Righi, Choupette and her maid Françoise Caçote, Brad Kroenig with his wife Nicole and their sons Hudson and Jameson. His faithful seamstresses were also there, led by *première* Anita Briey, who had worked alongside the designer for over fifty years, since his early days at Chloé.

There was no priest presiding over the ceremony. None of Lagerfeld's relatives were invited, not even his half-sister Thea's daughter Thoma Schulenburg or his sister Christel's daughter and two sons in the United States. It was a secret gathering. Still, there were between sixty and eighty people standing by the roadside when the hearse drove past carrying the black coffin to the Crématorium du Mont-Valérien.

During the memorial service in the austere hall, Princess Caroline recited a poem called 'Ave' by Lagerfeld's favourite lyricist Catherine Pozzi. The poem was included in one of the first books he published with his L.S.D. imprint: 'Très haut amour, s'il se peut que je meure / Sans avoir su d'où je vous possédais, / En quel soleil était votre demeure / En quel passé votre temps, en quelle heure / Je vous aimais', 'Exalted love, were I to die / Without knowing from where I possessed you, / In what sun you dwelt, / In what past your times were, in what hour / I loved you'.[1] She had barely reached the end of this first verse in French when her voice began to crack.

Karl Lagerfeld hated funerals. He once made a joke about what would happen when his time came: 'There will be no funeral. I'd rather die.'[2] Before he passed away, the designer said that he wanted his ashes to be mixed with those of his mother and of Jacques de Bascher. The man tasked with making him disappear without a trace was Sébastien Jondeau. He scattered or buried the ashes somewhere in France a few days after the cremation. And, true to his word, he didn't tell a single soul exactly where or how he did it. There is no memorial site.

Lagerfeld's fashion legacy was guaranteed. Countless designers have tried to replicate his work ethic, and many designers were inspired to take up the profession because of the example he set. And not only that: now he had been succeeded at Chanel by his chosen candidate, Virginie Viard, nearly five decades after the passing of Coco Chanel in 1971 there was a woman back at the helm of France's most important fashion house. Lagerfeld's legend lived on in other collections in the year of his death. Jackets inspired by the Chanel look were everywhere to be seen at the fashion shows in February and March – at Marc Jacobs, Donatella Versace, Hedi Slimane (Celine) and Alessandro Michele (Gucci). Fashion journalist Bridget Foley described this as 'the best kind of homage'.[3] Finally, there was another reminder of the late designer. In summer 2019, the LVMH Prize for Young Designers changed its name to the Karl Lagerfeld Prize. The first winner of this new award was Hed Mayner, a talented young Israeli, who won 150,000 euros and an exclusive mentorship programme. Lagerfeld believed in the LVMH Prize because his career had also begun after winning a fashion award.

Two weeks after Lagerfeld's death, on 5 March, it was time for the Chanel ready-to-wear show that would be his parting message to the world.[4] Lars Eidinger stepped out in a black Chanel jacket. The piece, equal parts classic and relaxed, was actually designed for women – but, worn by a man, it surrounded him with a strange aura of inverted emancipation. Coco Chanel based her famous tweed suit on men's tailoring, hence the four patch pockets. And now here was this German actor, blurring gender lines in the other direction. He called Lagerfeld 'insanely free and downright anarchic'.

No other item of clothing could have been more fitting for this day in the Grand Palais. The show was unveiling the last collection designed by a man who had produced countless variations of the Chanel suit over the course of thirty-six years. It was honouring a designer who knew all the rules of fashion and took pleasure in breaking them; someone who refused to follow earthly categories such as age, gender or background. Up next at 10.30 a.m. this Tuesday in

March: the Chanel autumn/winter 2019–2020 show. Lagerfeld would continue to create an impact with his designs well into the next year.

He had even come up with the concept for the set: a winter wonderland with wooden chalets, like in Switzerland, where Coco Chanel lived for several years after the war. The guests kicked up the snow as they made their way to their seats, the chimneys smoked, and the little fir trees were dusted with snow. The words 'Chalet Gardenia' were written in ornate lettering on the house at the top end of the catwalk, named after the plant with white blossoms that also grows at high altitudes. The flower had lent its name to one of Coco Chanel's perfumes in 1925: Gardénia.

It was a familiar scene, as at any major Chanel show. Actress Kristen Stewart wore a black jumpsuit printed with CC logos and took a seat next to singer Janelle Monáe, who was sporting a colourful Ancient Egyptian look from the last Métiers d'Art collection. Anna Wintour arrived in a pale pink Chanel suit, not opting for black like so many of the other guests. Lars Eidinger posed for a selfie with Claudia Schiffer. People took videos and shared posts, chatted and joked. This time there was no sign of false sentimentality, not even in the front row.

The show began with the chiming of a bell, almost like a church service. Coats, suits, dresses, hats: oversized. Bags: flat, stitched, with diamond quilting and the trademark interlocking CC clasp. The new Chanel 19 bag, designed by Karl Lagerfeld and Virginie Viard, was a message for posterity and a classic like the 2.55. The number is also significant: the Chanel 19 is named after the year of its launch, and like the Chanel No 19 perfume it references Coco Chanel's date of birth, 19 August 1883. When they came up with the name for this new bag, they of course did not know the impending year (2019) or day (19 February) of Lagerfeld's death.

The bells, the minute of silence, the devotion: it was all 'very spiritual' according to Lars Eidinger. To him, this fashion show felt like a secular service: 'Karl Lagerfeld tells us what it is like to die, and he does it with a sense of humour.' The last models wore round 'snowball dresses'. When people remember this collection in the future, they will picture Penélope Cruz or Kaia Gerber floating through the glass palace like balls of cotton. A fashion creation story had reached its finale: ideas became reality, designs came into effect, moments stretched into eternity. The oversized capes covered the models' footsteps in the artificial snow. Karl Lagerfeld wanted to disappear that way, too – without a trace. And on the morning of the Chanel show, that's exactly what he did.

Karl

Family Tree

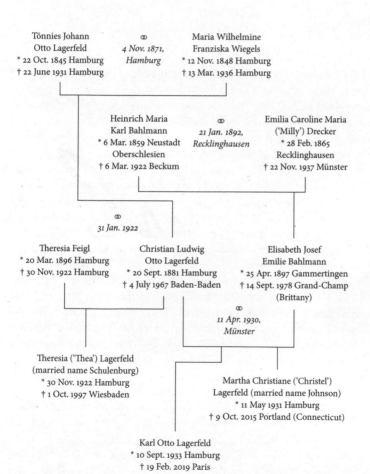

Tönnies Johann
Otto Lagerfeld
* 22 Oct. 1845 Hamburg
† 22 June 1931 Hamburg

∞
4 Nov. 1871,
Hamburg

Maria Wilhelmine
Franziska Wiegels
* 12 Nov. 1848 Hamburg
† 13 Mar. 1936 Hamburg

Heinrich Maria
Karl Bahlmann
* 6 Mar. 1859 Neustadt
Oberschlesien
† 6 Mar. 1922 Beckum

∞
21 Jan. 1892,
Recklinghausen

Emilia Caroline Maria
('Milly') Drecker
* 28 Feb. 1865
Recklinghausen
† 22 Nov. 1937 Münster

∞
31 Jan. 1922

Theresia Feigl
* 20 Mar. 1896 Hamburg
† 30 Nov. 1922 Hamburg

Christian Ludwig
Otto Lagerfeld
* 20 Sept. 1881 Hamburg
† 4 July 1967 Baden-Baden

Elisabeth Josef
Emilie Bahlmann
* 25 Apr. 1897 Gammertingen
† 14 Sept. 1978 Grand-Champ
(Brittany)

∞
11 Apr. 1930,
Münster

Theresia ('Thea') Lagerfeld
(married name Schulenburg)
* 30 Nov. 1922 Hamburg
† 1 Oct. 1997 Wiesbaden

Martha Christiane ('Christel')
Lagerfeld (married name Johnson)
* 11 May 1931 Hamburg
† 9 Oct. 2015 Portland (Connecticut)

Karl Otto Lagerfeld
* 10 Sept. 1933 Hamburg
† 19 Feb. 2019 Paris

Appendix
Acknowledgments

I would like to thank: Marietta Andreae (Hamburg), Fritz Andresen (Freising), Nancy Antonelli (Palm Beach Gardens), Sybille Baumbach (Hamburg), Peter Bermbach (Paris), Claudia Bessler (Frankfurt), Sylvia Blankenburg (Neustadt in Holstein), Rainer Blasius (Munich), Peter W. Boveleth (Hünxe), Detlev Brandt (Berlin), Ruth Brandt (Schmallenberg), Hans-Joachim Bronisch (Bad Bramstedt), Michael Bührke (Münster), Paul Caranicas (New York), Yavidan Castillo (Paris), Stefan Clauser (Beckum), Caroline Cnocquaert (Paris), Corinna Cramer-Feuerbach (Berlin), Godfrey Deeny (Paris), Barbara Dieudonné (Dortmund), Victoire Doutreleau (Paris), Markus Ebner (Paris), Lars Eidinger (Berlin), Ulla Ertelt (Frankfurt), Silvia Fendi (Rome), Leonie Feuerbach (Frankfurt), Stephan Finsterbusch (Frankfurt), Helmut Fricke (Frankfurt), Christel Friedrichs (Bad Bramstedt), Claudia Frobenius (Hamburg), Michel Gaubert (Paris), Christine Gensmantel (Frankfurt), Nicola Gerber Maramotti (Reggio Emilia), Baptiste Giabiconi (Paris), Tan Giudicelli (Paris), Inga Griese (Berlin), Rose-Maria Gropp (Frankfurt), Michael Haentjes (Hamburg), Maria Hagedorn (Beckum), Philippe Heurtault (Paris), Wolfgang Hölker (Münster), Manfred Jacobsen (Bad Bramstedt), Sylvia Jahrke (Hitzhusen), Sébastien Jondeau (Paris), Karin Joop-Metz (Potsdam), Wolfgang Joop (Potsdam), Donna Jordan (New York), Elfriede von Jouanne (Hagen), Thomas Karlauf (Berlin), Peter Kempe (Saint-Rémy-de-Provence), Marina Krauth (Hamburg), Catherine Kujawski (Paris), Günter Lagerfeld (Henstedt-Ulzburg), Wilhelm Lange (Neustadt in Holstein), Sophie de Langlade (Paris), Caroline Lebar (Paris), Rosemarie Le Gallais (Paris), Hervé Le Masson (Paris), Heidelore Litty (Lübeck), Julia Löhr (Berlin), Stefan Lubrina (Paris), Inge Ludwig (Neumünster), Laura Lusuardi (Reggio Emilia), Philippe Morillon (Paris), Eckhard Müller (Münster), Jürgen Müller (Munich), Tina Müller (Düsseldorf), Clara Munch (Paris), Sarah Obertreis (Frankfurt), Christopher Pfleiderer (Baden-Baden), Stéphanie Primet (Paris), Matthias Prinz (Hamburg), Adelheid Rasche (Nürnberg), Ariel de Ravenel (Paris), Alexandra von Rehlingen (Hamburg), Patricia Riekel

(Munich), Sandra Riggs-Schnakenbourg (Paris), Warren Riggs (Los Angeles), Pier Paolo Righi (Amsterdam), Carine Roitfeld (Paris), Melanie Christina Röttig (Hamburg), Evelyn Rumstedt (Hamburg), Ursula Scheube (Berlin), Claudia Schiffer (London), Anke Schipp (Frankfurt), Peter-Philipp Schmitt (Frankfurt), Donald Schneider (Berlin), Thoma Schulenburg (Hamburg), Alexandra Schumacher (Munich), Stefanie Schütte (Hamburg), Hans Wilhelm Seyfrid (Hamburg), Andrei Sidorov (Vladivostok), Miles Socha (Paris), Géraldine-Julie Sommier (Paris), Gerhard Steidl (Göttingen), Bernd Steinle (Frankfurt), Rudolf Stratmann (Münster), Hans-Josef Susenburger (Frankfurt), Werner Thiele (Holm), Gloria von Thurn und Taxis (Regensburg), Corey Grant Tippin (New York), Céline Toledano (Paris), Ralph Toledano (Paris), Gordian Tork (Palm Beach Gardens), Daniela Tran (Paris), Ashley Tschudin (New York), Jürgen Udolph (Leipzig), Christian Ullrich (Baden-Baden), Marga Ullrich (Baden-Baden), Dirk van Versendaal (Hamburg), Karl Wagner (Bad Bramstedt), Christoph von Weyhe (Paris), Jennifer Wiebking (Düsseldorf), Michaela Wiegel (Paris), Andrea and Matthias Wirthwein (Mannheim), Andreas Wirwalski (Munich), Stefan Wittenbrink (Beckum), Eric Wright (New York), Georg Wurzer (Wilhelmsdorf), Yorn (Paris) and Renate Zatsch (Paris), as well as my mother, my sister, my wife and my son.

Notes

In Loving Memory

1   For more background in relation to this paragraph, see Alfons Kaiser, '"Die Kleider tragen uns." Die Modewelt erinnert an Karl Lagerfeld – nicht in einer Trauerfeier, sondern in fröhlichem Gedenken', *Frankfurter Allgemeine Zeitung*, 22 June 2019, p. 8.

2   I would like to thank Sybille Baumbach from DokuSearch in Hamburg and Georg Wurzer in Russia for their help on the archival work for this book. I am also particularly grateful to Gordian Tork, Claudia Frobenius and Thoma Schulenburg for allowing me to consult the family archives for my research.

Prologue

1   Paul Sahner, *Karl* (Munich: 2019), p. 58.

2   'Hamburg ist mir familiär und fremd', *Bild am Sonntag*, 14 February 2015.

3   For an earlier version of this chapter, see Alfons Kaiser, 'Wie Lagerfeld begann', *Die 100 Größten* (supplement), *Frankfurter Allgemeine Zeitung*, 3 July 2019, p. H8.

4   An advertisement in the local newspaper attests to this line of business: 'Expelled from their monastery "La Grande Chartreuse" and stripped of their trademarks, which were sold at public auction in France, the outraged Carthusian monks took their secret with them to Tarragona (Spain), where they now produce their liqueur. The beverage is sold in bottles with the name "Liqueur des Pères Chartreux".' Tönnies Otto Lagerfeld signed the notice in his capacity as an 'Agent for Hamburg, Bremen and Exports'. *Hamburger Nachrichten*, 15 June 1907, p. 3.

5   Obituary notices in the *Hamburger Nachrichten* newspaper on 24 June 1931 and 15 March 1936. The notices were found by family researcher Evelyn Rumstedt: http://rumstedt-familie.de

6   Hildegard von Marchtaler, *Chronik der Firma Van Dissel, Rode & Co. Nachf.,*

Hamburg, gegründet 1893, und deren Vorgänger in Venezuela, gegründet 1852 (Munich: 1953), Stiftung Hanseatisches Wirtschaftsarchiv, Hamburg.

7   Sylvia Blankenburg, 'Wenn der Karl sich auf seine Wurzeln besinnen würde', *Lübecker Nachrichten*, 10–11 March 2002, p. 27.

8   Conversation with Thoma Schulenburg, 24 February 2020.

9   Blankenburg, 'Wenn der Karl sich auf seine Wurzeln besinnen würde', p. 27.

10   Sahner, *Karl*, p. 42.

11   Conversation with Thoma Schulenburg, 24 February 2020. References to conversations will only be given in the Notes section after the first quote from the respective speaker in that chapter.

12   Otto Lagerfeld was still in San Francisco when his brother Carl died at home in Hamburg on 14 December 1906 aged thirty-four. This is indicated by the addition of 'San Francisco' after Otto's name in the obituary for his brother, which was published in the *Hamburger Nachrichten* newspaper on 16 December 1906.

13   The residence permit is dated 11 December 1907. See Russian State Historical Archive of the Far

East in Vladivostok (Российский Государственный Исторический Архив Дальнего Востока, фонд 1 опись 3 дело 1062 'Русские билеты, 1906–1907гг').

14   Email from Andrei Sidorov, 14 May 2019.

15   See Russian State Historical Archive of the Far East in Vladivostok (Российский Государственный Исторический Архив Дальнего Востока, фонд 1 опись 12 дело 478 'Германские и австрийские подданные, 1914г').

16   See Russian State Historical Archive of the Far East in Vladivostok (Российский Государственный Исторический Архив Дальнего Востока, фонд 1 опись 12 дело 521 'Прошения германских подданных, 1914г').

17   See Russian State Historical Archive of the Far East in Vladivostok (Российский Государственный Исторический Архив Дальнего Востока, фонд 1 опись 12 дело 572 'Отказы в прошениях высылаемых немцев о подданстве, 1914г').

18   Eleanor L. Pray, *Letters from Vladivostok, 1894–1930*, ed. Birgitta Ingemanson (Seattle and London: 2014), p. 162. The author was one of the people standing on the platform in Vladivostok on 8 September 1914, when she waved goodbye to some of her German friends ('Tolle, Lagerfeldt, Wübbens and one other ... whose only crime is that they are German').

19   Extensive research in the National Archive of the Republic of Sakha (Yakutia) proved unfruitful. Only one mention of Otto Lagerfeld was found on a list of people who were exiled to the Irkutsk Governorate, which encompassed Verkhoyansk. Telephone communication from Nataliya I. Baischeva to Georg Wurzer, 23 September 2019.

20   Otto Lagerfeld, 'Milch in Scheiben', reader's letter in the *Frankfurter Allgemeine Zeitung*, 10 March 1956, p. 18.

21   Blankenburg, 'Wenn der Karl sich auf seine Wurzeln besinnen würde', p. 27.

22   See the Hamburg State Archives: Staatsarchiv der Freien und Hansestadt Hamburg, HRA 20 537, Signatur A1 Band 84. There is no indication of when the two men left the company. Both their names are still included in the listing in the Hamburg directory for 1925.

23   Wibke Bruhns, 'Der gestiefelte Kater. Was macht eigentlich so ein Modemann?', *Stern*, 12 October 1978.

24   Blankenburg, 'Wenn der Karl sich auf seine Wurzeln besinnen würde', p. 27.

25   Christian Meurer, 'Bad Bramstedt vor Augen, Paris im Kopf', *Frankfurter Allgemeine Zeitung*, 5 September 2008, p. 9.

26   Staatsarchiv Hamburg, Bestandsnummer 221-11, Fa 14 840. Otto Lagerfeld received his salary and bonus from the General Milk Company Inc. in New York.

27   Conversation with Wilhelm Lange, 5 November 2019.

28   See Wilhelm Lange, *Cap Arcona. Dokumentation* (Neustadt in Holstein: 2014), p. 94.

29   Conversation with Thoma Schulenburg, 24 February 2020. Otto Lagerfeld's name is nowhere to be found on the list of prisoners held at Neumünster prison during those years. There is no way of knowing whether he might have been provisionally detained pending trial. The relevant holdings for this period do not include any information relating to pre-trial detainment or any supplementary files. Information provided by the Landesarchiv Schleswig-Holstein (state archives) in Schleswig on 23 and 27 April 2020. Karl Lagerfeld believed that a competitor had denounced his father. See Raphaëlle Bacqué, *Kaiser Karl* (Paris: 2019), p. 24.

30   Ulrich Herbert, *Geschichte Deutschlands im 20. Jahrhundert* (Munich: 2014), p. 597.

31   The Glücksklee headquarters at 36 Mittelweg is now the office of the Hamburger Institut für Sozialforschung (Hamburg Institute for Social Research). When the building was acquired by the institute in 1986, the 'Glücksklee' name still stood above the entrance as a reminder of its former use. Communication from Reinhart Schwarz, archive manager at the Hamburger Institut für Sozialforschung, 4 October 2019.

32   Interview with Karl Lagerfeld on German television, hosted by Carlheinz Hollmann: 'Das ist Ihr Leben.

Stationen eines Lebens im Spiegel der Erinnerungen. Carlheinz Hollmann stellt Karl Lagerfeld vor', ZDF, 12 January 1978.

33 'Hamburg ist mir familiär und fremd', *Bild am Sonntag*, 14 February 2015.

34 Interview with Karl Lagerfeld on German talk show 'Beckmann', ARD, 5 July 2004.

35 Quoted in Blankenburg, 'Wenn der Karl sich auf seine Wurzeln besinnen würde', p. 27.

36 Kurt Lagerfeld, the son of Otto Lagerfeld's brother Johannes Paul, moved from Hamburg to Neustadt with his wife Gisela in 1938 and became the manager of the milk factory there. Their children Margaret (born 1939) and Günter, who was two years younger, were delighted whenever they saw their great-uncle's car because the chauffeur brought them gifts. Little Günter was also happy after the war, when he was allowed in the back of the four-door Mercedes and it took him to Neustadt marketplace. 'Hardly anyone had a car like that back then.' Conversation with Günter Lagerfeld, 14 July 2019.

37 G. M., 'Allgäuer Alpenmilch liegt gut im Markt', *Frankfurter Allgemeine Zeitung*, 7 June 1963, p. 22.

38 K. B., 'Glücksklee will das Frühstück reformieren', *Frankfurter Allgemeine Zeitung*, 19 August 1967, p. 8.

39 See the information boards in the Haus der Manufakturen, Neustadt in Holstein.

40 See Christiane Arp and Christoph Amend, 'Ich bin im Grunde harmlos. Ich sehe nur nicht so aus. Karl Lagerfeld – Das Interview', *Vogue* (German edition), January 2018.

41 Conversation with Thoma Schulenburg, 24 February 2020.

42 Registration card for Otto Lagerfeld, Stadtarchiv Baden-Baden.

43 Sahner, *Karl*, p. 134 f.

44 Interview with Karl Lagerfeld on German talk show 'Markus Lanz', ZDF, 17 March 2011.

45 See Inga Griese and Jennifer Wilton, 'War doch schön', *Welt am Sonntag*, 1 December 2013, p. 22.

46 Otto Lagerfeld obituary, *Frankfurter Allgemeine Zeitung*, 6 July 1967, p. 20.

47 Conversation with Günter Lagerfeld, 14 July 2019, also witnessed by his sister Margarete.

48 Communication from the cemetery administration at the Evangelical Lutheran Parish of Nienstedten, 22 July 2019.

49 'Markus Lanz', ZDF, 17 March 2011.

50 Interview by Alfons Kaiser, 'Der Zopf bleibt dran', *Frankfurter Allgemeine Magazin*, October 2015, p. 88.

51 Amy Larocca, 'Karl Lagerfeld on His Mother, €3 Million Cat, and Being a "Fashion Vampire"', *The Cut*, 31 March 2015.

52 Andrew O'Hagan, 'The Maddening and Brilliant Karl Lagerfeld', *T Magazine*, 12 October 2015.

53 Sahner, *Karl*, p. 27.

54 Ibid., p. 33.

55 Ibid., p. 313.

56 Ibid., p. 131.

57 LAV NRW, Abt. Westfalen, Best. Regierung Münster, Nr. B 49.

58 See the state commissioner's questionnaire for the denazification and categorization of the Hanseatic City of Hamburg ('Fragebogen des Staatskommissars für die Entnazifizierung und Kategorisierung der Hansestadt Hamburg'), Staatsarchiv Hamburg, Bestandsnummer 221-11, Signatur 75 271.

59 'Since I do not have any cash assets to speak of due to the effects of inflation, and since my widow's pension is my main source of income, I would like to request, if possible, that the state cover the full costs of the move.'

60 Conversation with Ruth Brandt, 24 August 2019.

61 Conversation with Gordian Tork, 15 October 2019. Karl Lagerfeld's aunt Felicitas died on 15 February 1978, seven months before her sister Elisabeth. The grave of Felicitas and Conrad Ramstedt is in the Lauheide Forest Cemetery in Münster, Section VII Nr.22 DB.

62 Kaiser, 'Der Zopf bleibt dran', p. 88.

63 Larocca, 'Karl Lagerfeld on His Mother, €3 Million Cat, and Being a "Fashion Vampire"'.

64 O'Hagan, 'The Maddening and Brilliant Karl Lagerfeld'.

65 Sahner, *Karl*, p. 83.
66 Conversation with Gordian Tork, 7 April 2020.
67 Meurer, 'Bad Bramstedt vor Augen, Paris im Kopf', p. 9.
68 Conversation with Thoma Schulenburg, 24 February 2020.
69 Herbert, *Geschichte Deutschlands*, p. 237.
70 Ibid., p. 234.
71 Conversation with Karl Lagerfeld, 28 January 2015.
72 Ibid.
73 Sahner, *Karl*, p. 39.
74 This information is according to the directory for Cologne and the surrounding area from 1930: 'Adressbuch von Köln und Umgegend 1930', Erster Band, erster Teil (Greven's Kölner Adressbuch-Verlag), 31. Elisabeth Bahlmann's name does not appear in the 1929 address book, and there is no mention of her in the address book from 1931.
75 Letters from Elisabeth Bahlmann in Cologne to her mother Milly Bahlmann in Münster, 7 and 8 April 1929. Courtesy of Gordian Tork's archive.
76 Conversation with Karl Lagerfeld, 28 January 2015.
77 The address on the wedding announcement is 'Sülldorfer Weg 53a' in Blankenese, where Otto Lagerfeld was registered until he moved to 70 Elbchaussee in October 1926.
78 Standesamt Münster, Urkunde Nr. 197/1930.
79 Maike and Ronald Holst, *Blankeneser Frauen* (Hamburg: 2013), p. 69. According to the records for Greater Altona, Otto Lagerfeld registered on 9 July 1930 and his wife officially followed on 30 July.
80 Ibid., p. 72. The address 'Baurs Park 3' only appears on the letterhead in Otto Lagerfeld's communications with the authorities until 1935. After that, the address reads 'Gut Bissenmoor' (Bissenmoor Estate). See the Bad Bramstedt municipal archives: Stadtarchiv Bad Bramstedt, Nr. 937.
81 Alicia Drake, *The Beautiful Fall: Fashion, Genius and Glorious Excess in 1970s Paris* (London: 2012, first pub. 2006), p. 70.
82 Conversation with Helmut Junge, 14 December 2019.
83 Conversation with Thoma Schulenburg, 24 February 2020.
84 It seems that, in general, Elisabeth Lagerfeld was easily affected by her environment. For instance, in a letter to her mother from Cologne in 1929, she writes: 'I really do think that the climate in Münster makes me rather melancholy.' Letter from Elisabeth Bahlmann in Cologne to Milly Bahlmann in Münster, 7 April 1929. Gordian Tork's archive. Karl Lagerfeld gave another reason for the move: apparently he wasn't allowed to spend too much time in Blankenese as a small child because it was so humid there. He claimed his doctor told him: 'You'll be hard of hearing at fifty.' Quoted in Bernd Skupin, 'Karlstadt. Lagerfeld hat Hamburg früh verlassen – aber nie so ganz', *Vogue* (German edition), July 2019, pp. 177–81: 180.
85 Interview with Karl Lagerfeld on German talk show 'Beckmann', ARD, 5 July 2004.
86 Conversation with Karl Wagner, 24 April 2019.
87 Conversation with Sylvia Jahrke, 23 April 2019.
88 Quoted in Drake, *The Beautiful Fall*, p. 173.
89 O'Hagan, 'The Maddening and Brilliant Karl Lagerfeld'.
90 Ibid.
91 Maureen Orth, 'Kaiser Karl: Behind the Mask', *Vanity Fair*, February 1992.
92 Sahner, *Karl*, p. 38.
93 Orth, 'Kaiser Karl: Behind the Mask'.
94 Information provided by aviation expert Jürgen Schelling, 23 December 2019.
95 Orth, 'Kaiser Karl: Behind the Mask'.
96 Raphaëlle Bacqué, *Kaiser Karl*, trans. from the French by Caroline Beamish (Suffolk: 2020), p. 43.
97 Alice Rawsthorn, *Yves Saint Laurent: A Biography* (New York: 1996), p. 29.
98 Conversation with Andrea and Matthias Wirthwein, 12 March 2019.
99 Larocca, 'Karl Lagerfeld on His Mother, € 3 Million Cat, and Being a "Fashion Vampire"'.
100 Rodolphe Marconi (dir.), *Lagerfeld Confidential*, 2007.

101 Conversation with Daniela Tran, 26 April 2020.

102 Philip Utz, '"All the other designers hate me..." Karl Lagerfeld gets ready to tell all', *Numéro*, 12 April 2018.

103 'I'm very much against people openly discussing their inner life – if they have one, that is.' Interview with Karl Lagerfeld on the German talk show 'Gero von Boehm begegnet... Karl Lagerfeld', 3sat, 12 September 2005.

104 Interview with Alfons Kaiser, 'Bei mir wird nicht diskutiert', *Frankfurter Allgemeine Sonntagszeitung*, 13 March 2011, p. 54.

105 'Beckmann', ARD, 5 July 2004.

106 Kaiser, 'Bei mir wird nicht diskutiert'.

107 Conversation with Daniela Tran, 26 April 2020.

1933 to 1951

1   Sahner, *Karl*, p. 34.

2   Herbert, *Geschichte Deutschlands*, p. 319.

3   Ibid., p. 308.

4   Ibid., p. 319.

5   Conversation with Gerhard Steidl, 7 March 2020.

6   Conversation with Peter Kempe, 1 October 2019.

7   Conversation with Gordian Tork, 12 November 2019.

8   'Karl Lügenfeld! Er machte sich fünf Jahre jünger' ['Karl Liarfeld! He made himself five years younger'], *Bild am Sonntag*, 7 September 2003, p. 20 f.

9   'Gero von Boehm begegnet... Karl Lagerfeld', 3sat, 12 September 2005.

10   Interview by Sylvia Jorif and Marion Ruggieri, 'L'homme sans passé', *Elle*, 22 September 2008.

11   Conversation with Sophie de Langlade, 1 October 2019.

12   Sahner, *Karl*, p. 34.

13   Based on a statement from the Standesamt Hamburg-Nord (Civil Register Office for Hamburg North), 14 April 2020. The retention term for births registered at the civil register office is 110 years. Once this period has lapsed, the Hamburg registers of births, deaths and marriages are transferred to the Staatsarchiv Hamburg and are no longer subject to the strict usage rules of the Personenstandsgesetz (German Civil Status Act).

14   'Lagerfeld pöbelt im TV', *Bild*, 7 December 2006.

15   Conversation with Karl Wagner, 24 April 2019.

16   Holst, *Blankeneser Frauen*, p. 70.

17   *Hamburger Nachrichten*, 12 September 1933. Original birth announcements can also be found in the private archives of Gordian Tork and Helmut Junge.

18   Sahner, *Karl*, p. 47.

19   According to first-name researcher Knud Bielefeld: https://www.beliebte-vornamen.de

20   Sahner, *Karl*, p. 52.

21   Jan-Uwe Schadendorf, *Alt-Bramstedt im Bild* (Bad Bramstedt: 1984), p. 56.

22   Conversation with Thoma Schulenburg, 14 December 2019.

23   See the Bad Bramstedt municipal archives: Stadtarchiv Bad Bramstedt, Nr. 937.

24   Ibid.

25   Letter from Nikita Gsovsky to the municipal office of Bad Bramstedt, 7 January 1979.

26   Invoice from Ernst Krebs KG, Neumünster, dated 22 January 1979.

27   Carl Swanson, 'Karl Lagerfeld's House of Provocation', *The Cut*, 9 December 2018.

28   Interview by Anne-Cécile Beaudoin and Elisabeth Lazaroo, 'Karl Lagerfeld. L'étoffe d'une star', *Paris Match*, 28 April 2013. See also 'Markus Lanz', ZDF, 19 July 2012. In his appearance on the German talk show, Lagerfeld said, 'I was a precocious child; I wanted to be thought of as a grown-up.'

29   Conversation with Elfriede von Jouanne, 24 April 2019.

30   See 'Fragebogen des Staatskommissars für die Entnazifizierung und Kategorisierung der Hansestadt Hamburg', Staatsarchiv Hamburg, Bestandsnummer 221-11, Signatur 75 271.

31 Letter from Elisabeth Lagerfeld in Bad Bramstedt to Milly Bahlmann in Münster, 26 August 1937. Gordian Tork's archive.

32 Conversation with Karl Wagner, 24 April 2019.

33 Conversation with Thoma Schulenburg, 14 December 2019.

34 Sahner, *Karl*, p. 55.

35 Conversation with Karl Lagerfeld, 28 January 2015.

36 According to information provided by Siegfried Werner's daughter Christel Friedrichs on 23 April 2019.

37 Sahner, *Karl*, p. 105.

38 Conversation with Sylvia Jahrke, 23 April 2019.

39 Sahner, *Karl*, p. 69. Sahner posits that 'Mule' is derived from the term for donkey because Lagerfeld was so stubborn as a boy.

40 Letter from Elisabeth Lagerfeld in Bad Bramstedt to her sister Felicitas Ramstedt in Münster, 15 January 1937. Gordian Tork's archive.

41 'Gero von Boehm begegnet... Karl Lagerfeld', 3sat, 12 September 2015.

42 Marconi, *Lagerfeld Confidential*.

43 Conversation with Karl Lagerfeld, 28 January 2015.

44 The original painting from 1850 was destroyed in World War II. It was burned, along with several other works from the Kaiser-Friedrich-Museum's art gallery, in May 1945 while being stored – ironically for safekeeping – in a flak tower in Friedrichshain public park.

45 Bertrand du Vignaud, 'Interview de Karl Lagerfeld', in Karl Lagerfeld, *Collection Lagerfeld Vol. 1: Important mobilier et objets d'art* (Monaco and New York: 2000), p. 17. Elsewhere, however, Lagerfeld said that he was seven or eight years old at the time. This is probably because he was trying to claim he was younger than his years. One time he even said that he wanted the Round Table painting when he was three years old. See Bruhns, 'Der gestiefelte Kater. Was macht eigentlich so ein Modemann?'

46 Werner Busch, *Adolph Menzel: The Quest for Reality* (Los Angeles: 2017), p. 138.

47 The architectural plans show that the house at 46 Innocentiastrasse had been built in 1909 for I. H. Andersen. When Otto Lagerfeld died, his tenant Hans Wilhelm Seyfrid bought the property. In the year of Karl Lagerfeld's death, there was an initiative calling for the park or a street to be named after the designer because he lived here for a few years as a boy and said that the area was one of his favourite parts of Hamburg.

48 Sahner, *Karl*, p. 66.

49 Letter from Elisabeth Lagerfeld in Bad Bramstedt to her sister Felicitas Ramstedt in Münster, 15 July 1942. Gordian Tork's archive.

50 Letter from Christel Lagerfeld in Bad Bramstedt to her aunt Felicitas Ramstedt in Münster, 23 December 1942. Gordian Tork's archive.

51 Staatsarchiv Hamburg, Bestandsnummer 221-11, Signatur Fa 14 840.

52 Kennedy Fraser, 'The Impresario: Imperial Splendors', *Vogue* (US edition), September 2004.

53 Interview by Marc-Olivier Fogiel, 'Le Divan', France 3, 24 February 2015.

54 Conversation with Sylvia Jahrke, 23 April 2019.

55 Communication from Manfred Jacobsen, 23 October 2019.

56 Sahner, *Karl*, p. 66.

57 Conversation with Karl Wagner, 24 April 2019.

58 For more information on this paragraph, see Holger Heims and Hark Lenze, 'Bad Bramstedt im Zweiten Weltkrieg', *Schriftenreihe der Jürgen-Fuhlendorf-Schule, Heft 6* (Bad Bramstedt: 1982).

59 Herbert, *Geschichte Deutschlands*, p. 502.

60 Quoted in Drake, *The Beautiful Fall*, p. 332.

61 Bacqué, *Kaiser Karl* (trans. Beamish), p. 20.

62 Ibid., p. 24.

63 Stadtarchiv Bad Bramstedt, Nr. 2565 I.

64 Herbert, *Geschichte Deutschlands*, p. 553.

65 The photograph is kept in the archives of Gordian Tork, the grandson of Elisabeth Lagerfeld's sister Felicitas Ramstedt.

66 Communication from Manfred Jacobsen, 18 November 2019.

67 Staatsarchiv Hamburg, Bestandsnummer 221-11, Signatur Fa 14 840.

68 Communication from Horst Gies, 11 February 2020.

69 See Jürgen W. Falter, *10 Millionen ganz normale Parteigenossen. Neue Forschungsergebnisse zu den Mitgliedern der NSDAP 1925–1945* (Mainz: 2016), p. 14. The findings of this research indicate that around 90 per cent of new members were male in the period from 1933 to 1938.

70 See Björn Weigel, '"Märzgefallene" und Aufnahmestopp im Frühjahr 1933. Eine Studie über den Opportunismus', in Wolfgang Benz (ed.), *Wie wurde man Parteigenosse? Die NSDAP und ihre Mitglieder* (Frankfurt: 2009), pp. 91–109.

71 See Gustavo Corni and Horst Gies, *Brot – Butter – Kanonen. Die Ernährungswirtschaft in Deutschland unter der Diktatur Hitlers* (Berlin: 1997), p. 53 ff.

72 Staatsarchiv Hamburg, Bestandsnummer 221-11, Signatur Fa 14 840.

73 Staatsarchiv Hamburg, Bestandsnummer 221-11, Signatur 75 271.

74 Gordian Tork's archive.

75 See Falter, *10 Millionen ganz normale Parteigenossen*, p. 25.

76 Communication from Gerda Kessemeier, 3 April 2020.

77 Conversation with Thoma Schulenburg, 24 February 2020.

78 Letter from Elisabeth Lagerfeld in Bad Bramstedt to her sister Felicitas Ramstedt in Münster, 15 January 1937. Gordian Tork's archive.

79 Conversation with Gordian Tork, 26 April 2020.

80 Interview on German talk show 'Johannes B. Kerner', ZDF, 9 June 2009.

81 'Markus Lanz', ZDF, 19 July 2012.

82 Peter A. J. Bendixen, *Jahreszeiten. Stationen und Episoden aus meinem Leben* (Berlin: 2012), p. 174.

83 Ibid., p. 174 f.

84 Karl Lagerfeld, 'Editorial', *Welt am Sonntag*, 1 December 2013, p. 2.

85 'Hamburg ist mir familiär und fremd', *Bild am Sonntag*, 14 February 2015.

86 Sahner, *Karl*, p. 79.

87 Conversation with Karl Lagerfeld, 28 January 2015.

88 Conversation with Ursula Scheube, 1 November 2019.

89 Conversation with Christel Friedrichs, 23 April 2019.

90 Sahner, *Karl*, p. 67.

91 On this paragraph, see Ernst Neumann, '50 Jahre Jürgen-Fuhlendorf-Schule', in *Festschrift zum 50-jährigen Bestehen der Jürgen-Fuhlendorf-Schule in Bad Bramstedt* (Bad Bramstedt: 1958).

92 Conversation with Hans-Joachim Bronisch, 23 April 2019.

93 Alfons Kaiser, 'Karl Lagerfeld als Karikaturist', in Karl Lagerfeld, *Karlikaturen* (Göttingen: 2019), p. 6.

94 Conversation with Inge Ludwig, 25 April 2019.

95 Conversation with Barbara Dieudonné, 1 August 2019.

96 Bert Krüger, 'Modezar Karl Lagerfeld: Seine Jahre auf Gut Bissenmoor', in *Heimatkundliches Jahrbuch für den Kreis Segeberg* (Bad Segeberg: 1991), pp. 104–6: 104.

97 Kaiser, 'Karl Lagerfeld als Karikaturist', p. 8.

98 'Johannes B. Kerner', ZDF, 9 June 2009.

99 Conversation between Roger Willemsen and Karl Lagerfeld at 'lit.Cologne' literary festival, Cologne Opera, 16 March 2012.

100 Bendixen, *Jahreszeiten. Stationen und Episoden*, p. 172.

101 Conversation with Fritz Andresen, 3 November 2019.

102 Sahner, *Karl*, p. 136; see also 'Beckmann', ARD, 5 July 2004.

103 Bendixen, *Jahreszeiten. Stationen und Episoden*, p. 160 f.

104 Neumann, '50 Jahre Jürgen-Fuhlendorf-Schule'.

105 Conversation with Karl Wagner, 24 April 2019.

106 Conversation with Fritz Andresen, 6 November 2019.

107 Bendixen, *Jahreszeiten. Stationen und Episoden*, p. 172.

108 Krüger, 'Modezar Karl Lagerfeld: Seine Jahre auf Gut Bissenmoor', p. 105.

109 Didier Eribon, *Insult and the Making of the Gay Self*, trans. Michael Lucey (Durham and London: 2004), p. 15.

110 Ibid., p. 18.

111 Ibid., p. 16.

112 Ibid., pp. 19–20.

113 Dagmar von Taube, 'Karl Lagerfeld zwischen Genie und Diätcola', *Iconist*, 21 December 2010.

114 Griese and Wilton, 'War doch schön', p. 19; see also 'Beckmann', ARD, 5 July 2004, and interview by Bruce LaBruce in *Vice* magazine: https://www.vice.com/en/article/xdvd7w/karl-lagerfeld-369-v17n3

115 Bacqué, *Kaiser Karl* (trans. Beamish), p. 23.

116 Beaudoin and Lazaroo, 'Karl Lagerfeld. L'étoffe d'une star'.

117 Griese and Wilton, 'War doch schön', p. 19.

118 See Alfons Kaiser, 'Der letzte Modeschöpfer', *Frankfurter Allgemeine Zeitung*, 20 February 2019, p. 9.

119 Eribon, *Insult and the Making of the Gay Self*, p. 33.

120 Ibid., pp. 29–30.

121 Ibid., p. 35.

122 Sahner, *Karl*, p. 56.

123 Conversation with Sylvia Jahrke, 23 April 2019.

124 Graphological analysis. Copy dated 31 August 1936. Gordian Tork's archive.

125 Letter from Elisabeth Lagerfeld in Bad Bramstedt to her sister Felicitas Ramstedt in Münster, 20 July 1942. Gordian Tork's archive.

126 Conversation with Thoma Schulenburg, 27 August 2019.

127 Conversation with Sébastien Jondeau, 19 March 2020; see also Baptiste Giabiconi, *Karl et moi* (Paris: 2020), p. 116.

128 Ben Ashford, '"I have no family," designer Karl Lagerfeld has declared. But his secret American SISTER isn't hurt she hasn't seen him in 45 years – and would welcome him to her rural home town to share a Diet Coke', *Daily Mail*, 21 January 2015.

129 Sahner, *Karl*, p. 56.

130 Interview by Sven Michaelsen and Stefanie Rosenkranz, 'Vergebung zählt nicht zu meinem Wortschatz', in 'Adieu, Karl. Ein Nachruf', *Stern Extra*, February 2019, pp. 68–73: 72.

131 Christiane M. Johnson obituary, *Hartford Courant*, 14 October 2015.

132 Conversation with Marietta Andreae, 15 July 2019.

133 Conversation with Barbara Dieudonné, 1 August 2019.

134 Conversation with Thoma Schulenburg, 14 December 2019.

135 Willy Pötter, *Geschichte der Reinhardswaldschule – Berühungspunkte mit Menschen und Institutionen* (Fulda: 2011), p. 56.

136 Conversation with Gertrud Scheele, 31 July 2019.

137 Letter from Elisabeth Lagerfeld in Bad Bramstedt to her sister Felicitas Ramstedt in Münster, 20 July 1942. Gordian Tork's archive.

138 Information provided by Thoma Schulenburg, 5 August 2019.

139 *Hamburger Anzeiger*, 1–2 April 1944.

140 Conversation with Thoma Schulenburg, 14 December 2019.

141 See Lagerfeld, 'Editorial', p. 2.

142 Conversation with Thoma Schulenburg, 24 February 2020.

143 Josef Neckermann, *Erinnerungen*, transcribed by Karin Weingart and Harvey T. Rowe (Frankfurt and Berlin: 1990), p. 259.

144 Orth, 'Kaiser Karl'.

145 Communication from Gertrud Scheele, 14 July 2019.

146 Thoma Schulenburg's archive.

147 Sahner, *Karl*, p. 56.

148 'Markus Lanz', ZDF, 17 March 2011; see also Marconi, *Lagerfeld Confidential*.

149 Conversation with Gertrud Scheele, 31 July 2019.

150 Conversation with Thoma Schulenburg, 24 February 2020.

151 Letter from Elisabeth Lagerfeld in Paris to her sister Felicitas Ramstedt in Münster, 4 December 1972. Gordian Tork's archive.

152 Conversation with Thoma Schulenburg, 29 August 2020.

153 Conversation with Andrea and Matthias Wirthwein, 12 March 2019; and conversation with Christopher Pfleiderer, 25 March 2019. For an earlier version of this chapter, see Alfons Kaiser, 'Wie Karl Lagerfeld zum gläubigen Preußen wurde', *Frankfurter Allgemeine Magazin*, 14 April 2019, p. 20.

154 'Zur Ehre Gottes, zum Heile der leidenden Menschheit, zur Freude der Ärzte und Schwestern, zur Zierde

der Stadt Münster', *Die Geschichte der Raphaelsklinik* (Münster: 2008), p. 43.

155 'Johannes B. Kerner', ZDF, 9 June 2009.

156 Marconi, *Lagerfeld Confidential*.

157 Kaiser, 'Bei mir wird nicht diskutiert'.

158 Sahner, *Karl*, p. 73.

159 'Johannes B. Kerner', ZDF, 9 June 2009.

160 Martina Neuen, *Karl Lagerfeld – Mode als Religion*. A film by Martina Neuen. Vox, 7 September 2013.

161 According to information from the archives of the Evangelical-Lutheran Parish and confirmation records for Bad Bramstedt. See Archiv des Evangelisch-Lutherischen Kirchenkreises Altholstein in Neumünster, Konfirmationsbuch der Kirchengemeinde Bad Bramstedt, lf. Nr. 1948/17.

162 Based on verbal reports in the community. These cannot be confirmed by the Archdiocese of Hamburg due to post-mortem rights (the protection period for baptisms extends to 120 years after birth). Compare, however, 'Karl Lagerfeld', *Der Spiegel*, 21 September 1998, p. 284.

163 Kaiser, 'Der Zopf bleibt dran', p. 88; see also O'Hagan, 'The Maddening and Brilliant Karl Lagerfeld'.

164 Fragebogen des Staatskommissars für die Entnazifizierung und Kategorisierung der Hansestadt Hamburg, Staatsarchiv Hamburg, Bestandsnummer 221-11, Signatur 75 271.

165 Communication from the Catholic Parish of St Maria in Hamburg, 17 December 2019.

166 Laurent Allen-Caron, *Le Mystère Lagerfeld* (Paris: 2017), p. 158.

167 Kaiser, 'Bei mir wird nicht diskutiert'.

168 Communication from Dior, 11 June 2019.

169 Griese and Wilton, 'War doch schön', p. 19.

170 Christian Dior, *Dior* (Frankfurt: 1956), p. 175.

171 '80 Modelle unter Polizeiaufsicht. Christian Diors Kollektion traf ein – Constanze begrüßte', *Hamburger Abendblatt*, 12 December 1949, p. 3. Other sources for the following paragraphs: 'Erbauende und belehrende Kleiderschau', *Hamburger Abendblatt*, 13 December 1949, p. 3; Erika Müller, 'Die Garçonnes von der Seine. Des

Pariser Modekünstlers Dior Sendboten in Hamburg', *Die Zeit*, 22 December 1949; 'Man könnte sie sonst schreien hören', *Der Spiegel*, 15 December 1949; 'Er schickte seine schönsten Frauen', *Constanze*, 1950, vol. 1, pp. 8–12; Marie Hélène Bourdil, 'Und dann weinte er vor Freude', *Constanze. Die Mode 1950. Sonderheft mit zwei Schnittmusterbogen*, 1950, p. 14 f.

172 Christian Dior, *Christian Dior and I*, trans. from the French by Antonia Fraser (New York: 1957), p. 167; see also Dior, *Dior*, p. 175.

173 See Arp and Amend, 'Ich bin im Grunde harmlos'.

174 Ibid.

175 *Constanze. Die Mode 1950. Sonderheft mit zwei Schnittmusterbogen*, p. 14 f.

176 Sahner, *Karl*, p. 91.

177 'Hamburg ist mir familiär und fremd', *Bild am Sonntag*, 14 February 2015.

178 Sandra Brant and Ingrid Sischy, 'Ich bin total improvisiert. Ein Gespräch über Paris, Papier-Passion und die Freiheit, Karl Lagerfeld zu sein', in 'Karl Lagerfeld. Modemethode', *Vogue Special*, May 2015, pp. 12–17: 16.

179 Sahner, *Karl*, p. 40.

180 Herbert, *Geschichte Deutschlands*, p. 696.

181 According to Elisabeth Lagerfeld, the family was still living in the Pension Bristol at 52 Feldbrunnenstrasse at the beginning of 1950. See official denazification survey: Fragebogen des Staatskommissars für die Entnazifizierung und Kategorisierung der Hansestadt Hamburg, Staatsarchiv Hamburg, Bestandsnummer 221-11, Signatur 75 271.

182 Conversation with Thoma Schulenburg, 14 December 2019.

183 Sahner, *Karl*, p. 90.

184 'Beckmann', ARD, 5 July 2004.

1952 to 1982

1 From the press release for the Chanel Cruise collection show in Paris on 3 May 2019. Lagerfeld came up with the concept for the set: a railway station. See Alfons Kaiser, 'In einem Zug. Virginie Viard, die Nachfolgerin von Karl Lagerfeld, zeigt in Paris ihre erste eigene Kollektion für Chanel', *Frankfurter Allgemeine Zeitung*, p. 4. May 2019, p. 8. Lagerfeld's name is not mentioned in any of the student lists for the Lycée Montaigne, which he claimed to have attended. He probably never went to secondary school in Paris. See Sahner, *Karl*, p. 93.

2 Podcast 3.55, *Monocle* magazine.

3 According to the account from Karl Lagerfeld's cousin Kurt Lagerfeld, quoted in Blankenburg, 'Wenn der Karl sich auf seine Wurzeln besinnen würde'.

4 See Beaudoin and Lazaroo, 'Karl Lagerfeld. L'étoffe d'une star'.

5 Karl Lagerfeld, *Off the Record* (Göttingen: 1994), n.p. See also Beaudoin and Lazaroo, 'Karl Lagerfeld. L'étoffe d'une star'.

6 Podcast 3.55, *Monocle* magazine.

7 Lagerfeld, *Off the Record*, n.p.

8 Ibid.

9 Interview by David Slama and Thierry Billard, 'Karl Kapital!', *Paris Capitale*, March 2008, pp. 54–59: 57.

10 Beaudoin and Lazaroo, 'Karl Lagerfeld. L'étoffe d'une star'.

11 Ibid.

12 Brant and Sischy, 'Ich bin total improvisiert', p. 16.

13 Slama and Billard, 'Karl Kapital!', p. 57.

14 Brant and Sischy, 'Ich bin total improvisiert', p. 16.

15 Walter Benjamin, *The Arcades Project*, ed. Rolf Tiedemann, trans. from the German by Howard Eiland and Kevin McLaughlin (Cambridge, MA: 1999), p. 420.

16 Karl Lagerfeld in conversation with Bridget Foley at the 'WWD Apparel and Retail CEO Summit', New York, 8 January 2013.

17 Slama and Billard, 'Karl Kapital!', p. 54.

18 Benjamin, *The Arcades Project*, p. 421.

19 Ibid., p. 427.

20 The quotes in this chapter are taken from conversations with Peter Bermbach on 14 April, 20 August and 6 December 2019.

21 Eribon, *Insult and the Making of the Gay Self*, p. 29.

22 'Boulevard Bio', ARD, 5 November 1996.

23 See Matthias Waechter, *Geschichte Frankreichs im 20. Jahrhundert* (Munich: 2019), p. 274 ff.

24 Peter Bermbach, 'Mein Karl', Z magazine, *Frankfurter Allgemeine Zeitung*, 26 March 2011, p. 24.

25 'Beckmann', ARD, 5 July 2004.

26 Sahner, *Karl*, p. 95.

27 Ibid.

28 See 'The Divine History of the International Woolmark Prize' (no year), The Woolmark Company.

29 'Beckmann', ARD, 5 July 2004.

30 See WWD Staff, 'Woolmark Spins a New Yarn in Tribute to Karl Lagerfeld', *Women's Wear Daily*, 4 February 2020.

31 'Beckmann', ARD, 5 July 2004.

32 Sahner, *Karl*, p. 100.

33 'Das ist Ihr Leben. Stationen eines Lebens im Spiegel der Erinnerungen. Carlheinz Hollmann stellt Karl Lagerfeld vor', ZDF, 12 January 1978.

34 'Johannes B. Kerner', ZDF, 17 December 2005.

35 Sahner, *Karl*, p. 100.

36 Bermbach, 'Mein Karl', p. 24 f.

37 Quoted in Peter Stanford, *Bronwen Astor: Her Life and Times* (London: 2000), p. 119.

38 Ibid.

39 Conversation with Victoire Doutreleau, 3 March 2020.

40 Victoire Doutreleau, *Et Dior créa Victoire* (Paris: 1997), p. 263.

41 Ibid., p. 293.

42 Ibid., p. 268.

43 Ibid., p. 269.

44 See Rawsthorn, *Yves Saint Laurent*, p. 2.

45 Allen-Caron, *Le Mystère Lagerfeld*, p. 63 f.

46 Conversation with Peter Kempe, 30 April 2020.

47 Michaelsen and Rosenkranz, 'Vergebung zählt nicht zu meinem Wortschatz', p. 72.

48 See Allen-Caron, *Le Mystère Lagerfeld*, p. 71 f.; and Bacqué, *Kaiser Karl* (trans. Beamish), p. 49.

49 Michaelsen and Rosenkranz, 'Vergebung zählt nicht zu meinem Wortschatz', p. 72.

50 Rawsthorn, *Yves Saint Laurent*, p. 36.

51 Ibid., p. 54.

52 'Das ist Ihr Leben. Stationen eines Lebens im Spiegel der Erinnerungen. Carlheinz Hollmann stellt Karl Lagerfeld vor', ZDF, 12 January 1978.

53 Conversation with Peter Kempe, 18 April 2020.

54 Conversation with Peter Bermbach, 27 August 2019.

55 'Pariser Frühling in Samt und Seide', *Münchner Illustrierte* (10), 5 March 1960, cover and p. 12.

56 Griese and Wilton, 'War doch schön', p. 22.

57 Florentine Pabst, 'Karls neue Kleider. Wie ein listiger Hamburger seine modischen Einfälle in Paris durchsetzte', *Stern*, 20 September 1973, pp. 184–90.

58 Silke Wichert, 'Das tapfere Schneiderlein. Sie waren jung und wollten die Welt: Große Designer erzählen von ihren kleinen Anfängen', *Süddeutsche Zeitung Magazin*, 7 September 2012, p. 46.

59 Podcast 3.55, *Monocle* magazine.

60 Sahner, *Karl*, p. 115.

61 Karl Lagerfeld and Dr Jean-Claude Houdret, *The Karl Lagerfeld Diet* (New York: 2005), p. 21.

62 Sahner, *Karl*, p. 113.

63 'Beckmann', ARD, 5 July 2004.

64 Sahner, *Karl*, p. 96.

65 Conversation with Peter Bermbach, 14 April 2019.

66 Bermbach, 'Mein Karl', p. 24 f.

67 See Waechter, *Geschichte Frankreichs im 20. Jahrhundert*, p. 311 ff.

68 Ibid., p. 377.

69 Ibid., p. 371.

70 Ibid., p. 372.

71 Conversation with Christoph von Weyhe, 1 July 2019.

72 See Marie-Claire Pauwels, 'Karl le magnifique', *Le Point*, 7 July 2005, p. 76.

73 Interview by Thierry Ardisson, 'Anti-portrait chinois: Karl Lagerfeld', Antenne 2, 24 March 1990.

74 See, for example, Sahner, *Karl*, p. 50 ff.

75 Quoted in Drake, *The Beautiful Fall*, p. 171.

76 According to name specialists Jürgen Udolph and Judith Pfaff, it is quite common in Sweden to form compound names based on this pattern. Bay leaves appear on all the other coats of arms for families whose surnames begin with 'Lager', even though bay trees are rare in Sweden because the plant is only frost-resistant under certain conditions. Communication from Jürgen Udolph, 15 April 2020.

77 The first mention of Tönnies (Anton) Lagerfeld(t) appears, as a sailor, in the oldest surviving record of protected Burghers (Staatsarchiv Hamburg 1: 411-2_I 221, Schutzverwandte St. Pauli 1755–1837, S. 51, Nr. 244). Protected Burghers benefitted from the protection of a community without belonging to that community.

78 Pat Cleveland, *Walking with the Muses: A Memoir* (New York: 2016), p. 228.

79 Michael Gross, 'The Stranger. Lagerfeld makes his marks', *New York Magazine*, 20 August 1990, pp. 24–26: 24.

80 Utz, '"All the other designers hate me..."'. See also Ryan White, 'Karl Lagerfeld insults just about everyone in this outrageous interview', *i-D*, 13 April 2018: https://i-d. vice.com/en_uk/article/paxxjz/ karl-lagerfeld-virgil-abloh-alaia-numero

81 Conversation with Marga and Christian Ullrich, 20 November 2019.

82 Conversation with Peter Bermbach, 14 April 2019.

83 Conversation with Thoma Schulenburg, 24 February 2020.

84 Interview by Dirk van Versendaal, 'Ich mag es nicht so gern erdnah', *Stern*, 9 October 2014, p. 114.

85 Interview by Mira Wiesinger, 'Wenn ich geradeaus gucken muss, schlafe ich ein', *Welt Online*, 24 November 2012.

86 Ibid.

87 Van Versendaal, 'Ich mag es nicht so gern erdnah', p. 114.

88 Wiesinger, 'Wenn ich geradeaus gucken muss, schlafe ich ein'.

89 Sahner, *Karl*, p. 96.

90 'Markus Lanz', ZDF, 19 April 2012.

91 Sahner, *Karl*, p. 97.

92   'Markus Lanz', ZDF, 19 April 2012.
93   Van Versendaal, 'Ich mag es nicht
      so gern erdnah', p. 114.
94   'Markus Lanz', ZDF, 19 April 2012.
95   Van Versendaal, 'Ich mag es nicht
      so gern erdnah', p. 115.
96   Thadée Klossowski de Rola, *Vie rêvée*
      (Paris: 2013), p. 223.
97   The quotes in this chapter are taken
      from conversations with Rosemarie Le
      Gallais on 27 November 2019, 16 January
      2020 and 1 February 2020.
98   Some sources claim that he started
      working for the brand in 1963. However,
      the earliest sketch of his to be found
      in the Chloé archive is for the autumn/
      winter 1964 collection and dates to 1964.
99   Conversation with Peter Bermbach,
      14 April 2019.
100   Conversation with Géraldine-Julie
      Sommier, 21 January 2020.
101   In Miles Socha and Laure Guilbault,
      'Chloé Founder Gaby Aghion Dies at 93',
      Women's Wear Daily, 29 September 2014.
102   Pabst, 'Karls neue Kleider'.
103   Drake, *The Beautiful Fall*, p. 77.
104   Lagerfeld, *Off the Record*, n.p.
105   See Sarah Mower, *Chloé: Attitudes*
      (New York: 2013), p. 86.
106   Bruhns, 'Der gestiefelte Kater. Was
      macht eigentlich so ein Modemann?'
107   See Mower, *Chloé: Attitudes*, p. 96.
108   Conversation with Ariel de Ravenel,
      1 February 2020.
109   Conversation with Corey Grant Tippin,
      5 January 2020.
110   Bill Cunningham, in *Antonio Lopez 1970:
      Sex Fashion & Disco*, documentary film
      by James Crump, 2017.
111   Conversation with Rosemarie Le Gallais,
      27 November 2019.
112   *Vogue Paris*, February 1970, cover
      and p. 3.
113   See Adrien Gombeaud, 'Je vous
      embrasse. K. L.', *Vogue Paris*, December
      2016, p. 160 ff.
114   Conversation with Renate Zatsch,
      25 September 2019.
115   Bruhns, 'Der gestiefelte Kater. Was
      macht eigentlich so ein Modemann?'
116   Peter Bermbach recalls that Lagerfeld
      earned the equivalent of 7,000 marks
      per month in his early years at Chloé.
      This sum increased considerably with

      the success he achieved in the 1970s.
      Conversation with Peter Bermbach,
      1 May 2020.
117   'NDR Talk Show', NDR, 6 January 1984.
118   Conversation with Claudia Bessler,
      5 February 2020.
119   Karl Lagerfeld in conversation with
      Bridget Foley at the 'WWD Apparel
      and Retail CEO Summit', New York,
      8 January 2013.
120   See WWD Staff, '"Karl For Ever": A Joyful
      Celebration of Karl Lagerfeld's Legacy',
      Women's Wear Daily, 20 June 2019.
121   Interview by Alfons Kaiser, '"Ich bin
      nicht sein Klon". Silvia Fendi über
      Karl Lagerfeld', *Frankfurter Allgemeine
      Magazin*, August 2019, p. 35.
122   Conversation with Eric Wright,
      8 September 2019.
123   Kaiser, '"Ich bin nicht sein Klon".
      Silvia Fendi über Karl Lagerfeld', p. 35.
124   Alfons Kaiser, 'Furore um die Fourrure.
      Fendi zeigt Pelzmode bei der Couture –
      zu Ehren von Lagerfeld, zum Ärger der
      Tierschützer', *Frankfurter Allgemeine
      Zeitung*, 10 July 2015, p. 6.
125   Sahner, *Karl*, p. 133.
126   Conversation with Laura Lusuardi,
      14 June 2019.
127   Nathalie Mont-Servan, 'Taille fine
      et prêt-à-porter d'hiver', *Le Monde*,
      15 April 1972.
128   Communication from Peter Kempe,
      20 April 2020.
129   '"I have it in the blood." Karl Lagerfeld
      on his success at Chanel', CNN,
      19 October 2011.
130   Conversation with Ulla Ertelt,
      6 April 2020.
131   Conversation with Peter W. Boveleth,
      5 January 2020.
132   Karl Lagerfeld in conversation with
      Bridget Foley, 'WWD Apparel and Retail
      CEO Summit', New York, 8 January 2013.
133   Conversation with Tan Giudicelli,
      2 March 2020.
134   Drake, *The Beautiful Fall*, p. 91 f.
135   Conversations with Corey Grant Tippin
      on 31 December 2019 and 5 January 2020.
136   Cleveland, *Walking with the Muses*,
      p. 234.
137   Quoted in Drake, *The Beautiful Fall*, p. 86.
138   Jerry Hall, *My Life in Pictures* (London:
      2010).

139 Antonio Lopez, *Antonio Lopez: Instamatics* (Santa Fe: 2011), n.p.
140 Ibid.
141 Conversation with Renate Zatsch, 25 September 2019.
142 Cleveland, *Walking with the Muses*, p. 219.
143 Conversation with Rosemarie Le Gallais, 27 November 2019.
144 Marie Ottavi, *Jacques de Bascher. Dandy de l'ombre* (Paris: 2017), p. 64.
145 Drake, *The Beautiful Fall*, p. 103.
146 Conversations with Corey Grant Tippin on 31 December 2019 and 5 January 2020.
147 O'Hagan, 'The Maddening and Brilliant Karl Lagerfeld'.
148 Ottavi, *Jacques de Bascher*, p. 64.
149 Laurence Benaïm, *Yves Saint Laurent: A Biography* (New York: 2019), p. 241.
150 Drake, *The Beautiful Fall*, p. 105.
151 Bacqué, *Kaiser Karl*, p. 77.
152 For a full account of this paragraph, see Drake, *The Beautiful Fall*, p. 106 ff.
153 Klossowski de Rola, *Vie rêvée*, p. 35.
154 Communication from Paul Caranicas, 28 January 2020.
155 See Paul Caranicas, *Antonio's People* (New York: 2004).
156 Conversation with Ariel de Ravenel, 1 February 2020.
157 Bill Cunningham, in *Antonio Lopez 1970: Sex Fashion & Disco*.
158 Conversation with Rosemarie Le Gallais, 13 February 2020.
159 Bill Cunningham, in *Antonio Lopez 1970: Sex Fashion & Disco*.
160 Conversation with Eric Wright, 8 September 2019.
161 Wolfgang Joop, *Die einzig mögliche Zeit* (Hamburg: 2019), p. 301.
162 John Colapinto, 'In the Now. Where Karl Lagerfeld lives', *New Yorker*, 19 March 2007.
163 See Drake, *The Beautiful Fall*, p. 135.
164 Beaudoin and Lazaroo, 'Karl Lagerfeld. L'étoffe d'une star'.
165 'Beckmann', ARD, 5 July 2004.
166 Ottavi, *Jacques de Bascher*, p. 17.
167 Drake, *The Beautiful Fall*, p. 163.
168 Ottavi, *Jacques de Bascher*, p. 38.
169 Ibid., p. 41.
170 Ibid., p. 33.
171 Ibid., p. 26.
172 Günter Erbe, *Der moderne Dandy* (Cologne, Weimar and Vienna: 2017), p. 258.
173 Joop, *Die einzig mögliche Zeit*, p. 297.
174 Ottavi, *Jacques de Bascher*, p. 70.
175 Ibid., p. 87.
176 Klossowski de Rola, *Vie rêvée*, p. 130.
177 Ottavi, *Jacques de Bascher*, p. 75.
178 Joop, *Die einzig mögliche Zeit*, p. 296.
179 Conversation with Victoire Doutreleau, 3 March 2020.
180 Bruhns, 'Der gestiefelte Kater. Was macht eigentlich so ein Modemann?'
181 'Markus Lanz', ZDF, 19 April 2012.
182 Conversation with Patricia Riekel, 20 November 2019.
183 Ottavi, *Jacques de Bascher*, p. 41.
184 Marc Rioufol, *Tox. Comment je suis mort et ressuscité* (Paris: 2011), p. 46.
185 Conversation with Wolfgang Joop, 20 February 2020.
186 Ottavi, *Jacques de Bascher*, p. 111.
187 Conversation with Philippe Heurtault, 5 January 2020.
188 Ottavi, *Jacques de Bascher*, p. 123.
189 Conversation with Karin Joop-Metz, 20 February 2020.
190 See Bacqué, *Kaiser Karl* (trans. Beamish), p. 119.
191 See Alexandre Debouté and Véronique Richebois, *Pierre Bergé. Le Pygmalion* (Paris: 2020), p. 187.
192 Conversation with Claudia Frobenius, 14 April 2020.
193 Lagerfeld, *Off the Record*, n.p.
194 Rioufol, *Tox. Comment je suis mort et ressuscité*, p. 74.
195 Drake, *The Beautiful Fall*, p. 220.
196 Klossowski de Rola, Vie rêvée, p. 197.
197 See Debouté and Richebois, *Pierre Bergé. Le Pygmalion*, p. 199.
198 Ottavi, *Jacques de Bascher*, p. 173.
199 Drake, *The Beautiful Fall*, p. 246.
200 Ibid., p. 247.
201 Conversation with Rosemarie Le Gallais, 16 January 2020.
202 Ottavi, *Jacques de Bascher*, p. 260.
203 Conversation with Ariel de Ravenel, 1 February 2020.
204 Karl Lagerfeld, 'Souvenirs pour l'imaginaire à venir', in Philippe Morillon, *Une dernière danse? 1970–1980. Journal d'une décennie* (Paris: 2009), pp. 4–5: 5.

205 Ottavi, *Jacques de Bascher*, p. 264.
206 Conversation with Eric Wright, 8 September 2019.
207 Conversation with Caroline Lebar, 18 April 2019.
208 Ottavi, *Jacques de Bascher*, p. 273.
209 'Beckmann', ARD, 5 July 2004.
210 Karl Lagerfeld, 'Nordfleisch', in *Helmut Newton* (Munich: 1982), pp. 7–15: 10.
211 O'Hagan, 'The Maddening and Brilliant Karl Lagerfeld'.
212 Alfons Kaiser, 'Das Lagerfeld-Alphabet. Der Modeschöpfer buchstabiert seine Welt – von A wie "Armani" bis Z wie "Zukunft".' Transcribed by Alfons Kaiser, *Frankfurter Allgemeine Sonntagszeitung*, 11 February 2007, p. 55.
213 Conversation with Karl Lagerfeld, 28 January 2015.
214 Ibid.
215 Conversation with Carine Roitfeld, 1 October 2019.
216 Pabst, 'Karls neue Kleider'.
217 Conversation with Peter Bermbach, 21 February 2020.
218 Conversation with Gloria von Thurn und Taxis, 13 August 2019.
219 'Beckmann', ARD, 5 July 2004.
220 Lagerfeld, 'Nordfleisch', p. 10.
221 Bruhns, 'Der gestiefelte Kater. Was macht eigentlich so ein Modemann?'
222 Conversation with Peter Bermbach, 21 February 2020.
223 'Beckmann', ARD, 5 July 2004.
224 Conversation with Wolfgang Joop, 20 February 2020.
225 See Carole Blumenfeld, 'Karl Lagerfeld: The Colour of the 18th Century', *La Gazette Drouot*, 21 February 2019.
226 Information provided by local residents and the Grand-Champ town hall, 4 October 2019.
227 Bacqué, *Kaiser Karl* (trans. Beamish), p. 133.
228 Communication from Philippe Heurtault, 12 January 2020.
229 Conversation with Karin Joop-Metz, 20 February 2020.
230 Joop, *Die einzig mögliche Zeit*, p. 297.
231 Bacqué, *Kaiser Karl* (trans. Beamish), p. 119. See also Ottavi, *Jacques de Bascher*, p. 157 f.
232 Drake, *The Beautiful Fall*, p. 195.
233 Interview by Lorenz Maroldt, '"Ein bisschen Humor tut immer gut". Treffen zweier Macher. In Paris diskutieren Karl Lagerfeld und Bread & Butter-Chef Karl-Heinz Müller über den Erfolg ihrer Marken, Designer aus Berlin und die Hosenlängen der Kanzlerin', *Tagesspiegel*, 6 July 2011, p. 28.
234 According to information provided by estate trustee Paul Caranicas on 12 September 2019, however, the drawings are not in Antonio Lopez's estate.
235 Conversation with Corey Grant Tippin, 5 January 2020.
236 Letter from Elisabeth Lagerfeld in Paris to Felicitas Ramstedt in Münster, 30 December 1972. Gordian Tork's archive.
237 Letter from Elisabeth Lagerfeld in Paris to Felicitas Ramstedt in Pfatter (Upper Palatinate), 11 August 1969. Gordian Tork's archive.
238 Conversation with Renate Zatsch, 25 September 2019.
239 Conversation with Peter Bermbach, 14 April 2019.
240 Letter from Elisabeth Lagerfeld in Paris to Felicitas Ramstedt in Münster, 14 April 1974. Gordian Tork's archive.
241 Letter from Elisabeth Lagerfeld in Paris to Felicitas Ramstedt in Münster, 30 December 1972. Gordian Tork's archive.
242 Letter from Elisabeth Lagerfeld in Paris to Felicitas Ramstedt in Münster, 14 April 1974. Gordian Tork's archive.
243 Letter from Elisabeth Lagerfeld in Paris to Felicitas Ramstedt in Münster, 13 April 1976. Gordian Tork's archive.
244 Conversation with Rosemarie Le Gallais, 1 February 2020.
245 Bacqué, *Kaiser Karl* (trans. Beamish), p. 123.
246 Bruhns, 'Der gestiefelte Kater. Was macht eigentlich so ein Modemann?'
247 Pauwels, 'Karl le magnifique', p. 77.
248 Conversation with Rosemarie Le Gallais, 6 January 2020.
249 Kennedy Fraser, 'The Impresario: Imperial Splendors', *Vogue* (US edition), September 2004. See also Pauwels, 'Karl le magnifique', p. 78.
250 See Ottavi, *Jacques de Bascher*, p. 274.

251   Conversation between Peter-Philipp
      Schmitt and Matteo Thun, 15 April 2019.
252   Karl Lagerfeld, in Sotheby's auction
      press release, Monaco, 13 October 1991.
      Lagerfeld took delivery of the goods
      in 1982.
253   Sotheby's auction press release, Monaco,
      13 October 1991.
254   A. H. (Angelika Heinick), 'Stuhl für's
      Museum. Art déco und Memphis in
      Monaco', *Frankfurter Allgemeine Zeitung*,
      19 October 1991, p. 35.
255   Jean Bond Rafferty, 'Living Lagerfeld',
      Art+Auction, September 2008, n.p.
256   Du Vignaud, 'Interview de Karl
      Lagerfeld', p. 17 f.
257   Ibid., p. 18.

258   Bruhns, 'Der gestiefelte Kater. Was
      macht eigentlich so ein Modemann?'
259   See Chanel Prêt-à-Porter Spring/Summer
      2010 and Karl Lagerfeld, *Collection
      Lagerfeld Vol. 3: Old Master Pictures*
      (Monaco and New York: 2000), p. 70 ff.
260   Communication from Godfrey Deeny,
      28 January 2020.
261   Bruhns, 'Der gestiefelte Kater. Was
      macht eigentlich so ein Modemann?'
262   Conversation with Karl Lagerfeld,
      28 January 2015.
263   *Lagerfeld, Collection Lagerfeld Vol. 1*, p. 15.
264   'Gero von Boehm begegnet… Karl
      Lagerfeld', 3sat, 12 September 2005.
265   Bond Rafferty, 'Living Lagerfeld', n.p.
266   Ibid.
267   Ibid.

1983 to 1999

1   Quoted in Bacqué, *Kaiser Karl*
      (trans. Beamish), p. 54.
2   Quoted in Allen-Caron, *Le Mystère
      Lagerfeld*, p. 83.
3   Bruhns, 'Der gestiefelte Kater. Was
      macht eigentlich so ein Modemann?'
4   Conversation with Rosemarie Le Gallais,
      13 February 2020.
5   Conversation with Eric Wright,
      8 September 2019.
6   Lagerfeld, 'Souvenirs pour l'imaginaire
      à venir', p. 5.
7   Waechter, *Geschichte Frankreichs
      im 20. Jahrhundert*, p. 431.
8   'Neues vom Kleidermarkt', NDR,
      15 August 1984.
9   'Zu Gast in Hamburg: Karl Lagerfeld', in
      'Nordschau Hamburg', NDR, 30 July 1982.
10   'Hamburger Journal', NDR, 4 December
      1985.
11   Conversation with Caroline Lebar,
      18 April 2019.
12   Conversation with Rosemarie Le Gallais,
      27 November 2019.
13   See 'Gero von Boehm begegnet… Karl
      Lagerfeld', 3sat, 12 September 2005.
14   Conversation with Michel Gaubert,
      15 April 2019.
15   Marconi, *Lagerfeld Confidential*.
16   Conversation with Céline Toledano, 27
      March 2020; see also Arnaud Maillard,

      *Karl Lagerfeld und ich. 15 Jahre an der
      Seite des Modezaren* (Munich: 2007),
      p. 86.
17   Conversation with Sophie de Langlade,
      1 October 2019.
18   Marconi, *Lagerfeld Confidential*.
19   Conversation with Ralph Toledano,
      28 March 2020.
20   Maillard, *Karl Lagerfeld und ich*, p. 78.
21   Conversation with Pascal Brault,
      1 February 2020.
22   Conversation with Tommy Hilfiger,
      20 June 2019.
23   Hilfiger CEO Fred Gehring became
      a shareholder in the Karl Lagerfeld
      label, as did Hong Kong billionaire
      Silas Chou, who helped to build the
      Michael Kors label, and the G-III
      Apparel Group, whose brands include
      Donna Karan. Other shareholders
      included the US-based clothing
      company PVH and the holding
      company Apax Private Equity.
24   The menswear line has been distributed
      by F. D. Fashion Design Herrenmode
      GmbH in Miltenberg am Main for
      decades, and is now also sold in stores
      and on the Karl Lagerfeld brand website.
25   Conversation with Pier Paolo Righi,
      25 September 2019.

26 Conversation with Hun Kim, 25 September 2019.

27 Conversation with Rosemarie Le Gallais, 27 November 2019.

28 Brant and Sischy, 'Ich bin total improvisiert', p. 16.

29 Quoted in Michael Gross, 'Chanel Today', *New York Times Magazine*, 28 July 1985.

30 Conversation with Géraldine-Julie Sommier, 21 January 2020.

31 Karl Lagerfeld in conversation with Bridget Foley at the 'WWD Apparel and Retail CEO Summit,' New York, 8 January 2013.

32 Douglas Kirkland and Karl Lagerfeld, *Mademoiselle – Coco Chanel / Summer 62* (Göttingen: 2009), n.p.

33 Edmonde Charles-Roux, *Chanel. Ihr Leben in Bildern*, translated into German from the French by Eva Plorin (Munich: 2005), p. 28.

34 Ibid., p. 67.

35 Coco Chanel opened her fashion house at 31 Rue Cambon in 1918. This is still the address of the head office, which houses a large boutique on the ground floor, a couture salon on the first floor, Coco Chanel's apartment on the second floor, the design studio on the third floor, and the couture ateliers on the upper floors.

36 Waechter, *Geschichte Frankreichs im 20. Jahrhundert*, p. 190.

37 Doutreleau, *Et Dior créa Victoire*, p. 269.

38 Kirkland and Lagerfeld, *Mademoiselle – Coco Chanel / Summer 1962*, n.p.

39 See Hal Vaughan, *Sleeping with the Enemy: Coco Chanel's Secret War* (New York: 2011).

40 Waechter, *Geschichte Frankreichs im 20. Jahrhundert*, p. 272.

41 Conversation with Marietta Andreae, 15 July 2019.

42 Conversation with Sophie de Langlade, 1 October 2019.

43 Gross, 'Chanel Today'.

44 Christopher Petkanas, 'Lagerfeld Tackles Couture', *Women's Wear Daily*, 19 January 1983, pp. 1 and 4 f.

45 Sahner, *Karl*, p. 207.

46 Brant and Sischy, 'Ich bin total improvisiert', p. 16.

47 Conversation with Eva Campocasso, 22 March 2020.

48 Petkanas, 'Lagerfeld Tackles Couture', pp. 1 and 4 f.

49 Conversation with Gerhard Steidl, 7 March 2020.

50 Natasha Fraser-Cavassoni, *After Andy: Adventures in Warhol Land* (New York: 2017), p. 246.

51 Drake, *The Beautiful Fall*, p. 316.

52 Interview by Alfons Kaiser, '"Ich will das so, dann geht das so". Designer Karl Lagerfeld über die Mode und das Leben', *Frankfurter Allgemeine Zeitung*, 4 October 2011, p. 9.

53 In addition to the *flou* atelier in haute couture, there is also a *tailleur* (tailoring) atelier for suit materials, skirts, trousers and tweed clothing. The atelier is also divided into *flou* and *tailleur* in ready-to-wear, so at the time there were four ateliers in total. This number increased over time: by 2020 there were four ateliers for haute couture and three for ready-to-wear.

54 Fraser-Cavassoni, *After Andy: Adventures in Warhol Land*, p. 255.

55 Conversation with Gloria von Thurn und Taxis, 13 August 2019.

56 'Neues vom Kleidermarkt', NDR, 15 August 1984.

57 *Hinter den Kulissen von Chanel. Künstler, Ateliers und Werkstätten*, reportage by Laetitia Cénac, illustrations by Jean-Phillipe Delhomme, translated into German from the French by Cornelia Panzacchi (Munich: 2019), p. 7.

58 Conversation with Eric Wright, 8 September 2019.

59 Conversation with Wolfgang Joop, 20 February 2020.

60 Kaiser, 'Bei mir wird nicht diskutiert', p. 54.

61 Chanel's acquisitions included studio embroiderers Lesage (2002), shoemaker Massaro (2002), milliner Maison Michel (1997), decorative flower and feather maker Lemarié (1996), pleating specialist Lognon (2013), jewelry maker Desrues (1985), gold and silversmith Goossens (2005), silk spinning specialist Riotord (2016), lining silk specialists Denis & Fils (2016), silk dyeing and finishing specialists Hugotag (2016), glovemaker Causse (2012), Scottish knitwear

specialist Barrie (2012) and the Bodin-Joyeux tannery (2013).

62 *Hinter den Kulissen von Chanel. Künstler, Ateliers und Werkstätten*, p. 221.

63 Alfons Kaiser, 'Eine Jacke, die allen passt. Chanel macht mit einer Foto-Ausstellung Station in Berlin – und Bruno Pavlovsky, der Mode-Chef, erklärt die Luxusmarke', *Frankfurter Allgemeine Zeitung*, 22 November 2012, p. 9.

64 Kaiser, 'Bei mir wird nicht diskutiert', p. 54.

65 Ibid.

66 Patricia Riekel, 'Karl Lagerfeld, der Deutsche, der die Welt verzauberte', *Focus*, 23 February 2019, p. 30.

67 In 2019, for instance, they bought the Italian tannery Conceria Samanta and acquired stakes in the leather goods makers Renato Corti and Mabi, and in 2018 they invested in Sulapac (a Finnish start-up specializing in biodegradable packaging) and also acquired a minority stake in the small Boston-based company Evolved by Nature, which develops environmentally friendly textile coatings. The Wertheimer brothers also treated themselves to some wineries.

68 Karl Lagerfeld in conversation with Bridget Foley at the 'WWD Apparel and Retail CEO Summit', New York, 8 January 2013.

69 Conversation with Eric Wright, 8 September 2019.

70 Conversation with Gerhard Steidl, 7 March 2020.

71 Conversation with Julia Stegner, 20 February 2019.

72 Conversation with Eric Pfrunder, 21 June 2019.

73 Hubertus Gassner, 'Von der Kunst der Künstlichkeit. Über die Fotografie des Karl Lagerfeld', in *Karl Lagerfeld. Fotografie, Kunstmuseum Moritzburg Halle (Saale)* (Göttingen: 2020), pp. 13–39: 32.

74 Karl Lagerfeld, 'Le Rêve brisé de la Modernité', in Karl Lagerfeld, *Villa Noailles, Été 1995* (Göttingen: 1995), n.p.

75 Gassner, 'Von der Kunst der Künstlichkeit'.

76 See Karl Lagerfeld, *Moderne Mythologie* (Göttingen: 2014).

77 See *Karl Lagerfeld. Fotografie*, p. 96 ff.

78 Karl Lagerfeld, *Cassina as seen by Karl* (Göttingen: 2018).

79 Interview by Viola Keeve and Dirk van Versendaal, 'Ich bin die Unschuld vom Lande', *Stern*, 14 December 2006, pp. 116–21: 117.

80 See *Karl Lagerfeld. Fotografie*, p. 80 ff.

81 Karl Lagerfeld, *Paris Photo by Karl Lagerfeld* (Göttingen: 2017).

82 Conversation with Eric Wright, 8 September 2019.

83 'Neues vom Kleidermarkt', NDR, 15 August 1984. This is roughly equivalent to the US$300,000 estimated by other sources. See Bacqué, *Kaiser Karl*, p. 197.

84 Inès de la Fressange, 'Profession Mannequin', *Conversations avec Marianne Mairesse* (Paris: 2002), p. 106 ff.

85 Benaïm, *Yves Saint Laurent*, p. 350.

86 Orth, 'Kaiser Karl: Behind the Mask'.

87 Inès de la Fressange, 'Comme tous les génies, il n'aimait pas qu'on lui résiste et il voulait l'exclusivité', *Paris Match*, 21 February 2019, p. 67.

88 Conversation with Eric Wright, 8 September 2019.

89 Orth, 'Kaiser Karl: Behind the Mask'.

90 Communication from Claudia Schiffer, 22 April 2020.

91 Conversation with Sophie de Langlade, 1 October 2019.

92 Conversation with Eric Wright, 8 September 2019.

93 Conversation with Marietta Andreae, 24 February 2020.

94 Conversation with Matthias Prinz, 9 May 2019.

95 Conversation with Alexandra von Rehlingen, 9 May 2019.

96 Conversation with Gloria von Thurn und Taxis, 13 August 2019.

97 Sahner, *Karl*, p. 129 f.

98 Conversation with Eric Wright, 8 September 2019.

99 Communication from Michael Haentjes, 3 April 2020.

100 Loïc Prigent, 'Karl Lagerfeld symbolise la mode dans ce qu'elle a de plus extraordinaire...', *Vogue Paris*, April 2019, pp. 236–40: 240.

101 Anke Schipp, 'Seemannsgarn. Der verlorene Sohn ist zurück: Nicht reumütig, sondern mit Pauken und Trompeten präsentiert Karl Lagerfeld in der Elbphilharmonie eine Chanel-Kollektion', *Frankfurter Allgemeine Zeitung*, 8 December 2017, p. 8.

102 Conversation with Inga Griese, 21 June 2019.

103 Conversation with Caroline Cnocquaert and Stéphanie Primet, 26 November 2019.

104 Conversation with Matthias Prinz, 9 May 2019.

105 Fern Mallis, *Fashion Lives: Fashion Icons with Fern Mallis* (New York: 2015), p. 307 ff.

106 Communication from Alice Schwarzer, 9 July 2019.

107 Giabiconi, *Karl et moi*, p. 141.

108 Conversation with Marietta Andreae, 24 February 2020.

109 Conversation with Godfrey Deeny, 17 April 2019.

110 Ute Dahmen, *Aenne Burda. Wunder sind machbar* (Munich: 2011), p. 401.

111 'Markus Lanz', ZDF, 19 April 2012.

112 'Beckmann', ARD, 5 July 2004.

113 'Markus Lanz', ZDF, 17 March 2011.

114 Michaelsen and Rosenkranz, 'Vergebung zählt nicht zu meinem Wortschatz'.

115 See Lauren Alexis Fisher, 'Karl Lagerfeld's Wittiest, Most Iconic, and Most Outrageous Quotes of All Time', *Harper's Bazaar*, 19 February 2020: https://www.harpersbazaar.com/fashion/designers/a26405187/karl-lagerfeld-quotes/

116 'Johannes B. Kerner', ZDF, 9 June 2009.

117 Conversation with Ariel de Ravenel, 1 February 2020.

118 Lagerfeld, 'Nordfleisch', p. 11.

119 Anna Wintour, 'My Brilliant Friend', *Vogue* (US edition), April 2019, p. 40.

120 Minouflet de Vermenou, 'Ex libris', *Vogue Paris*, February 1979, p. 233 ff.: 233. See also 'Der Modemacher als Literaturkritiker', *Der Spiegel*, 19 February 1979, p. 185.

121 Conversation with Matthias Prinz, 9 May 2019.

122 Conversation with Elfriede von Jouanne, 24 April 2019.

123 Unless otherwise indicated, all quotes in this chapter are taken from a largely unpublished interview with Karl Lagerfeld on 28 January 2015.

124 'Gero von Boehm begegnet... Karl Lagerfeld', 3sat, 12 September 2005.

125 Conversation with Caroline Lebar, 18 April 2019.

126 Conversation with Rosemarie Le Gallais, 1 February 2020.

127 Conversation with Ralph Toledano, 28 March 2020.

128 Karl Lagerfeld, *Karlikaturen* (Göttingen: 2019), p. 77.

129 Conversation with Hervé Le Masson and Catherine Kujawski, 21 June 2019.

130 *La Blonde et Moi: Une journée dans la vie de Karl Lagerfeld*, documentary film by Alexandra Golovanoff, Paris première on 18 October 2009.

131 Conversation between Roger Willemsen and Karl Lagerfeld at 'lit.Cologne' literary festival, Cologne Opera, 16 March 2012.

132 Slama and Billard, 'Karl Kapital!', p. 54.

133 Conversation with Caroline Lebar, 18 April 2019.

134 Conversation with Gerhard Steidl, 7 March 2020.

135 Slama and Billard, 'Karl Kapital!', p. 59.

136 Conversation between Roger Willemsen and Karl Lagerfeld at 'lit.Cologne' literary festival, Cologne Opera, 16 March 2012.

137 Conversation with Marina Krauth, 9 May 2019.

138 Conversation with Wolfgang Hölker, 9 July 2019.

139 'Des Kaisers neue Kleider', *Das Märchen von Hans Christian Andersen, illustriert von Karl Lagerfeld* (Münster: 1992 / new edn 2019).

140 Conversation between Roger Willemsen and Karl Lagerfeld at 'lit.Cologne' literary festival, Cologne Opera, 16 March 2012.

2000 to 2019

1   Conversation with Werner Thiele, 14 December 2019.

2   Bruhns, 'Der gestiefelte Kater. Was macht eigentlich so ein Modemann?'

3   Conversation with Rosemarie Le Gallais, 27 November 2019.

4   Bruhns, 'Der gestiefelte Kater. Was macht eigentlich so ein Modemann?'

5   Lagerfeld and Houdret, The Karl Lagerfeld Diet, p. 79.

6   Ibid., p. 167.

7   Ibid., p. 61.

8   'Beckmann', ARD, 5 July 2004.

9   Lagerfeld and Houdret, The Karl Lagerfeld Diet, p. 73.

10 Pauwels, 'Karl le magnifique', p. 76.

11 Conversation with Caroline Lebar, 18 April 2019.

12 'Beckmann', ARD, 5 July 2004.

13 'Markus Lanz', ZDF, 19 April 2012.

14 Loïc Prigent, 'Sébastien Jondeau, l'ange gardien de Karl Lagerfeld: "Parler avec lui, je ne pensais pas que ça me manquerait autant"', Madame Figaro, 9 February 2020.

15 Sahner, Karl, p. 312.

16 Alfons Kaiser, 'Aus der Vorstadt in die Mode. Er war sein Leibwächter, Assistent und Vertrauter: Vier Monate nach dem Tod von Karl Lagerfeld hat Sébastien Jondeau nun eine neue Aufgabe', Frankfurter Allgemeine Sonntagszeitung, 16 June 2019, p. 14.

17 'Boulevard Bio', ARD, 5 November 1996.

18 Pabst, 'Karls neue Kleider'.

19 Kaiser, 'Der Zopf bleibt dran', p. 88.

20 Ibid.

21 Kaiser, 'Bei mir wird nicht diskutiert', p. 54.

22 Kaiser, 'Der Zopf bleibt dran', p. 88.

23 Nathalie Mont-Servan, 'Haut les cols', Le Monde, 17 January 1976.

24 Brandt and Sischy, 'Ich bin total improvisiert', p. 15.

25 Conversation with Philippe Zubrzycki, 27 November 2019.

26 Kaiser, 'Der Zopf bleibt dran', p. 88.

27 Karl Lagerfeld in conversation with Bridget Foley at the 'WWD Apparel and Retail CEO Summit', New York, 8 January 2013.

28 Alfons Kaiser, 'Karl Lagerfeld trägt und macht Schmuck', Frankfurter Allgemeine Magazin, 9 December 2017, p. 20.

29 Interview by Charlie Rose and Harrie Mays, 'The Charlie Rose Show', Bloomberg Television, 10 February 2006.

30 Hinter den Kulissen von Chanel. Künstler, Ateliers und Werkstätten, p. 163.

31 'Beckmann', ARD, 5 July 2004.

32 'Markus Lanz', ZDF, 17 March 2011.

33 Griese and Wilton, 'War doch schön', p. 18.

34 See interview by Bruce LaBruce in Vice magazine: https://www.vice.com/en/article/xdvd7w/karl-lagerfeld-369-v17n3

35 Pauwels, 'Karl le magnifique', p. 75.

36 Kaiser, 'Bei mir wird nicht diskutiert', p. 54.

37 Tilman Allert, Gruß aus der Küche. Soziologie der kleinen Dinge (Frankfurt: 2017), p. 217.

38 Prigent, 'Sébastien Jondeau, l'ange gardien de Karl Lagerfeld'.

39 Beaudoin and Lazaroo, 'Karl Lagerfeld. L'étoffe d'une star'.

40 'Markus Lanz', ZDF, 19 April 2012.

41 Conversation with Gloria von Thurn und Taxis, 13 August 2019.

42 Conversation with Donald Schneider, 25 March 2020.

43 Conversation with Caroline Lebar, 18 April 2020.

44 Conversation with Eric Wright, 8 September 2019.

45 Conversation with Carine Roitfeld, 1 October 2019.

46 Conversation with Caroline Lebar, 19 March 2020.

47 Conversation with Sophie de Langlade, 1 October 2019.

48 Interview by Dirk van Versendaal, 'Mode lebt von Hysterie', Stern, 18 November 2004, p. 282.

49 For this chapter, see Alfons Kaiser and Julia Löhr, 'Auf allen Kanälen. Karl Lagerfeld wird mit seinen vielen Kampagnen gerade zu einer der größten Werbe-Ikonen', Frankfurter Allgemeine Zeitung, 16 April 2011, p. 16.

50 See 'Gero von Boehm begegnet... Karl Lagerfeld', 3sat, 12 September 2005.

51 Kaiser, 'Bei mir wird nicht diskutiert', p. 54.

52 As of the 1990s, Lagerfeld only drank Pepsi Max, a low-calorie, sugar-free cola drink. He stopped drinking Coca-Cola: 'They've put an additive in Cola Light in France recently,' he claimed. 'Now it tastes like mouthwash.' In Michaelsen and Rosenkranz, 'Vergebung zählt nicht zu meinem Wortschatz', p. 72.

53 Kaiser, 'Bei mir wird nicht diskutiert', p. 54.

54 Conversation with Tina Müller, 7 January 2020.

55 Drake, The Beautiful Fall, p. 200.

56 Ibid., p. 215.

57 Vanessa Lau, 'May 10, 1978: La Vie En Rouge', Women's Wear Daily, 29 November 2010.

58 Allen-Caron, Le Mystère Lagerfeld, p. 266 ff.

59 Quoted in ibid., p. 266.

60 Conversation with Godfrey Deeny, 17 April 2019.

61 Keeve and van Versendaal, 'Ich bin die Unschuld vom Lande', pp. 116–21.

62 Kaiser, 'Das Lagerfeld-Alphabet', p. 55.

63 Debouté and Richbois, Pierre Bergé. Le Pygmalion, p. 207.

64 Benaïm, Yves Saint Laurent, p. 446.

65 Conversation with Peter Kempe, 1 October 2019.

66 Pierre Bergé, Lettres à Yves (Paris: 2010), p. 15.

67 Ibid., p. 78.

68 Ibid., p. 38.

69 Ibid., p. 39.

70 Joop, Die einzig mögliche Zeit, p. 297.

71 Conversation with Philippe Heurtault, 5 January 2020.

72 Benaïm, Yves Saint Laurent, p. 361.

73 Giabiconi, Karl et moi, p. 31 ff.

74 Ibid., p. 75 f.

75 Conversation with Gerhard Steidl, 7 March 2020.

76 Giabiconi, Karl et moi, p. 114 ff.

77 Ibid., p. 116 f.

78 Ibid., p. 192.

79 Ibid., p. 14 f.

80 Ibid., p. 160.

81 See ibid., p. 178.

82 Ibid., p. 183.

83 Ibid., p. 183 f.

84 Karl Lagerfeld, Metamorphoses of an American: A Cycle of Youth 2003–2008 (Göttingen: 2008).

85 Golovanoff, La Blonde et Moi: Une journée dans la vie de Karl Lagerfeld.

86 'Gero von Boehm begegnet… Karl Lagerfeld', 3sat, 12 September 2005.

87 Ingrid Sischy, 'The Boy Who Loved Chanel', Vanity Fair, September 2015, pp. 300–3: 302.

88 Kaiser, 'Bei mir wird nicht diskutiert', p. 54.

89 Conversation with Karl Lagerfeld, 13 November 2017.

90 Sischy, 'The Boy Who Loved Chanel', p. 303.

91 For an earlier version of this chapter, see Alfons Kaiser, 'Die große Show', Frankfurter Allgemeine Magazin, 14 September 2019, p. 58 ff.

92 Conversation with Rosemarie Le Gallais, 27 November 2019.

93 Conversation with Eric Wright, 8 September 2019.

94 Conversation with Stefan Lubrina, 1 February 2020.

95 Conversation with Michel Gaubert, 15 April 2019.

96 Karl Lagerfeld in conversation with Bridget Foley at the 'WWD Apparel and Retail CEO Summit', New York, 8 January 2013.

97 See the postscript of the paperback edition: Drake, The Beautiful Fall, p. 378 ff.

98 Keeve and van Versendaal, 'Ich bin die Unschuld vom Lande', p. 117.

99 Maillard, Karl Lagerfeld und ich.

100 Ibid., p. 252.

101 'Johannes B. Kerner', ZDF, 9 June 2009.

102 Twitter: @sibelschick

103 Karl Lagerfeld in conversation with Bridget Foley at the 'WWD Apparel and Retail CEO Summit', New York, 8 January 2013.

104 'Hier habe ich die Hosen an!', Lagerfeld, Karlikaturen, p. 47.

105 Ibid., p. 93.

106 Ibid., p. 128. See also https://wwd.com/fashion-news/fashion-scoops/karl-lagerfeld-skewers-german-leader-in-cartoon-portraying-hitler-11025370/

107 Ibid., p. 135.

108 Christophe Ono-dit-Biot, 'Karl Lagerfeld: "La mort, c'est pour les autres qu'elle me derange"', *Le Point*, 9 May 2018.

109 Conversation with Gloria von Thurn und Taxis, 13 August 2019.

110 Conversation with Wolfgang Joop, 20 February 2020.

111 Thomas Schmid, 'Lagerfeld in dumpfen Wassern', *Die Welt*, 13 November 2017, p. 3.

112 Joelle Diderich, 'Karl Lagerfeld Talks Jewelry, Weinstein – and Acupuncture', *Women's Wear Daily*, 13 November 2017, p. 2.

113 Sahner, *Karl*, p. 313.

114 'Karl Lagerfeld: the creations and the controversy,' interview with Cathy Newman, *Channel 4 News*, 11 October 2012.

115 See Alfons Kaiser, 'Ein zurückgegebenes Geschenk. Prominente haben Hemden zum Gedenken an Karl Lagerfeld entworfen, die für einen guten Zweck verkauft werden', *Frankfurter Allgemeine Zeitung*, 28 September 2019, p. 9.

116 See Emmanuel Paquette, 'L'argent voyageur de Karl Lagerfeld', *L'Express*, 5 January 2016.

117 Conversation with Gerhard Steidl, 7 March 2020.

118 Fabrice Lhomme and Hervé Gattegno, 'Le testament de Jean-Claude Méry, financier occulte du RPR', *Le Monde*, 21 September 2000.

119 Laurent Mauduit, 'Le redressement fiscal de M. Lagerfeld a été réduit de moitié', *Le Monde*, 27 September 2000.

120 See 'Dominique Strauss-Kahn avait suivi l'avis du fisc sur le dossier Lagerfeld', *Le Monde*, 6 October 2000.

121 Maillard, *Karl Lagerfeld und ich*, p. 184 f.

122 Conversation with Wolfgang Joop, 20 February 2020.

123 Giabiconi, *Karl et moi*, p. 166.

124 Ibid., p. 166.

125 Conversation with Baptiste Giabiconi, 25 September 2019.

126 Giabiconi, *Karl et moi*, p. 169.

127 Ibid., p. 169.

128 'Markus Lanz', ZDF, 19 April 2012.

129 Podcast 3.55, *Monocle* magazine.

130 Conversation with Ashley Tschudin, 9 September 2019.

131 Karl Lagerfeld, *Choupette by Karl Lagerfeld* (Göttingen: 2019), n.p.

132 Larocca, 'Karl Lagerfeld on His Mother, €3 Million Cat, and Being a "Fashion Vampire"'.

133 Podcast 3.55, *Monocle* magazine.

134 O'Hagan, 'The Maddening and Brilliant Karl Lagerfeld'.

135 Utz, 'All the other designers hate me...'.

136 Lagerfeld, *Choupette by Karl Lagerfeld*, n.p.

137 Van Versendaal, 'Ich mag es nicht so gern erdnah', p. 115.

138 Conversation with Tina Müller, 7 January 2020.

139 Larocca, 'Karl Lagerfeld on His Mother, €3 Million Cat, and Being a "Fashion Vampire"'.

140 Giabiconi, *Karl et moi*, p. 171.

141 For the following paragraphs, see Elisabeth Lazaroo, 'Sébastien Jondeau: Le gardien des secrets de Karl Lagerfeld', *Paris Match*, 19 December 2019, p. 98 ff.

142 Conversation with Sébastien Jondeau, 19 March 2020.

143 For the following paragraphs, see Kaiser, 'Aus der Vorstadt in die Mode', p. 14.

144 Marion Ruggieri, '"Il est mort dans ma main": le garde du corps de Karl Lagerfeld se confie sur son décès', *Elle*, 24 September 2019.

145 Lazaroo, 'Sébastien Jondeau: Le gardien des secrets de Karl Lagerfeld', p. 98 ff.

146 Conversation with Caroline Lebar, 13 March 2019.

147 Lazaroo, 'Sébastien Jondeau: Le gardien des secrets de Karl Lagerfeld', p. 105.

148 Conversation with Frédéric Gouby, 20 June 2019.

149 Conversation with Karl Lagerfeld, 13 November 2017.

150 *Hinter den Kulissen von Chanel. Künstler, Ateliers und Werkstätten*, p. 39.

151 Conversation with Patricia Riekel, 20 November 2019.

152 Giabiconi, *Karl et moi*, p. 201.

153 Conversation with Gerhard Steidl, 7 March 2020.

154 Conversation with Patricia Riekel, 20 November 2019.

155 Conversation with Miles Socha, 18 April 2020.

156 Conversation with Caroline Cnocquaert, 26 November 2019.

157 'Markus Lanz', ZDF, 17 March 2011.
158 Conversation with Caroline Cnocquaert, 26 November 2019.
159 Interview by Martina Neuen, '"Er hat gekämpft wie ein Krieger." Ein Jahr nach dem Tod von Karl Lagerfeld spricht sein enger Vertrauter Baptiste Giabiconi über das Leben an der Seite des Modeschöpfers', *Stern*, 20 February 2020, p. 100.
160 Giabiconi, *Karl et moi*, p. 217.
161 Lazaroo, 'Sébastien Jondeau: Le gardien des secrets de Karl Lagerfeld', p. 105.
162 Giabiconi, *Karl et moi*, p. 220.
163 See Stefan Blatt, 'Erbkrieg um Choupette', *Bunte*, 28 March 2019, p. 24 ff.: 26.
164 See Claudia Fromme, 'Schöne Nachrichten', *Süddeutsche Zeitung*, 20 April 2019, p. 57.

Legacy

1 Catherine Pozzi, *Die sechs Gedichte. Les six poèmes. The six poems*, trans. Friedhelm Kemp (Göttingen: 2002).
2 Utz, 'All the other designers hate me…'.
3 Bridget Foley, 'The Chanel Influence on Fall. For fall, numerous designers found inspiration in the Chanel jacket. The timing was mere coincidence', *Women's Wear Daily*, 5 April 2019.
4 See Alfons Kaiser, 'Prêt-à-Partir. Im Grand Palais in Paris wird Karl Lagerfelds letzte Chanel-Kollektion gezeigt', *Frankfurter Allgemeine Zeitung*, 6 March 2019, p. 7.

Picture Credits

akg-images/picture alliance/Eventpress p. 330

Francis Apesteguy/Getty Images p. 189

Hans-Joachim Bronisch Archive p. 75

Chloé Archive p. 146

Giovanni Coruzzi/Bridgeman Images p. 303

Victoire Doutreleau Archive/Lagerfeld heirs
p. 119

Helmut Fricke/FAZ pp. 236, 252, 280, 284, 338,
344

Helmut Fricke/FAZ/Max Mara Archive p. 157

Claudia Frobenius Archive pp. 16, 86

Sean Gallup/Getty Images p. 295

Anthony Ghnassia/Getty Images for Karl
Lagerfeld p. 8

Pierre Guillaud/AFP/Getty Images p. 251

Philippe Heurtault pp. 181, 186

Helmut Junge Archive pp. 49, 55

Alfons Kaiser pp. 101, 197, 228

Keystone-France/Gamma-Keystone/Getty
Images p. 115

Patrick Kovarik/AFP/Getty Images p. 315

Karl Lagerfeld/Frankfurter Allgemeine Magazin
p. 324

Karl Lagerfeld/Eric Pfrunder p. 274

Bertrand Langlois/AFP/Getty Images p. 297

Rosemarie Le Gallais Archive p. 141

Manuel Litran/Paris Match/Getty Images p. 245

The Estate of Antonio Lopez and Juan Ramos
pp. 164, 167

Münchner Illustrierte p. 127

Pierre Perrin/Gamma-Rapho/Getty Images
p. 208

Vittoriano Rastelli/Corbis/Getty Images p. 153

Bertrand Rindoff Petroff/Getty Images p. 308

Adalberto Roque/AFP/Getty Images p. 313

Jürgen Schadeberg/Getty Images pp. 206, 214

Max Scheler/Estate/Agentur Focus pp. 2, 162

Ursula Scheube Archive p. 82

Thoma Schulenburg Archive p. 104

Andrei Sidorov Archive p. 20

Daniel Simon/Gamma-Rapho/Getty Images
p. 270

Gordian Tork Archive pp. 29, 44, 50, 66, 137

Andrea and Matthias Wirthwein Archive,
Repro Frank Röth p. 94

Index of Names